NEW-YORK HISTORICAL SOCIETY.

PUBLICATION FUND.

V.

COMMITTEE ON PUBLICATIONS.

AUGUSTUS SCHELL,
EVERT A. DUYCKINCK,
GEORGE H. MOORE.

COLLECTIONS

OF THE

NEW-YORK HISTORICAL SOCIETY

FOR THE YEAR

1872.

PUBLICATION FUND SERIES.

NEW YORK:
PRINTED FOR THE SOCIETY.
MDCCCLXXIII.

Officers of the Society, 1873.

PRESIDENT,

FREDERIC DE PEYSTER, LL.D.

FIRST VICE-PRESIDENT,

WILLIAM CULLEN BRYANT, LL.D.

SECOND VICE-PRESIDENT,

JAMES W. BEEKMAN.

FOREIGN CORRESPONDING SECRETARY,

WILLIAM J. HOPPIN.

DOMESTIC CORRESPONDING SECRETARY,

EVERT A. DUYCKINCK.

RECORDING SECRETARY,

ANDREW WARNER.

TREASURER,

BENJAMIN H. FIELD.

LIBRARIAN,

GEORGE HENRY MOORE, LL.D.

EXECUTIVE COMMITTEE.

FIRST CLASS—FOR ONE YEAR, ENDING 1874.

EDWARD F. DE LANCEY, WILLIAM T. BLODGETT,
JOHN ADRIANCE.

SECOND CLASS—FOR TWO YEARS, ENDING 1875.

J. TAYLOR JOHNSTON, ERASTUS C. BENEDICT, LL.D.,
ROBERT LENOX KENNEDY.

THIRD CLASS—FOR THREE YEARS, ENDING 1876.

AUGUSTUS SCHELL, EVERT A. DUYCKINCK,
JAMES WILLIAM BEEKMAN.

FOURTH CLASS—FOR FOUR YEARS, ENDING 1877.

SAMUEL OSGOOD, D.D., WILLIAM R. MARTIN,
CHARLES P. KIRKLAND, LL.D.

CHARLES P. KIRKLAND, LL.D., *Chairman.*
GEORGE H. MOORE, LL.D., *Secretary.*

[The President, Recording Secretary, Treasurer, and Librarian, are members, *ex officio*, of the Executive Committee.]

COMMITTEE ON THE FINE ARTS.

JONATHAN STURGES,	WILLIAM J. HOPPIN,
A. B. DURAND,	JOHN A. WEEKS,
ANDREW WARNER,	EDWARD SATTERLEE.

JONATHAN STURGES, *Chairman.*
ANDREW WARNER, *Secretary.*

[The President, Librarian, and Chairman of the Executive Committee, are members, *ex officio*, of the Committee on the Fine Arts.]

THE LEE PAPERS.

VOL. II.

1776-1778.

THE LEE PAPERS.

To Patrick Henry.

Williamsburg, May 7th, 1776.

Dear Sir,

If I had not the highest opinion of your Candour and liberal way of thinking, I should not venture to address myself to you, and if I was not equally perswaded of the great weight and influence, which the transcendent abilities you possess, must naturally confer, I should not give myself the trouble of writing, nor you the trouble of reading this long letter. Since our conversation yesterday, my thoughts have been solely employed, on the great question, whether independence ought, or ought not to be immediately declared? Having weigh'd the arguments on both sides, I am clearly of opinion, that we must (as we value the liberties of America, or even her existence) without a moments delay declare for Independence. If my reasons appear weak you will excuse 'em, for the disinterestedness of the Author; as I may venture to affirm that no man on this Continent will sacrifice more than myself by the separation—But if I have the good fortune to offer any arguments which have escaped your acute understanding and they should make the desired impression I shall think I have render'd the greatest service to the Community. The objection you made yesterday (if I understood you right) to an immediate declaration, was by many degrees the most specious (indeed it was the only tolerable one) that I have yet heard—you say (and with great justice) that we ought previously to have felt the pulse of France and

Spain—I more than believe, I am almost confident that it has been done—at least I can ascertain upon recollection that some of the Committee of Secrecy have assured me, that the sentiments of both these Courts or their Agents had been sounded, and were found to be as favorable as could be wished. But admitting that we are utter strangers to their sentiments of the subject, and that we run some risk of this Declaration's being coldly received by these powers, such is our situation, that the risque must be ventur'd. On one side there are the most probable chances of our success, founded on the certain advantages which must manifest themselves to French understandings by a treaty of Alliance with America. The strength and weakness, the poverty & opulence of every state are estimated in the scale of comparison with her immediate Rival; the superior commerce and marine force of England, were evidently established on the monopoly of her American trade—The inferiority of France, in these two capital points, had its source, consequently from the same origin; any deduction of this monopoly, must bring down her Rival in proportion to the deduction, as the total annihilation of this Commerce, must reduce her to an inferiority, or perhaps total subjection. The French are & always have been sensible of these great truths. Your idea that they may be diverted from a line of policy which ensures 'em such immense and permanent advantages, by an offer of partition from Great Britain, appears to me, if you will excuse the term, an absolute Chimera. They must be wretched politicians indeed, if they wou'd prefer the uncertain acquisition, and the precarious expensive possession of one or two provinces to the greater part of the Commerce of the whole besides were not the advantages from the latter so manifestly greater than those that would accrue from the imagin'd partition Scheme. It is notorious, that acquisition of Territory or even Colonial possessions which require either men or money to retain, are entirely repugnant to the spirit and principles of the present French Court; it is so repugnant indeed, that it is most certain, they have lately entertain'd thoughts of abandoning their West India Islands, *le commerce et le œconomie* are the cry down from the king to the lowest Minister, from these considerations, I am myself convinced, that they will immediately and essentially assist us, if Independence is declared. But allowing that there can be no certainty, but mere bare chances in our favor, I do insist upon it that these chances render it your duty to adopt the measure, as by procrastination our ruin is inevitble; should it now be determined to wait the result of a previous formal negociation with France a whole year must pass over our heads before we can be acquainted with the result. In the meantime we are to struggle through a Campaign without arms, ammunition, or any one necessary of war—disgrace and defeat will infallibly ensue; the soldiers and officers will become so dispirited that they will abandon their Colours and probably never be perswaded to make another effort. But there is another consideration still more cogent. I can assure you, Sir, that the spirit of the people (except a very few in these lower parts of Virginia whose little blood has been suck'd out by musketoes) cry out for this Declaration, the military in particular, men and officers are outrageous on the subject—and a man of your excellent discernment need not be told, how dangerous it would be in present circumstances to dally with the spirit, or disappoint the expectations of the bulk of the People—may not despair, anarchy, and finally submission be the bitter fruits? I am perswaded firmly that they will, and in this perswasion I most devoutly pray, that you may not merely recommend, but positively lay injunctions on your servants in Congress to embrace a measure necessary to Salvation. God Almighty bless you, Sir, and make your Councils whatever they may be, as beneficial to your Country as your capacity to serve it is undoubted.

Yours most entirely
CHARLES LEE.

From Major Josiah Parker.

Dear General,

I arrived at this place on Friday Evening after taking care that all the Houses, Plank, Vessels &c of the Sheddens, Goodrich's, Jamiesons and Sprowles, were totally demolished, every day I kept annoying the Enemy at their breast work, where they were as busily engaged as possible in fortifying themselves; indeed they are now as secure as it is possible for to be, the Otter is near it on the East side as she can lay, the Dunmore on the N.W. and all their Tenders around it, they have now six pieces mounted which they always kept playing upon us when near it, without any damage except one man who receiv'd a Grape shott in his body which I had cut out and he in a fair way of doing well; I found it impracticable to do anything there as the Enemy wou'd not venture out, I thought after we were gone perhaps they might; but here I am baulk'd, for since their train of intelligence is cut off, they expect the woods are lined with men and they keep close in their dens, as I have had parties out every day which cannot discover a soul stirring. All their Merchant Ships are removed below the Mills, which I think indicates fear of something, I hope the Philadelphia Fleet If they come, from their Force, and being so well manned, I think them certain of victory, as not one of those ships at Norfolk are half compleat of men except the Otter, added to this the number of impress'd Seamen who would of course turn of our side provided they saw the glimmering of Victory; in order that you may inform the Congress, if you think proper I will give, a state of the Naval force in Norfolk Harbour & Hampton Road; provided the Roebuck is on shore on Delaware which I am informed she is, from a Capt. Johnson, a prisoner on parole from the Fleet and a Woman which our party picked up yesterday from the Fleet. If their story is true there only remains the Liverpoole of 28 9 & 6 pounders in Hampton road, the Otter of 20 six & four pounders, the W^{m} of six 4 pounders, the Dunmore of 14 from 4 to 9 pounders, the Fincastle Sloop of 10, 4 pounders, & twenty Tenders from two to six small guns, with about Eighty sail of Merchantmen, supposed to be worth 1,500,000 £ currency, indeed their value to us cannot be ascertained, the immensity of warlike stores, salt, &^{c} which are articles so hard to come at, I think deserves the most vigorous push. I am told that Dunmore is so much alarmed, that without speedy assistance he intends to join Cornwallis who is arrived at South Carolina and convey all those valuable effects to the main and grand squadron of this Continent. I have sent you enclosed as good a sketch of Dunmore's lines, the Harbours branches &^{c} as I am capable of drawing myself, which tho' incorrect may serve to give you a faint Idea of a place, which many are unacquainted with. [In the margin is the following.] ☞ I proposed sending you a plan of their Fortification, but as you have seen it and I have not now time to do it as Capt. Grier waits shall defer it 'till another opportunity. The Engineer was with me the other day and had every view he could wish of their Fortifications, he thinks them strong & no possibility of keeping them, if taken without the ships cou'd be got off, if that was the case before they would go, they cou'd carry off their military utensils on a prodigious raft which they have got which will bear at least 300 men, on which they could easily bear off their cannon or anything else in a few minutes, as it is not above 300 yards from their lines, and may be brought within fifty, the Engineer thinks it might be taken by forming a rolling battery, without loss, but the ground itself is of no use. It is true we might destroy their bake houses, which to them are very valuable. I agree with him that it may be accomplished in that manner, and am willing and ready to execute it provided you think proper, as I ever shall be to obey all your commands. As old Goodrich is a prisoner I must beg leave to give you some information which I collected with respect to him—After his son Wm Goodrich had arrived with the Countrys powder from St Eustatia, and the old man hunted about and threatened as he was by Lord Dunmore, in order to make peace with him, and keep us in darkness, he went to him, confessed his fault, opened the plan, and begg'd forgiveness which was granted by his Lordship, who gave him a permit to go to the West Indies; he all this while was passing betwixt Dunmore and us, we thought he was keeping himself out of the Enemy's way, while he was divulging all the secrets of the Cabinet which he could get at, he after some time went to Carolina to go as he inform'd the Committee of Safety to settle the matter and procure the ballance of the Powder, however as he was going out of Ocracock, he was taken by Lieut. Jones of the King Fishers Tender who pay'd no respect to Lord Dunmore's pass but brought him round to Norfolk; when Dunmore understood it he opened the Budget to Montague and they agreed to give him his parole, to go in quest of more news, a better pimp they not have got, for his diligence, at last Convention, made Dunmore esteem him as his first favourite, the Part he has taken since is so glaring, it's needless for me to mention it—this information I received from Captn Eastwood, who was the Capt. who brought in the powder under Wm. Goodrich, and was taken off Ocracock by Lieut. Jones with old Goodrich. He tells me he expected instant death when taken, Goodrich discovered his uneasiness, begg'd him to be compos'd that all was safe by his pass from Lord Dunmore. Eastwood informs me that Goodrich was used ill by Lieut. Jones, from his character as from his pass he cou'd not bear the double dealing of such a traitor. I am informed Col^{o} Peachy has resigned, if so, I do not know in what manner our officers rise in rank, whether by Regiment, by the line, or will of Congress, should they be promoted according to Seniority I am satisfied, if by the Regiment, I know in what manner, but if by merit or caprice of Congress, I must beg that you will remember that no field officer has attended the Regiment but myself since embodyed; I confess myself as high in rank as I could wish and higher than I am capable of executing so well as I cou'd wish; but at the same time I feel that pride, which every officers breast ought to bear.

I am Dr General
Your mo. obdt. & very hble Servt.
J. PARKER.

To EDMUND PENDLETON.

Williamsburgh, May ye 8th 1776.

SIR,

As the enclosed Copy of the result of a Council of Officers this day assembled will not only inform the convention of the measures taken for the security of the Province in my absence, but also comprizes a petition with respect to the serious consequences which may attend the leaving the counties of Princess Ann and Norfolk county in their present situation I take the Liberty of offering it to the consideration of the house, I have received their commands relating to Mr Wormley and have sent orders to Colonel Dangerfield to put 'em in execution.

I am Sir with the greatest respect
Your most obedt humble
CHARLES LEE.

To the Honble Edmd Pendleton
President of the Convention

PROCEEDINGS OF A COUNCIL.

Williamsburgh, May 8, 1776.

As General Clinton has undoubtedly landed, and some transports of the enemy are arrived in North

Carolina, General Lee thinks it his duty immediately to repair to that Province, to take measures for defeating their schemes; but before his departure he esteems it his duty to digest some plan for the safety and security of Virginia. To this end he thinks it necessary to call a Council of all the General and Field Officers at Williamsburgh.

In consequence of these Summonses a Council of the following officers was formed.

Major General Lee

Brig. Gen. Lewis	Brig. Gen. Howe
Coloner Buckner	Colonel Christian
L[t] Col. McClanachan	Lieut Col. Bullit.

General Lee proposes the following questions:

What posts not occupied should be occupied?

What posts now occupied may be abandoned?

1st Does not the Great Bridge seem to be a post of importance?

The Council unanimously agreed that it is a post of the greatest importance, and that it should be maintained by at least four hundred men.

It being agreed that the Great Bridge should be garrisoned the Council are consequently of opinion that Suffolk must likewise be maintained, and that the different defiles between Suffolk and the Great Bridge (which will hereafter be pointed out to the Engineers) be fortified.

The Council consider Suffolk to be of such import ance they unanimously agree that a battalion at least should be kept to defend that post and its dependencies.

2ndly. Does it appear that Kemp's Landing without great risk to the body there stationed, can be supported? Is the importance of this post so great as to counterbalance the risk? But if it is thought necessary to abandon Kemp's Landing, should not the Convention be petitioned to put in execution the former resolve of the Committee of Safety (now rescinded) of obliging all the slaves of a military age, as well as of the white inhabitants who are not manifest active partisans of liberty, to evacuate the counties of Norfolk and Princess Anne, lying between the Great Bridge, ocean, and Currituck Sound; as likewise those residing in that tract between the Eastern and Southern Branches, and those of the lower parts of Nansemond and the Western branch, who have taken the oath to Lord Dunmore.

The Court are of opinion (with only one dissentient) that Kemp's Landing cannot be supported without the greatest risk; that when it is evacuated the whole stock would consequently fall into the hands of the enemy; and therefore the male slaves and all the inhabitants of a military age who are not manifestly active partisans of the publick liberty, will be actively employed for her destruction; that both inclination and necessity will oblige them. In consequence of this opinion they beg leave humbly to petition the Convention to put in execution the resolve of the Committee of Safety (now rescinded) on this subject.

As the getting possession of the capital would give an air of dignity and decided superiority to the enemy which in a country abounding with slaves, is a point of the highest importance, ought not a considerable force be stationed at Williamsburgh and its dependencies, in which are included York, Jamestown, Burrel's Ferry and Hampton?

It is unanimously agreed as strong a force as possible ought to be stationed in the capital and its dependencies.

As, from a consideration of the present weakness of the army in this Province it is impossible to station a force adequate to this purpose, and at the same time to aim at defending the vast extent of country open to the insults of the enemy, can a battalion be spared for the Northern Neck?

The Council are of opinion that only two companies can be spared to be stationed on the Northern Neck, but that they should be reinforced by some companies of Minute-men.

CHARLES LEE, President.

FROM GENERAL JOHN ARMSTRONG.

Charleston, S. C. 8th May, 1776.

SIR,

Your surprise probably may be such as mine was, when on the third Inst. I arrived here, and found that in South Carolina there is not a single soldier on the Continental Establishment, nor have the Commissions of Congress been accepted by any of its Officers.

The Military department which by virtue of the Resolutions of the Provincial Congress had been assigned to the Council of Safety—upon the dissolution of that Body, and forming a new Constitution for the Colony, is assigned by an Ordinance of the Legislature to his Excellency the President from whom the Officers derive their Commissions as well those of the Provincial Regimts as of the Militia.

The President assures me that this separate or Provincial footing of theirs with the reasons inducing them thereto, are at full length laid before the Continental Congress and everything submitted to the decision of that Body, and says he expects an early answer, desiring as I believe the officers generally do, that I wou'd wait until it come. I have now wrote to Congress desiring their further Orders &c and mentioned my waiting the answer unless I should receive your particular Orders to any other Post, which I now begg or at least to be favoured with your advice. Shou'd the Enemy land in No Carolina I intend repairing immediately there where I may expect to see you in person, but shou'd the attack begin here, I am more at a loss what to do, at least until Continental Troops come forward.

The reasons given by this Government for adhering

to their own Military System, are first that the Articles or regulations for discipline, drawn up by Congress, are defective, too mild for the perverse Soldiery of this meridian, to whom 39 lashes wou'd prove but a light breakfast. The drumming out an Officer gives great disgust—difference in the time enlisted for by them which was longer than that directed by Congress—Danger in discharging their troops which they considered as a pre-requisite to their becoming Continental, &c. These are the principal all of which I presume might have been obviated without the least risque to the Service, and they now on the common footing, entitled both to rank & pay, their government making up the Surplus, wch most of the Officers now wish for, and the Governmt have apply'd some time ago to Congress for Continental Rank & pay.

From Georgia I have only heard that the Battalion there has arisen to about four hundred Men, which join'd by their Militia may make about one thousand. I take it for granted you are informed of the late accession to the Fleet at Cape Fear, & the reasons to believe that North Carolina is the first mark in yr district, which is probable—Yet may these appearances vanish & this Colony be the first object, as the Troops at St Augustine said to be two thousand may instigate the Indian Tribes by the aid of their Deputy Superintendent (which some say is in agitation)—join to these Malcontents, and peradventure the domesticks.

I find this Colony have voted four thousand Troops, but about two thousand are yet raised, these stationed at various Posts, and officers out a recruiting—Of the Militia, two hundred & fifty doing duty in Town performed by a monthly rotation.

The propriety of opening the Ports at present has been doubted and altercated in the Legislative Councils here—yielded to on the whole. The greater part of this Province and I hear also of Georgia are for independence—Georgia has also form'd a new Constitution—The Battalion Continental.

I'm called by principles of gratitude and common justice to inform you that the President, Council, and Officers of the Army have treated me with friendship and every mark of civility—have asked kindly for you & much wish your arrival here with one or two thousand Troops.

I am Sir, with great respect
Your most Obedt. humb[le] Serv[t]
JOHN ARMSTRONG.

General Lee.

FROM GENERAL WASHINGTON.

New York, May [9th], 1776.

MY DEAR LEE,

Your favour of the 5th ult. from Williamsburg, the first I have received from you since you left this city, came to my hands by the last post. I thank you for your kind congratulations on our possession of Boston. I thank you for your good wishes in our future operations, and hope that every diabolical attempt to deprive mankind of their inherent rights and privileges, whether made in the East, West, North, or South, will be attended with disappointment and disgrace, and that the authors in the end will be brought to such punishment, as an injured people have a right to inflict.

General Howe's retreat from Boston was precipitate, beyond any thing I could have conceived. The destruction of the stores at Dunbar's camp after Braddock's defeat was but a faint image of what was seen at Boston; artillery carts cut to pieces in one place; gun carriages in another; shells broke here; shot buried there, and every thing carrying with it the face of disorder and confusion, as also of distress.

Immediately upon their embarkation, I detached a brigade of five regiments to this city, and upon their sailing, removed with the whole army hither, except four regiments at Boston, and one at Beverley, &c., for the protection of those places, the stores and barracks there, and for erecting works for defending the harbour of the first. Immediately upon my arrival here I detached four regiments by order of Congress to Canada, (to wit, Poors, Patterson's, Greaton's and Bond's) under the command of Brigadier Thompson, and since that, by the same authority, and in consequence of some unfavourable accounts from that quarter, General Sullivan and six other regiments, namely, Starke's, Reed's, Wain's, Irvine's, Wind's and Dayton's have moved off for that department; the four last regiments are of Pennsylvania and New-Jersey. The first brigade arrived at Albany the twenty-fourth ultimo, and were moving on, when accounts came from thence the twenty-seventh. The other brigade must all be at Albany before this, as some of the regiments sailed ten days ago, and the last four, and the winds very favourable. This has left us very weak at this place, whilst I have my fears that the reinforcement will scarce get to Canada in time, for want of teams to transport the troops, &c. to Fort George, and vessels to convey them on afterwards.

We have done a great deal of work at this place. In a fortnight more, I think the city will be in a very respectable posture of defence. Governor's Island has a large and strong work erected, and a regiment encamped there. The point below, called Red Hook, has a small, but exceeding strong barbet battery; and several new works are constructed, and many of them almost executed at other places.

General Ward, upon the evacuation of Boston, and finding that there was a probability of his removing from the smoke of his own chimney, applied to me, and wrote to Congress for leave to resign. A few days afterwards, some of the officers, as he says, getting *uneasy* at the prospect of his leaving them, he applied for his letter of resignation, which had been committed to my care; but, behold! it had been carefully forwarded to Congress, and as I have since learnt, judged so reasonable, (*want of health* being the plea,) that it was instantly complied with. Brigadier Fry, previous to this, also conceiving that there was nothing entertaining or profitable to an old man, to be marching and counter-marching, desired, immediately on the evacuation of Boston, (which happened on the 17th of March,) that he might *resign his commission on the* 11*th of April:* the choice of the day became a matter of great speculation, and remained profoundly mysterious till he exhibited his account, when there appeared neither more nor less in it, than the completion of three calendar months; the pay of which he received without any kind of compunction, although he had never done one tour of duty, or, I believe, had ever been out of his house from the time he entered till he quitted Cambridge.

So much for two Generals: I have next to inform you that the Pay-master-general, Colonel Warren, not finding it convenient to attend the army, from the varinous employments and avocations in which he was engaged, also resigned his commission, and is succeeded by your old aid, Palfrey.

When I was speaking of the distressed situation of the king's troops, and the tories, at their evacuation of Boston, I might have gone on, and added, that their misfortunes did not end here. It seems upon their arrival at Halifax, many of the former were obliged to encamp, although the ground was covered deep with snow; and the latter, to pay six dollars a-week for sorry upper-rooms, and stow in them, men, women, and children, as thick comparatively, as the hair upon their heads. This induced many of these gentry to return, and throw themselves upon the mercy and clemency of their countrymen, who were for sending them immediately back, as the properest and severest punishment they could inflict; but death being preferred to this, they now wait in confinement, any other that may be thought due to such parricides.

All the ships of war have left this place, and gone down to the Hook, except the Asia, which lays five miles below the Narrows, and about twelve or fourteen from hence. I could have added more, but my paper will not admit of it. With compliment, therefore, to the gentlemen of my acquaintance with you, and with the most fervent wishes for your health and success,

I remain, Your most affectionate,

G. WASHINGTON.

Major General Lee.

TO EDMUND PENDLETON.

Williamsburg May 9th, 1776.

SIR,

As I am obliged by the arrival of the Enemy to repair to North Carolina, and am not less prompted by my zeal and affection for this Province, than oblig'd by my duty to take every precaution for its safety before my departure; on this Principle, I beg leave to lay before the Convention, the following measures which I conceive to be necessary.

1st To devise some means for establishing a Corps of Cavalry, without which, an army is so extremely defective in every part of the world, and in none more than in this, for reasons which it might be tedious to enumerate.

2ndly. Without delay to order some able Pilots of every River to examine accurately the narrowest part of the channel of each river, what is the nature of the Shoals which form these Channels? whether they are solid, firm, sand, gravel, or rock? What is the distance of the nearest part of the Channel from either shore? What is the nature of the shore, whether it is high or low? for I am sanguine enough to hope when these circumstances are ascertain'd, the navigation of most of the Rivers may be shut up to the Enemy, by means of batteries either floating or fixed.

3rdly As these purposes cannot be effected without

a large body of Carpenters, Smiths, & Artificers, of every sort, to establish some Companies of 'em subject to the military laws, as without a coercive power, it is difficult in this part of the world to prevail upon 'em to work.

4thly As I understand there are prodigious stocks of Sheep and Cattle on the Islands near the Eastern shore, and as my authority does not extend to whatever concerns property, that you will order immediately all this stock to be transported to the Continent, and if this is impracticable to kill them, as otherwise they must indisputably fall into the hands of the Enemy.

5thly As the Eastern Counties are from their great abundance of all the necessaries of Life, so tempting objects to the incursions of the Enemy, & as I understand that there will be no difficulty in procuring good men, I would humbly propose to the Convention, to augment Col. Flemings Regiment to the same strength of numbers with the other Battalions. I must now Sir, beg leave to mention to the Gentlemen of the Convention a very important matter of consideration, no less than the preservation of the lives of your soldiers. The Continental allowance to Surgeons & Surgeons Mates of the Regiments is so miserably small, and at the same time the common country practice of Surgeons is so very lucrative in this Province, that it is not possible to find men qualified for the station who will accept: and as I cannot venture to propose to the Continental Congress the increase of the pay of the Surgeons of the whole army, merely because this increase is necessary in my division, I must submit it to the judgment of the Convention whether such an addition, as to bring up the pay of these Gentlemen to the original Provincial Ordinance will not be money well and necessarily expended.

I am Sir, with the greatest Respect

Yours &c,

CHARLES LEE.

To the President of Congress.

Williamsburg, May ye 10th 1776.

Sir,

Inclosed is a Packet I have just received from North Carolina, as likewise a Resolve of the Convention of Virginia in consequence of this intelligence. I had before detached a Battalion of Riflemen to Halifax for which place I intend to set out myself the day after tomorrow—there is a noble spirit in this Province pervading all orders of men, if the same becomes universal we shall be saved. I am fortunately for my own happiness, & I think for the well being of the community on the best of Terms with the Senatorial part as well as the People at large—I shall endeavour to preserve their confidence and good opinion, I am extremely distress'd for Engineers, and the two that I have tell me that they will be under the necessity of resigning, as they cannot subsist on their present military pittance. I hope the Congress will think proper to increase their salary and their number—May I without presumption urge to the Congress the absolute necessity of straining every nerve to possess themselves of Niagara at least, if not Detroit?

I am Sir, with the greatest respect,

Your most ob^{t} hum: ser^{t},

Charles Lee

Copy of the Resolve referred to in the foregoing.

In Convention, May 10, 1776.

Resolved, that 1150 men consisting of minute men and militia, be immediately rais'd in the following Counties, & Proportions, that is to say: Albemarle 100, Amherst 50, Amelia 100, Brunswick 100, Buckingham 50, Cumberland 50, Dinwiddie 50, Charlotte 50, Halifax 100, Hanover 100, Louisa 50, Lunenburg 100, Maclenburg 100, Prince Edward 50, Sussex 50, Pittsylvania 150, and sent to the assistance of North Carolina.

TO GENERAL WASHINGTON.

Williamsburgh, May 10, 1776.

MY DEAR GENERAL:

The most compendious method to give you an idea of the state of your Province is to enclose you the result of a council of officers, every article of which is approved by your Convention. We have just received an express from North Carolina informing us of the arrival of eight large transports in Cape Fear River, on the whole containing as it is supposed about two thousand men. I had before on a suspicion of their arrival detached a battalion of riflemen and shall set out myself the day after to morrow. The Convention has ordered 1200 militia or Minute-men to that Province. My command (as you may easily perceive) is extremely perplexing from the consideration of the vast extent of vulnerable parts of this country intersected by such a variety of navigable waters and the expedition with which the enemy (furnished with canvass wings) can fly from one spot to another. Had we arms for the minute men and half a dozen good field Engineers, we might laugh at their efforts; but in this article (like the rest of the Continent) we are miserably defficient. Engineers, we have but two, and they threaten to resign, as it is impossible they should subsist on a more wretched pittance than common carpenters or bricklayers, can earn. I have written to Congress entreating them to augment the pay: a word from you would, I make no doubt, effect it.

I wish, my dear General, you would send me Captain Smith, on condition the Congress make it worth his while, otherwise I have not conscience to propose it. I am well pleased with your officers in general, and the men are good, some Irish rascals excepted. I have formed two companies of grenadiers to each regiment; and with spears of thirteen feet long, their rifles (for they are all riflemen) slung over their shoulders, their appearance is formidable, and the men are conciliated to the weapon. I am likewise furnishing myself with four-ounced rifled amusettes, which will carry an infernal distance; the two-ounced hit a half sheet of paper at five hundred yards distance. So much for military.

A noble spirit possesses the Convention. They are almost unanimous for independence, but differ in their sentiments about the mode; two days will decide it. I have the pleasure to inform you that I am extremely well in the opinion of the Senatorial part, as well as of the people at large. God send me the grace to preserve it. But their neighbors of Maryland (I mean their Council of Safety) make a most damnable clamor (as I am informed) on the subject of a letter I wrote to the Chairman of the Committee of Baltimore, to seize the person and papers of Mr. Eden, upon the discovery which was communicated to me of his treacherous correspondence with the Secretary of State; it was not only a measure justifiable in the eyes of God and men, but absolutely necessary. The Committee of Safety here are indeed as deep in the scrape as myself. The Congress must, and will, I dare say, support and vindicate the measure. Captain Green and his party are upon their march, as you ordered. I was a damned blockhead for bringing them so far, as their accounts will be intricate; but I hope not so intricate as not to be unriddled.

I send you an account of the money I advanced to the different officers—to Captains Smith, Lunt, and Green. I have taken the liberty to appoint a Sergeant Denmark of the Rifle battalion to do duty as an Ensign. He is a man of worth, and I beg that you will confirm his commission. Another Sergeant of the same battalion I have promoted to the rank of Second Lieutenant in the artillery of this Province. He is a German, his name Holmer, and very deserving. If little Eustace cannot be provided for with you, I could wish, if there is a cheap method of doing it, you would send him to me, as I have it in my power to place him and quite doat upon him. My love to M[rs] Washington, Gates, and her bad half, to Moylan, but Palfrey is a scoundrel for not writing. Adieu, my dear General

Yours, most Sincerely

C. Lee

To General Washington.

To Richard Henry Lee.

Williamsburgh, May 10, 1776.

My Dear Friend,

Your brother and I think, from the language of your letters, that the pulse of the Congress is low, and that you yourself, with all your vigour, are by collision, somewhat more contracted in your hopes than we wished to have found. If you do not declare immediately for positive independence, we are all ruined. There is a poorness of spirit and languor in the late proceedings of Congress that I confess frightens me so much that at times I regret having embarked my all, my fortune, life, and reputation, in their bottom. I sometimes wish I had settled in some country of slaves, where the most lenient master governs. However, let the fate of my property be what it will, I hope I shall preserve my reputation, and resign my breath with a tolerable degree of grace. God bless you. I cannot write more at present. "Ah, Cassius, I am sick of many griefs."

Yours, most entirely,

Charles Lee

Honourable Richard Henry Lee.

To Edmund Pendleton.

Williamsburg, 10th May, 1776.

Sir,

We remain, after consideration, of opinion, that the Inhabitants of the Counties of Norfolk & Princess Anne from their dangerous & exposed situation & notorious disaffection to the common cause of America, ought immediately to be removed; that such of them as are nearest the Enemy, should first be attended to and without the least delay be compell'd to withdraw with their property to an interior part of this, or some other Colony; and that even those who being near our Guards may not venture, or being distant from the Enemy can with less convenience supply them, should be obliged directly to drive off their stocks and carry all their slaves fit to bear arms to a place of Safety. The Inhabitants who may be permitted to remain longest at their habitations, are those who reside on that side of the Great Bridge next to Carolina along ye Road to the Northwest Landing and down the Neck of Land to Carratuck sound, and those between the Bridge of Suffolk who are not immediately in the power of the Enemy (which by reference to the enclos'd rough sketch of the country will more fully appear). Above all, we consider the Inhabitants of that tract of Country, between the Eastern & Southern Branches as most dangerous to the Community both from their Situation and Principles, & that they ought first to be remov'd.

We are Sir, with great Respect
Your most obt humble Servants

Charles Lee,
Robert Howe.

The Hone Edmund Pendleton,
President of the Convention.

To Major Hendricks.

Williamsburg, May 11, 1776.

Sir,

I join with you entirely that a flag of truce ought to be esteemed sacred, and much approve your good sense and spirit in remonstrating against their irregular and insolent proceeding if it is repeated. I wou'd have you consider the respect due to the flag annihilated by the improper mode of conducting it. I am likewise of your opinion that these people who come ashore on their parole are extremely dangerous. I have put a stop to it at Kemp's Landing and desire you will do the same at Hampton, when our powder arrives you shall have some of it, the Artillery Officer will be down with you in a few days, the eighteen pounders which are good must be sent up here, as I think you can have no use for 'em at Hampton. When you write again address yourself to Brig.[r] Lewis as I shall set out for Halifax to-morrow. You are to put in execution the sentence on a Deserter from Capt.[n] FitzGerald's Comp.[a]—it is a just & good sentence.

I am Sir, with the greatest respect,

Your most ob.[t] Serv.[t]

Charles Lee.

Major Hendrick

Com.[t] at Hampton.

To Edmund Pendleton.

Williamsburg May 11.th 1776.

Sir,

Upon consulting with General Howe, I find it will be most conducible to the Service to order your militia to Halifax, where they shall receive further Orders from me. The difference of the Continental Establishment and that of the Province, will occasion, I am afraid, much confusion—for instance, the pay of the Artillery here is two shillings per diem—that of the Artillery in the Army to the Eastward no more than other soldiers—if we should attempt to reduce it, this Company so essentially necessary for the service, will consequently be dissolved, and to propose the augmentation of it to the Congress wou'd appear perhaps unreasonable, as it wou'd put them under the necessity of raising the pay of this Corps universally. I therefore, Sir, must beg leave to lay my perplexity on this head before the Convention. Mr. Agnew who was lately tryed by the Committee, and is allowed to be a most irreclaimable Enemy was seen the day before the Enemy made their last predatory expedition to Hog Island in consultation with Mr. Holt a suspected Tory on the very scene of their depredations—shou'd a man so dangerous be suffered at large? a Mr Wright in Glocester may as I informed do, & has done much mischief.

I am Sir, with the greatest Respect,

Your most obt humble Servant,

CHARLES LEE

To the Hon. Edmund Pendleton,

President of the Convention.

TO COL. WILLIAM WOODFORD.

Williamsburg, May 11th 1776.

DEAR COLONEL,

I pitty you most sincerely for your damn'd employment, but so far from flattering you with being relieved of the burthen, that I may announce to you, its growing more irksome and difficult—the convention have order'd the first Resolve of the Committee to be put rigidly in execution. You must proceed therefore with vigor if the Suffolk carts do not come down they must be press'd—Colonel Stephen will receive an order on this subject. have you order'd Muhlenberg's Regiment to march for Halifax? I hope to God, you have, for no time is to be lost, as we have certain news of the Enemy's arrival in the River Cape Fear. I set out tomorrow myself. so you must direct your Letters on Virginia Business to General Lewis. let Muhlenburg have the waggons & provisions necessary as far as Halifax. I hope he has a Quarter master who is capable of acting as Commissary for so small a body as one Regiment, Capt[n] Knox will follow the Regiment, so the Colonel must not wait for him. You may inform him that I have also order'd stores of all kinds for his Regiment to Halifax—once more, I entreat he may march immediately. I desire no more prisoners on their Parole may be admitted on shore. They do mischief. I have left your Canteens with Colonel Finney. but have taken the liberty to exchange the bottles as your's are larger than mine. Adieu D[r] Colonel. God bless you.

C. Lee.

My compliments to all your People. If the Baron has set the works of the bridge agoing—send him to Halifax, but you must furnish him with the money he wants to discharge his Debts at the Bridge, and bear his expenses on the Road. Your Regiment & the 2[d] will be relieved as soon as possible.

Col. William Woodford,
Kemp's.

From Richard Henry Lee.

Philadelphia 11th May 1776.

My dear Friend,

Since I wrote you last nothing of consequence hath happened, unless it be, that the Roebuck & Liverpoole coming up the river Delaware, were met a few miles above New Castle by the 13 Gondolas of this city, and after a cannonade of 3 hours each day for two successive days, the ships returned down the river, and the Gallies to their former Station—The latter unhurt, and the former repulsed after being pretty well pepper'd with shot from 18 to 32 pounders. My friendship for you is so strong, and the sense I have of the obligations America is under to you so high, that I shall ever pray the liberty of being full and free on every subject that materially concerns you. I find a spirit prevailing here, which leads its possessors to regard with a jealous eye, every instance of deviation (in a military or naval Commander) from the line of instructions, and every undertaking productive of expense which is not warranted by express order of Congress. Thus animated, I find some Gentlemen expressing dissatisfaction at your having promised forage and rations to such Cavalry as might be assembled in Virginia, & likewise because of the boats you had ordered to be built for the security of the Rivers. You know my friend that the spirit of liberty is a jealous spirit, and that Senators are not always wise and candid, but that frequently they are governed by envy, enmity, and a great variety of bad passions—Upon these considerations, may it not be prudent when it can be done, without danger, to the common cause previously to obtain the Consent of Congress, where much deviation from the usual rotine of business is requisite, and especially where expence is created thereby. Such is the opinion entertained of you, that when you press a thing as necessary, if it is in the power of Congress, I am inclined to think a majority of that Body will readily adopt the measure. What I hear and see has induced me to say thus much —I am satisfied that *verbum sapienti sat est*—some still continue to gape for Commissioners, altho' there is no more reason to expect any than to look for virtue from a Tory, or wisdom from a fool. I fancy the Hessian, Hanoverian, & Highland Commissioners, will shortly give us a different kind of treaty from the one that has been expected. We have no very late authentic accounts from Canada, but those we have, do not remove all hope of Quebec being ours before assistance can reach it.

The Proprietary Colonies do certainly obstruct and perplex the American Machine—Those who wish delay, and want nothing done, say, let the people in the Colonies begin, we must not go before them—Tho' they well know the language in the Country to be, Let the Congress advise. In fact, the other Colonies must do what is right, and on giving proper and positive orders to their Servants in Congress, the Proprietary men will be obliged to pursue the right road. Before this reaches you I suppose the powder and medicines will be arrived, and the Blankets and shoes will quickly follow. We have had 23 Tons of powder, and a good deal of Saltpetre arrived within these 10 days. Since writing the above, a french Gentleman, who appears sensible and clever, has been with us. His letter is enclosed. He has been bred to Cavalry, and wishes to serve in Virginia. As a Committee of Congress has already reported against having Continental Cavalry in North Carolina, I suppose the same opinion will prevail respecting Virginia. But the measure is so wise and necessary for the defence of our Colony, that I wish and hope a few squadrons will be formed on Colonial expence, in which case, this Gentleman w[d] answer well as an Instructor & Commander.

Farewell my dear friend,

Richard Henry Lee.

To General Washington.

Williamsburgh, May 11, 1776.

Dear General:

I should be deficient in gratitude as well as duty if I did not recommend in the strongest terms, Captain

Grier. He has shown so much care, industry, zeal, and activity, that I entreat you will patronize him in the most particular manner. You will oblige me, therefore, in the highest degree, by taking him under your protection.

I am, dear General, affectionately and entirely yours,

CHARLES LEE.

To His Excellency General Washington.

FROM CHRISTOPHER FRENCH.

Hartford, 13th May 1776.

SIR,

You, no doubt remember that, when you pass'd through this Place in January last, you made a Bett of Ten Guineas with me that Quebec would be taken by the Provincials in the Course of the current Winter; That event has not happen'd (nor is there now the least prospect that it ever will, as there are accounts, not only of its having been reinforc'd by a part of His Majesty's Fleet, and a large Body of his Troops, but that His Excellency Genl Carleton has drove them entirely from before it) &, indeed, your own Papers, unaccustom'd as they are to communicate to the Public anything which argues against their Successes, have lately inserted some very desponding Letters from that Quarter; They also regret that you was not sent there to command them, and though, as you are become our Enemy, I cannot be so gross as to wish you had with success, yet I am not so much yours, as to envy you the Honor you might have acquir'd by a well concerted Retreat which, though you might not have effected, yet I know you would have attempted, a circumstance which, from your being at the head of such raw & undisciplined Forces could only have added to the brilliancy of your measures. You will be pleas'd to direct Mr Lawrence, Treasurer here, to pay me, which will much oblige

Sir,

Your most obt. hble. Servant

CHRIS. FRENCH.

To Genl Lee,
Williamsburg
Savannah, Georgia.

FROM BRIG. GEN. JAMES MOORE.

Wilmington, No Carolina, May 19, 1776.

SIR,

Since sealing my letter to you by the Express, Col. Nash (who is with a detachment about 11 Miles from Fort Johnson) writes me that the Enemy have landed 1700 Men & some pieces of Artillery & formed a Camp ¾ of a Mile back from the Fort. There is between sixty and 70 Sail of Topsail Vessels in this River, and the following Ships of War, viz: The Solbay, & Action, 28 Guns each, Spinx and Mercury 20 Guns each, Scorpion and Falcon 14 Guns each, & the Bristol of 50 Guns laying off the bar. Sir Peter Parker has hoisted his flag on board the Solbay. I have the honor to be

Sir,

Your obedt hble. Servant

JA. MOORE.

Major Genl Lee.

FROM HENRY STUART, ETC.

GENTLEMEN,

Sometime ago Mr Cameron & myself wrote you a letter by Mr Thomas & inclosed you the talk we had with the Indians respecting the Purchase which 'tis reported you lately made of them for the Rivers Wattauger, Nolichucky &c. We are since informed that you are under great apprehensions of the Indians doing Mischief, but it is not the design of his Majesty to set his Friends and Allies the Indians on his liege subjects. Therefore, however if you are willing to join his Majesty's forces as soon as they arrive at the Cherokee Nation by repairing to the Kings Standard, shall find protection, and their Families and Estates be secure from all Danger whatever. Yet that his Majesty's Officers may be certain which of you are willing to take up Arms in defence of the Kings just rights, I have thought fit to recommend it to you every one that is desirous of preventing inevitable ruin to himself and Family immediately to subscribe a written Paper, acknowledging their Allegiance to his Majesty King George, and that they're ready and willing whenever call'd on to appear in Arms in defence of the British Rights in America, which Paper as soon as it is assigned send to me by some safe hand, should any of the Inhabitants be desirous of knowing how they are to be kept free from every kind of insult or danger, inform them that his Majesty will immediately land an Army in West Florida, and march them through the Creek Nation to the Chicasaws where 500 Warriors from each Nation are to join them and then come by the Cherokees, who have also promised their Assistance, then take possession of the Frontiers of North Carolina, & Virginia, at the same time that his Majesty's Forces make a Diversion on the coasts of them Provinces. If any of the Inhabitants have Cattle, Pack Horses, Flour to spare by applying to us they shall have a good price for them as soon as his Majesty's troops are embodied.

I am Gents, &c

HENRY STUART,
Deputy Superintendent.

Wattauger, ss.

This day came Nathaniel Reed before me one of the Trustees assigned to keep the Peace for the district aforesaid, and make Oath on the Holy Evangelist and Almighty God, that a Stranger rode up to Mr Robertson's yesterday in the Evening. Who he was he did not know and delivered a letter, a true copy of which is above.

Given under my hand this 19th May 1776.

JOHN CARTER.

Test: Jas Smith.

A true Copy of a letter laid before the Virginia Convention.

EDM^D PENDLETON, P^r.

TO BRIGADIER GENERAL MOORE.

Halifax, May ye 20th 1776.

SIR,

In consequence of a letter from the Committee of Safety of your Province, apprizing us of the arrival of several transports in Cape Fear River, as also of the weakness of the Province from the consideration of the number of Enemy's lodged in your bosoms (the Highlanders and Regulators) the Convention of Virginia voted immediately a body of thirteen hundred militia and minute men to march for this Province, on my part, I order'd a Battalion of Riflemen to rendezvous at Halifax. I suppose they will arrive tomorrow. I shall then march without delay to Newbern, unless I am inform'd on the rout that the Enemy are reimbark'd, which I am inclin'd to think will be the case, for since the overthrow of their scheme by Colonel Caswell's victory I cannot see what advantages they can propose to themselves by any operations in North Carolina, it is probable Rage and revenge (which at present alone seem to actuate the King and his accursed instruments) may inspire 'em before their departure with the lust of destroying Wilmington—but I am in hopes you are already strong enough to prevent the accomplishment. The Assurances which you may give your people that a body is on their march to support them, will probably add to their natural spirit and vigor. You may easily conceive, Sir, how perplexing is my situation—it is my duty to superintend the Security and safety of four wide extended Provinces, the enemy being furnished with canvass wings can fly with expedition from one quarter to ano^r I may of course be in the North when apparently I ought to be in the South, or in the South when I ought to be in the North; I may be censur'd without any real demerits—this consideration gives a check to my motions which wou'd otherwise be more rapid, for instance, cou'd I be assur'd that it was the intention of the Enemy to lodge themselves seriously in this Province, I wou'd post night & day to join you. * * * * *

To Brig. Gen. Moore,
at Cape Fear.

From Richard Henry Lee.

Philadelphia, 21st May, 1776.

My dear Friend,

As I wrote you yesterday by your Express, I have now only to thank you for your favor by last post. If you discovered any languor in my letters it must have been merely corporeal, the mental powers having been just as vigorous as ever. Excessive writing and constant attention to business afflicts me a good deal I own, but they are far from depressing my spirits in the great cause of America, and if you were to consult with our *moderate men* in and out of doors you would think me possessed of something else than languor. The mischievous instructions from some Colonies have indeed fettered Congressional Councils, but many of these are done away, and the rest will be so immediately The

[late] Resolve of Congress respecting government hath wrought a great change hereabouts, and very soon the Public affairs will wear a different aspect, and be directed with better spirit. I expect an expedition to Detroit will be undertaken, Niagara will probably be suspended, as the Indians thereabout wish it to continue a place of trade yet awhile. A Gentleman just from N. York, tells us that 70 sail of Transports with 10,000 troops were arrived off the Hook; and that Gen. Washington was dispatching an Express to Congress, a confirmation is hourly expected. They have made the works about N. York very strong, and tho' the detachment of 10 Battalions to Canada, has not left above 8,000, yet 10, or 12000 militia may be thrown in, so that we apprehend no danger from that quarter.

Farewell, my dear Sir,

RICHARD HENRY LEE.

Early in April I gave you an Account of the affair of the Annapolis Council.

General Lee, Commander of the Continental Forces in the Southern Department, at Williamsburg, Virginia.

PROCEEDINGS OF THE MARYLAND CONVENTION.

In Convention, Annapolis, May 24th 1776.

Resolved, that it is the opinion of this Convention that the Council of Safety of this province, upon the subject of the late intercepted letters to Governor Eden, duly & properly exercised the powers delegated to them.

Resolved, that it is the opinion of this Convention, that upon the evidence before them of the correspondence which his Excellency Governor Eden has from time to time held with Administration, it does not appear that such correspondence has been with an unfriendly intent or calculation to countenance any hostile measures against America.

Whereas by a late intercepted letter from Lord George Germain, one of the Secretaries of State, to his Excellency the Governor, it appears that a great armament of land and sea forces was in readiness to proceed to the Southward, in his Lordships expression "in order to attempt the restoration of legal government in that part of America," but in effect to invade and subdue the Southern Colonies, which Armament was to proceed in the first place to North Carolina, and from thence to South Carolina, or Virginia, as circumstances of greater, or less advantage should point out, if to the latter, it might have very important consequences to this province, and therefore, in the said letter, his Excellency is called on well to consider of every means by which he may, in conjunction with Lord Dunmore give facility and assistance to the operations of the said Armament. And Whereas the Governor must, if he remains in the exercise of the powers of government, fulfill and execute the instructions of Administration, or hazard the displeasure of the King, which it cannot be expected he will do; And Whereas by Act of Assembly of this Province, the powers of Government, in the absence of the Governor, devolves upon the President of the Council, and therefore the Governor's departure cannot occasion a dissolution, or suspension of the present established form of Government within this province which this convention doth not think ought now to be changed.

Therefore Resolved, that it be signified to the Governor that the publick quiet and safety in the judgment of this convention require that he leave this province; & that he is at full liberty to depart peaceably with his effects.

Resolved, that a Committee of five persons be appointed to wait on his Excellency with a copy of the above resolutions, together with the following Address, to wit:

To His Excellency Robert Eden, Esq. Governor of Maryland.

May it please your Excellency,

We are commanded by the Convention to wait upon your Excellency to communicate to you the Resolutions they have this day entered into, & are instructed to assure your Excellency that the Convention entertains a favorable sense of your conduct relative to the affairs of America since the unhappy differences have subsisted between Great Britain and the United Colonies, as far as the same hath come to their knowledge, and of their real wishes for your return to resume the government of this province whenever we shall happily be restored to peace and that connection with Great Britain, the interruption and suspension of which have filled the mind of every good man with the deepest regret. From the disposition your Excellency hath manifested to promote the real interests of both Countries, the Convention is induced to entertain the warmest hopes and expectations, that, upon your arrival in England, you will represent the temper and principles of the people of Maryland with the same candour you have hitherto shewn; and that you will exert your endeavours to promote a reconciliation, upon terms that may be secure and honourable both to Great Britain and America.

Extracts from the Minutes:

G. Duvall.

To Edmund Pendleton.

Halifax, May ye 24th 1776.

Sir,

The disorderly mutinous and dangerous disposition of the soldiers of the 8th Reg^t^ have detain'd me longer in this place than I cou'd have wish'd more particularly as We hear (tho the accounts are not well authenticated) that the whole fleet of Transports under Lord Cornwallis is arrived at Cape Fear. We have at length after infinite trouble got this Banditti out of the Town and of course I set out myself immediately, on the road I expected an express from General Moore ascertaining me of the Enemy's motions and intentions, as it is more than probable that They will re-embark and bend their course towards Virginia I shall proceed slowly, that on the supposition They do re-embark my journey back may require less time—but as it is still possible that They may seriously have thoughts of lodging themselves in this Province, I wish to be so near that I can join General Moore in forty eight hours—Newbern for these reasons seems a proper station untill I can obtain some further lights with regard to their designs—the spirit of desertion in these back Country Troops is so alarmingly great that I must submit it to the wisdom of the Convention whether it is not of the utmost importance to devise some means to put a stop to it before it spreads, by enjoining the Committees of the different Counties to seize every Soldier who cannot produce an authentic discharge or pass and throw him into the County jail until He can be convey'd to the Reg[t] to which He belongs—or by some other means—but the Convention are much better Judges than I can possibly be of the proper method to be pursued. I can only affirm that unless some effectual method is devis'd and adopted it will be impossible for us to keep the Field—the old Countrymen particularly the Irish whom the officers have injudiciously inlisted in order to fill up their Companies have much contaminated the Troops; and if more care is not taken on this head for the future the whole Army will be one mass of disorder, vice, and confusion—altho' I have so great reason to complain of the misconduct of this Reg[t] I must do the officers, particularly the Field officers the justice to say that their conduct is in general very satisfactory.

The Gentlemen of this Province with whom I have convers'd seem to me a little too secure in the perswasion that the Highlanders and Regulators are incapacitated from acting. General Howe as well as myself is of a different opinion, so that upon the whole the vote of Virginia Convention to march the Militia may be attended with most salutary effects, and cannot with any bad ones—had I not consider'd the spirit of desertion [of a] very alarming nature, I should not have troubled the Convention with this letter—As you will perceive that it contains no other matter of sufficient importance for their perusal—but I once more request that They will take this affair into their consideration and devise some means of stifling the evil before it get too great a head.

I am Sir, Yours,

CHARLES LEE

TO COLONEL ——.

Tarborough, May ye 25th 1776.

DR COLONEL—

I have so great a reliance on your discretion and the zeal of a great part of your officers that I am perswaded the directions I leave will be literally (and without confusion) followed.

It is my intention that you shall march to Duplins Court House and there encamp (as you have no tents) in the Indian manner as conveniently to your people as possible.

You will find all necessaries both for your men and horses at proper stations 'till you arrive at Harrison's on Bears Creek where the roads fork, here you will meet with a Mr Miller who will repair to this fork, conduct you to the Court House, and supply you with all kinds of provisions for your Corps—At this Camp you must wait for further orders.

I am myself oblig'd to proceed by the way of Newbern. I hear that two of your officers have behav'd extremely ill; for God's sake send them about their busyness quietly—if They consent to be dismiss'd quietly—but if They are refractory leave 'em in arrest at this place under the care of Colonel Erwin till They can be brought formally to a Court Martial. I wish you much more ease and satisfaction in your march than you have hitherto experienced.

Yours

CHARLES LEE.

Send some officer to Mr Miller who lives six miles from the fork to apprise him of your arrival and your wants.

You will put the Waggon with the Intrenching tools under the direction of Colo Irwin of this Place, who will forward them under a Guard of a party of his Regiment to Wilmington.

I desire you will not halt in this Town, without you find it absolutely necessary, and then only for a little time.

TO EDMUND PENDLETON.

Tarborough, May ye 25th 1776.

SIR,

As I think it my duty to convey every information of the motions and intentions or even the surmises of the motions and intentions of the Enemy to the Convention of Virginia of whom I have so high an opinion, and for whom my veneration increases daily, I take the liberty to inclose Copies of the letters I have received from General Moore and Mr Rutledge—from the import of these letters you will see that the most probable conjecture is that their first object is S. Carolina—You will of course have time to put your Province in some state of defence. I hope and conjure that no time may be lost in attempting to raise batteries on the shoals and banks of the rivers which form their respective channels, I must likewise urge the necessity of immediately raising a body of Horse, the necessity of which I feel every day more sensibly—We cannot really do without them. We met on the road two officers from S. Carolina, a Mr Drayton and Mr Elliot, whose busyness is to petition your Convention to permit them to recruit in Virginia, it not being possible to find Men in their Province—it appears to me that on one hand it is absolutely necessary for the common safety that this permission shou'd be given, on the other that many inconveniences will result from it—their bounties are so high that it may render the recruiting of the Virginia Regiments more difficult. The Men may grow exorbitant in their demands—the case is perplexing, but of two evils We must chuse the least. Suppose, Sir, for I confess I speak at a venture, you were to order a draft of Volunteers from the different Regiments, that the Caroliners were to refund the bounty money which had been given to your men, and to add as a temptation what They think proper. I do not believe that by adopting this method many of the native Virginians will offer themselves—the Irish, I am perswaded in crowds—to this, one objection may be made, that you will purge your Army of bad subjects at the expense of another Province—but I must observe that the ordinances of S. Carolina are much better calculated to keep these sort of refractory spirits in order than the Continental Ordinances—their laws are more severe, and severity is necessary for an Irish soldiery—I'm well acquainted with their dispositions, and know that the lenient measures and familiar manners adapted to the genius of your people only tend to inspire the Irish with the Spirit of stubbornness and mutiny—I must repeat, Sir, that I only offer an opinion, and wou'd not be thought to advise—it is so late at night that you will pardon the conciseness of this letter, and believe me to be with the greatest respect Sir,

Your most obedt and humble Servt

CHARLES LEE.

P. S. The personal civil things to me express'd by

M[r] Rutledge are left as they are not through vanity, but I really had not time to [erase] them—As it is possible that the mode I have hinted may occasion some discontent to the officers who have taken pains to form Companies, it may not be amiss previously to any resolution to consult with the Colonels.

From Isaac Reed to Gen. Lewis.

Smithfield, May 25, 1776.

Dear General,

I reached Smithfield this afternoon from Williamsburg, and am informed (I think from good authority) that Lord Dunmore with his Fleet, intends takeing possession of Kent Island in the Province of Maryland, just below Annapolis, and opposite to the Mouth of Patuxent, which affords a fine harbour for it; the Island is about thirty miles long, contains a great variety of live stock, and promises an exuberant harvest of grain. I have taken the liberty of giveing you this intelligence, in expectation that something may be done immediately to prevent their progress in landing and fortifying themselves; this Island lies on the Eastern shore of that province, where the inhabitants it is said, are allmost all Tories, and possibly will make little or no opposition. A report prevails here, that an engagement has very lately happened at Cape Fear, brought on by an attempt of the Enemy to land, in which they sustain'd a loss of four or five hundred men, and their landing prevented. I can't vouch for the truth of this report, but on the contrary am induced to discredit it.

I have the honor to be, Sir,

Y[r] mo. obt. Servant

Isaac Reed.

To Brigadier General Lewis,
in Williamsburg.

From Brigadier General Moore.

Wilmington, May 26, 1776.

Sir,

Your letter of the 20 instant I have received and wished it was in my power to give you such information as might enable you to penetrate the real designs of the Enemy. General Clinton has been assured by one Campbell, who a few days since went on board the Palliser, Transport, laying at Fort Johnson, that he had been authorized by the Highlanders and Regulators to let him know they wou'd immediately join him if he would march into their Settlements; how far he may be induced to take a step of this Nature, I am not able to Judge. The person who gave this information further informs me the Enemy are landed and Encamp'd about ½ a Mile from the Fort, with several pieces of Cannon and that he saw one Waggon on shore. I have reason to believe that Governor Martin uses his utmost endeavours to prevail with the General to make this Province the scene of Action, while Lord William Campbell is not less Solicitous for having the War immediately carried into South Carolina; the latter I am of opinion will be the object of Genl. Clinton's Attention, it being almost impossible for him to march far into this Province without a considerable number of horses and waggons. I have the greatest reason to believe the King's Troops, now landed, do not exceed 3,250 Men, Marines included. A number so inconsiderable I conceive, can never be intended to act against a province so populous as Virginia, which confirms me in the opinion that South Carolina is the place of their destination. Should the Battalion of Riflemen mentioned in your letter, join the Regular Troops and Militia here, I believe we shall not have occasion for the Minute Men and Militia voted by the Convention of Virginia for this Service. I shall take every possible step to discover the course of the Enemys should they leave this River, and will advise you of the same; from my belief of their intentions against South Carolina I have had intelligent persons stationed on the banks of the sea near little River to watch their course if they should appear that way, and to send an Express for Charles-Town. I shall do the same to the Northward, & advise you as early as possible, and follow your directions in every particular.

The Enemies out posts will be attacked to night, with about 200 Men under the command of Col[l] Nash.

I have the honor to be, Sir,

Your obedt. hble Serv[t]

JA. MOORE,

Brig[r] Gen[l]

Major Gen. Lee

at Newbern.

ADDRESS FROM INHABITANTS OF NEWBERN.

To his Excellency General Lee, Esq. Commander in Chief in the Southern Department of the United American Colonies.

May it Please your Excellency:

The Committee and other Inhabitants of the town of Newbern impressed with a Lively sense of your generous and manly exertions in defence of American Rights and Liberties, are happy in having an opportunity of paying our gratefull tribute of thanks and of offering our most cordial Congratulations on your arrival among us.

At a time when this Province is actually invaded by a powerfull fleet & army, the anxiety natural on the occasion, is not a Little alleviated by the Command of the forces destined for its protection being placed in the hands of a gentleman of your distinguished character.

The Inhabitants of this Province tho' different in

point of discipline, are as sensible of the inestimable blessings of freedom as our Neighbors—and we flatter ourselves under your prudent arrangement will as successfully oppose the hostile designs of our Enemys.

And we Beg your Excellency will do us the Justice to believe that nothing in our power shall be wanting to add strength and facility to your opperations in this Province.

May 27th 1776.

From General Andrew Lewis.

Williamsburg, May 27th 1776.

Dear General,

On the 23rd instant I was informed that the Enemy had abandoned their Post at Portsmouth and that their Fleet had fell down to the Mouth of James River, and ranged themselves opposite to Hampton, to which place I rode on the 24th and found them as reported. On the 25th in the Evening they got under sail and fell down to the Road. On the 26th early in the morning they appeared to stand out to sea, but instantly tacked about and ran up the Bay, having a strong and fair wind, by one o'clock about 50 of the Fleet reached the Mouth of Peanketank. Col. Dangerfield marched what men he had towards the Fleet; when within a mile and a half of them, he met a flag from Dunmore requesting liberty to water and purchase provision, which was refused. I have ordered all of Col. Dangerfield's Battalion on this side York River to join him with all possible speed. I am not apprehensive of any other ill consequences attending from the present station of the Fleet, than their possessing themselves of what stock is upon Gwins Island at the mouth of Peanketank. Had I known of such Island and stock, which is said to be considerable, I should have (long e'er now) ordered every Thing that could have contributed to the support of the Enemy to be removed. I send you a Letter I received from Col° Reed, who thinks his information may in a great measure be depended on. Its more than probable Lord Dunmore is but too well informed, that the Marylanders are greatly divided in sentiment with Regard to the measures necessary to be pursued in Defence of the Common Cause (the Curse of Scotland attend the disaffected for such they must be who endeavour to throw obstructions in the way of such who are declaring for Independence) this may prompt him to take post in Kent Island. He may have something further in view, in case General Clinton and he have concerted a Plan, by which Clinton is to act in this Government with his Army, he may hope, that our Troops will be drawn from their present stations in order to oppose him where he may take post, or endeavour to distress the Inhabitants by the advantage he has of armed vessels, which would give Clinton an opportunity of effecting his Purposes without much opposition. Since I wrote the above we have the disagreeable news from Quebec, which you will receive with this. Mortifying indeed, that our cannon, small arms, and powder should fall into the Hands of our Enemies without Resistance. This unhappy affair will I am afraid fix the Indians (who were too much inclined to our Enemies) against us. We have most alarming Intelligence from the Cherokee Nation, many emissaries being amongst them with a very large quantity of powder, and their declared Intention of acting against us. The Companies of the 4th and 5th Battalions that were in this Quarter have marched to Suffolk and the great Bridge, those of the 1st and 2nd, whom they were to relieve, or have by this time relieved, not come, nor do I know that they are got on their march—Col° Mercers are on their march, this Day they were to leave Fredericksburg, so that at present (Col. Dangerfields being on their march to join him) we have but very few to do Duty of any kind, and must remain so untill those ordered to this Place reach us. Mr Stradler reports that it would take two or three hundred men several months to make such works at Batchelors Point as would prove effectual, this being the Case in our present weak state cannot undertake it. We cannot by any means spare more than two Companies at Burwell's Ferry, so that the works at that Place must go on but slowly, until we are reinforced. M[r] Hunter is directed to send down the large Rifles as soon as possible. The Quarter Master General is causing slings to be made for the Grenadiers. The small number of Smiths we have are not at all equal to the work, nor have I been able to procure more. I have advertised for some Smiths. I wish it may prove a means of procuring those very necessary workmen—M[r] Stradler for want of proper Instruments (as he tells me) has not been able to make a satisfactory Report of the Practicability of erecting a Battery to correspond with that at James Town. The works at York and Hampton goes on as well as can be expected from the number at those Stations. I expect M[r] Madison who was sent to the back country to purchase Rifles down soon with what he has purchased the number not yet known, but I am told pretty considerable—since you left us a considerable number of firelocks has been brought from Pensylvania, but so exceedingly bad that they could not be received, and are carried back. I have this moment by express from Col. Dangerfield Information that two or three hundred of the Enemy have landed on Gwins Island, and still continue to land fast. It's said that the Distance between the Island and mainland is near $\frac{1}{4}$ of a mile, that there are some thousands of Sheep, great stocks of cattle and 10 or 12 poor Families. Is it not strange that none of the Gentlemen who were acquainted with those circumstances ever reported the Case, for my part I may with the greatest Truth say, that I never heard of such a Place before the Enemy reached it. Capt. Seyars has finished the works at Cumberland very compleatly. The Brigantine Industry and Cargo recommended by Capt. Lilly is paid for and I suppose by this time fitted for his Purpose, but circumstances at present will

not permit the Experiment. I am with great respect
Dr General

Your most obt. and very Humble Servt
ANDw LEWIS.

FROM RICHARD HENRY LEE.

Philadelphia 27 May 1776.

MY DEAR FRIEND,

The inclosed intelligence lately received from England, will give you a better idea of the designs of our enemies than any we have before received. In a letter I have seen from London of unquestionable authority is the following paragraph—" A General of the first abilities and experience would come over if he could have any assurance from the Congress of keeping his rank, but that being very high, he would not submit to have any one but an American his superior, and that only in consideration of the confidence due to an American in a question so peculiarly American." Let me have your opinion of this matter. Prince Ferdinand's recommendation of the General mentioned above is in these words " Si l'on veut un Officier aprouvé, intelligent, et brave; je ne scai si on peut trouver un autre qui le vaille."

There is no person in America can answer this paragraph so well as yourself. Our friend Gates, who with Generals Washington and Mifflin (the latter lately made a Brigadier, and Mr Gates, a Major General) are now here, is of opinion that the officer desiring to come to America is Major General Beckwith. But this is merely conjecture, founded on the mans political principles, and his abilities as a Soldier. The papers I formerly sent you, with the evening post now enclosed, will shew you the political convulsions of this Province, but I incline to think that this sensible spirited people, will not long be duped by Proprietary Machinations, whatever may be the fate of Maryland. Apropos, what do you think of the representative bodies of this latter Province? Of all the extraordinary Phenomena of this extraordinary age, these are the most extraordinary! Is the Convention of Maryland, a Conclave of Popes, a mutilated legislature, or an Assembly of wise Men? By the manner in which they dispense with Oaths, it w^d seem they conceived of themselves as the first of those, for surely a mutilated legislature, an unorganized government cannot do what these men by their Resolve of May the 15th have undertaken—Nor is their 2^d resolve of the 21st better founded, unless they can shew, which I believe is not in their power, that the people had in contemplation these things when they chose them, and elected them accordingly. What do these folks mean by a "Reunion with G. Britain *on constitutional principles?*" I profess I do not understand them, nor do I believe the best among them have any sensible ideas annexed to these terms. But I have done with them being satisfied they will never figure in history among the Solons, Lycurgus's, or Alfred's. Our Commissioners in Canada seem to be on the fright, but I hope Thomas, Sullivan, Thomson, &^c will restore the spirits with our affairs in that Province. The disgrace apart, our late capture of the valuable Transport to the Eastward, much more than compensates for the loss before Quebec. The Continental armed Ship, Franklin has certainly taken & secured a most valuable Transport with 75 Tons of Gunpowder 1000 stand of arms, and a variety of other useful articles valued at £50,000, this money. The sensible and manly resolve of Virginia of the 15th instant has gladdened the hearts of all wise and worthy men here. It will powerfully contribute to sett things right in these Proprietary governments. We have here 4 Tribes of the Six Nation Indians, and yesterday we had between 2 & 3 thousand men paraded on the Common to their great astonishment and delight. We hope effectually to secure the friendship of these people.

Farewell dear Sir, and be assured you have my hearty wishes for success and happiness. Can't Clinton (if he is on shore) be disturbed before the rest of his Myrmidons join him?

My compliments to Gen. Howe.

RICHARD HENRY LEE.

Gen. Lee.

Commander of the Continental Armies in the Southern Department at Williamsburg, Virginia

---

RICHARD HENRY LEE TO THOMAS LUD LEE.

Philadelphia, 28th May 1776.

MY DEAR BROTHER,

This is Post morning and I am obliged on a Committee of conference with the Generals Washington, Gates, & Mifflin by 9 on the operations of this Campaign, so that I cannot possibly write to many of my friends and particularly Col° Mason. Pray make my compliments to him, let him have the news sent, and apologize for me. Col° Nelson is not arrived, but I suppose he will by this day sennight, about which time I shall sett out for Virginia, and after resting at home a day or two, will attend the Convention at Williamsburg. The sensible and spirited resolve of my Countrymen on the 15th has gladdened the heart of every friend to human nature in this place, and it will have a wonderful good effect on the misguided Councils of these Proprietary Colonies. What a scene of determined rapine and roguery do the German treaties present to us, and Ld Dartmouths answer to the Duke of Graftons motion, 16th March, has shut the mouths of all Gapers after Commissioners. The transport Prize taken to the Eastward is extremely apropos. The vessel and Cargo are valued at £50,000. We are not without hopes of getting some more of the same flock, if fortune should have separated them from the Shepherd, they will most probably fall. This is the Campaign that we shall be most tried in probably, and we should endeavour as far as human care can go to be more invulnerable than Achilles, not exposing even the heel, where the stake is so immense. We have not lately heard from Canada, but we hope for better news soon than our last. A potent push will assuredly be made there this Summer by our enemies, and if we can prevent them from communicating with the Upper Country, and thereby debauching the Indians, we shall answer every good purpose there. The Roebuck is gone from here crippled, but the Liverpoole remains thinly manned and in want of provisions. It is to be hoped that the death of the King of Portugal will produce something in Europe favorable to us. Let no consideration interrupt your attention to the making of Common Salt, Salt Petre & Arms; and every kind of encouragement should be given to all sorts of useful manufacture.

Farewell my dear brother
RICHARD HENRY LEE.

Our brothers in London were well, the 13. Febry. last. I write Gen. Lee by this post—do see that the letter is forwarded from Williamsburg.

R. H. LEE.

Thomas Lud Lee, Esquire
at Williamsburg, in Virginia.

FROM LIEUT. COLONEL S. ELBERT.

Savannah 28th May, 1776.

SIR,

A few days since, I received a pacquet from Thomas Bullett, Esq. Deputy Adjutant General of the Southern District, directing that a return of the Georgia Battalion of Continental Troops be immediately made to your Excellency; in compliance therewith I take the first opportunity of Inclosing the same.

The number of Men we have at present, tho' far short of the Compliment, by much Exceed our expectations, considering the Infant state of the Colony, and at the same time a much larger Bounty given by our Neighbouring Province, in their Provincial Service, however, this you may depend upon, Sir, that the Officers & what Soldiers we have are unexceptionable, and such as will acquit themselves with Honor, whenever put to trial; pity it is, that they are badly armed, worse clothed, and have no Camp Equipage at all, notwithstanding which I am certain, so hearty are they in the Glorious Cause of their Country, that they would Chearfully take the Field when necessary, tho' they should have no other covering but the Canopy of Heaven.

We have undoubted Information of about a Thousand Ministerial Troops being the other day at St. Augustine, an Hundred of them with proper Officers have marched for the Creek Nation of Indians, with intent, no doubt, to be assisted by those Savages in making a diversion on our Western Boundary.

This being the only Province from which our Enemies could get fresh provisions, on account of our inability to oppose them, I submit to your Excellency's Judgment, whether an immediate additional Force might not be necessary to prevent them, should they make an attempt, in order to supply their Friends, who may be acting against the Carolina's & Virginia which 'tis very probable they intend by having such a force in the above Garrison. Our Colonel McIntosh is at present on some business to the Southward of the province, he is expected to return in a few days when, I have no doubt, he will give you every necessary information in his power. I have the Honor to be Respectfully.

Your Excellency's most obed[t] Serv[t]

S. Elbert—Lieu[t.] Col.

of the Georgia Battalion Continental Troops.

His Excellency Major General Lee.

From Edmund Pendleton.

Wmsburg, June 1, 1776.

Sir,

I had the honor of laying your favor of the 24th before the Convention, who were much [conce]rned to hear of the mutinous temper of the Troops in [the] 8th Regiment, and will consider of some remedy to check the progress of that alarming evil. The still uncertain destination of Genl Clinton's Troops would have made it proper for us to continue the assistance of our Minutemen and Militia, formerly ordered to North Carolina; but unluckily a few days ago on a report that the Enemy had certainly left Cape Fear, and that you were on your return to this Colony, the convention ordered Expresses to be sent to stop the march of those men, directing them to Rendezvous at certain places and wait for Orders to repair to any part of this Colony, where they might be wanting. This step, encouraged by the opinion of the two Gentlemen from North Carolina, that the assistance was not wanting there, I hope may not prove detrimental to the Service.

I am with great regard, Sir,

Your mo. obedt Servant

Edmd Pendleton, Pr

Hon. Major Gen. Lee.

To Edmund Pendleton.

Wilmington, 1 June, 1776.

Sir,

The whole enemy's fleet have sailed from Cape Fear, the first division on Wednesday, the last yesterday; but it is far from being ascertained whether they have steered their course to the northward or to the southward. The people here are all of opinion that Charleston is their object. For my own part I do not see on what they ground this persuasion. However, as South Carolina is weaker in numbers than Virginia, I have ordered Muhlenberg's regiment, at a venture, to Charleston immediately; as also a detachment of seven hundred men from this place. I have been also under the necessity of stripping this Province of sixteen hundred pounds of gunpowder, which I must replace from Virginia.

As this colony is now apparently no longer in danger, I shall send an express to stop your militia, as they may be wanted more in their own Province, and will now be an unnecessary expense.

I shall myself set out for Charleston tomorrow, but at the same time confess, I know not whether I shall go to or from the enemy; but if that capital is really their object, their whole force will be collected in one point, their operations will be more regular, and, consequently, my presence as Commander-in-chief of the district, more requisite; whereas, if Virginia is their object, it is possible and probable their operations may be merely predatory and piratical. If such are their intentions, I am confident that your own officers will have little or no occasion for the advice or assistance (such as they are) of, Sir, &c

CHARLES LEE.

P. S. As I have not much time, and indeed there being no absolute necessity of troubling the Congress with any circumstances farther than expressed in this letter, I must entreat, Sir, that you will send a copy of it to the Congress.

FROM BRIG. GEN. ANDREW LEWIS.

Williamsburg, June 3rd 1776.

Dr Genl

Mr Massenburg sets out to wait on you after being detained several Days by sickness. I am obliged to give him an Order on the Quarter Master for a Horse, and tho' he has received to the value of twenty Pounds from Col. Woodford, which amounts to more than his pay, that sum being necessarily expended, I have given him an order on the Paymaster for twenty five dollars, thinking it necessary he should wait on you with all possible expedition. In my last to you I mentioned the Enemy's landing on Gwin's Island. I lost no Time in going to discover the situation of the Enemy. I found them in possession of the Island. They had thrown up part of a strong like Battery with some out works, exclusive of an Intrenchment across a narrow part of the Island, and had several armed vessels between the Island and the Main Land, this was a circumstance which I little expected, as I had been told our men could wade to the Island, and at the very place where we found armed sloops and Tenders get in without the least obstruction. This being the case, all I could do was to post Col. Dangerfield's Battalion so as to prevent as much as possible any connection between Lord Dunmore's Banditti and the disaffected & Negroes. I ordered a Battery to be erected at the Narrows to prevent the Vessels getting out, as they must return within sixty yards of our works, there being a shoal that makes out at the lower end of the Island two miles towards the Bay, but this cannot be waded but at low water, and then up to the mens Breasts, and that for four Miles exposed to the Fire of as many of the Fleet as the Enemy might think proper to lay near the shoals. I have ordered down four pieces of Cannon, and hope to be able to oblige the Enemy to burn the Vessels that have got in to the Narrows. I propose sending three companies to reinforce Col. Dangerfield's battalion or more should I find Dunmore reinforced, but this will not be an easy matter to come to the knowledge of. The Fleet being so frequently in motion, some running out and others returning every Hour. I shall do everything in my power to prepare for the Reception of the Enemy. I am extreamly willing to wish you a pleasing Tour and every satisfaction you can wish for, but its morally impossible it can be the case.

I am Dr General

Your most obedt. and very humble Servt.

ANDW LEWIS

Br Genl.

P. S. On being properly informed I find the stock on the Island much less than at first represented, the Cattle under 200, the sheep not more.

A. LEWIS,

On the Service of the United Colonies.

To the Honble Charles Lee,

Major Genl. and Commander in Chief of the Continental Army in ye Southern District

p Mr Massenburg.

Mr. Massenburg has received fifteen dollars more than mentioned within, in ye whole forty dollars.

FROM PRESIDENT RUTLEDGE.

June 4, 1776—5 o'clock, P.M.

DEAR SIR,

I this moment received yours by Captain Mouat. I wish you and a powerful reinforcement were now here. For God's sake lose not a moment. There are fifty sail or vessels at anchor off the bar, within sight of the town, which will, I suppose, come in with to-morrow's tide, if the wind is not unfavourable. Bring us all the forces you can collect, to cope with this armament, either from North-Carolina, Virginia, or any part of this Province you pass through. I send this express to you, and send on the roads, and at the several ferries, to facilitate your march.

In haste, Yours sincerely

J. RUTLEDGE.

To the Honourable Major-General Lee.

TO THE PRESIDENT OF CONGRESS.

Little River on the road to Charlestown,
June 6th, 1776.

SIR,

You will perceive from the inclosed letters* the necessity of reinforcing this Province & Georgia—the Enemy will probably make it the Seat of war—Two thousand men at least ought to be dispatch'd from Pensylvania and Maryland to replace the Regiments I shall order from Virginia. [Ten thousand weight of powder is arrived safe at Charlestown.]

I am Sir, with the greatest Respect
Your most ob^t hum^ble Servant

CHARLES LEE.

The Hon John Hancock.

* The letters inclosed were two from Gen. Armstrong, with the foregoing letter from President Rutledge, giving information that the enemy had arrived off the bar at Charleston within sight of the town.

To Brigadier General Lewis.

Little River on the Road to Charlestown,
6th. June, 1776.

Dear Sir,

On the receipt of this you must order as large a body of the Regulars as can possibly be spared to march to Cross Creek in North Carolina—you may either do it by Regiments or Detachments—it is now I think certain that South Carolina & Georgia are their object—lay these inclosed Letters before the Convention—send Copies of them to the Convention of Maryland—perhaps that Province can spare a Battalion or two for the defence of Virginia which may be replaced from Pensylvania.

I am Dear General,
Yours
Charles Lee.

Br^r Genl Lewis, Williamsburg.

P.S. The Letter for the Congress should be dispatch'd immediately—if any Cavalry are raised detach them.

To Colonel Moultrie.

Thursday Morning, six o'clock. [June 6, 1776.]

Sir:—I am extremely obliged to you for your activity and alertness. I beg you will order Long Island to be reconnoitred well, and perhaps you will see a probability of attacking them with advantage from the main; but this must be left to your own prudence. I have ordered the two rascally carpenters who deserted, to be searched for; if they can be found, I shall send them bound to you. I do not myself much like the scheme of retreating by boats; it cannot, I think, be done without confusion. But I think you ought to have two means of retreat; for which reason I must beg that you will be expeditious in finishing the bridge; and all the boats I can procure shall be likewise sent to you. If possible I will visit you to day.

I am, dear Sir, yours,

CHARLES LEE.

To Col. Moultrie.

TO COLONEL MOULTRIE.

Charlestown, 8 o'clock, June 8th.

SIR: As we have received information that a body of the enemy have landed, and are lodging themselves on Long Island, and as the nature of the country is represented to me as favourable to Riflemen, I must request that you immediately detach Thompson's and Sumpter's regiments, Captains Alston's, Mayham's and Coutirier's companies, to that Island, with orders to attack, and, if possible, dislodge this corps of the enemy; but you must, above all, take care that their retreat across the breach from Long-Island to Sullivan's Island is secured to them in case of necessity. For which purpose, you are desired to move down to the point commanding the breach two field pieces; the sooner it is done the better. You are, therefore, to exert yourself in such a manner that the attack may be made at break of day.

I am Sir, Yours,

CHARLES LEE,
Major-General.

To Col. Moultrie.

TO COLONEL MOULTRIE.

Charlestown, June 8, 1776.

SIR,

I have ordered a considerable reinforcement of Riflemen to join Colonel Thompson, which, with the advantages of ground, ought to make you totally secure. I shall be with you as soon as possible in the morning. Mr Bellamy will, I hope, be able to finish you a bridge to morrow.

I am, Sir, your most Obedient Servant

CHARLES LEE.

To Col. Moultrie,
Sullivan's Island

PRESIDENT RUTLEDGE TO COLONEL MOULTRIE.

June 9th 5 o'clock

The command of all the Regular forces and Militia of this Colony, acting in conjunction with them, being invested in Major-General Lee, orders issued by him are to be obeyed.

J. RUTLEDGE.

To Col. Moultrie.

TO COLONEL MOULTRIE.

June 10, 1776.

SIR,

You will receive a number of flats, ropes, and planks, for the construction of bridges for your retreat. You are to give a receipt, and be answerable for them.

I am Sir, yours

CHARLES LEE,
Major General.

Col. Moultrie.

P. S. I find my last night's letter was not sent. I beg you would send a few expert scouts to discover what the enemy have done, or are doing; If it can be done with the least probable advantage, put my last night's orders in execution to-night.

From Colonel Moultrie.

Sullivan's Island, 7 o'clock June 10, 1776.

Sir:

I just now received your orders for detaching Thompson and Sumpter's regiments, Allston, Maham, and Coutirier's companies. By date of your letter, it seems as if you intended this business to have been done this morning, but your letter came too late to hand for that purpose. I shall send the detachment to our advance guard, there to remain with their boats for crossing them, hid till night, then shall embark them for Long-Island, where they may be reconnoitring till day-light. I shall be obliged to your Excellency to send us some person to finish our gate.

I am, Sir, your most obedient
William Moultrie,
Col. 2[d] Regiment

To General Lee.

To Colonel Moultrie.

June 10, 6 oclock P.M.

Sir:

I am just returned from an excursion into the Country. As the large ships are now over the bar, and as your bridge must be finished; I would wish you would lay aside all thoughts of an expedition against Long-Island, unless your scouts bring such intelligence as almost to insure a successful stroke.

I am, Sir, Yours,
Charles Lee.

To Col. Moultrie, Sullivans Island.

To Colonel Moultrie.

June 10, 1776. 8 o'clock.

Sir:

As the Commodore's ship has passed the bar, and as it is absolutely necessary for your, and the common safety, that the bridge of retreat should be finished this night; I would have you, by all means, to lay aside all thoughts of the expedition against Long-Island; unless you receive assurances from your scouts, that you may strike an important stroke.

Yours

Charles Lee, Major General.

To Col. Moultrie.

To Colonel Moultrie.

June 11, 1776.

Sir:

As the main body of Horry's Regiment are at Point Haddrell, Mayham and Coutirier's companies should be included in the detachment to be sent to the main.

Charles Lee.

To Col. Moultrie.

To Colonel Moultrie.

June 11, 1776.

Sir: I was much surprised that this morning the Engineer should make a report to me that a bridge of retreat was impracticable, as I understand that a few days ago yourself and the other Field Officers gave it as your opinions that it might be effected. If I had boats, I should send them according to your request, but they are not to be had. The flats, ropes, and anchors, were sent in consequence of your former opinion. As I think your security will be much greater by posting a considerable body of Riflemen on the Continent than on the Island, I must desire that you will immediately detach 400 of them to the continent: They are to post themselves, or rather extend themselves, from the left of Point Haddrell towards Long Island; by which means they will be able to prevent the enemy from erecting works, to cut off your retreat. I would order the whole body off the Island, but apprehend it might make your garrison uneasy. You must order this body to be alert in patroling, and if there is not natural cover in this range, they must throw up artificial ones. I request that this order may be instantly obeyed—I am Sir, yours

CHARLES LEE.

To Colonel Moultrie.

I had rather you would make up this detachment 500. I hope the point of your Island, opposite to Long Island, is secured against the enemy lodging there. I have ordered boats to be found, if possible.

C. L.

FROM THOMAS BURKE.

Tyaquin, June 11th 1776.

SIR,

This moment yours of the first Instant came to my Hand. The Note Inclosed, directed to the Commanding Officer of the Corps of Virginia Forces, Intended for the Station of Hillsborough, I will use my best endeavours to Transmit so soon as I can learn who he is, or from what part of Virginia they are ordered, of both I am now entirely uninformed having heard nothing of such destination until I received your Letter. If I can get no information in my neighbourhood I will send your Note to the Commanding Officer of Halifax or Mecklinburg County which lyeing contiguous to this, are most likely to have received orders to march hither. I cannot say Sir, that I rejoice that the enemy have abandoned their design on This Colony. Their Force could not have effected much against us, but they may prove troublesome to some of our Southern Neighbours who are probably not so well provided for Defence as we are.

I beg leave Sir, to wish you all possible Success in your Generous efforts for the Defence of the undoubted Rights of Mankind, had the scene of action been where we first Expected I intended to have put myself a volunteer under your command, and to have contributed my little assistance towards that success which I am assured would have attended your command. Remote as the scene may be I shall not bear absence from it with much patience, and were it not almost ruin to my private affairs, no campaign should pass without receiving the little assistance I could personally give, for tho' I am no military character, nor ambitious of such Distinction, the cause in which we are now engaged, and in which I have unremittingly struggled since the stamp act makes me anxious to be a witness, and an actor however Inconsiderable in every scene of Importance, whether Military or Civil which may relate to it.

I have the honor to be with singular respect, Sir,

Your obed[t] Servant,

Genl. Lee. THO[s] BURKE.

FROM COLONEL ——.

Newbern, 12th of June, 1776.

SIR,

I had the Honour to receive y[r] Excellency's Commands from L[t] Col Irwin, relative to the March of the Regiment under my Command; be assured, I shall at all times with the greatest punctuality obey any orders issued by you, or any commanding Officer.

Since the receipt of the above, I have been favored with a Letter from the Adjutant General direct^{g} Me by your Orders to march with all possible dispatch to Wilmington; which I shou'd instantly have complied with, but for a very obvious Reason; the great want of Money to pay the Soldiery, the Bounty Money, & advance pay, I beg leave to be very candid with y^{r} Excellency: when the Regiment was in Edenton, with the greatest difficulty I restrained their Inclination for desertion, by assuming to pay all their debts in that Town; by a promise to see their demands properly satisfied on their arrival at Newbern and to prevent any desertion on the Road; assured them that the Regiment shou'd not proceed to Wilmington without their receiving satisfactory payments—being fed up with these Expectations, they behave themselves well, & I flatter myself that I shall have it in my power to march to Wilmington complete Company's. As there has not been any Person deputed to meet the Regiment in Newbern, I am compelled to send an Express to Colo. Blount at Halifax for the necessary sum of money. So soon as officers and men are satisfied in their just demands, I pledge my honor for their instant March. I sincerely wish your Excellency all possible success, and I am with much Respect

Sir, Your obed. Ser^{t}

On the Continental Service: Favored by Col. Salter.

To His Excellency Major General Lee.

From Gen. Andrew Lewis.

Williamsburg, June ye 12th 1776.

Dear General,

I received your Favour dated Wilmington the first of June, which was the first notice I had of Clinton's sailing from Cape Fear. As he has not yet appeared on our Coast I have all the Reason imaginable to believe he has steered his course for Charles Town or more Southernly. I had before the receipt of your Letter wrote you twice (the first dated May the 27th, the last June the 3rd) informing you of the Enemy's abandoning their Post at Portsmouth, and the whole Fleet sailing to Gwin's Island, &c to which Information I can only add, that they are still in possession of that Island. I have ordered several Pieces of Cannon at Gloucester Town to be mounted, which the workmen are about, in order to have them mounted opposite the Enemy, and if possible to prevent some small armed Vessels getting out which lie between the mainland and the Island. I have sent under the Command of Col° Mercer three companies to reinforce Col° Dangerfield's Battalion, and shou'd (e'er now) have sent more, had it not been to us very uncertain what steps Clinton might take. We have all the Inclination you could wish to get on the Island, if we can by any probable means make the attempt, this must altogether depend on Circumstances. Col. Stephens has taken Post at Portsmouth, thinking it would answer better Purposes to maintain that Ground than throw up works at the great Bridge, as he took this step without any application to me, I make no doubt of his having given you Information and expects Instructions on that head. I never being on that ground cannot judge of the propriety of his Measures. The Convention having had Mr Stadlers Case under Consideration refused making any addition to his Pay, but on my Representation to the House, they without a dissenting voice have allowed him all he asked, but under this restriction no longer than he serves in this Colony. He is now throwing up some works opposite to the Island, he thinks it will be exceedingly difficult to make a battery opposite to that at James Town, from which any thing can be expected. I have information that six waggon Loads of Powder have crossed this colony for the

Carolina's, but this wants confirmation. A small vessel having got up safe to Fredericksburg (an account of which you must have seen before this Time in the Papers) has landed five tons of powder for Continental use. Should I find that the Seat of War for this season is to be rather in Carolina than here, I shall order what you think proper of the five Tuns to be hastened to you, at all events shall order two Tuns immediately. As the three Companies of Col° Mercer's Battalion at Alexandria are to be relieved by two companies of the new raised men, the powder can be escorted by them to this place, and ordered to Halifax, where I hope it will be received by a Guard and forwarded. Your directions for a Guard from that Place might be necessary. The Committee of Safety knows of a Resolve of Congress that 5000 blankets should be bought and sent here, and some private Letters say that they are bought. That's all we know of them. We have not linen sufficient for our small army in this Colony, I shall send 100lb of bark with the powder. I shall write the Congress as you direct, Doctor William Rickman is appointed Director and Chief Physician of the General Hospital. He arrived yesterday. None of the row-gallies yet fitted out, but some of them soon will. Capt. Lilly's preparations have been much more tedious than I expected, he says he will be able to make some attempt next week. We have got some more armorers and hope to have soon an addition to the number. Our men took a small sloop endeavouring to get out of the Narrows between the Island and our breast-work. She having run a Ground, a few men in two small Canoes boarded her, five men who were all her crew endeavoured to escape by swimming—three of which were shot from the shoar and sunk. Two hogsheads of Brandy, ½ Ditto of Rum, some tools and ropes with some provisions were taken out for the use of our Troops there, who were in need of the brandy and rum, as the water is very bad. Deserters say that Lord Dunmore is in dayly expectation of two Regiments—a great mortality among the Enemy, some of both white and black are discovered floating every Day. Adieu Dear General, may Heaven prosper you. My Compliments to General Howe and the Gentlemen of your Family.

I am with great Respect
Your most obedt & very hble Serv[t]
ANDW LEWIS.

The Honble Charles Lee,
Major Genl & Com[r] of the Cont[l] Army in the
Southern District of North America.

Since I closed this letter I received a commission for Hugh Mercer, Esq. appointing him Brig. Genl. he is ordered to N. York immediately. This gives me both pleasure & pain. A. LEWIS.

GENERAL ORDERS.

12th June, 1776.

UPON any alarm the different corps are to repair to the following places of rendezvous.

The artillery regiment, and militia acting as artillery, to their stations heretofore allotted them. The remainder of the town militia to the State House. The country militia, in that part of Lynch's pasture, nearest the town.

The North-Carolina troops, in a distinct line on the more remote part; at least two hundred yards in the rear, of the country militia.

The town-militia are to receive their orders from Brigadier General Armstrong.

The country militia, from Brigadier General Howe.

The North-Carolina forces are to be considered as a corps of reserve; and to be under the immediate command of General Lee.

From Colonel Gadsden.

Fort Johnson, 12 June, '76.

Sir,

I have the Honour to send to your Excelly by Colo Pinckney a Return of Colo Huger's and my Regt besides these Capt. Stones Company of James Island militia is also under my Command consisting of about sixty men, thirty of which are kept constantly on the Patrol Duty watching the Enemy's motions at the different Landings within seven Miles of us, the other thirty are always in readiness to assist at the Western Battery. We have 43 Cannon mounted at this Fort & the Battery, and as Col. Hugers men are all just rais'd, & thirty-six of my own Regiment, new recruits, none of which have been used to Cannon, they must be extremely awkward thereat. Many of our Cannon are very heavy & require a great number of men, & should we have warm work, and the Enemy attempt to land we can spare but a very small body to oppose them without leaving many of the Cannon.

Our Carpenters & Labourers have deserted us many Days since, which has put our works entirely to a stand, were it not for this, in a very few days more I cou'd have the Curtain of the upper Battery compleate, so that the Platform might be ready to be laid the moment the plank arrived.

I beg leave to refer your Excelly. to Colo Pinckney for any Thing relative to the Regimt I shall be always ready with the greatest Pleasure to execute any of your Excellys Commands, & am

Yr. Excellys most obed. hble Servant

Chrisr Gadsden.

P. S. One of the Enemy's Tenders drove by the Gale almost in reach of our Cannon, the Enemy thought proper to abandon her, about half an hour ago, and one of our Pilots has taken possession of her, and is bringing her up. I am in hopes this Storm will do the Enemy's Business yet.

'Tis now the 13th The above is what I intended to have sent to yr Excelly. yesterday but the weather prevented me. The two large ships of the Enemy that were at Anchor off the Bar are drove from their anchors and not to be seen. A sloop also of theirs we imagine must be drove ashore, as we see nothing of her.

To His Excellency Major Gen. Lee,
Commander in Chief of the Continental
and Colonial Forces acting in conjunction
from Virginia to South Carolina

To Colonel Moultrie.

Charlestown, June 13, 1776.

Sir:

As I am extremely solicitous for the honour and safety of you and the troops under your command, and as I am myself persuaded that your danger or safety depends entirely on the strength or weakness of the corps stationed on the other side of the creek; I must request that when the necessary works proposed are finished, you will detach at least another hundred men to strengthen this corps. I wish you would send me an exact state of your ammunition, that you may be supplied accordingly. His Excellency the President complains that several boats have been lost at your station: As so much depends on these boats, I must desire that you will put them under a sufficient guard: Oblige the officer commanding the guard, to give a receipt for their number, and be accountable for them.

I am, Sir, your most obedient Servant

Charles Lee.

To Colonel Moultrie.

To Colonel Horry.

Charlestown, June ye 14th, 1776.

Sir,

I consider the safety of the Fort and Garrison on Sullivan's Island as entirely depending on your Post, and on the activity and vigilance of the Corps of Riflemen extending from the left of your post along that Creek that separates Sullivan's Island from the Continent. This Corps I would still further reinforce, but have it not at present in my power; they are, however, so formidable a Body of men, that with your Spirit and Industry there is the greatest probability that they will be able to check, if not totally defeat any attempt of the Enemy on that side.

As the old field where you are stationed (if I recollect right) affords no natural shelter for Riflemen, I would recommend it to you to intersect it with a number of small trenches, at the distance of sixty or seventy yards, one in the rear of the other. They should be shallow, and the dirt thrown out towards the enemy, as otherways when possessed of, they would serve the enemy for protection, as well as they had done for yourselves. I desire that you will be very punctual in making a Report when anything extraordinary happens, and constant in making returns of your own corps. I am, sir, your most ob't humble servant,

Charles Lee

To Col. Horry,
Hattoral's Point.

To Colonel Moultrie.

Haddrell's Point, June 15, 1776.

Sir;

I have stationed Brigadier General Armstrong at this place; You are to make all your reports to him, and in all respects to consider him as your commanding officer.

I am, Sir, your most obedient Servant

CHARLES LEE

To Col. Moultrie

GENERAL ORDERS.

15th June, 1776.

THE Guards henceforward, are to be composed of the following numbers:

One field-officer, 3 captains, 9 subalterns, and 200 rank and file, are to form the main guard, at the State-House.

One captain, 3 subalterns, 4 serjeants, and 72 rank and file, at the Distillery to the left of the Magazine.

A captain, with the same number as the former, to mount at Gadsden's wharf.

A subaltern, 2 serjeants, 2 corporals, and 24 privates at the Magazine.

A subaltern, with the same number as the former, at the point behind Gibbes' wharf.

One subaltern, 2 serjeants, 2 corporals, 24 privates, at the fleche which is thrown up a little to the right of Grimball's Battery.

One subaltern, 2 serjeants, 2 corporals, with the same number of privates, in the rear of Grenville's Bastion.

One subaltern, 2 serjeants, 2 corporals, 24 privates, at the Exchange.

One subaltern, 2 serjeants, 2 corporals, with the same number of privates, at Rose's wharf.

One captain, 3 subalterns, 4 serjeants, 72 rank and file at St. Philip's Church.

The two brigades, are to post the centries of the different guards, in such a manner, that the whole may furnish an equal proportion.

Every Corps de Guarde which mounts on the quais, is to throw up fleches cannon-proof, at their respective stations; after the model of that, to the right of Grimball's Battery.

A field-officer of the day, is to be immediately warned; who is to be received by all the guards as well as the centries, with rested arms: he should be furnished with some mark of distinction—for instance, a spontoon, or halfpike, in his hand.

The guards are to turn out, and rest their arms when his Excellency the President or the Major General pass by; but this only once a day to each.

The Brigadiers, are to be received by the guards, with shouldered arms.

The Major General, wears a blue ribbon; as a badge of his rank, and by which he may be known.

The Brigadier Generals, a pink ribbon.

Rounds, are to go five times a night, and are to be regulated in the following manner. The field-officer, commanding the main guard, to go at eleven. The field-officer of the day, to go at twelve. The three captains of the main guard, at half past one, three, and at day-break. The countersign will be sent by the field-officer of the day, to the field-officer commanding the main guard at retreat beating: who, is to send it enclosed, and sealed, to the officers of the different guards.

No person, either military or resident, of this town, to pass the centries after nine, and tattoo beating; without giving the countersign.

16th June 1776.

Patrols, are to go, every hour of the night; from the beating of the tattoo, to the revellie.

Of the main guard, to consist of a serjeant and 12 men.

The patrol of each captain's guard, to consist of a corporal and 6 men.

The patrol of a subaltern, of a lance corporal, and 3 men.

The patrol of the main guard, to take Broad-street and Old Church-street, from the State House, to the two extremities and back, as likewise Queen and Tradd-streets.

The patrol at Gadsden's wharf guard, is to pass to and from the Governor's Bridge.

The patrol of the subaltern's guard at the Governor's Bridge is to pass to and from Cannon's Battery—that of Cannon's Battery, to and from Philip's Battery—that of Philip's Battery, to and from Lyttleton's Bastion—that of Lyttleton's Bastion, to and from the guard on the right of Wilkins' Battery—to and from Gibbes' wharf; and communications behind the barricadoes will be opened for this purpose.

The patrol on Gibbes' wharf, to pass to and from the Distillery.

The patrol of the Distillery, to pass to and from Cummings' Battery, from thence to the new Carolina Barracks.

The captain's guard, which will be posted some where in Squirrel-street, is to take patrol up and down George-street; and from the New Barracks, to St Philip's Church, as likewise the whole of the Boundary-street from one extremity to another.

These different patroles are to prevent disorders, and any number of people assembling together; likewise, to oblige all those who keep public-houses, to send away their guests, at the hour prescribed by his Excellency the President in Council.

To President Rutledge.

Charlestown, June 16th 1776.

Dear Sir,

I shou'd leave the Parole & Countersign entirely to you, as I think it due to your rank & presidency in your own Province; but as it is perhaps politic at this juncture to hold up in all the Colonies the Continental Officers as objects of the greatest respect, We will give them alternately if you have no objection to it—the Adjutant General will repair to you for the Parole this day before orderly time—if busyness calls you out you can leave it seal'd up for him. He will before retreat beating repair to you in like manner for the Countersign—to morrow I shall give them—As the admitting boats after sunset into all parts of the Town, may be attended with much danger, I wish you wou'd appoint one particular place where they alone can be admitted.

I am Dear Sir, &c
CHARLES LEE.

P. S. Don't you think, Sir, it wou'd be right to order all the tipling Houses to be shut up before tat-too beating.

To His Excellency John Rutledge,
President and Commander in Chief
of the Province of South Carolina.

FROM COLONEL PATTEN.

Little River, 17th June 1776.

SIR,

On my march from Wilmington to Little River the Express from Philadelphia came up with me on the Road: I being some Distance ahead of the Troops, had it not in my power to write, but desired him to acquaint you what time I should be at the Boundary. Capt Gray of the 3rd Regiment came with me within eight Miles of the Boundary on his way to Charlestown, but left the Regiment without acquainting me of his going of, but I expected he would have waited on your Excellency to Lett you know of my arrival—have likewise Wrote by the Post, but by receiving no orders from you Imagine they have all fail'd: that now I send by Express—agreeable to Gen[l] Mores Orders have placed a Subaltoons guard on the Bank to watch the motions of the fleet, but have made no Discoveries. I have nothing in particular to acquaint you off—Except forty head of Cattle that was Drove from the Neighbourhood of Lockwoods Folley the Day before I marched, through their to the men of Warr: which that and many other Reasons Convinces me that the most part of that Neighbourhood are Torreys. I took a Prisoner there that had been sent from on Board the Man of Warr, to watch our motions, and delivered him to the Capt. of the Militia to send to Wilmington, but as soon as I was gone was sett att Liberty—think it would not be amiss to place a few Continental Troops their to keep them in order. I have Reconnighted this place as Well as I could and find that their is an Inlett, Eight Miles to the Southward of Lockwood's Folley called Shelott, that their is Fourteen feet of Water over the Barr, and Twelve feet over the Barr of Little River—that any of their small Vessells might come in and suplie the Whole Fleet with fresh Provisions; as the stocks of cattle is Large their—Exceept their is a force to Repell them. Should be glad of Your Orders by the Bearer,

Am Your most hble Serv[t]

John Patten

General Orders.

Charles-town, June 19th, 1776.

As it now appears almost a certainty, (from the intelligence of some deserters,) that the enemy's intention is to make an attack on the city; and as the General is confident, that the numbers and spirit of the garrison will prevent their landing, it only remains to guard against the injury which the city may receive from their cannon.

The continental troops, provincials, and militia, are, therefore, most earnestly conjured to work with no less alacrity, than fight with courage. Courage alone will not suffice in war: true soldiers and magnanimous citizens must brandish the pick-axe and spade, as well as the sword, in defence of their country; one or two days labour, at this critical juncture, may not only save many worthy families from ruin, but many worthy individuals from loss of limbs and life. On this principle the General does not, simply in his capacity of commanding officer, order, but entreat the whole garrison, (those on the necessary duties excepted,) to exert themselves in forwarding the requisite works of protection.

The colonels or commanding officers of the corps are to review their men's arms this evening at roll calling; to take care they are in as good order as possible, and that they are furnished with good flints. The officers commanding the different guards are to do the same with their respective guards.

For the future it must be observed, as an established rule, that no artillery officer fires a single cannon without previously acquainting the General.

To Colonel Gadsden.

Charlestown, June 19th, 1776.

Dear Sir,

As from the intelligence we have received from Deserters, we have the strongest reason to believe that the Tyrants Troops have not the least idea of attacking your Fort—but that their Scheme is in two Corps to make an attempt on the Town at the same time on Point Huteral or Fort Sullivan, and, as now your Western Battery is given up, it appears that you have actually more men than your Fort will contain—I must request that you will immediately reinforce the Town (which is much too thinly garrison'd) with Col[l] Huge's Regiment—if indeed you wish to retain a subaltern and twenty-five to man the three Guns of the Western Battery—I have no objection—I rely so much on your good sense, calmness and discretion, that I flatter myself when the Enemy pass your Fort not a single Gun will be fired at too great a distance—not a single Gun, but when you have the greatest probability of its being fired with effect.

I am Dear Sir,

Your most Obed[t] Servant,

CHARLES LEE.

Colonel Gadsden, Fort Johnson.

TO COLONEL PATTEN.

Charlestown, 19th June, 1776.

SIR,

It is extremely unfortunate that General Moore shou'd not in consequence of my last Letters have order'd you forward to this place—I must therefore entreat that you will march with all possible expedition as it is of the last importance.

I am Sir,

Your Most Ob[t] Servant

CHARLES LEE.

To Colonel Patten, or Officer Commanding the division of North Carolina Troops at the Boundary House.

To Colonel Thompson.

Charlestown 21st June, 1776.

Sir,

It is a certain truth that the Enemy entertain a most unfortunate apprehension of American Rifle Men —it is equally certain that nothing can contribute to diminish this apprehension so infallibly as a frequent ineffectual fire—it is with some concern therefore that I am inform'd that your Men have been suffer'd to fire at a most preposterous distance; upon this principle, I must entreat and insist that you consider it as a standing order that not a man under your Command is to fire at a greater distance than an hundred and fifty yards at the utmost—in short that they never fire without almost a moral certainty of hitting their object—distant firing has a double bad effect, it encourages the Enemy, and adds to the pernicious perswasion of the American soldiers—vizt *that they are no match for their Antagonists at close fighting*—to speak plainly, it is almost a sure method of making 'em Cowards—once more I must request that a stop be put to this childish, vitious & scandalous practice—I extend the rule to those who have the care of the Field Pieces—four hundred yards is the greatest distance they should be allowed to fire at—a transgression of this rule will be considered as the effect of flurry and want of courage. Those who are accused of transgressing will be proceeded against as acting from these principles: I have, Sir, the greatest opinion of your good sense and spirit and flatter myself that you will not only issue orders of restriction on this head, but that you will be attentive that they are rigorously put in execution, and am Sir,

Your most obet humble Servant

Charles Lee.

P. S. I am likewise informed that your men pass without order or orders to Long Island—Is this wise?

is it Soldier like? is it to shew the Enemy where our weakness is? I confess I am astonish'd at such enormities—I positively order, Sir, that an immediate check be put to these abominations. I expect compliance, & will not excuse such violation of discipline for the future.

To Colonel Thompson,
at Sullivan's Island.

To Colonel Moultrie.

Charlestown, 21st June, 1776.

Sir,

Inclosed is a Letter for Colonel Thompson; I send it open that you may read it, for allowing for the difference of his circumstances as a Rifle Officer, the spirit of the orders is to extend to the whole—no vague uncertain firing either of Rifles, Muskets or Cannon is to be permitted—Soldiers running at random wherever their folly directs is an absolute abomination not to be tolerated—for Heaven's sake, Sir, as you are in a most important Post—a Post where you have an opportunity of acquiring great honor—exert yourself—by exerting yourself, I mean, when you issue any orders, suffer 'em not to be trifled with—every body is well perswaded of your Spirit and zeal, but they accuse you of being too easy in command—that is, I suppose too relaxed in Discipline—than which in your situation give me leave to say, there cannot be a greater vice—let your orders be as few as possible—but let 'em be punctually obeyed. I wou'd not recommend teizing your Men & Officers with superfluous duties or labor, but I expect that you enforce the execution of whatever is necessary for the honor and safety of your Garrison—shou'd any misfortune happen which can be attributed to negligence or inertness on this head, the weight [of] censure will scarcely fall less heavily upon you, than should it arise from a deficiency of Courage—but as you are known to possess sufficiently of this last attribute, your Friends are only apprehensive on the other score. You will excuse the prolixity and didactick stile of this Letter, as it arises not only from my anxiety for the public, but in some measure from my concern for the reputation of a Gentleman of so respectable a Character as Colonel Moultrie—but enough of this at present. Before you employ your Engineer in any work, satisfy yourself well that he understands the principle of the work he undertakes, and the mode of executing it—for instance: does he understand what is the necessary degree of talus for the Traverse in the Fort? if I recommend the construction of an advanced Fleche on the right flank of your Fort to impede the Enemy's approaches, will he comprehend it? if he does not, I will send Mr. Byrd—I shall order some timber for this purpose to be carried to you. I desire you will put a commission'd officer (and a good officer) at the breach to prevent the monstrous disorders I complain of.

I am Sir, with the greatest respect

Your most humble Servant,

CHARLES LEE.

To Colonel Moultrie,
Sullivan's Island.

TO COLONEL MOULTRIE.

June 21st, 1776.

SIR:

I am extremely concerned to hear that the traverse which I had ordered to be thrown up, and which is really of the greatest importance, should be so illy executed as to threaten a speedy fall; surely Mr. De Brahm, the Engineer, must be acquainted with the de gree of talus necessary in all works—For God's sake enjoin him to correct the evil before it is too late—At any rate devise the means of preventing its ruin—I must likewise express my concern when I am told that your gunners are suffered to fire at the enemy when it is almost impossible that their fire should have any effect. I must desire you, Sir, that you must establish it as an eternal rule, that no piece of ordnance, great or small, should be fired at a greater distance than four hundred yards; but all orders will be in vain unless you make an example of the first who disregards your orders. Is Bellamy with you? Has he begun the second bridge? I hope you will keep him on the Island until he has finished the work.

I am, Sir, your most obedient Servant

CHARLES LEE.

To Colonel Moultrie.

P. S. Those two field pieces at the very end of the Point are so exposed that I desire you will draw them off to a more secure distance from the enemy; in their present situation, it appears to me, they may be carried off whenever the enemy think proper.

To Colonel Moultrie.

Charlestown, June 21st 1776.

SIR:

I hope you will excuse the style of my last letter. I must once more repeat that it did nöt arise from any diffidence in your judgment, zeal, or spirit; but merely from an apprehension that your good nature and easy temper might, in some measure, counteract those good qualities which you are universally known to possess. As you seem sensible that it is necessary to exert your powers, I do not, I cannot, wish this important post in better hands than yours: once more therefore, excuse my manner of writing. I wish Mr Bellamy had (when he was desired to give in a list of all he wanted) left nothing to ask for at this time. Mr Cochran is now employed in finding out the planks he requests; you shall have it as soon as possible. Captain Tuffts was ordered to put himself under the command of General Armstrong. I shall write to the General to night, to order him to station him in such a manner as to be of the greatest use to you, as likewise to spare you all the necessary assistance. Tomorrow I expect Muhlenburg's Regiment and I flatter myself that we shall be able to devise some means of baffling the enemy, should your post be really their object.

I am, Sir, with the greatest respect,
Your most obedient humble Servant,
CHARLES LEE.

To Col Moultrie,
Fort Sullivan.

P. S. We have hoes and spades, but no helves to them; so General Armstrong must return those he borrowed: We shall endeavour to replace them.

To President Rutledge.

Charlestown, June 22nd, 1776.

DEAR SIR,

As I confess, I never cou'd from the conversation I have had with the different Gentlemen here, well understand on what principle Sullivans Island was first taken possession of and fortify'd, or on what principle it is to be maintain'd I shou'd be extremely oblig'd to you if you will sometime this day convene the Gentlemen of the Council, that I may be able to form an opinion whether or no, it will be prudent to risk so many men, and encounter so many difficulties in attempt ing to support it.

I am Dear Sir, Yours

CHARLES LEE.

To His Excellency John Rutledge,
President & Com^r in Chief of the
Province of South Carolina.

To Colonel Moultrie.

Charlestown [5 o'clock] 23rd June, 1776.

SIR,

I have sent Captn Cochran (a very active man) to your Island to devise the means of establishing a second communication with the Continent—Pritchard's Flat he says is already at the Island—Muhlenburg's Regiment will be here to night; We shall be then very strong. I will be down with you tomorrow with a Body of Workmen & put you I hope in a state of great security —Upon the whole I think you will be safe, if your people do their duty—there can be nothing to fear to night. I hope your Garrison will remain in spirits; on my part, I promise every attention.

I am Sir, [with the greatest truth]
Your most ob^t Servt

CHARLES LEE.

To Col. Moultrie,
Sullivan's Island.

General Orders.

Fort Sullivan, June 24th 1776.

GENERAL LEE positively orders, that the screen behind the aperture of the traverse be immediately begun and finished with all possible expedition; that a breast-work of timber, six feet high, be raised on the rampart, so as to form a continuation of the traverse; that a banquet be raised behind the traverse, so as to enable the musquetry to fire over. The present work round the near guard room to be considerably strengthened: the parapet raised, and the ditch deeper and wider; a screen to be thrown up behind the entrance; a facade of fascines, or old timber, is necessary to keep up the light sand of which the breast-work of this rear-guard is composed.

To Colonel Moultrie.

Charlestown, June 25 1776.

Sir:

The gentleman that delivers you this letter is Baron Massenbourg, one of the Continental Engineers. I desire you will furnish him with the number of workmen, and with every material he may require to carry on his works.

I am, Sir, your most obedient, humble Servant,

Charles Lee.

To Col. Moultrie,
Sullivans Island.

To Colonel Moultrie.

[June 25, 1776]

Sir,

I have sent you the carpenter; it is your fault if he escapes again; keep a guard over him. Send the express boat back immediately.

Yours,

Charles Lee.

To Colonel Moultrie.

P. S. Finish the bridge.

To President Rutledge.

Charlestown, June 25th. 1776.

Dear Sir,

I have just received a Letter from the Baron who seems frighten'd out of his wits at the dangerousness of the situation of our Troops on the Island where retreat is so precarious—however he is setting himself to work to do the best he can—I have desired Colonel Laurence to send immediately to the Island fifty men for work—I must entreat your Excellency to give order that a sufficient number of the Palmeto logs necessary for the completion of the Bridge, may without loss of time be forwarded.

I am Sir, with the greatest Respect
Your most obt. hum: Servant
Charles Lee.

His Excellency John Rutledge.

From Alexander White.

Winchester 27th June, 1776.

Sir,

Your favour of 10th April did not reach me 'till 22nd Inst. I that day wrote you an Answer by one Mr Campbell, who was on his way to Williamsburg, and who promised to give my letter a Conveyance if he did not see you. I informed you that I saw no objection to your paying off the Incumbrances on your Land and the future payments to Mr Hite whenever it is convenient for you to do so, except £400, which is to be retained 'till the title to part of the Land is compleated. I prepared a Mortgage for securing to Mr Hite the future payments agreeable to Contract, and offered it to Mr Thos Hite who would not accept it on account of a recital which he supposed would prejudice the frivolous suit commenced against you, though it was drawn in common form before I had the most distant expectation of such a suit ever being commenced. The Mortgage is a sterling Debt, the Agent a Resident of Maryland. I therefore presume Virginia Paper will not be acceptable, and perhaps some difficulty may arise in these times of Confusion respecting the rate of Exchange I settled it with Mr Hite in V. C. at 25 p. c^t.

I should be happy to see the Important Subject of the Independence of N. A. discussed in the perspicuous and able manner you are capable of. I have troubled you with some of my crude thoughts, to afford you an opportunity when leisure will permit and inclination lead you to explain my mistakes and correct my errors. From the commencement of the present unhappy Dispute I considered the shedding of blood (if that event should take place) as the Era at which would terminate the British Empire in America or the Colonies be subjugated to the absolute Dominion of Parliament, and when hostilities commenced my mind was only agitated with the means of defending ourselves and forming a Constitution which would secure substantial Liberty to the People; but when I found the Congress entertained different views, that they had again petitioned the King for reconciliation, and declared to their fellow subjects throughout the Empire that their only end in taking up Arms was to procure a Redress of Grievances, and secure their properties and Constitutional Rights, solemnly disclaiming every Idea of establishing an Independent Empire, it gave a different turn to my thoughts. I reflected that our Ancestors have fought many Battles and shed Torrents of Blood in support of their Constitutional Rights, and whatever may have been the fate of Arbitrary Princes, the Constitution was ever held sacred, the instance of Charles's Reign only excepted. The Whigs were then obliged to join with the Tories in Restoring Royalty in its Lustre, to get rid of a Phantom which the Independents had raised under the name of Liberty. The

Hope of a Re-union with our Brethren of G. Britain and of the encreasing Grandeur and Prosperity of the whole Empire to me, I confess, had something agreeable in it. I therefore with eagerness investigated the proposed Plan of operations to enable me to judge of the probable Event, and I found, or thought I found, the security of our Liberties in connection with Great Britain almost certainly attainable, at any rate more practicable than the establishing an Independent State; for the following among other Reasons, that the People of America were determinately united in support of that measure; that every insult and injury from Administration only tended to animate and cement. That the greatest Trading Cities and most respectable characters in England are our Friends. That even our Enemies in Parliament dare not stand the attack on the proper ground, but in order to carry their point have always insisted we were aiming at Independency. That the belief of this, is the sole reason we have any Enemies among the People of England, and though I am of opinion the Governing Powers of Britain would rather lose the Colonies totally, than yield one Iota of their pretensions, the people will think very differently when convinced our views extend no further than to the Security of those Rights which they themselves hold essential to Liberty. That it would be impossible for Government to carry on a war against the inclinations, and so destructive to the Interests of the People, as the present must obviously appear, when it is remembered, the Cause of our Contest is the assumed Power of Parliament to tax the Colonists, to alter our forms of government, to transport us to Britain for the Trial of supposed offences, and to make laws regulating our Internal Police. That the sword would even drop from the hand of a British Soldier, if he believed it pointed against the Breast of a man contending for his birthright. That an attempt to establish an Independency would unite England as one Man against us, and though she is burdened with an enormous debt and deprived of a most valuable branch of Commerce, she has still great Resources, and it is not easy to foresee the consequences of the utmost exertions of her Powers. Besides, it appears to be the Interest of Europe that America should remain dependent. The power and Importance of England (which by a defection of the Colonies she would lose) is necessary in the European System, Holland and Portugal I think owe their Political Existence to her. And even those states which might wish to see her depressed were their Interests confined to Europe, would dread greater evils from the Establishment of an Independent Empire in N. America, the certain consequence of which would be, I apprehend, the loss of Mexico, S. America, and the West India Islands to whomsoever belonging. But it is a necessary enquiry, on what terms can our differences be adjusted which will secure us from future contests? I answer, it is impossible. The nature of Human Affairs is such that no political system can be established which the folly of weak or ambition of wicked men will not in time subvert. Let G. Britain relinquish her Claim of Internal Legislation and Taxation. Let stated times be limited for the holding and duration of Assemblies, and Councillors dependent on the Crown be deprived of Legislative Powers or hold their places during Life, and let Supreme Judges be appointed in each Colony to hold their places during good behaviour with certain and adequate salaries. All this would be no real injury to England, the only advantage she ever did, or ever can receive from America is her Commerce, an Equitable share of which ought to be secured to her by a grand Commercial System to be agreed on by the Legislatures of the two Countries, and to remain unalterable except by mutual consent. Such a plan of accommodation I think, offers as fair for the permanent security of Peace Wealth and Liberty as any I have heard or can devise for the government of America in an Independent State. I take it for granted (as I have never heard it disputed) that a Popular or Democratic Government must take place, which in its most perfect state, I think much inferior to the mixed Government of Britain, for I hold it as a maxim, that wherever the Supreme Power is vested in one man, or one body of Men, the liberty of the subject is at best precarious. It appears from History, that popular fury is as formidable, and often exercised with as much injustice as Royal Indignation. Frequent Elections are no security in this case. The spirit of the People always influences the Representative Body and if a man becomes unpopular, however Innocent, his Ruin is inevitable. To you I need not give instances. Neither is it possible in such a Constitution to render the Judicial Powers totally independent. The same Body of Men who have the appointment of the Judges, having also the power of removing them, will carry popular prejudice even to the Seats of Justice. In this Respect England has the advantage of all other Nations. In cool dispassionate hours the three Branches of the Legislature concur in enacting Laws for the general Good of the Community. The meanest subject cannot be punished unless he transgresses these Laws. Neither can the Judges be displaced for faithfully executing them, without the like concurrence. This protects Individuals equally from popular Violence and the Arbitrary Measures of Kings and Courtiers. But is America capable of receiving a Democratic Government? Have we that Industry, Frugality, Economy, that Virtue which is necessary to constitute it? Laws and Constitutions must be adapted to the manners of the People, they do not, they cannot form them. Whenever the manners change the laws change with them, or lose their Force. Is not N. America too extensive for a popular Government? But I find the spirit of the times is against a union; we must then become a Confederacy of Republicks, each having Supreme Powers within itself. Does not this afford a prospect of perpetual wars and Internal Feuds 'till some one Colony or perhaps one man becomes

Master of the whole Continent? Recur to the Historic page, and point out the age and Country where this under similar circumstances has not been the case. The United Provinces being surrounded by more powerful States materially distinguishes their situation from that of these Colonies. A Congress or General Council for regulating the affairs of the whole Confederacy will hardly be sufficient to maintain peace. There was a general Council of the English Heptarchy yet that Island was an uninterrupted scene of blood and slaughter 'till united under one head. There is a General Diet of the German Empire, yet every one knows the Princes of the Empire submit to its decrees just as far as suits their own purposes. Greece had her Amphictyons, yet was not without intestine Wars.

The Country being called to Arms for the Express Purpose of defending and securing her Constitutional Liberty, Is there not an Inconsistency in employing those Arms to quite different Purposes, at least 'till it is known whether the Original End be attainable? and surely the most sanguine could not expect that Point so soon determined; or that we could force England to a Compliance with our Terms in the course of one Campaign. An apology might well be expected for this trouble, if I had a good one to offer, you should have it. Some slight touches on the subject with several Expressions of Regard interspersed through your Letters of Business emboldened me to take this Liberty and further to request an answer. I am one of those who have ever wished and gloried in the Honour and Prosperity of the British Empire, but if a separation takes place, Interest, Inclination, Every Consideration will induce me to take part with my Native Land, and my best endeavours shall not be wanting to render the Americans a free and happy People. Any Lights which you may throw on the subject shall be faithfully improved to that Purpose as far as in my narrow sphere (and it is a very narrow one) permits. The Arguments of Pamphleteers and News Paper Scribblers on both sides of the Question, have been so absurd, fallacious, or at least superficial, that very little instruction or pleasure could be derived from reading them. Heartily wishing you success in every patriotic Exertion of your abilities, I remain with great Esteem, Sir

Your very humble Servant

ALEX[R] WHITE.

Genl. Lee.

TO GENERAL ARMSTRONG.

Charlestown 27th. June, 1776.

DEAR GENERAL,

As the deputy Adjutant General had contrary to my intentions & order put a great part of Muhlenberg's Regiment on duty, it is impossible to send 'em as I proposed this morning—You must therefore prevail upon the Remainder of Horry's Regiment to take this duty upon them—for as I suppose the Bridge is finish'd, and the risk apparently less—these pretty Gentlemen may probably be prevail'd upon—as to giving a positive order to men of such sensibility and delicacy—it wou'd be harsh & cruel—You must therefore, I say, endeavour to prevail upon them—if your endeavours do not succeed, I shall try some other figure of Rhetorick.

I am Dear General, Yours

CHARLES LEE.

Brigad[r] General Armstrong,
at Hadral's Point.

P.S. I wish you wou'd in my name thank Colonel Thompson's Regiment for the cheerfulness and alacrity with which they have done very hard duty.

To Colonel Moultrie.

Charlestown, June 27th 1776.

Dear Sir: Could you not contrive this night to take up the enemy's buoys? I have ordered General Armstrong to send a hundred volunteers to ease Colonel Thompson's Regiment of their heavy duty; for I find that a part of Colonel Horry's Regiment had most magnanimously refused to take this duty on them. We shall live I hope to thank them—I am in hopes your bridge will be finished this night; you can then be reinforced at pleasure.

I am, dear Sir, Yours,

Charles Lee.

To Col. Moultrie.

To Colonel Moultrie.

Charlestown June 27, 1776.

Dear Sir,

Some boats will possibly pass by you to-night from town on a scouting expedition, before 12 o'clock at night; their orders are to intercept some of the enemy's boats, and gain some important intelligence; I must desire, therefore, that you enjoin the whole sentinels on your Island not to challenge any boats passing from town, or to fire upon them, which would defeat the whole scheme; on their return, if they meet with any success, they shall have orders to greet you with two cheers; and if the wind or tide is against their return to town, they will put into your post, and remain with you this night. I hope your bridge is finished, as I intend to reinforce you considerably.

Yours

Charles Lee.

To Col. Moultrie.

To Colonel Moultrie.

June 28, 6 o'clock, A.M.

Dear Col.

I shall send you immediately a reinforcement. If the bridge cannot be finished without taking down the old——take it down without ceremony, but it would be better to have both.

Yours,
Charles Lee.

To Col. Moultrie.

To Colonel Moultrie.

Point Haddrell, June 28th 1776.

Dear Colonel:

If you should unfortunately expend your ammunition without beating off the enemy, or driving them on ground, spike your guns, and retreat with all the order possible; but I know you will be careful not to throw away your ammunition.

Charles Lee,
Major General.

To Col. Moultrie.

To Colonel Moultrie.

Armstrong's June 28th, 3 o'clock P.M.

Dear Col.

Major Byrd makes reports of your conduct which does you infinite honour; they are, indeed, such as I expected. I have sent for more ammunition for you;

and ordered a large corps of Riflemen to reinforce Col. Thompson.

Yours,

CHARLES LEE.

To Col. Moultrie.

TO COLONEL MOULTRIE.

Charlestown June 29th 9 o'clock.

DEAR COLONEL,

I shou'd have thank'd you & your brave Garrison this morning *viva voce* at the Fort—but am prevented by a great deal of busyness—I do most heartily thank you all and shall do you justice in my Letters to the Congress—I have apply'd for some Rum for your Men. They deserve every comfort that can be afforded to them—We have sent for more Powder—inform me of all your Wants.

I am Dear Colonel, Yours,

CHARLES LEE.

Colonel Moultrie, at Sullivan's Island.

I desire Colonel Thompson will send over as soon as he can, a Return of all occurrences in his part of the Island.

TO THE PRESIDENT OF THE CONVENTION OF VIRGINIA.

Charleston, June 29th 1776.

SIR:—

I took the liberty of detaining your Express, Mr Page, concluding that something material must before this have arrived: but as I imagine you are extremely anxious for the fate of this important Capital, I think it my duty to dispatch him with a very compendious, or rather imperfect account of our present situation. Yesterday about eleven o'clock the Enemy's Squadron, consisting of one fifty, one forty, and six frigates came to anchor before Fort Sullivan, and began one of the most furious cannonades I ever heard or saw: their project was apparently at the same time to land their troops on the East end of the island; twice they attempted it, and twice were gallantly repulsed: the ships continued their fire over the fort till eleven at night. The behavior of the Garrison, both men and officers, with Colonel Moultrie at their head, I confess astonished me; it was brave to the last degree. I had no idea that so much coolness and intrepidity could be displayed by a collection of raw recruits, as I was witness of in this garrison. Had we been better supplied with ammunition, it is most probable their Squadron would have been utterly destroyed—however, they have no reason to triumph; one of their Frigates is now in flames, another lost its bowsprit, the Commodore and a forty gunship had their mizzens shot away, and are otherwise much damaged—in short, they may be said in this their first essay on South Carolina to have been worsted, but presume they will make another attempt. Our loss is ten killed, twenty two wounded, seven of whom have lost their legs or arms. The defences of the fort have received no injury, only one gun dismounted. I shall write when the affair is finished, a more accurate relation to your Convention and to the Congress; in the meantime I think it but justice to publish the merits of Col. Moultrie and his brave Garrison. Col. Thompson of the South Carolina Rangers acquitted himself most nobly in repulsing the troops who attempted to land at the other end of the Island. I know not which Corps I have the greatest reason to be pleased with, Muhlenberg's Virginians, or the North Carolina troops —they are both equally alert, zealous and spirited. I must now, Sir, entreat that you will forward to Wilmington as much powder as can possibly be spared from your province, to supply the place of that which I shall draw from North Carolina; shoes, shirts, and blankets are likewise absolutely necessary for the North Carolinians, who are quite naked. I request, Sir, that you will order these necessaries with the greatest expedition. You will excuse the shortness of my letter, as you may easily conceive that I have a good deal of employment on my hands. I shall not write to the Congress, till the operations of the enemy are brought to something more like a decision. If you, Sir, think this short relation of importance sufficient, you will, of course, transmit it.

I am, Sir, with the greatest respect,

Your most obedient, humble Servant

CHARLES LEE.

TO THE PRESIDENT OF THE PROVINCIAL CONGRESS OF NORTH CAROLINA.

Charlestown, June 29th, 1776.

SIR,

I have written a short account of our situation to the Convention of Virginia, with directions to be open'd for your perusal—I must entreat, Sir, that you will forward to this place with the greatest expedition all the powder you can spare, it will I hope be soon replaced from Virginia.

I am Sir, with the greatest Respect

Your most ob^{t} hum: Servant

CHARLES LEE.

TO BENJAMIN RUSH.

Charlestown, June ye 29th 1776.

MY DEAR RUSH,

I appriz'd you some time ago that you must not expect letters from me as often as I wish'd to write 'em my inclination wou'd prompt me to persecute you every

Post I seize now a leisure moment. You will excuse the conciseness of the scroll—We had yesterday a very severe party of Cannonade with the Tyrant's Mercenaries—They attack'd with eight ships of War a very imperfect and ill plan'd Fort on Sullivan's Island—and were fairly repuls'd, I really believe with very great loss—the Commodore's Ship and another Forty Gun, suppos'd to be the Roe Buck, were both dismasted of their mizens, another Frigate lost its Bowsprit—and the Acteon was set on fire and this morning blew up—They must have suffer'd greatly in men—Our People, tho' quite raw Recruits behav'd like the decima Legio—it was a severe tryal for any Troops. I have been in a good deal of fire, but never in a hotter or more incessant. We had only ten kill'd on the Spot—and twenty two wounded, seven of whom lost their limbs—A Colonel Moutrie commanded who has gain'd eternal credit. I thought it necessary as I was not acquainted with the merit of these brave fellows to appear amongst 'em. They were pleas'd with my visit but did not want encouragement if you are acquainted with Lewis Morris the Delegate congratulate him in my name in having such a son—amongst other becoming qualities He is a full inch taller in the midst of a hot Cannonade than at other times, tho' He is generally pretty upright. Upon my soul He is a fine Boy, as is my other Aid-de-Camp Byrd; I believe They will go down to Tartarus for the three-headed Dog of Darkness if I order 'em. You are not to think the affair I am speaking of is decisive—On the contrary I expect an other and more serious attack—I must not forget that their land Forces attempted at the same time that the ships attack'd to land on the East end of this Sullivan's Island, and were repuls'd twice by a Colonell Thompson of the S. Carolina Rangers—What their loss was I have not yet learnt. We have fortify'd this extensive Town against a surprise at least—Upon the whole I think it safe—I beg you will give my love to Robert Morris and that I will write to him by the next Express—Communicate this letter to him and to Colonel Lee as likewise to Mr Rutledge from whom I have not heard a word this age—What poor mortals are these Maryland Council men! I hope the Congress will write a letter to the People of that Province at large advising 'em to get rid of their damn'd Government—Their aim is to continue feudal Lords to a Tyrant. I am much pleas'd with your operations against your sad Dogs of the Assembly.

Adieu, My Dr Rush *fac ut valeas et me ames*,

C. Lee.

To D. Benjamin Rush,
Philadelphia.

To General Gates.

Charlestown June ye 29th 1776.

My Dr Gates—

I have just read that the General and your Excellency are arriv'd at Philadelphia—my love and respects to the General that I shall send an express to him in a few days—with a minute account of our situation—and the smites of a double repulse the Tyrant's mercenaries have met with—their squadron has been roughly handled—the Commodore and the Roebuck dismasted of their mizens—one frigate lost its Bowsprit and another (the Acteon) blown up, Rush will give you a compendious detail of it—our Troops (tho raw behav'd most nobly) the fire was extremely hot and incessant. Their Troops attempted to land twice and were twice repuls'd by the S. Carolina Rangers. Our loss in the Fort was ten kill'd, twenty two wounded seven of whom lost their limbs, but They encouraged their Comrades after the loss of their limbs—to stand to the cause of liberty. My two young Aid de Camps Byrd and Morris stand fire most nobly—Young Old Jenifer and little Nourse strutted like Crows in a gutter—the fire was I assure you very hot—I am much pleas'd with the Troops—men and officers—and really believe 'em braver than the Enemy—but I wou'd not be understood that this affair was decisive—it was most probably only the prelude to a more serious one—the event of which the great God of Battles only knows—I mean the truly great and universal God not the partial God of the Jews—inclos'd is a return (I dare say not the most perfect) of our strength—apropos—I cannot send it just now, for the Adjudant General who is in love has forgot a whole Regt. You shall have it in a few days. We have about five thoushand men—if I had a thoushand light Horse I could protect these Colonies completely—urge the General to urge it—I am tir'd of writing on the subject. Yours my Dr Gates

C. LEE.

FROM RICHARD HENRY LEE.

Williamsb[g] 29th June, 1776.

MY DEAR FRIEND,

The desire of being here at the formation of our new Government brought me from Philadelphia the 13th of this month. I have been in this City a week where I have had the pleasure to see our new plan of Government go on well. This day will put a finishing hand to it. 'Tis very much of the democratic kind, altho' a Governor and second branch of legislation are admitted, for the former is not permitted voice in Legislation, he is in all things to be advised by his Privy Council, and both are by joint ballot of both houses to be chosen annually, altho' the Governor may be continued in Office 3 years, after which he is not eligible for 4 years. Both the Houses of the Legislature are chosen by the whole body of the people—Our former House of Burgesses, now called the House of Delegates to be chosen annually in the usual manner. The other House, now called the House of Senators is to be 24 in number and to be chosen from Districts into which the Country is to be laid off. One fourth of this Body go out annually by rotation, and the vacancy filled by the District whence they came. The Judges and other Great Officers of State are to be chosen by Joint ballot of both houses, and to hold their Offices during good behaviour. These are the outlines of our political machine, which I hope is sufficiently guarded against the Monster Tyranny. When I left Philadelphia the Military arrangement stood thus—For N. York 10,000 regular troops joined by 15,000 militia—For Canada 7,000 regulars joined by 6,000 militia and 2000 Indians, a Flying Camp of 10,000 in the middle Colonies—11 Battalions in the eastern Colonies and 23 in the Southern. Gen. Wooster had so misconducted matters in Canada, that with very little opposition our Troops were obliged to retreat to the mouth of Sorell, and a Regiment posted at the Cedars, 12 miles above Montreal was shamefully surrendered to a party of the Enemy coming from Niagara. The letters by this post from Phil[a] tell us that our affairs in that Country were recovering fast, and that Gen. Thompson, with 2000 men was gone down to Dechambeau or Falls of Richelieu, to dispossess 300 regular Troops there, and recover that important post. I incline to think our friend Genl. Gates will be sent to Canada as Chief Commander, poor Thomas having died at Chamblée of the small pox. We have already taken three transports with Highlanders—The 217 that have fallen to our share are distributed thro' this Colony, a few in each County, and permitted to hire themselves out to labour, thus to become the Citizens of America instead of its enemies. Great distress prevails in the British West Indies, and the French preparations in that part of the World, formidable. The news of Phil[a] when I came away was that the Court of France had stopt the Hessians &[c] from coming here. I have not the least doubt but that Independence will, in a few days, be publicly announced by the General Congress. All restraining instructions are now removed except from Maryland, and there, the people were up, and instructions sending from all parts to their Convention, which met 10 days ago, expressly directing to rescind their instructions and pursue a different line of political conduct. I incline to think therefore that Independence will carry it nem. con. and Foreign Alliance immediately sought. The business of Confederation will also then be set on foot.

I shall return to Chantilly in a few days and remain there until the last of August, when I go to Philadelphia. It will give me a singular pleasure to hear from you when your leisure will permit, because there is nothing I more sincerely wish than to know that you are happy and successful.

Remember me to M[r] President Rutledge, and tell my friend Gen. Gadsden, that I remember him with much affection.

Farewell my dear friend
RICHARD HENRY LEE.

Col[o] Harrison and M[r] Braxton are left out of our delegation to Congress, the other 5 continued—This Convention voted 6 Troops of Horse.

Major General Lee,
Commander of the Continental Armies in the Southern Department, at Charleston, South Carolina.

FRAGMENT—TO RICHARD HENRY LEE.

[Charlestown, July 1776.]

* * * misconduct from old Wooster. I think you ought to send your plate into Canada, for if W. lose that we lose everything. If my scheme of raising cavalry is found censurable by the Congress, I do not know what can pass uncensured. It was the most œconomical plan that can be devised; but it was said that I should

have previously laid it before them—As [no time] was to be loss'd, not a single minute, and as I was assured by divers members of the Convention, that if the Congress did not thus—to be at the expense of Forage—the Province wou'd—it was impossible, at least it was dangerous to wait the result of the resolves of the Congress on this head. Do you know, that we have been near losing this Province from the want of cavalry? We must have a large body. I request as I have not time you will justify me to Congress on this subject—you shall * * *

To General Washington.

Charlestown, 1 July, 1776.

My Dear General,

I have the happiness to congratulate you on a very signal success (if I may not call it a victory), which we have gained over the mercenary instruments of the British tyrant. I shall not trouble you with a detail of their manœuvres or delays, but defer it to another time, when I have more leisure to write, and you to attend. Let it suffice, that having lost an opportunity (such as I hope will never again present itself) of taking the town, which, on my arrival, was utterly defenceless, the Commodore thought proper, on Friday last, with his whole squadron, consisting of two fifties, six frigates, and a bomb (the rates of which you will see in the inclosed list), to attack our fort on Sullivan's Island.

They dropped their anchors about eleven in the forenoon, at the distance of three or four yards before the front battery. I was myself, at this time, in a boat, endeavouring to make the Island; but the wind and tide being violently against us, drove us on the main. They immediately commenced the most furious fire I ever heard or saw. I confess I was in pain, from the little confidence I reposed in our troops; the officers being all boys, and the men raw recruits. What aug mented my anxiety was, that we had no bridge finished for retreat, or communication; and the creek, or cove, which separates it from the continent, is near a mile wide. I had received, likewise, intelligence that their land troops intended at the same time to land and assault. I never in my life felt myself so uneasy; and what added to my uneasiness was, that I knew our stock of ammunition was miserably low. I had once thoughts of ordering the Commanding officer to spike his guns, and when his ammunition was spent to retreat with as little loss as possible. However, I thought proper previously to send to town for a fresh supply, if it could possibly be procured, and ordered my Aid-de-Camp Mr. Byrd, (who is a lad of magnanimous courage) to pass over in a small canoe, and report the state of the spirit of the garrison. If it had been low, I should have abandoned all thoughts of defence. His report was flattering. I then determined to maintain the post at all risks, and passed the creek or cove, in a small boat, in order to animate the garrison *in propriâ personâ*; but I found they had no occasion for such encouragement.

They were pleased with my visit, and assured me they never would abandon the post but with their lives. The cool courage they displayed astonished and enraptured me, for I do assure you, my dear General, I never experienced a hotter fire. Twelve full hours it was continued without intermission. The noble fellows, who were mortally wounded, conjured their brethren never to abandon the standard of liberty. Those who lost their limbs deserted not their posts. Upon the whole they acted like Romans in the third century. However, our works were so good and solid, that we lost but few; only ten killed on the spot, and twenty-two wounded, seven of whom lost their legs or arms. The loss of the enemy as you will perceive by the enclosed list was very great. As I send a detail to the Congress, I shall not trouble you with a duplicate; but, before I finish, you must suffer me to recommend to your esteem, friendship, and patronage my (though young) Aids-de-Camp, Byrd and Morris, whose good sense, integrity, activity, and valor, promise to their country a most fruitful crop of essential services. Mr. Jenifer, of Maryland, a gentleman of fortune, and not of the age when the blood of men flows heroically, has shown not less spirit than these youngsters. I may venture to recommend in these high terms, because the trial was severe.

Colonel Moultrie, who commanded the garrison, deserves the highest honors. The manifest intention of the enemy was to land, at the same time the ships began to fire, their whole regulars on the east end of the Island. Twice they attempted it, and twice were repulsed by a Colonel Thompson, of the South Carolina Rangers, in conjunction with a body of North Carolina regulars. Upon the whole, the South and North Carolina troops and Virginia Rifle battalion we have here, are admirable soldiers. The enemy is now returned to their old station on this side the bar. What their intention is, I cannot divine. One of the five deserters, who came over to us this day, is the most intelligent fellow I ever met with. The accounts of their particular loss and situation are his, and I think they may be depended upon.

For God's sake, my dear General, urge the Congress to furnish me with a thousand cavalry. With a thousand cavalry I could insure the safety of these Southern Provinces; and without cavalry, I can answer for nothing. I proposed a scheme in Virginia for raising a body almost without any expense. The scheme was relished by the gentlemen of Virginia, but I am told the project was censured by some members of the Congress on the principle that a military servant should not take the liberty to propose any thing. This opinion I sincerely subscribe to, when our distance from the sovereign is so small, and the danger so remote, as to admit of proposing, deliberating, resolving, and approving; but when a General is at a vast distance, and the enemy close to him, I humbly conceive that it is his duty to propose and adopt anything, without other authority than the public safety. From want of this species of troops, we had infallibly lost this Capital, but the dilatoriness and stupidity of the enemy saved us.

I this instant learn that the Commodore is fixing buoys on the bar, which indicates an intention of quitting the place. It is probable that they will bend their course to Hampton, or Chesapeake Bay.

I am extremely happy, dear General, that you are at Philadelphia, for their counsels sometimes lack a little military electricity.

I have ordered the Adjutant General to send you a return; I mean only a return of the strength of this place. I suppose it will be imperfect, for it is an Herculean labor, to a South Carolina officer, to make any detail. God bless you, my dear General, and crown you with success, as I am,

Most entirely and affectionately, Yours,

CHARLES LEE.

P. S. I am made quite happy by the resolution of Congress to keep Canada. Had it been relinquished, all would have been lost.

MEMORANDUM BY GENERAL LEE.

When a Bridge of Communication between Fort Sullivan and the Main is constructed it is absolutely necessary for its protection that two redoubts shou'd be thrown up—on or near the spots determin'd by General Lee and Baron Massenback, the Engineer—these redoubts will likewise answer the essential purpose of preventing the Enemy's landing betwixt the fort and the Point of the Island corresponding with Haderal's Point—A good strong Redoubt shou'd be likewise constructed on Point Haderel, as an open Battery is always subject to be seiz'd by a light Party of the Enemy and turn'd against us—As it appears to me extremely practicable for the Enemy to land on the strand betwixt the East Point of the Island and the Fort and make their approaches on that side I shou'd think it prudent to throw up a chain of redoubts at proper distances on the natural ridge of Sand-hill. They shou'd be so constructed that the most distant be cannonaded by the next that by the Third and the nearest to the Fort by the Guns of the Fort. As it is impossible from the nature of the ground on Sullivan's Island to surround the Post by any sort of a Ditch some other methods must be devised of securing it against an Escalade—1 strong deal well form'd abbatis wou'd in my opinion best answer the purpose—but this abbatis must be so sunk as not to be expos'd to be destroy'd by Cannon—but as a thorough knowledge of all the avenues, creeks and landing Places which lead to Point Haderel, are of the last importance—it is to be hoped that Colonel Gadsden will recommend it to his officers to make themselves masters of it—as also to reconnoitre all the neighbouring Islands —that on the supposition the Enemy shou'd again lodge themselves in any of 'em, We may know how to attack 'em with advantage.

It is almost superfluous to mention the necessity of an   of Communication betwixt the Fort and Bridge or a Tete de Pont on the Hederel Side, and of a strong redoubt at the   as these works must appear to every man indispensably necessary, [*the following is not in Lee's autograph*] but above all the necessity of a strong Redoubt at the advanced Guard is evident.

To Colonel Moultrie.

Charlestown, July 1st 1776.

Dear Colonel,

Huger's Regiment have offer'd themselves to work at your Fort. I believe a Corps of Blacks wou'd have answer'd better, but the President & Vice President think otherwise. You must desire the Baron to throw up the redoubt I order'd near or on the beach to prevent their landing—the Carpenters will I hope soon finish the Gate. I have applied for six horses and hope I shall procure 'em for you. Five deserters are just arrived here from the Ships of War; inclosed I send you a list of the murders your Garrison has now to answer for, but I hope it will sit light on their consciences.

I am Sir,
Your most ob[t] hum: Servant
CHARLES LEE.

Colonel Moultrie,
at Sullivan's Island.

P. S. I must request that your Garrison may be kept more vigilant than ever, and that Colonel Thompson and his Corps do not relax, for it is almost proverbial in War, that we are never in so great danger, as when success makes us confidently secure—let the bridge be finished without delay.

To President Rutledge.

Charleston July 1st 1776.

DEAR SIR,

It is not impossible that the late repulse of the Enemy may be fatal to us. We seem now all sunk into a most secure and comfortable sleep—Not a mortal of any kind, black or white at work—much is to be done for the security of the Town and the Island of Sullivan—in the Town, the Barricades shou'd all be considerably highten'd and thicken'd—the parapet which encircles the whole shou'd likewise be strengthen'd and rais'd—I wish your Excellency wou'd give order that a sufficient number of Men shall be collected for these necessary works,—I am afraid Huger's Regiment will not answer the purpose in Sullivan's Island half so well as a Corps of Blacks, besides will it not unhinge the whole system of our present duties? As I intend to write to the Congress tomorrow, it will be necessary I shou'd have ready an Express.

I am Dr Sir, &c.
CHARLES LEE.

FROM ARCHIBALD BULLOCK, PRESIDENT OF GEORGIA.

Savannah July 2d 1776

SIR,

As the Gentlemen that were deputed to wait upon you, in order to confer on the best Measures for the defence of this Province are not returned, I have sent to his Excellency the President a Copy of a Letter, I have just received from Lieut. Colonel McIntosh—I have desired he would communicate the Contents to you—I have not the least doubt of your perfect Knowledge of the whole scheme of ministerial operations against the Continent and that you are well informed of our helpless situation—The Importance of this Colony to the American cause is very great & therefore I'm persuaded we shall claim part of your attention—Your presence here would give a most happy & favorable Complexion to our affairs—The Post-Boy is waiting & I can only wish that the Lord of Hosts, the God of Armies may be your guide & protection.

I am, Sir, respectfully your
Most obedient & very humb. Servt
ARCHD BULLOCK.

His Excellency Genl Lee,
at Charleston.

To the President of Congress.

Charlestown, July 2nd, 1776.

Sir,

I shou'd have done myself the honor sooner of informing the Congress of the attack made by the Enemy's Squadron on Sullivan's Island and their repulse—but conjectur'd that by waiting a day or two I might probably be furnished with the means of sending a more minute, full, and satisfactory account—my conjecture was right, for yesterday five seamen made their escape, one of whom is a more intelligent Fellow than is commonly found amongst men of his level—inclosed is a copy of their Narrative, some parts of it are perhaps too whimsical & trivial to merit the attention of Congress, but I think it my duty to present it as it is without adding or curtailing a circumstance—I think, Sir, I may venture to congratulate the Congress on the event; not only the advantages must be considerable, but the affair reflects no small credit on the American Arms.

On Fryday about eleven o'clock, the Commodore with his whole squadron consisting of two line of battle ships and six Frigates (the rates of which are mark'd in the enclosed narrative) anchor'd at less than half musket shot from the Fort, and commenced one of the most furious and incessant fires I ever saw or heard—it was manifestly their plan to land at the same time their whole regulars at the east end of the Island and of course invest the Fort by Land and Sea—as the Garrison was composed entirely of raw Troops both Men & Officers, as I knew their ammunition was short, and as the Bridge by which we cou'd reinforce or call off the Troops from the Island was unfinished you may easily conceive my anxiety—it was so great that I was in suspense whether I should evacuate it or not—fortunately while I was in this State of Suspense some ammunition arriv'd from the Town, and my Aid de

Camp M[r] Byrd returning from the Island with a flattering report of the Garrison's spirit, I determin'd to support it at all hazards—On this principle I thought it my duty to cross over to the Island to encourage the Garrison by my presence, but I might have saved myself that trouble, for I found on my arrival they had no occasion for any sort of encouragement; I found 'em determin'd and cool to the last degree, their behaviour wou'd in fact have done honor to the oldest Troops—I beg leave, Sir, therefore to recommend in the strongest terms to the Congress the Commanding Officer Colonel Moutrie and his whole Garrison as brave soldiers and excellent citizens—nor must I omit at the same time mentioning Colonel Thompson who with the South Carolina Rangers and a detachment of the North Carolina Regulars repulsed the Enemy in two several attempts to make a lodgment at the other extremity of the Island.

Our loss considering the heat and duration of the fire was inconsiderable, we had only ten men killed on the spot and twenty two wounded, seven of whom lost their limbs, but with their limbs they did not lose their spirits for they enthusiastically encouraged their Comrades never to abandon the standard of Liberty and their Country—this I do assure you, Sir, is not in the stile of Gasconading Romance usual after every successful action, but literally fact; I with pleasure mention the circumstance as it augurs well to the cause of freedom—At eleven the fire ceas'd, having continued just twelve hours without the least intermission. What the Enemy's intentions are now, it is impossible to divine. I am inclin'd to think they will (if they can repass the Barr) bend their course to Cheasepeack or Hampton Bay, perhaps shame & rage may prompt their land Forces to some attempt before their Departure; on my part I shall spare no pains to discover their intentions and baffle their schemes.

As Georgia is a district of the Command with which you have honor'd me, I thought it prudent to request some of their members to a conference with the president of this province and myself—They accepted the Invitation and gave us great satisfaction from their intelligence and good sense—inclosed is the substance of their deliberation.

The Province is certainly of the last importance to the common cause, and the mode of protecting it pointed out by these Gentlemen, is in my opinion in all its parts wise and necessary. They had conceived a notion that I had powers to augment their establishment. I assured 'em I had no such powers, but both Mr. Rutledge and myself gave it as our opinion that any expenses manifestly beyond their faculties which they might incurr in the common cause, wou'd be repaid by the Congress, and in this perswasion we ventured to encourage them to augment their Cavalry without loss of time and make the proposed present of Cattle to the Indians—Indeed, Sir, without a strong Corps of cavalry I do not see how it is possible to protect these Southern Colonies, and with one thousand good cavalry, I think I cou'd ensure their protection—from the want of this species of Troops Charlestown & its dependencies had certainly been lost if the Enemy had acted with the vigor and expedition we had reason to expect, but a most unaccountable langour and inertness on their parts have saved us—if the scheme I proposed in Virginia had been approved and adopted it wou'd have been not only a security but considerable economy—the forage was to have been the only expense—now I am upon the subject, I cannot help mentioning that I have been inform'd that the project has been considered by some Gentlemen as a sort of presumption in me in arrogating such a power but I fancy the affair was not properly understood; I saw the immediate necessity of such a corps—I knew they cou'd be rais'd immediately by these means, and at the same time I was given to understand by several Gentlemen of the Virginian Convention, that shou'd the Continental Congress disapprove of the expense (trifling as it was) there was little doubt of their Convention defraying it—but in fact, Sir, the measure seem'd necessary for the Salvation of the Provinces; and not a day was to be lost, which I hope will fully justify my Conduct, and I must beg leave to repeat my assertion that without Cavalry these Provinces cannot easily be defended. I wish some means cou'd be devised of reducing East Florida to an American Province—had I force sufficient, I should, with your permission, certainly attempt it—the advantages must be great and manifold.

The augmentation of the Georgian Cavalry I sincerely hope may be approved of by the Congress—inclos'd is the establishment and pay proposed for 'em—I think the terms not high.

I shall Sir, conclude with expressing the high satisfaction I have received from the zeal, activity and public spirit of the Gentlemen and Inhabitants of this City and Province, from the President & Council down to the lowest order of the People, and with assuring you that I have not in my military capacity met with the least obstruction or difficulty, but that we have all worked in concert and harmony for the common good. I will earnestly request you will pay my respects to the Congress, and be perswaded Sir, that I am most entirely and devotedly

Your most Obedient Servant

CHARLES LEE.

To The Hon[a] John Hancock,

President of the Continental Congress.

The Georgia Troopers have according to the establishment of their Congress fifty Shillings sterling ℔ man, rations for themselves, but find arms, horses, and forage—the Captain's pay is Ten Pounds sterling ℔ month—the Lieutenants Six pounds—the Quarter Master four pounds.

P. S. Lord Dunmore has with him I believe at present only one ship of War—if any part of the Continental Fleet shou'd happen to visit Hampton Bay at this juncture, it would defeat the whole scheme of the Enemy's operations at least for this Campaign—but it is impossible to say how long his Lordship may remain in this weak condition.

NARRATIVE, ETC.

[*Inclosed in the foregoing letter.*]

Narrative, by Thomas Burnitt, of Col. Davidson's Massachusetts Regiment, Daniel Hawkins of Boston, Robert Scott and Edmund Alston of New Hampshire, and James Scott of Virginia, deserters from the fleet which attacked and were beaten off by the Fort at Sullivan's Island, on Friday, the 28th [June], 1776. They are all Americans, and had been taken by the enemy at sea: Burnitt, Hawkins, and Scott in the Sloop Sally, Hawkins and Alston in the Brigantine Friendship.

The Bristol of 50 guns, commanded by Sir Peter Parker, greatly damaged in her hull, large knees and timbers shot through and smashed:—if the water had not been very smooth, it would have been impossible to have kept her from sinking; all the carpenters in the fleet have been called to her assistance.

Mizen mast shot away, main mast badly wounded by 3 several shots, foremast by 2, rigging sails and yards much damaged.

The Captain of the Commodore lost his left arm above the elbow; he was sent yesterday (30th June) to England in a brig. The Commodore's breeches torn off—his back side laid bare, his thigh and knee wounded; he walks only when supported by two men. 44 men killed, and 30 wounded, among whom were many Midshipmen, and inferior Officers; 20 of the wounded dead since the action—talked in the fleet that the two large ships would go over the Bar again, and proceed to English harbour in Antigua to be repaired. The Bristol, when lightened as much as possible, draws 18 feet 7 inches water.

Experiment of 50 guns on 2 decks, all 12 pounders; a slighter built vessel than the Bristol exceedingly damaged in her hull—several ports beat in, and her mizzen mast hurt, but uncertain of particulars. 57 killed, of whom the Captain was one, 30 wounded, several of whom since died; draws when lightened 17 feet water; the general opinion that neither of these large ships will go safely over the Bar again.

Solbay 28 guns, 2 men killed, and 4 wounded; D'Active, 28 guns, Lieutenant killed, and 4 wounded; Acteon, 28 guns, Sphynx, 20 guns, Syren, 28 guns, all got aground, the first in coming up, the two latter in running away; the Sphynx cut away her bowsprit, the Syren got off, Acteon (by the assistance of 20 English seamen) remained fast, burnt and blown up by her own people (whilst she was on fire, Mr. Milligan, one of our [Carolina] Marine Officers, and a party of men boarded her, brought off her colors, the ship's bill, and as many sails and stores as three boats could contain.)

The Thunderbomb lay at a considerable distance, throwing shells at the fort, and by overcharging had shattered her beds, and damaged the ship so much, as to render it necessary for her to go into dock before she can act again. The Friendship, a hired armed vessel of 26 guns of various sizes, covered the Bomb, as did the Syren, who also fired briskly at the Fort Briocket [ricochet] shots; the whole fleet badly manned and sickly, particularly the Syren's men at two-thirds short allowance of provisions and water; they have had no fresh meat since their arrival, the 1st of June.

Lord Wm. Campbell had been very anxious for the attack, and proposed taking all the forts with only the Syren and Solbay. Lord Cornwallis has the chief command of the land force. He and Gen. Clinton are both on shore with the troops at Long Island. His Lordship had sometime ago urged Sir Peter Parker to attack on the seaside, otherwise he would march up, attack, and take the Fort, and complain of Sir Peter's tardiness. The Commander replied: Cornwallis might march his troops, when he pleased, but the fleet required a fair wind; the first that happened he would proceed against the Fort. The general at that time believed we had no troops out of garrison, but he was soon better informed, being since repulsed and drove back with loss. He remained quiet, and left the Commodore to enjoy the glory of being defeated alone. This must be a mistake, from Lord Cornwallis having the command when the fleet left Ireland.

A Negro Pilot [who is exceedingly caressed, was on board the Commodore and] was put down with the Doctor out of danger;—when they sailed from Ireland the number of men 4000—11 transports parted from them had not been heard of since—which with desertions reduced them to 1500 or 2000 at most. They began to steal off between 9 and 10 of the clock, made no noise, nor waited to heave up, and not slipt cable. The Commodore has only one anchor and cable left. 2 o'clock on Friday the Fort, waiting for a supply of powder—the men of wars men mistaking the unavoidable delay for surrender, cried "they have done fighting." "By God," says others, "we are glad of it; for we never had such a drubbing in our lives. We had been told the Yankees would not stand two fires, but we never saw better fellows."—All the common men in the fleet spoke loudly in praise of the garrison, brave, fine fellows; the men in general very desirous of getting on shore to join the Americans.

Conference with the Georgia Deputies.

[*Inclosed in the preceding Letter to Congress.*]

The Deputies sent from Georgia by Desire of His Excellency General Lee to confer with him upon the State of that Colony in order to devise the best Method of putting it in a proper Posture of Defence beg leave to represent, That from the weak and defenceless situation of the Colony, surrounded as it is with Enemies, It stands in immediate need of Assistance from the General Congress. And when they consider that however small the Colony may be of itself in a comparative Point of View, yet that from the great Plenty of Provision—numerous stocks of Cattle—excellent Inlets—Harbours and Rivers (perhaps equal to any upon the Continent) with which the Colony abounds—and above all the firm attachment of its Inhabitants to the American cause—they are led to trust that the Protection and Security of that Colony will be held an object of considerable Importance.

No one of the thirteen United Colonies is so weak within or so much exposed from without. To the East the Inhabitants suffer the Ravages of British Cruizers—their Negroes are daily inveigled & carried away from their Plantations. British Fleets may be supplied with Beef from several large Islands well stocked with cattle which line their Coast, and round which large ships may sail—To the South they have the Province of East Florida—the Inhabitants and Soldiery in which must of Necessity make Inroads upon Georgia for the Article of Provision with which they have heretofore been chiefly supplied. Georgia here stands as a Barrier to South Carolina—and effectually secures that Province against the like Depredations—the Southern Parts of Georgia contain vast stocks of Cattle and our most valuable Rice Plantations lie that way, by some late computations there are said to be upwards of 30,000 of Head of black Cattle in the Province, and Hogs &c without Number. We have certain Accounts of their being at this time upwards of 1000 British Troops in St Augustine.

To the West and almost down upon the Georgia Line are the most numerous tribes of Indians now in North America—to wit the Creeks, Cherokees, Choctaws and a number of small Tribes, in the whole at least 15,000 Gun-Men—All these Nations have been much tampered with by the Emissaries of Government and without the utmost Exertions of Prudence on our side it is feared may be brought to act against us—they are so situated as to make it extremely convenient for our Enemies to supply them from E. & W. Florida, with Ammunition and every thing else they want. Our last accounts from the Indians are rather unfavorable, and when we consider their natural Principle of Infidelity and how much more able our Enemies are to purchase their Friendship by presents &c than we are, there seems to be the greatest Reason to apprehend a Rupture with them—in such a Case the Fate of Georgia may be easily conceived. Add to all these considerations the vast Numbers of Negroes we have, perhaps of themselves Sufficient to subdue us—in Point of Numbers the Blacks exceed the Whites; and the ready Channel of Supply and secure retreat which St Augustine affords render them much to be dreaded. The Conquest of Georgia would doubtless be considered as a great acquisition by Gt Britain. It is a most excellent Provision Country—abounds with Ship-Timber and Lumber of all kinds and is most conveniently situated for a Place of Rendezvous to their Shipping.

Under all these Circumstances it must certainly appear indispensably necessary that Measures be immediately taken for the Defence and Security of that Province, but the low situation in Point of Means or Ability of its Inhabitants puts it out of their Power to do so of themselves, more especially as they have been already put to a very great Expense in consequence of the late descent upon them. The great objects seem to be, Men, Fortification and a good understanding with the Indians. We would therefore beg leave to propose.

1st That his Excellency General Lee be requested to state the peculiar situation of the Province of Georgia to the General Congress and to obtain directions from them to raise and take into Continental Pay so many Men as may be conceived to be sufficient to defend that Province—in our opinion less than Six Battalions will not answer the Purpose. But as we do not conceive any of these Men can be recruited in Georgia we would apprehend it full as eligible (if that can be done) to order some of the Regiments already raised to march thither, and further that the four Troops of Horse already raised be augmented to a Regiment and put upon the Continental Establishment. Part of these Battalions and Troops may be so stationed—as to serve equally for the protection of Georgia and South Carolina agst the Indians, and above all may entirely shut up the Communication between them and our Enemies to the Southward, which will certainly be the most effectual Means of preventing an Indian War.

2ndly That the sum of sterling be granted by the General Congress for building Fortifications and Guard Boats in the Province of Georgia—the reason why we conceive this ought to be a general Charge because it is evident the *same* will serve against attacks from the South and for Cutting off the Communication between E. & W. Florida and the Indians upon which the Peace of the back Inhabitants of Georgia So Carolina, No. Carolina & Virginia depends—Besides It seems to be a Part of the plan of Administration to throw Forces into the Indian Country where they expect to be Joined by considerable Numbers of the Savages, and in this Event there is no Province or Place through which they can so conveniently pass as thro' Georgia.

3rdly It is a fixt Principle with the Indians to be paid for their good offices, and in this Controversy we conceive they will expect to be well paid even for Neutrality. The articles they prefer will doubtless be ammunition and Cloathing but these we have it not in our Power to give them. We would then propose *Cattle* as a substitute, and are inclined to think if the Communication between them & our Enemies were cut off they would soon be brought to be well satisfied with a Present of this Kind. It is therefore submitted to the General Congress whether it w[d] not be worth while to give Directions that a Number not exceeding 5000 Head of Cattle be purchased, and Distributed among the Indians by the Commissioners. We are of Opinion this step would answer many valuable Purposes and would have a tendency not only of attaching them to our Interest from Gratitude, but would also be a Means of civilizing them, and by fixing the Idea of Property would keep them honest and peaceable with us for Fear of Reprizals.

JONATHAN BRYAN,
JOHN HOUSTOUN,
LACH[N] M[c]INTOSH.

Endorsed by General Lee: Result of a Conference of the Georgian Deputies.

TO ROBERT MORRIS.

Charlestown July 2[d] 1776.

DR MORRIS

I shall not trouble you with a detail of the Enemy's late attack on Sullivan's Island and their repulse, if I may not call it a defeat. You will have the whole from my letter to the Congress—let it suffice that our men acted much better than I had any conception raw troops would do. The advantage must be considerable and the credit to our Arms undoubtedly great—the slaughter on the side of the Tyrants mercenaries was not trifling—but they deserv'd it. I want my dr. friend to talk a little on my own affairs—it is true I cannot positively and formally prove that my fortune is confiscated—but I have the strongest reason to believe it and have no means of proving it—In short my situation with regard to circumstances is more whimsical and disagreeable than any man's on the Continent. I have really nothing that I can call my own—the half of the Estate pay'd for is more properly yours than mine. I have this morning been conversing with Mr Rutledge on the subject—He is of the opinion that the Congress ought of their own Accords at least to have advanced the whole purchase money of this Estate—that it is indelicate to keep me in this most rigid state of dependency than other men. He is now writing to Mr Lynch and his brother Ned to urge 'em to a motion of this kind—there is one circumstance to be consider'd, how am I to pay the interest of the money borrow'd for the purchase? how I am to pay the interest due on the different mortgages? I am sensible that the Congress have made a hard bargain but they were pleased to think otherwise—Upon the whole my friend for my ease and let me add for the credit of the Congress, I must intreat and request that you will exert yourself in concert with my other Friends particularly Rutledge, the Lee's, Dickinson and the Adams's to compass the payment for the full purchase money—not only that borrow'd and pay'd but to clear off the incumbrances, and likewise one thousand pounds or five hundred to set the Estate agoing—let me have some realized property—altho' not half I have stak'd and most probably lost—and I shall be easy. I shall then bustle with double vigor, for to confess the truth I have hours of great uneasiness on the subject—besides will not the bargain the Congress have made in me appear still harder when the whole bill comes upon 'em at once principal and interest—not to be prolix—put yourself in my place, and tell me wou'd you not think it a duty to yourself to realize something? I have already shewn the highest confidence in the honour of the Congress. I have still the same confidence, but it is composed not only of mortal but changeable men. Once more therefore let me intreat you to exert yourself in this (to me) so important a point. I must beg you will communicate this letter to the Gentlemen I have mentioned and to any other members you think proper and relieve my uneasiness folly or whatever name you chuse to give it. Adieu God bless you and all your family.

Yours entirely and affectionately
CHARLES LEE.

My two young aid de camps Byrd and Morris stand fire charmingly. I have a third aid de camp a Mr. Jenifer a young gentleman of about five and fifty who is no flincher, the little secretary Nourse behaved likewise very calmly and sedately.

TO GENERAL WASHINGTON.

Charlestown, July 2, 1776.

SIR:

My having early in life engaged in the last war under you, and the present one we are engaged in appearing to be an affair that will not be very shortly settled, induces me to solicit your notice and patronage in obtaining a promotion of rank in some measure adequate to my long service and rank last war. In this I flatter myself with your notice to Congress, as otherwise I may pass altogether unnoticed amongst the many promotions taking place; and my principal having left a vacancy by his promotion, hope this application will not be out of time. I am, with the utmost respect,

Your obedient, humble servant,
THOMAS BULLITT

DEAR GENERAL:

You must consider this as a Postscript, and at the

same time recommendatory letter of your old friend Thomas Bullitt. He is certainly a man of merit, and entitled, from his length of services, zeal, and valour to higher rank than he enjoys.

C. Lee.

To the President of the Convention of Virginia, Etc.

Charlestown, July ye 3rd 1776.

Sir,

Our affair on the 28th was much more important than I at first conceiv'd—inclosed is the narrative of some Deserters, one of whom is a very intelligent fellow —I think it is my duty to send this account in its proper form neither adding nor curtailing a single circumstance. I congratulate you Sir, and the public on an event which certainly does great credit to the American Arms and I hope must be attended with very great advantages.

I am Sir, &^c

Charles Lee.

I must beg Sir, you'll be very expeditious in forwarding the powder to this place.

To the Honorable The President of the Convention of Virginia, & to the President of the Council of North Carolina enclosing to each of 'em a Narrative of the late Engagement, Enemy's loss, &c, as taken from some Deserters.

To Sir Henry Clinton.

Charlestown July ye 3rd 1776.

Sir,

A Certain Walker was by a most whimsical concurrence of wind and tide hurried into the midst of our

Sentinels at the end of Sullivan's Island. He says he is Master of a Brig Transport and has the principal property in the Vessel—as the man wou'd probably be ruin'd by this odd accident, Mr. Rutledge President of the Province and myself would propose to you an exchange of this Walker for Ethan Allen, or if he is not at present in your Fleet or Army for any two of the Connecticut privates who were taken prisoners with Allen, I confess honestly to you, Sir, that I am extremely desirous of redeeming Allen and his whole party—you I am sure are liberal enough to compassionate the sufferings of those who think at least they are engaged in a righteous cause—In this perswasion I propose to you an exchange man for man of these People with the Soldiers of the 14th who were taken Prisoners at the Great Bridge in Virginia—if therefore any of this party are at present in your Custody you will oblige me much in releasing 'em. I pledge my word and honor that an equal number of the fourteenth shall be sent from the place of their confinement to Lord Dunmore's Camp or wherever you think proper.

I take the liberty to request you'll accept of a small quantity of fruit and vegetables which perhaps in your situation are not easily procur'd—This I hope you will consider as a testimony of the regard I have for your personal qualities—the President joins with me in a high opinion of Mr. Clinton.

I have, I am told, an intimate Friend and Comrade in your Corps, Captain Primrose Kennedy of the 44th—I intreat you will assure him of my love and Friendship and send him a small portion of the Fruit.

Mr. Byrd, one of my Aid de Camps is the Flag, who I am confident will be treated with all the respect due to his character.

I am Sir,

Your most Obt Servant

CHARLES LEE.

To Major Genl. Clinton.

(Sent by a flag of truce.)

To Lieut. Col. Palfrey.

Charlestown, July y^e 3rd 1776.

My DR Palfrey,

The old observation that [money] spoileth the [wit] is not exemplify'd in you—on the contrary, you never [were] in your life so brilliant as since you were Master of twice fifty Dollars $p^{'r}$ month—God inspire the Congress with the whim of increasing your store, that you may become still a more entertaining Correspondent—if it was not for this consideration I cou'd wish you with us. We often long to laugh with the gallant Palfrey—but you wou'd only afford us half the Amusement you did formerly—for you must remember that not only the quantity of good things which came out of your mouth but the quantity of good things which went into your mouth furnish'd us with matter of wonder and pleasure—but, alas, were you with us you wou'd be totally eclips'd in one of these branches—We have a little Secretary that cou'd eat up you and your whole Family. We have a considerable wager now depending, Spada is to fast thirty six hours and the Secretary twelve. They are then to start together on a course of roast Beef. I have laid on Spada, but the majority of those who are acquainted with the abilities of the two gentlemen, are clear that I shall lose. You will hear of a snub We have given Sir P. Parker. I assure you it was hot busyness. My two Aid de Camps Byrd and Morris stand fire most divinely—Upon my Soul they are spirited lads. I must now intreat, My Dr. Palfrey, that you will assist Capt. Grere in unravelling his accounts with the men of the different Regiments otherwise I must [ask] Whitcombe. Adieu. Write to me often—My love to Morland and Beyler.

Yours most affectionately

Charles Lee.

To Lieut. Col. Palfrey,
Paymaster General.

To President Rutledge.

Charlestown 5th July 1776.

Dear Sir,

There is so much confusion arising from Commands issuing from different Quarters, that I must request that the Quarter Master General has the sole direction of all which is properly in his Department; the house for instance where the Tools are kept, is shut up to him —Powder is sent to the Posts without letting me know, in short we are playing at Duke & No Duke, and throwing everything into confusion and anarchy—I do not mention these things from any jealousy of command, but really and literally for the good of the service and wish that everything military was conducted thro' one proper Channel. I am Dear Sir,

Your most Obt Servant
Charles Lee.

To John Rutledge, Prest. &c

The necessary works are all at a stand, and have been at a stand these seven days.

From Col. Richard Henry Lee.

Williamsbg 6th July, 1776.

My dear Friend,

The inclosed form of Government will shew you that this Country has in view a permanent system of Liberty. Mr Henry is chosen Governor, and a Privy Council is appointed to assist him in the discharge of his important duty—A new Great Seal, adapted to our State is ordered to be made, and now, we have in all respects a full and free Government which this day begins the exercise of its powers. The Convention of Maryland has rescinded the mischievous instructions with which they had bound their Delegates, empowered three of them to join the other Colonies in a vote of Independence, Foreign Alliance, Confederation, &c. By this time I expect the two former are settled in Congress—Before this reaches you, no doubt you will have heared of our having taken in this Bay a Transport with 217 Highlanders, and by this Post we learn that 5 Transports more with the same kind of Cattle have been carried into the Eastern Ports—But this good news is allayed by more adverse fortune in Canada—Gen. Thomson with 2000 men went to dislodge 300 Regular Troops at the three Rivers whence he was met by Gen. Burgoyne with a considerable force—Thomson's forces were routed himself and Col. Irwin taken prisoners, with the loss of 150 men killed, wounded, & taken prisoners. The rest joined our Army at the mouth of Sorel. In short, our affairs in Canada, at present wear but an indifferent aspect. We learn by this post that a very extensive conspiracy (pushed on by British gold) has been detected at New-York—General Washington was to have been assassinated, the magazine blown up, and the cannon spiked—'Tis said the Mayor of N. York was concerned in the Plot. Many are now in Jail for this nefarious business. Lord Dunmore still remains on Gwin's Island where Caterpillar like, we hear he has devoured everything in that place, so that it is probable force of some kind or other will shortly drive him thence but where he will fasten next we cannot guess. We are concerned here at not hearing from you, and are obliged to comfort ourselves with the consideration that no news is good news. I shall return to Congress about the last of August, and in the meantime nothing will more contribute to my happiness than to hear that you are healthy, happy, and successful. Our cause is the cause of Virtue and mankind, and well supported as it is, I have no doubt of its success. Farewell my dear Friend

RICHARD HENRY LEE.

My direction is at Chantilly, Westmoreland County, Virginia.

FROM COL. LACHLAN McINTOSH.

SIR,

Since I came to Savannah we hear from the Southward that a number of Regulars & Indians to the amount of 5 or six hundred are come from S[t] Augustine to the River S[t] Marys with Intention it is said to cross that River & enter this Province. A party of Militia were ordered in consequence of this Intelligence to assist the Rangers in repelling them from whom we had no acco[t] yet—and the out Detachments of my Battalion brought in for the protection of the Town, least the attempt from the Southward may be intended to facilitate, & co-operate with an attack from Sea, which seems probable—We are further informed that some of the Foreign Troops are lately arrived in S[t] Augustine—that they have many Indians there also who are regularly trained every Day. This I thought proper to mention to your Excellency that you may be better able to Judge of the Enemy's Intention by Comparing their motions here with their Manœuvres in Carolina.

I shall be glad to receive your particular Orders on this and every other Matter that occurs, and have the Honor to be your Excelly[s.]

Most ob[t] Hble Servant

LACH[N] McINTOSH.

Savannah in Georgia, 7 July, 1776.

The Bearer of this is Lieu[t] Col[o] Elbert of the Georgia Continental Battalion.

Since I wrote the above an acco[t] is just rec[d] p. Express that the Indian's has killed one Capt[n] Smith & his Family on little River abo[t] 150 Miles west of this Town, and have taken several Family's prisoners at & near Kecowee Fort Prince George, and carry'd them over the Hills to Cameron Stewarts Commissary

To His Excellency Charles Lee, Esq. Major General & Commander in Chief of the American Forces in the Southern District Charleston S[o] Carolina.

To Colonel Moultrie.

Charlestown, 7th July, 1776.

Dear Colonel,

I am extremely concern'd that the materials are not provided, which are necessary for carrying on, and finishing the works proposed in your Fort and Island; but at the same time I think the Negroes you have with you may be usefully employ'd—they may fill up the Merlons which are not yet full—they may palisade (for I believe you have palisades sufficient) the low, and most accessible parts of the Embrasures & angles—Is your Gate finish'd? How is the Bridge? I beg you will inform me, and am Dr Colonel

Your most ob^t^ Servt

Charles Lee.

To Colonel Moultrie,
at Sullivan's Island.

To General Armstrong.

Charlestown, July ye 7th, 1776.

Dear General,

I think, with you, that General Clinton is not a Soldier of so poor a stamp, as to abandon all thoughts of making an impression either on the Town Forts or your Post merely because the Commodores Squadron was the other day repulsed—I am extremely uneasy in not being able to put all these places hors d'insult—but an Angel from Heaven cou'd not get the better of the indolent & procrastinating spirit of these people—six days have I been assur'd that Palmeto logs in abundance were provided, and not a single log is (as I can discover) procur'd. Fascines, I have order'd to be made, but no Tools are to be found for the purpose—in short, the whole is sunk into one universal sleep.

As you very prudently propose fortifying your post, I must desire you will inform me whether you want Guns—what size and number? I must request likewise that you will announce in public orders, that for the future if any Militia men attempt to quit their station without orders, they will be treated as Mutineers and Deserters on the spot without waiting for a formal Tryal.

I think the Guard in Tufts Schooner shou'd be order'd not to suffer any of 'em to pass without proper authority and if they attempt to pass by force to fire upon 'em—but previous to this order the whole must be apprized of it.

I am Dear General,
Your most ob[t.]
CHARLES LEE.

To Brigadier General Armstrong,
Hadrals Point.

To EDMUND PENDLETON.

Charlestown July y[e] 7th. 1776

SIR,

M[r] Rutledge will inform you by this Express of the outrages committed by the Cherokees which must be construed as the commencement of a war.

As it is now certain that a capital and favourite part of the plan laid down by his most excellent and clement majesty George the Third, is to lay waste the Provinces, burn the habitations and mix men women and children in common carnage by the hands of the Indians; and as this part of his plan tho' of a piece in humanity is certainly more big with mischievous consequences than the rest, It appears to me absolutely necessary to crush the evil before it arises to any dangerous height—indeed if we avail ourselves of the event, it may prove a fortunate one—perhaps we ought in policy to have a wish for it.

We can now with the greatest justice strike a blow which is necessary to intimidate the numerous tribes of Indians from falling into the measures of the Tyrant, and as these Cherokees are not esteemed the most formidable Warriors we can probably do it without much risk or loss. I think then Sir, that without a moments delay a body of your Frontier Riflemen shou'd be immediately furnish'd forth, and march into the Country of the Over hill Cherokees and make a severe lasting and salutary example of 'em. The Carolinas propose at the same time attacking their lower Towns and with the co-operation of Virginia entertain no doubt of success.

Clinton's Army and Parkers Squadron are pretty much in the same situation as when I wrote last—they daily indeed make some alterations in the position of their land Troops from one Island to another—perhaps for new air or water of which the Deserters say they are in great want—they tell us likewise that considerable sickness prevails in the Army and greater discontents from hard duty and bad diet—The spirit of desertion begins to shew itself; five soldiers came over these last last two nights, who assure us that were they not on an Island from which it is difficult to escape two thirds of their army wou'd soon be with us—I am myself inclined to believe 'em—upon the whole, when I consider the difficulties which the Enemy Generals have to encounter —the temper and disposition of their Troops, and the improving spirit of ours, I assure myself that the game is in our hands. God give us more grace than to shuffle it away. I am Sir

Your most obed humble Servant

CHARLES LEE.

To The Hon^{o} Edm^{d} Pendleton

President of the Convention of Virginia.

P. S. I must request that any letters I address to your Convention may be forwarded to the Congress when you think 'em of sufficient importance.

To the President of the Congress of North Carolina.

Charlestown 7th July 1776.

Sir,

Mr Rutledge will inform you by this Express of the Outrages committed by the Cherokees which must be now construed as the commencement of a war.

As it is now certain that a capital and favourite part of the plan laid down by his most excellent and clement Majesty George the Third is to lay waste the provinces, burn the habitations &c &c &c without much risk or loss (as the foregoing letter to the Convention of Virginia) I think then, Sir, that without a moments delay a Body of Riflemen from your Province shou'd be immediately furnish'd forth, to act in conjunction with the South Carolinas against the lower Nation, whilst the Virginians march against the Upper—I make no doubt of your being able to make a severe lasting & salutary example of them.

Clinton's Army and Parkers Squadron &c (as the foregoing Letter to the Convention of Virginia)—God give us more grace than to shuffle it away.

I am Sir, Your most obt. humble Servant

Charles Lee.

To the Honorable the President
of the Provincial Council of
North Carolina.

To Colonel Moultrie.

Charlestown, July 7th, 1776.

General Lee's compliments to Colonel Moultrie, and desires he may come to town as soon as he thinks proper; he hopes the air will cure his gout.

To President Rutledge.

Charlestown July 9th, 1776.

Dear Sir,

Colonel Moutrie informs me that not a Palmeto log is yet arrived in the Island—Upon my Soul we have all a great deal to answer for—ten days have been suffer'd to pass over our heads without adding the least to our strength. I wish your Excellency wou'd order some of your People to make enquiries on this head—even the Timber for the Gate has not been sent, altho' it has been promis'd many days, from, Dear Sir,

Your most obed[t] humble Servant

Charles Lee.

To His Excellency John Rutledge.

To President Rutledge.

Charlestown, July 12th 6 o'clock, 1776.

Dear Sir,

Colonel Gadsdens proposal shews undoubtedly a noble disposition, but it is really so repugnant to common prudence to make an attempt this night, that I cannot consent to it—the Enemy must be greater Dunces that I can yet conceive 'em if they are not by this time hors d'insult—an hours work is sufficient to ensure 'em against a surprise of this kind—I am however extremely happy to see this military ardor prevailing amongst your men and officers, and if they trust to me it shall be avail'd of to the public Service.

I am D[r] Sir, Yours

Charles Lee.

To His Excellency Jn[o] Rutledge.

FROM JOHN PAGE.

W^ms^burg, July ye 12th 1776.

MY DEAR GENERAL,

Your kind concern for my Health made me happy, & the high Approbation you Express of my public conduct highly gratified my Pride—I had the pleasure of receiving your letter which did me so much honour about the 9th of last Month—I was then at Mr Harrison's near Petersburg, where I had gone with Mrs Page for the recovery of her health—Our Trip happily has answered our Wishes—& we are once more fixed in Wmsburg. It is now four Weeks since we have received any certain Account of the Situation of Affairs in either of the Carolinas—Even your Letter to Brigadier Lewis countermanding the March of the Troops did not arrive here 'till four weeks after it was written. The Regiments had just began their March, but had they not been scattered abroad on distant stations and badly provided with necessaries for such an Expedition, they would have reached the Place of their Destination before your Express could have stopped them—It will be worth your while to examine into the occasion of this. I thought it a matter of so much importance to have such Orders communicated with Dispatch, that I advised the Brigadier to send an Express to you immediately to inform you of the unaccountable Delay that yours had met with, & to recommend it to you to establish a Post throughout your District, but he was preparing for an Expedition against Gwyn Island—The Brigadier set out last Monday on his Way to our Camp, attended by the Cols. Woodford, Stephen, Buckner & Weedon, & some others, intending to examine into the strength of the Enemy, and submit the propriety of an Attack to a Council of War—they reached the Camp that Night, & the next Day finding that the Dunmore had changed Stations with the Otter, & had exposed herself very prettily to the very Place where we had been preparing a Battery for the Otter, they determined not to lose this good opportunity of beginning their Cannonade in which they might severely & principally chastise the noble Earl—at 8 o'clock A.M. Capt. Arundel, & Lieut. Denny saluted the Dunmore & Otter with 2 18 Pounders—the very first Shot at the Otter, though a full Mile from our Battery struck her as is supposed between Wind & Water, for she did not return the Fire but was towed off on the Careen—the Dunmore fired a Broad side & then was towed off, having received 4 shot through her Sides, whilst she was in Tow she received a 5th through her stern which raked her—scarcely a shot was fired which did not do execution in some part of the Fleet—a Schooner lost one of her masts—whilst Lieut Denny was firing on the Fleet, their Battery on the Island, began to play on him, & a Ball passed through his Embrasure, on which he immediately turned his Cannon on their Battery (for he had taken the precaution to have scope enough to take in the Fleet & that part of their Battery) & fired 3 Times successively into their Embrasure, which 3 Rounds completely silenced that Part of the Battery. The other Part facing our Lines on the Haven, was almost as soon silenced by our Battery erected against it with 4 Nine and 3 Six Pounders—Part of their Camp was a little exposed to both of our Batteries which fired a few rounds into it—this Fire was as well directed as that against their Ships for it beat down many of their tents and threw their Camp into the utmost Confusion. When this was discovered the Brigadier ordered Cannows to be brought down to enable his men to pass over into the Island—for unhappily we had not a Boat on the shore—these could not be procured 'till the next day, when a smart Cannonade began between the Batteries, but as soon as our men had manned their Boats, their Fire ceased, & they retreated with precipitation to their Boats, and escaped safely to their ships having first broken off the Trunnions &^{c} of their Cannon—there were 3 Tenders up the Haven which could not pass our batteries, these they abandoned—they endeavoured to burn one but our Men boarded it & extinguished the Flames. I understand that all of them have their swivels in them, but it is reported that they had thrown the Guns overboard—We are now in Possession of the Island—The Fleet has retired but is in sight—This might have been a complete Affair if proper Measures had been preconcerted & the whole well conducted—However our men behaved well—Our Artillery was admirably served, & we have disgraced and mortified our Enemies. In this affair we lost not a man—but most unhappily poor Capt. Arundel was killed by the bursting of a wooden Mortar he was endeavouring to throw shells into the Fleet from—his Loss is irreparable! He behaved with great spirit and activity, & was so hearty in our Cause that he is universally lamented. Col. Stephen is just returned from Gwyns Island, he says the Enemy carried off all their cannon from their Batteries except one Six pounder which they spiked—they left 6 Carriage Guns in one of the Tenders—several Negroes and a few whites were taken—2 Negroes & one of the 14th Regiment deserted to us—The Prisoners inform that Lord Dunmore's Mate was cut in two by a double headed 18 Pounder which also took off one Mans Arm & another's Leg, & drove a splinter into his Lordship's Leg—Tom. Byrd was ill of a Fever, & was carted off to a Boat just before our People landed—they were obliged to burn two fine small Vessels that Day & at Night in the Mouth of the River—they burnt also a large ship supposed to be the Dunmore as she was not with the Fleet next Morning—it was the Logan—The Fowey it is said was with the Fleet but did not chuse to come within reach of our Guns—The Roe-buck was at the Mouth of Rappahanock. The Colonel says when he came away the whole Fleet had sailed & were out of sight, & it was uncertain where they are gone—Some suppose to Maryland—they went off in a bad Plight without Biscuit or Water—Their Works were found of excellent Construction & considerable extent—they were preparing to build Houses and a Windmill—they had made a vast Collection of Materials for different works—Their Tents, which they moved off except one markee which was left in their Hurry and through which a Cannon Ball had passed, were capable of containing about 700 or 800 Men—from many circumstances it is evident they meant to stay there a considerable Time. I have been interrupted in writing & before I could return to my scrawl—I had the Happiness to receive your Letter of the 3rd July. I most heartily congratulate you on your Success—it was a most glorious Affair—a noble Defence! The british Navy has been happily checked in her proud career & has received a most just & compleat chastisement. What must the *Tyrant* think of himself now? The whole Continent in Arms against him, 750 of his favourite Highlanders in our Possession & his Fleets repulsed & disgraced along our Coasts for 2000 Miles! Doubtless the Hand of the Lord is upon him—I hope he will repent & be contented to put up with the Loss of America, or if he does not, that he may be turned out like Nebuchadnezzar to graze—but enough of him. The Marylanders were roused up by the Resolve of our Convention & have lectured their Representatives so well that they have unanimously voted for Independency—they have no occasion for our Rifle Men on that Account—however I can assure you on the Eastern shore of Maryland there has been a considerable Insurrection of Tories in so much that Col. Fleming has been obliged to march with 120 Men to quell them—we have not yet heard the Event of that Affair—a considerable Number of those Wretches with Eden were in the Fleet when we put them to the Scamper—Our affairs are managed most scandalously in Canada—for God's sake advise them what to do, for they seem to be quite at a loss. Did you ever recommend it to Congress to set on Foot an Expedition against Detroit and Niagara? I think our Augusta men assisted by the Pensylvanians would readily undertake the Reduc tion of Detroit—if they were allowed all the Plunder they can take, & were to have a Premium in Land. Our Governor has been extremely ill of a bilious Fever ever since his appointment, he is still unable to do Busyness—but by the Ordinance we are enabled to transact public Busyness without him, in such cases. I have just heard that the Congress declared for Independency on y[e] 2nd of this month—I have written so long and confusedly at full speed that it is time to stop. Tom. Lee is gone home. My complts. to Brig. General Howe, Col. Bullett, & the Gent[n] with him—

I am most sincerely yours

JOHN PAGE.

P. S. I have scratched off & inclosed a little miserable sketch of Gwyns Island, as it appeared to me when M[r] Andrews and myself reconnoitred about 3 Weeks ago, & with our Quadrants measured the distance from our Lines to their Battery—We find it 475 yards—We then were of opinion that with the 2 18 Pounders and 4 9's, a Cannonade might do the Busyness for the Ships & Camp, which was then extremely exposed, & that a Raft might be made in 24 Hours to carry over Men enough to make Prisoners of every Man on the Island, but the Cannon were not mounted —3 of our Cruizers and one Row Galley are at last come down the Rivers. J. P.

The Dunmore left 2 Cables & Anchors—the Fleet 7 fine Cables & Anchors, worth at least £1200. I had sealed my letter but opened it June 13th. to add a few words more.

Lieut Denny who had been bred a seaman had served on board a Man of War, & had commanded an armed schooner on the Lakes, desired leave to take one of the Prizes—The Lady Charlotte Tender, & cruise out to reconnoitre the Fleet—he was permitted to do so, and sailed down within a Mile of the Otter, gave her a Broadside, & then returned, bringing home with him a fine anchor weighing 800lb & a Cable of 90 Fathom. The Fleet is gone into the Mouth of Potomack. We have just received your Letter by Page, dated June 29th. I am delighted with your description of the bravery of Col. Moutrie & the Garrison of Fort Sullivan. It is not Flattery my dear General when I tell you, that most of us here attribute the glorious Display of Bravery on that Day to the animating Presence of a Commander, who independent of his great military Abilities & experience appeared to be the Evil Genius of Clinton, who had followed him, & from whose presence he had seemed to retire & retreat along the Coast from Boston to Chas Town. All that I could do as there were not Gent^{n} enough in Town to make a Council was to desire Brig^{r} Lewis to send immediately to North Carolina all the Powder that could be spared out of the Magazine, about 4 thousand lbs will be sent. We have a large Quantity on the eastern shore which we have ordered over—for Gods sake establish a Post through your District.

Once more adieu.

J. P.

From Col. Adam Stephen.

W^{m}burg, 13th July, 1776.

My Dear General,

In the words of that zealous Grecian who run himself to death, to announce at Athens the successful Event of the Battle of Marathon; I do most cordially congratulate you; *χαιρετὲ! χαιρωμεν!* Rejoice! Let us Rejoice! Upon which expression, the Athenian expired; but there I beg leave to be off; and will patiently wait to hear more Joyful news from you.

The Event of that dreadful Cannonade is most astonishing. Porto Bello, Boccochico, & the other Castle at Carthagena were compelled to yield to Vernon: Fort Lewis in St Domingo yielded to Knowles's mettle:

Pray, of what stuff is Fort Sullivan made to resist so many 12 & 18 pounders, for so long a time?

It is to be wished that Sir Peter Parker may quarrel w[h] Cornwallis, for not crossing the gutt, whilst he was exerting his utmost Force by water: & no doubt, but Cornwallis will find some pretence for blameing him, but then Sir Peter can produce his Breeches in Evidence.

I have been on Sullivans Island; but do not remember the distance of Long Island from the main: The youth and fire of Cornwallis, will 'tis to be hoped give you an advantage: If it is an easy matter to make a descent upon Long Island, the passage from Sullivan to Long Island is far from being impracticable, so that reinforcing Sullivans Island before you make that descent, It may be possible to put him between two fires. But the number & convenience of procuring Boats, the situation of his Camp and the ground contiguous, will determine the propriety of the attempt. At any Rate, I hope it will be in your power to assist the Musketoes in keeping his Soldiers awake in the night.

I refer you to M[r] Page for politicks.

The Congress—the Officers—the Soldiers are to be blamed for the loss of Canada.

The force sent thither, was not adequate, to the Reduction or defence of that Country.

The Enemy has now got possession of a Territory that will supply their army with provision. Our conduct there, is productive of the most extensive ill consequences. I am in pain about N. York, & am of opinion that we have not half force there.

On the 9th inst. the Anniversary of Braddock's defeat, a day which I will always remember, we attacked Lord Dunmore by Sea & Land. The Ship Dunmore lying nearest our Battery, the first shot destroyed his Lordships China, & spoil'd his dancing by driving a splinter into his Leg. The second double-headed shot cut his Boatswain asunder, and limb'd his Gunner by the knee. The vessels soon begun to tow off, and were so much damaged, that the Enemy were oblig'd to burn three of them, one of which is said to be the Dunmore. They slipt their Cables, made the best of their way, and were drove to Sea without water, or one Biscuit aboard, as we were inform'd by the pilots and prisoners. They have prize flour and salt provisions enough.

They steer'd towards the Tangier Islands. We soon produced great Confusion in their Camp, and if we could have procured Boats—I run mad for Boats!—we could have kill'd or taken every one of the Negroes & Tories, & possessed ourselves of all their Cannon, Arms, & Ammunition. We have taken three of their Tenders, & one Row Galley would have enabled us to destroy great part of their fleet.

We have taken a Nephew of Capt. Squire's prisoner, rescued two pretty French Gentlemen, who were taken by Dunmore bringing in 500 barrels of powder for our use. We have likewise in custody Tom Jenn [ings] late Attorney General in Maryland. He arrived, as he says, at St Augustine from London, and was taken by Lord Dunmore in his Way to Maryland.

Poor Arundel has knock'd himself in the head by trying Experiments. Governor Eden was in the Fleet ready to sail for England, and made the best of his way in beginning the Cannonade. I offer my Compliments to the gentlemen with you, beg that you will get the people of the Carolinas to establish a better Correspondence with us, and have the honor to be

Dr General

Your most obet hble Servt.

ADAM STEPHEN.

' P. S. Dunmore was building Houses, Ovens, and Windmills in the Island—you may call them Castles in air. Gwins Island would have been a convenient place for Sr Peter to have mended his Breeches in.

This moment we are informed by Express that Dunmore is arm'd in Potowmack River.

We have taken eight hundred of Fraser's highlanders at different times & places. General Wooster is in Philadelphia, & blames the Congress for not supporting him, as much as they can blame him.

N.B. There is a hellish plot discovered at New-York. Tryon, Davis, the Mayor of the City, and several principal persons concerned—one of Genl. Washington's Guard is already Executed for it. Three Commissioners sworn to Secrecy, sit daily in Examining & prosecuting the discovery. Upon the arrival of the Enemy's fleet They were to assassinate the General and other principal Officers, blow up the Magazine, spike the Cannon, and admit the Enemy into the City.
It is said that this Enquiry will discover many Enemies to America in N. York, Jerseys & Pensylvania.

To General Lee,
S. Carolina.

To General Armstrong.

Charlestown July ye 14th 1776.

Dear General,

I am extremely concerned to hear that the Virginians and North Carolina Troops are falling down in sickness—I attribute it to three causes—being expos'd to the Sun in the day time, lying on the damp ground at night, and bad water—I have prevail'd on the President to order 'em boards which will remedy the evil arising from their lying on the damp ground—a quantity of rum is ordered over as an antidote to the bad water, and the third evil that of being expos'd to the sun, I shou'd think you may remove by stationing 'em in the wood on your left instead of the old field where they at present are.

Adieu, Dear General. I shall see you to-morrow.

Yours

CHARLES LEE.

To Brig[r] General Armstrong.

TO COLONEL GADSDEN.

Charlestown, July y[e] 15th 1776.

DEAR COLONEL,

As it now appears almost certain [that the Enemy] are upon their departure, I cou'd wish you wou'd apprize your officers that it is very probable I may regale 'em with a march very soon to stretch their legs after their long confinement.

I am Dear Colonel

Yours

CHARLES LEE.

To Colonel Gadsden,
at Fort Johnson.

TO PRESIDENT RUTLEDGE.

Charlestown 15 July, 1776.

DEAR SIR,

It now appears certain that the Tyrant's Fleet and Army are now on their departure—Wou'd it not be prudent immediately to order your Pilot Boat through the Gut and Stono River to watch their motions, that we may be ascertain'd which way they steer their course?

Yours Dear Sir

CHARLES LEE.

To His Exc'y John Rutledge.

From Daniel of St. Thomas Jenifer.

Annap[s] July 17, 1776.

My dear Sir,

I am obliged by your favor of the 7th ult[o] which only came to hand the 12th Inst. Your offences committed against the ruling powers in this Province are done away. Governor Eden's behaviour after he went on board the Fowey, justified in a great degree your sentiment of his being seiz'd; but the manner in which you directed it to be done was not palatable, and therefore the measure was not adopted. Your Excellency directed Purviance—Purviance of his own authority ordered Capt. Smyth, & Capt. Nicholson ordered his Lieut. all exercising absolute and distinct authority from the plenitude of their own power—add to this, Purviance's writing to the President of the Congress a letter, taking to himself the merit of everything that had been done in Maryland; asserting that the Council of Safety were timid & terrified at his boldness, this letter was read in Congress. Our Delegates demanded a Copy of it. M[r] Hancock said it was anonymous & confidential & desired to be excus'd; this brought on a debate, & a question, whether the letter should be delivered or not, carried 6 Colonies to 4, that it should be left to the Presidents option—the Lower Counties were divided, Jerseys not represented—Our Delegates applied to M[r] Hancock out of the House, & pushed matters so far as to become almost serious. M[r] Hancock it seems to screen his friend, had declared in the House that the letter was anonymous; but Purviance has given from under his hand, that it was not, and that his name was subscribed—thereby betraying the President as he had before done you, by delivering to the Council your Letter, and indeed as he also had his Country by prevailing upon the Committee of observation at Baltimore Town, to allow one or two vessels that he expected to arrive after the 10th of Sept[r], liberty to Lade. The

Country people obliged the Committee to rescind their Order. Purviance then made use of his Interest with his Northern friends in Congress, but failed. All these things being known and accumulated of course raised the resentment, not only of those who were in power, but of those who were out. The first insult the Council of Safety received, was from the Committee of Virginia who wrote about this busyness to the Committee of Baltimore, which shew'd an Evident & unjust want of confidence, for although those in power had nothing more at heart than a reconciliation & restoration of peace with Great Britain, yet they were doing every thing in their power to be provided against the worst, and have so far succeeded, as not only to supply in a great measure their own wants, but to supply the Congress with some valuable articles. We have had within two months past three Vessels from the W. Indias with 6000—8000 & 19000[lb] of Gunpowder, 6000[lb] of Sulphur Lead & besides 17000[lb] powder & 6000[lb] sulphur for our friends of Virg[a] We have at present about 70,000[lb] of powder in our different magazines & Hourly expect 55,000 more, & 1500 stand of arms w[ch] our agents were shipping off for us. These [wise] provisions tho' never published to the world have attached the people of the Province to the Council of Safety, so far as to dispense with a Law respecting power, that half of the Council should go out at the meeting of every Convention, and as many new ones to be chosen in their stead; have continued them with a Cart blanch, notwithstanding the unprecedented appeal made by the Convention of Virginia to the people at large in Maryland against them. But you may Sir, depend upon it, that the people of Maryland, tho' the last on the Continent to declare independence will go as far as any Colony towards the general defence of the United States. Peace would have been their choice, but as that could not be had consistent with their safety they will risque every thing before they will submit.

I will now give you a specimen that does honor to

Maryland. The Congress have desired that we should raise, embody, and send to Jersey 3400 of our militia. We have agreed to do it, & commissioned Brigadier Dent and other officers. But as it must take up time to arm & equip the men, we have dispatched Col° Smallwood with his Battalion and three independ[t] Companies, the whole about 1000 men, well armed disciplined and equipped, and I think are equal if not superior to any Troops on the Continent. We shall replace them out of the men to be raised for the flying Camp, in the meantime we have called out part of our militia to take the stations of the Battalion & independ[t] Companies, and this we have done at a time when our Province was invaded by Ld. Dunmore with four men of war, upwards of 60 Sail of Vessels, and when too we had an Insurrection in Somerset County to quell. From the facts above related your Excellency will perceive that we have not been idle. I am still of opinion that it is our Interest to be united with Britain and that our Province instructed its Delegates to agree to unite with the other Coly[s] in declaring independence too soon. These opinions I know you will reprobate. It is better that the people at large should be before their Rulers than their Rulers to be before them; in the first instance you are sure to be supported, in the last you run the risque of being deserted.

Lord Dunmore has pitched his Camp upon S[t] Georges Island about 15 Miles up Potomack River, where I think he will not long remain. The ship he was on board at Gwinns Island was much shattered, 14 shot all 18 Pounders hulled her and passed through the Cabbin very near his Lordship.

I congratulate your Excellency on your Success at Charles Town. Adieu, God protect you, & believe me to be, Dear Sir,

Your affect[e] Friend

DANIEL OF ST THO[s] JENIFER.

Be pleased to present my Compliments to the

President & his Lady, to Mr Eugee & his, & to Mr. Middleton

Men of War with Ld Dunmore, Roebuck, Lively, Fowey, Otter, Dunmore, & many Tenders from 12 to 4 Guns. The Mate of the Roebuck was killed in a skirmish with our Militia.

To Archibald Bullock.

Charlestown, July ye 18th 1776.

Sir,

I feel most sensibly for the distress'd situation of your Province, and am determin'd to exert myself for its relief—I wish I had it in my power to spare you a larger force than I am afraid our present numbers will admit of, but the instant we are assur'd the Enemy will depart, I will order a Battalion or a number equal to a Battalion for Savannah—these added to your own, will I hope be sufficient to protect the Inhabitants from insult and prevent your cattle from falling into the hands of these hell hounds let loose by an accurs'd Tyrant on a people whose only crime is having been too long patient with his diabolical administration.—Two expedients are now on foot—one from this Province against the lower Cherokees, another against the Overhill Cherokees from Virginia—I flatter myself that these two active operations will be a greater Security to Georgia than cou'd the largest defensive Body—if the Enemy steer southward, I shall myself march for your Province with all the force I can muster—but I must regulate my motions by theirs.

I most sincerely wish to your Province security and prosperity, & to yourself health & happiness, and am Sir

Your most Obedient Servant

Charles Lee.

His Excellency Arch^d^ Bullock.
President, &^c^ of Georgia.

To Colonel McIntosh.

Charlestown, July 18th 1776.

Dear Sir,

As Colonel Elbert can inform you of the situation of our affairs here I shall not trouble you on the subject—be assured that I will do everything in my power for the security and tranquility of your Province—The Enemy I believe is now on its departure—The moment I am assured that they will leave the place, a Battalion or a number equal to a Battalion shall march to Savannah—If there appears any probability that the intentions of this army are against Georgia, I will repair thither with all the force I can muster.

I am Dear Sir,

Your most obt Servant

Charles Lee

To Colonel McIntosh

Savannah, Georgia.

To Lieut. William T. Coles.

Charlestown July ye 18th 1776.

Sir,

It is not only a Duty I owe to the Service and the Station I am in, but also to the character of officers in general, to bring this affair (in which you are accus'd of being the principal actor) to a tryal immediately—I have ordered a Court Martial accordingly to assemble tomorrow—I sincerely wish you may acquit yourself, but as the Tryal is to be so immediately I cannot consent to your appearing in Public 'till it is over, and am

Sir,

Your most obt Servant

Charles Lee.

William Temple Coles,

of Col. Poke's Regiment.

To Richard Henry Lee.

Charles-town, July 19th, 1776.

My dear Friend,

I have received yours, of the 28th of May, and did not think it possible that any thing could come from your hand to give me so disagreeable sensations. You tell me a dark, mysterious story of a certain great General of whom prince Ferdinand has declared, *si l'on veut un officier*, &c. this great General in the clouds, will, it seems, graciously condescend to serve America, on condition that Congress will give him assurances of stepping over the heads of every officer but one, and this he submits to, only on consideration of the confidence due to an American. You ask my opinion on this subject; but the palpable meaning of your letter is, to prepare me for a cession of my rank in favour of some impudent adventurer. Beckwith is the man, as you conjecture, from his known political principles and military abilities, which are so transcendent, that I ought for the public interest to make a second sacrifice. I am not, I believe, naturally proud; I do not think myself conceited of my talents; but to be put in competition, much more to be spurned aside, to make room for so despicable a character as Beckwith, a generally reputed coward, (and a b——d sycophant,) I say, to be kicked out of my station for such a creature as this, would swell a man more humble than myself into a trumpeter of his own merits. Great God! is it come to this? I am not, it seems, an American; but am I not, (if I may so express myself,) *Americanior ipsis Americanis?* Have I not, such has been my zeal for your cause, once already waived my military claims in deference to the whim and partiality of some of your members? Did I not consent to serve under an old church-warden, of whom you had conceived a most extravagant and ridiculous opinion? Your eyes were at length opened, and deacon Ward returned to his proper occupation; and would you now a second time, (do you think it consistent with decency, I may say, gratitude or common honesty) to load me a second time with a similar disgrace? Have I betrayed any ignorance in my profession? Have I shewn a deficiency in courage? Am I slackened in my zeal or industry? What have I done to merit such an indignity? What part of my conduct can justify your harbouring such an idea? Have not I staked my fortune, life, and reputation in your cause? Is there a service in Europe to speak proudly, (your injurious proposal forces me to it,) is there a service in Europe, where with some small reputation, and my powerful friends, I might not expect the same rank I now hold? Have I not made myself a voluntary slave for the insurances of American freedom? Have I, sleeping or waking, employed a single thought, but for her welfare, glory or advantage? But enough of this—You ask my opinion, and I will freely, explicitly, and concisely give it to you. If the Congress supercede me, I will, I must obey; but, I hope, in common justice, and for their own honour that, they will re-establish me, at least in part, in the easy fortune which I have forfeited, so as to enable me to retire from a service to which I am no longer thought adequate. Before I conclude, let me once more repeat confidentially to you, that if Beckwith is the man, in whose favour you meditate so gross a piece of injustice, you will make a very bad bargain, as he is certainly, unless fame belies him, neither possessed of courage, abilities, or integrity.

In God's name, if a real genius, or acknowledged hero, favoured by Heaven with a more than common portion of etherial spirit, should present himself, (*a la Lippe*, or *Bragansa*,) receive him with open arms, as an immediate present from God; invest him with the command of the whole. No man loves, respects, and reverences another more than I do General Washington. I esteem his virtues, private and public. I know him to be a man of sense, courage, and firmness, but if a hero should start up, endowed with the attributes, which, according to my persuasion reside in the two I have mentioned, and who would charge himself with the mighty task of your political salvation, General Washington ought, and, I am convinced, would resign the truncheon; but that a little, paltry, impudent adventurer should sneakingly stipulate for the second rank, when, if his motives were pure, he could be equally serviceable in the third, fourth, fifth, or sixth; it is not to be endured, it is a gross imposition on common understanding, and a grosser attempt to rob an individual. I must beg and conjure you, my dear friend, for such I am sure you are, to consider the delicate, perhaps, you will say, false notions in which soldiers are bred; and that you will be careful of putting to so severe a trial the sensibility of one, who is most sincerely, devotedly, and affectionately, Yours,

CHARLES LEE.

To Richard Henry Lee, Esq.

P. S. I am extremely shocked with the pallid complexion of your public councils; is it possible that such a despicable group as the Maryland Convention should lay an embargo on the great vessel of the commonwealth! Can you be so weak as to hunt for the chimæra, absolute unanimity! Why do you not advise the aggregate of the people to enfranchise themselves? Your idea of quitting Canada from want of specie is to me inconceivable, when you can or ought to command plate sufficient to purchase ten Canadas.

To PRESIDENT RUTLEDGE.

Charlestown, July ye 19th, 1776.

DEAR SIR,

When I requested you to collect a number of boats for the transportation of Troops to the Islands it was my intention to transport the greatest force I cou'd possibly muster, to take the command in person, and endeavor to bring the Enemy to a battle; had we been victorious, there would have been an end of all their Southern operations, had we been defeated, it is true the loss, wou'd have been great, but not irreparable: upon the whole, ballancing the important consequences of victory and the disadvantages of a defeat, I shou'd have been justifiable in risking a general action—but the number of boats collected wou'd never have answer'd this purpose—They would contain at the utmost only twelve hundred men, a body too small to be detach'd on such an errand, in fact Islands present such manifold advantages to the enemy over us that we must never venture on 'em without an insurance or great probability of a compleat victory, because if defeated we have no possibility of retreat—As the Post on Long Island and all Schemes of attack are now ended, I only mention these things to explain the motives of my putting you to the trouble of collecting the Boats, the whole may be now undoubtedly returned.

Captain Hatter tells me that in this fleet of Craft there is one wooden boat belonging to Major Capers which might with little alteration be converted into an excellent Galley as we all agree a fleet of Gallies may be of the greatest use, and that it should be established without loss of time, I should think that every boat which with little trouble can be thrown into that form ought to be purchased.

I am Dear Sir, Yours,

Charles Lee.

To His Excellency John Rutledge

I wish you would turn your thoughts to the defence of Georgia, and what Regiment can best be spared from your Province for that purpose.

To President Rutledge.

Charlestown 20th July, 1776.

Dear Sir,

I received your Letter with respect to the Boats yesterday very late—in consequence of this letter, I desired Mr Hatter to defer returning the boats till this day. I should otherwise have discharged 'em—for my own part I did not know that they cou'd be of any use in transporting the Troops to Georgia—the Baron & I shall tomorrow lay out the works we intend for Sullivan's Island. Your Excellency will take care that they are finished—I have not your Constitution with regard to the Military—am a Stranger to the extent of my authority over the Colonial Troops; but had I an unlimited Authority I should request your Excellency to settle which of your Regiments may with the greatest conveniency march to Georgia—I should think Thompsons and Sumpters are the best calculated—they will together make about the strength of a Battalion—the Continental Regiment may probably be called to the Northward.

I am Dear Sir, Yours,

Charles Lee.

To His Excellency the President.

P. S. Not a moment should be lost in preparing this Corps for Georgia.

To Edmund Pendleton.

Charlestown July ye 20th 1776.

Sir,

The Enemy's Fleet and Army are certainly on their departure from this place—the Commodore's Ship has repass'd the Bar, the whole Troops are re-imbark'd; it is impossible to say where they intend to direct their course—I am inclin'd to think your Province will be the next scene of their operations, for which reason Sir, I think it my duty to put you on your Guard, that you may be prepar'd for their reception—the moment I am ascertain'd of their designs I shall set out to assist in counteracting 'em.

I am Sir,

Your most ob[t] Serv[t]

CHARLES LEE.

To the Hon[o] Edm[d] Pendleton,
President of the Convention of Virginia.

[A copy of this letter was at the same time forwarded to General Lewis.]

To President Rutledge.

Charlestown, July the 20th 1776.

DEAR SIR,

As the expedition from Virginia against the Overhill Cherokees, and your expedition against the lower nation, have, I apprehend some relation or dependance on each other what shall I say on the subject in my letter to the Convention? Shou'd I not give 'em as minute a detail as possible of the Army now ready to march? Of their numbers, condition and the time when it may be expected they will be in the Enemy's Country?

And am Dear Sir,

Yours

CHARLES LEE.

To His Excellency John Rutledge.

To Edmund Pendleton.

Charlestown, July 20th, 1776.

Sir,

I think it my duty to apprize you that the Enemy's Fleet and Army are now, in all human probability on their departure from this Coast; their Troops are all re-imbarked; the Commodore's Ship and the Solebay have re-passed the Bar, the Experiment and five other ships alone remain on this side but are preparing to pass the next tide—it is impossible to say where they will bend their course—but I am myself inclin'd to think Virginia will be the scene of their operations—the deserters indeed assert that it is their intention to proceed to New York; but it appears to me from Lord George Germaine's intercepted letter, that General Clinton is restricted to these Southern Colonies—perhaps they may try Georgia, the weakness of which Colony and the expectation of a powerful co-operation on the part of their Indian Allies may allure them; but on the other hand, the distress'd situation of their Fleet and Army, from the want of good water, fresh provisions and vegetables will make the temptation of the Table which Lord Dunmore, I understand, has spread for 'em on Guyn's Island, irresistable—upon the whole, I must repeat that I am perswaded Virginia will be their object—I hope and and make no doubt, Sir, that you will be prepared for their reception.

I think it necessary for the common service to inform you, Sir, that a Corps of at least fifteen hundred men will be assembled on the Cherokee line in less than three weeks from the present date; this number is supposed to be adequate to the end proposed; that is, the destruction of the Crops of the lower Nation and of course striking a necessary terror into the minds of other Nations. I mention this, as I apprehend the expedition projected against the Overhill Cherokees from your Province, may have some dependence on the manœuvres of the Caroliners against the lower Nation, but altho' being ignorant of the Geography and circumstances of the Country, I speak in the dark, with regard to the relation which one expedition may have with the other, the informing you of the number of the Carolina Corps and the time they may be expected to enter the Enemy's Country can be of no service.

As soon as I can be ascertain'd of the Enemy's designs, I shall set out for the point of action in hopes to render all the service in my power to the place attack'd as well as the common cause.

I am Sir, with the greatest respect
Your most obed^t humble Servant
CHARLES LEE.

To The Hon. Edmund Pendleton,
President of the Convention of Virginia.

To Captain Hatter.

Charlestown, July 21st 1776.

Sir,

I never was so astonish'd in my life as at your strange proceeding in sending an officer of the Enemy through the Country without apprizing General Armstrong who commanded the nearest post—not only sending him thro' the Country but into the heart of the Town—to examine our weakness and make a report to the General accordingly. Your Conduct once more I must repeat astonishes me to the last degree.

CHARLES LEE.

From the President of Congress.

Philadelphia, July 22, 1776.

Sir:

Your favour of the 2d instant, containing the very agreeable intelligence of the success of the American Army under your command, I had the honour of receiving, and immediately laid the same before Congress.

It affords me the greatest pleasure to convey to you, by their order, the most valuable tribute which a free people can ever bestow, or a generous mind wish to receive—the just tribute of gratitude for rendering important services to an oppressed country.

The same enlarged mind and distinguished ardour in the cause of freedom, that taught you to despise the prejudices which have enslaved the bulk of mankind, when you nobly undertook the defence of American liberty, will entitle you to receive from posterity the fame due to such exalted and disinterested conduct.

That a handful of men, without the advantage of military experience, animated only with the sacred love of liberty, should repulse a powerful fleet and army, are circumstances that must excite gratitude and wonder in the friends of America, and prove a source of the most mortifying disappointment to our enemies.

Accept, therefore, Sir, the thanks of the Independent States of America, unanimously declared by their Delegates to be due to you and the brave Officers and Troops under your command, who repulsed with so much valour the attack that was made on the State of South Carolina, on the 28th of June, by the Fleet and Army of his Britannick Majesty, and be pleased to communicate to them this distinguished mark of the approbation of their country.

I have the honour, to be, with great respect, Sir,

Your most obedient and very humble Servant

John Hancock, President.

To Major General Lee,

Charleston, S. C.

[*Enclosed in the preceding letter.*]

In Congress, July 20th 1776.

RESOLVED,

That the Thanks of the United States of America, be Given to Major General Lee, Colonel William Moultrie, Colonel William Thompson, and the Officers and Soldiers, under their Command, who on the 28th June last Repulsed with so much Valour the Attack, which was that day made on the State of South Carolina by the Fleet and Army of his Britannic Majesty

That Mr President Transmit the foregoing Resolution to General Lee, Colonel Moultrie and Colonel Thompson. By Order of Congress

JOHN HANCOCK, Prest

FROM SIR HENRY CLINTON.

Off Charles-Town Bar, July 22, 1776.

SIR,

On my return to the fleet, I found a letter from you by a flag of truce, with some refreshments you were pleased to send me, in return for which I must beg your acceptance of a cask of porter, and some English cheese.

I have made enquiries concerning the person mentioned in your letter, who, it seems, has occasioned this correspondence between us, but can learn nothing further about him, than that he is not a master of a vessel, as he has represented himself to you: and you will have been already informed by Mr. Byrd that Ethan Allen, and those that were with them, are gone to the Northward. I am, Sir,

Your most humble servant,

H. CLINTON.

To Charles Lee, Esq. Major General
in the service of his Polish Majesty.

To President Rutledge.

Charlestown ye 22nd July 1776.

Dear Sir,

I am much concern'd and not a little surprised that the Council shou'd object to sending their Troops, when requir'd for the common defence, to a neighboring Province—is it reasonable? is it just that the other Colonies shou'd be oblig'd to march to their assistance, and refuse in their turn to assist others? I have long wish'd and wish now more ardently than ever that the Continental Congress wou'd suffer no Colonial Troops to exist—I must now, Sir, request in my capacity as General appointed by Congress to watch over the Safety of the Southern District, that you will order a number of your Troops equal to a compleat Battalion to march immediately to Savanna for the defence of Georgia—if the Council cannot comply with this requisition I should be glad to be inform'd of the reasons that I may lay 'em before Congress, and be able to exculpate myself if any calamities fall upon that, at present, defenceless country.

I am, Dear Sir, Yours,
Charles Lee.

P. S. The Inhabitants of this Town begin or rather continue to fleece the Army most unmercifully—Six pounds one & threepence is demanded for burying a Soldier of Muhlenberg's. I beg your Excellency will correct these abuses.

To His Excellency John Rutledge.

To President Rutledge.

Charlestown, July 23rd 1776.

Dear Sir,

I have this instant received your Excellency's letter with the opinion of the Council on the subject of detaching a number equal to a Battalion of the Colonial Troops into Georgia, and hope I shall not be thought rude in confessing, that I do not see the least weight in any one of their arguments; but that on the contrary, they furnish substantial reasons for once more urging the requisition.

That Charlestown and its harbour are capital objects in the eye of the Enemy, and that their security against the attempts of the enemy, is of the highest importance, is a truth, I believe no man will contradict; a truth of which not only the Council here are sensible of, but the whole Continent: The Convention of Virginia, the Council of North Carolina were so sensible of it, that without the least opposition, they saw themselves stripped of a considerable part of their force to defeat the Enemies designs against Charlestown and its harbour; Virginia actually sent out a large Corps of Militia in order to enable North Carolina to spare a greater number of her regulars to the assistance of South Carolina.

That the two Forts rais'd (at so great an expense) require a constant Garrison (at least as strong a Garrison as now station'd in them) I certainly shall not deny, nor have I given the Council the least reason to think that I have an intention to diminish them.

You say, Sir, that when necessity requires it you shall be ready to assist Georgia with the greatest alacrity. The Georgians tell us that this time of necessity is come. They cry out for assistance.

But it is said, that the Continental Troops ought to be detach'd to Georgia in preference to the Colonial Troops; that it is a matter totally immaterial to them, whether They are in Georgia or in this Province, as long as they are remov'd from the spot where they have been raised, that it will be a greater satisfaction to the Inhabitants that their own People shou'd be amongst 'em than the Continental Troops, and finally, that it is natural to suppose, that your own people in the day of battle, will act with more ardor as they fight in the presence of their wives & children.

To these arguments I shall beg leave to answer, that every point is material or immaterial according to the way of thinking of the party concerned—That the Continental Troops do think marching to Georgia at present a point material—consequently it is so; They conceive it but just and reasonable after having marched so great a distance for your safety, that your people should take their tour of fatigue and they in their turn be indulg'd with some repose.

As to the satisfaction it will give the Inhabitants, I shall not dispute it, but I do not see why the satisfaction of the Inhabitants of your Province should be consulted in these cases more than the satisfaction of the other Provinces—the North Carolina officers and those of the Virginia Regiment receive Letters every day from their friends and Relations expressing their hopes and impatience for their return—Do you believe, Sir, that it wou'd give satisfaction to those friends and relations of theirs to hear of their further removal? on the contrary, might it not possibly give them great uneasiness and umbrage? in short, Sir, if I was to act on the principle of giving satisfaction to the inhabitants of any one Province partially, the great system of general defence must be broke to pieces.

I must lastly take the liberty to observe that the idea of soldiers acting with more valour at their own doors is repugnant to facts drawn from history and common observation, *respectu suarum rerum, rerum communium obliviscuntur*, is a trite adage in every military man's mouth—the attention of the soldier is drawn off from the voice of the Officer by the cry of a hog or a scream of a hen from his own hamlet; in short, nothing is more certain than that Soldiers are more Soldiers in every respect the further they are remov'd from their homes.

You remind me, Sir, that an Indian War is breaking out, but you must recollect that in our conversations on this subject, you have always given me assurances that your Frontiers wou'd furnish more men than sufficient for this purpose—nor can I see that the detaching a Battalion into Georgia, can in the least tend to incapacitate you for this War.

The Council, Sir, observe with concern and surprise, that I shou'd mention it as a thing probable that the Continental troops may move Northward—and at the same time detach to a distance a number equal to a Battalion of your Colonial Troops, even whilst the Enemy are in view—You may be assured, Sir, that my duty to the public, my particular regard for this Province, or my own reputation, will not suffer me hastily to adopt any measure which may leave an open to the Enemy for possessing themselves of so rich a prize—I never harbour'd a thought of running blindfold after them with the whole Troops at my heels—When I leave this place I shall endeavour to leave it in a posture of security as far as my means will admit.

Your Excellency may recollect that this method of assisting and sending to the Province attack'd, from its immediate Neighbor, is literally agreeable to your own plan, and I am doubly concern'd therefore when your Province is call'd upon for this purpose that the measure shou'd meet with any opposition.

Upon the whole, Sir, when I consider the defenceless state of Georgia, when assistance is so loudly and pathetically call'd for by the Governor Council and People, I think that both duty and humanity oblige us to grant it.

I think that in reason, justice, and policy this succour ought to consist of the Colonial Troops and not of the Continental, and I once more earnestly request your

Excellency and the Council to order a Body equal to a Battalion in number to march immediately to Georgia.

I am much flatter'd with the good opinion the Council entertain of my abilities and shall labour to deserve it, and am D[r] Sir,

Yours

CHARLES LEE.

To His Excellency John Rutledge.

To Colonel Huger.

Charlestown, July y[e] 23rd 8 oclock.

SIR,

The bare possibility of the Enemy's making an attempt on Port Royal is a sufficient reason for moving a respectable force towards that quarter—As I have not only a great opinion of your capacity, but of your zeal for the public Service, I am perswaded you will accept this command with alacrity and pleasure—I must request therefore that you will prepare your Regiment to march as early as possible tomorrow—three hundred militia shall be added to your command, and a corps of Rifle Men as soon as they can be procur'd—If it appears a certainty that the Enemy have really a design on that district, I will myself follow with the Major part of the Army

I am Sir, Yours

CHARLES LEE.

Colonel Huger.

P. S. Order the Waggon Master to prepare Waggons sufficient.

To President Rutledge.

Charlestown 23rd July ½ past
Ten o'clock—Night.

Dear Sir,

I was already apprised of Colonel Bull's rank and merit, but cannot conceive that any officer of merit shou'd be disgusted by being superceded in command when there is visibly no intention to disgrace him—it must frequently happen in the course of service that men of the greatest merit must be superceded by men of very moderate reputations—at present this is certainly not the case—if such a false delicacy or sophisticated notion of honor really exists, the sooner it is eradicated the better—its existence wou'd throw everything into confusion—Colonel Bull, if he is the man of sense and zeal for the public as he is represented, cannot possibly be disgusted by such a common incident—I therefore see no reason or shadow of reason for altering my mind on this subject, and must entreat your Excellency to take the necessary measures for expediting the march of Colonel Huger and the corps propos'd, and am Dear Sir

Your most obedient
Charles Lee.

His Excellency Jno. Rutledge.

From Benjamin Rush.

Dear General,

It would take a Volume to tell you how many clever things were said of you, and the brave Troops under your command after hearing of your late victory. It has given a wonderful turn to our affairs—The loss of Canada had sunk the spirits of many people who now begin to think our cause is not desperate, & that we shall yet triumph over our enemies.

The declaration of independence has produced a new æra in this part of America. The Militia of Pennsylvania seem to be actuated with a spirit more than Roman. Near 2000 citizens of Philad[a] have lately marched towards New-York in order to prevent an incursion being made by our enemies upon the state of New-Jersey—The cry of them all is for BATTLE. I think M[r] Howe will not be able to get a footing in New-York, and that he will end the present or begin the next campaign in Canada, or in some one of the Southern Colonies—the only places in which America is vulnerable. We depend upon Gates in the North, & *you* oblige us to hope for great things from the South.

The tories are quiet—but very surly. Lord Howes proclamation leaves them not a single filament of their cobweb doctrine of reconciliation. The spirit of liberty reigns triumphant in Pennsylvania. The Proprietary gentry have retired to their Country Seats, and honest men have taken the Seats they abused so much in the government of our State.

The papers will inform you that I have been thrust into Congress. I find there is a great deal of difference between sporting a sentiment in a Letter or over a glass of wine upon politicks, & discharging properly the duty of a Senator. I feel myself unequal to every part of my new Situation except where plain integrity is required.

My former letters to you may pass hereafter for a leaf of the Sybills. They are full of predictions, and what is still more uncommon—some of them have proved true. I shall go on—and add that that I think the Declaration of independence will produce union and new exertions in England in the same ratio that they have done in this country. The present Campaign I believe is only designed to train us for the Duties of next Summer. What do you think of the States of America being divided between two or three foreign

States & of seeing the Armies of two or three of the most powerful Nations in Europe upon our Coasts?

Adieu, Yours Sincerely

B. Rush.

Phil[a] July 23[d] 1776.

P.S. I sent a copy of that part of your letter in which you commend M[r] Morris so highly to his father. My Complt[s] to the gallant youth.

Major General Lee,
Charlestown, S[o] Carolina.

To President Rutledge.

Charlestown, July y[e] 24th 1776.

Dear Sir,

I have receiv'd two letters from M[r] Bullock, one of which alone I have kept—inclosed is an extract from it—the other of a later date is much more urgent—I am sorry that the Council requires such formal evidence. I was in hopes my word wou'd have been sufficient—Col. M[c]Intosh has press'd me most pathetically in two letters not to delay a moment in sending some Force to their Province. The Gentlemen who were here were eternally urging the necessity—in truth, Georgia is in a most lamentable state of weakness and impotence, and I hope that your Excellency and Council will take the measures which appear to me as well as to all others with whom I have convers'd necessary at this juncture.

I am Dear Sir,
Your most ob[t]

Charles Lee.

To His Excellency John Rutledge.

To Cornelius Harnet.

Charlestown July y[e] 24th 1776.

Sir,

I intreat you will present my respects to the Council of Safety, and that I think myself extreamly happy in having obtain'd their good opinion—I shall labour to deserve it—I am, if possible, more concerned than you can be, that your light horse Companies are not put on the Continental establishment—They are a species of Troops more than usefull, they are in my opinion a *sine qua non*, particularly in these Southern Colonies—I have in all my letters to Congress urged the necessity of being furnish'd with a considerable Body of cavalry—I have even ventur'd to insure the safety and protection of my wide extensive Command, had I only a thousand good cavalry at my disposal; I have dwelt much on the extreme difficulty of securing ourselves from insult and danger without them; but I know not how it happens, the Congress has never made the least reply on the subject—to say the truth, unless a War office is establish'd, or a particular Committee appointed to superintend and regulate all military matters abstracted from all other business—our military affairs will hobble on in but a slovenly manner—however, I have wrote so strongly and repeatedly on this topick that I am in hopes to force their attention at last. I shall not cease dinning it in their ears.

Nothing gives me greater pain than the wretch'd condition your Troops are in from want of cloaths—will it not be possible to collect in the Province a sufficient quantity of woollen to protect 'em in some degree from the injuries of the weather? I sincerely wish you may be able to make such a provision—I do not mean to flatter, but upon my honor they are deserving of the greatest attention—such at least I am sure, they are entitled to, from, Sir, Your most Obed[t] humble Servant

Charles Lee.

To Cornelius Harnet, Esq.
President of the Council of Safety of North Carolina.

ORDERS TO COLONEL POKE.

Charlestown July 25th 1776.

SIR,

You are to march from hence with that part of your Regiment now under your Command to the other side of the Boundary line, where you are to station yourself in the manner the most convenient either to prevent the enemy making predatory incursions into the Country by way of the various Inlets; or to cut off their communication and correspondence with the disaffected inhabitants residing in that Tract of Country from Little River Inlet to Fort Johnson.

You are to apprize General Moore of your instructions and situation and receive whatever further orders that officer pleases to issue. I am Sir,

Your most obedient Servant,

CHARLES LEE.

To Colonel Poke, of the
4th Regt of North Carolina Troops.

TO COLONEL BULL.

Charlestown, 25th July 1776.

SIR,

The great importance of Port Royal made it very probable that the enemy wou'd make some attempts upon it—I therefore thought it expedient to detach Colonel Huger with the remains of his Regiment and three hundred militia to defeat any attempt of this kind—Colonel Huger is since Countermanded, but the Militia march under the command of Colonel Kershaw and will put themselves under your orders—the reason of Colonel Huger's being countermanded is a very whimsical one in my opinion—it is entirely against my own inclination, and I have so good an opinion of your zeal and understanding that I am perswaded you will yourself (tho' chiefly interested) disapprove of the principle on which Colonel Huger is prevented from proceeding.

It was urged by the Governor and Council that you wou'd resent being superceded—to which I reply'd (and I hope justly) that Colonel Bull was represented to me as a man of too much sense and public spirit to take amiss an incident that must daily fall out in the course of service—that it was impossible he cou'd entertain so sophisticated a notion of honor and false delicacy—that if such notions really did exist, the sooner they were eradicated the better—that if such a way of thinking became fashionable an embargo wou'd be laid on all service; that I protested against the principle, and dreaded the consequences of establishing the precedent; however, I suffer'd myself to be overborne, and think I ought to make some apologies to you, Sir, for a step which may imply a perswasion that you cou'd possibly harbour such narrow ideas as to think yourself disgrac'd by an incident inevitable in the course of service, as I have really the highest respect for your character and good qualities, and am sir, most sincerely

Your most ob[t] humble Servant

CHARLES LEE.

To Colonel Bull.

FROM JOHN DICKINSON

MY DEAR GENERAL,

I receive with pleasure every mark of your Friendship, and none with more, than when you freely communicate to me your Disapprobation of any part of my conduct. As long as you give me that proof of a sincere esteem for me, so long I shall most affectionately love you; and so highly do I value your Esteem, that if my frailties did not furnish sufficient opportunities to evidence your Esteem in that manner, I should be almost tempted voluntarily to err, that I might receive repeated Testimonies of so agreeable a Truth. I entertain as much veneration for your abilities and integrity, as it is possible for man to do; and yet, for my soul, I cannot agree with you, that a *Declaration of Independence at this time*, will promote the happiness of my Country. I have tried, I have toil'd to thrust the Belief of the Proposition into my Mind. I have represented to myself, that you and several other good and sensible men think it as clear as any axiom in Euclid—that my Reputation, at least my Popularity must inevitably be sacrific'd by my obstinate Heresy—yet I have so much of the spirit of martyrdom in me that I have been conscientiously compelled to endure in my political capacity, the Fires & Faggots of Persecution, rather than resign my impious Persuation. To add to my comfort, this Reflection occurs, when I consider the weight that is due to the sentiments of some of those who differ from me in opinion, that perhaps I am suffering for a most absolute Falsity. However, while I think as I do, the Falsity is sacred to me, and I dread nothing more than offering violence to my Integrity. "*Mea me virtute involvo*"—and I am sure this Virtue ought to be a very warm thick Cloak, for I am a Witness, that it brings many storms and hard blows upon us poor mortals.—Among the rest, and here, my dear Friend, I am serious—that it has deprived me of the little power I once possest, that now might be exalted in your Service, our Convention, since I have been in this place with my Battalion, have left me out of the new Delegation. But your right to obtain from Congress the satisfaction you mention is so manifest, that I have not the least doubt but they will immediately order the money to be paid. I have wrote on the subject to a particular friend of mine, who is a Delegate and a man of abilities, which I am convinced he will exert in your Cause. I most heartily wish you success in that Business, and in every other that can give you pleasure. I congratulate you on the Success in Carolina. Do crush the Enemies of Liberty to the Southward so effectually and quickly, that I may have the Pleasure of serving under you this Summer. Lord Howe and his Brother are now on Staten Island—Their Quarters are about five or six miles from this Place, at least the Generals are—Their advanc'd Posts about half a mile from ours—the Sound between—our Militia to the number of 22 hundred stationed along it—General Mercer commands—We are to be reinforced, and are preparing Boats &c to make a descent on the Island, all over which the Enemies are spread—their numbers said to be between 8 & 10 thousand—A smash upon them, before the rest of the Fleet arrives, may render their Efforts against New York, less effectual. I wish you were here to direct our operations in this affair—As far as I can judge, a good deal of Generalship will be necessary for giving success to the measure—the Island being much intersected by streams & morasses, besides the Sound that surrounds it, in the narrowest places twenty perches broad. May Heaven bless you, my dear Sir, is the Sincere Prayer of your ever affectionate,

JOHN DICKINSON.

Elizabeth Town in Jersey
July 25th 1776.

FROM COLONEL MCINTOSH.

SIR,

I was honor'd with your Excellency's Letter of the 18th Inst, by Col. Elbert, & well pleased that you had the Safety of this Colony so much at heart.

I send Lieut. Seixias of our Battalion Express to inform your Excelly. that I am just told by a Gentleman come up the River, that he saw a Fifty Gun Ship yesterday afternoon sailing over our Barr into the

River, where four other Ships Lay at Anchor, and five other Ships under sail outside, which fir'd several Guns, & are probably in by this time. This I thought proper to give your Excell^{y}. the earliest intelligence of, as I imagine those gentry will not be guilty a second time of the same delay as in Carolina, or allow us to prepare for them or your Excell^{y}. to meet here again. I have not any doubt myself but this is the fleet from Charlestown. I ever was of opinion they could not in Honor go away without attempting some thing, and no place so probable as Georgia. I will continually inform you of the movements of the Enemy, and if we should not see your Excellency here soon, which I hope will not be the case, I shall be glad of your orders.

I have the Honor to be your Excell^{ys}
most obt. Hble Servant,
LACH^{N} M^{c}INTOSH.

Savannah in Georgia, 25th July, 1776.

I enclose yesterday's Report.

His Excell^{y} General Lee, Charlestown.

A Report is just come to Town of an Engagement up the Country with the Indians in which some were killed on both sides, but particulars unknown.

p. Lieut. Seixas Express.

ROBERT MORRIS TO GENERAL GATES.

Phil^{a} July 25th 1776.

DEAR SIR,

I ought to have wrote you a fortnight ago, that Mrs. Gates with your son Bob, had gone for Virginia after about a Weeks stay with us, during which you had the misfortune to lose a horse. I believe he had been too hard drove, at least Bob thought that was the cause of his death, although the Servant would not allow it. Mrs. Gates bought another from M[r]. Hancock for which I am to pay him forty pounds, and shall charge it to your account. Mrs Gates did not take the money she wanted at home, but is to draw on me for it.

I hope you will be able to put our affairs at the Lakes on a more respectable footing than they have ever been since the days of poor Montgomery, certainly there has been great mismanagement in that department and I find some people attributing this to a source I never should have suspected, is it possible that a man who writes so well & expresses such anxiety for the Cause of his Country as Gen[l]. S——r does, I say is it possible that he can be sacrificing the Interest of that Country to his Ambition or Avarice. I sincerely hope it is not so, but such insinuations are dropped. I beg leave to recommend Major Wood to your Patronage you'l find him a bold intrepid officer & as Lt. Col[o]. Allen has resigned, I shall push for the Major to have that vacancy.

You'l be pleased with Lee's success at Carolina the Enemy were maul'd greatly and I think the repulse disgraces them, consequently reflects great honor on our People.

You are no doubt well informed of what passes at New York & as I have full employm[t] for my whole time I shall only assure you of the esteem and regard with which I am D[r] Sir,

Your affectionate h[ble] Servant,

ROB[T] MORRIS.

TO PRESIDENT RUTLEDGE.

Charlestown, July y[e] 26th 1776.

DEAR SIR,

It was always my opinion (as I dare say it was yours) that it is of the last importance to insure the success of the first expedition against ye Indians on this principle. I think it prudent to form a Corps de reserve to prevent the dreadful consequences of a defeat, shou'd such be the fate of your army marching against them; Mr. Obenion is of opinion that this army is not quite sufficient for the two purposes of attacking and defending the Frontiers—You had better question him minutely on the subject—if your Excellency approves of it, I will immediately order a body of Continentals to Prince's Fort or any other station which shall be thought the most judicious.

I am Sir,

Yours

CHARLES LEE.

To The President.

FROM ARCHIBALD BULLOCK.

Savannah, July 26th 1776.

SIR,

I really must make an apology for taking off so much of your Excellency's Attention from the business of the United Colonies, by the frequency of my Epistles; but I hope you will consider it, as arising from a desire of communicating to you, whatever appears necessary to be known for the good of the common cause. I gave you p. favor of Lieutenant Seixas some information, respecting the Ships of War appearing off our Coast. I received the Intelligence, as I thought, from the best Authority & embraced the first opportunity of writing to you—however from the Examination of sundry Persons since, I find we have nothing to apprehend from this invincible Armada, & that they are not as yet at Cockspar. The accounts I have just received of the Outrages of the Indians are very disagreeable, yet I think with the Assistance of the Battalion you are going to send us, we shall do extremely well.

I have sent this by my friend Mr Byrd who was

going to Charlestown, and who will give you the News of this Province. I am Sir,

Your most obedient and very hble Sert.

ARCH[D] BULLOCK.

His Excellency Genl. Lee, at Charlestown
fav[d] by the hon[ble] John Bryan, Esq.

TO PRESIDENT RUTLEDGE.

July y[e] 27th, 1776.

DEAR SIR,

As the affair of taking the Brigg was in my apprehension not a naval but rather an army or at least a conjunct operation, and as she was burn'd contrary to the orders of General Armstrong under whose command and auspices the Commanding officer of the Float ing Battery certainly acted, I conceiv'd it wou'd be proper that a Court of inquiry compos'd of officers of the line, shou'd examine previously to a Court Martial into the cause of the Vessels being thus destroy'd contrary to the General Order—if the guilt lay with the Navy officer I shou'd then have prosecuted him at the proper tribunal Navy Court Martial—A Court of Inquiry pronounces no sentence, but only finds that there is sufficient cause, or is not sufficient cause for a Court Martial—so that upon the whole I can see nothing unfair in wishing for or proposing this mode of proceeding—for my own part I am extremely well satisfy'd whatever mode is adopted—my only motive for troubling you on the subject was to prevent the jealousies (whether reasonable or unreasonable) which I thought I cou'd perceive brewing in some of the Officers breasts.

I wrote a line last night by M[r] Obenion expressing my opinion that it wou'd be prudent to form a Corps de reserve on or near the Cherokee Line—but you have not favour'd me with an answer. I wish you wou'd think on the subject that we may without loss of time arrange measures relative to the project; and am Dr Sir,

Yours
CHARLES LEE.

Colonel Bullitt grossly mistook my meaning if he gave your Excellency the least room to think that I wish'd or propos'd to bring a Navy Officer to a Court Martial of land officers—such an idea never enter'd my head—not when I mention'd a Court of Inquiry of Officers of the line, did I mean to exclude the Navy Officers from a seat in this Court of Inquiry—the operation as I observed was conjunct—the Court of Inquiry might of course with propriety have been conjunct.

TO PRESIDENT RUTLEDGE.

Charlestown, 27th July 1776.

DEAR SIR,

Inclos'd I send you two Letters, from Governor Bullock, and Col. McIntosh—I am much concern'd that I cou'd not obtain your Excellency's and the Council's concurrence with my scheme of detaching a number of your Provincials equal to a Battalion into Georgia—I have order'd all the North Caroliners and Colonel Hugers Regiment under the command of General Howe to march with all possible expedition to Purisbourg—I must entreat your Excellency to order the proper officers to press waggons for Hugers Regiment and two ton of powder.

You will oblige me when you have read the Letters, if you will return 'em.

I am Dear Sir,
Your most obt humble Servt
CHARLES LEE.

To His Excellency the President.

To President Rutledge.

Charlestown 27th July 1776.

Sir,

As in all probability I shall soon depart from the Province, I think it my duty to submit to the consideration of your Excellency and the Council some measures which I think necessary for the safety of the Province, and consequently for the common interest of the United Colonies.

1st As there is great reason to think that the Enemy will make another attempt on Charlestown, altho' probably not before winter—a magazine shou'd be establish'd somewhere not very distant from the Town, for the subsistence of at least six thousand men for three months, but I wou'd recommend it for ten thousand men—the necessary articles are Flour, some rice, salt provisions, rum or whiskey and straw, with a great number of boards which may serve either as flooring or as Tents.

2ndly I wou'd propose that Commissaries shou'd be immediately employ'd on or near the South Georgia Line to purchase a sufficient number cf Cattle for the establishment of this magazine—it will answer a double good purpose; the cattle will be cheaper, and the Enemy will be deprived of one of the means of subsistence—a Corps of Troops must be employ'd to protect the Commissaries in the collection of the cattle, and which may at the same time serve to dislodge the Enemy from the Post they have taken on St Mary's.

3dly To construct and equip as expeditiously as possible a number of row gallies and other small vessels for the protection of the harbour and the coast.

4thly To lose no time in finishing the works as laid down by the Engineer in Sullivan's Island. I am Sir,

With the greatest respect

Your most obt humble Servt

Charles Lee.

To His Excellency The President.

To President Rutledge.

Charlestown ye 28th July 1776.

Dear Sir,

I shou'd be very glad to have your Excellency's opinion on the subject I proposed—I mean forming a Corps de reserve near or on the Cherokee Line—no time shou'd be lost—Muhlenberg's Regiment is ready for a march—the Quartermaster General shou'd be authorized to press a very considerable number of Waggons and immediately—fifty will not be too many—

I am Dear Sir, Yours,

Charles Lee.

To His Excellency the President.

To Benjamin Harrison.

Charlestown July ye 28th 1776.

Dear Sir,

The Army here and in North Carolina are in the greatest distress from want of Continental currency—I must request therefore that you will without delay furnish us with an hundred thousand Dollars, if you have that sum in y^r hands—if you have not, that you will endeavour to procure it. I am inform'd that the Troops in Virginia have been on the brink of mutiny and general desertion from a discontent from not being regularly paid—I cou'd wish (if it were possible) always to have the Army three months in arrears—but every point must yield to a general clamor—I therefore entreat that for the future they may be more regularly paid.

I am Dear Sir,

Your most Obedient Servt

Charles Lee.

To Benjamin Harrison, Esqr

Paymaster General of the Southern District.

To President Rutledge.

Charlestown, July 29th 1776.

Dear Sir,

Wherever we have Troops we should have Waggons; it was certainly therefore a great oversight in your Waggon Master General, not to retain a certain number of 'em. We are now in a very awkward situation —it is not indeed impossible that some time or other a whole Province may be lost by such an omission. An Army which cannot march in twenty four hours is no Army—I must entreat your Excellency to hasten the people employ'd to press Waggons, for the powder is now lying expos'd to accidents of various sorts.

Lt Medici of the Light Horse will deliver this note; it is necessary that the officers of this Corps, when detach'd (as they have no money for the purpose) shou'd be furnished with an Order upon the Inhabitants where they pass for forage—They must give receipts—I beg your Excellency will furnish them with such an Order. As I am writing to Virginia by express, I shou'd be glad to have it in my power to inform 'em of what steps are taken for the most regular establishments of Posts—Will your Excellency and the Council point out the best method, and I will communicate the plan to North Carolina that they may do their part.

I wish you joy of the powder arriv'd and am Dr Sir,

Yours

Charles Lee.

His Excellency the President.

Shou'd not some Divers make another attempt to fish up the muskets which these Rascals threw over board?

To Gov. Patrick Henry.

Charlestown, July 29th 1776.

Dear Sir,

I us'd to regret not being thrown into the World in the glorious third or fourth century of the Romans; but now I am thoroughly reconcil'd to my lot: the reveries which have frequently for a while serv'd to tickle my imagination (but which when awaked from my trance as constantly I consider'd as mere golden castles built in the air) at length bid fair for being realiz'd. We shall now, most probably, see a mighty empire establish'd of Freemen whose honour, property and military glories are not to be at the disposal of a scepter'd knave, thief, fool, or Coward; nor their consciences to be fetter'd by a proud domineering Hierarchy—every faculty of the soul will now be put in motion—no merit can lye latent; the highest officers of the State both civil and military will now be obtain'd without court favour, or the rascally talents of servility and observance by which Court favour cou'd alone be acquir'd—sense, valour, and industry, will conduct us to the goal; every spark of ability which every individual possesses, will now be brought forth and form the common aggregate for the advantage and honor of the Community—the operations of war will be directed by men qualified for war, and carried on with that energy natural to a young People—true unartiz'd knowledge, unsophisticated learning, simple genuine eloquence and poetry will be carried to the highest degree of perfection—this to many, I am sensible, wou'd appear rant, but to you, who, I think, have congenial feelings with my own, it needs no apology—however, I shall now endeavour to deliver myself more like a man of this world.

I most sincerely congratulate you on the noble conduct of your Countrymen, and I congratulate your Country on having Citizens deserving of the high honor to which you are exalted, for the being elected to the first Magistracy of a free People is certainly the pinnacle of human glory, and am perswaded (altho Virginia is so well stock'd with excellent citizens) that they cou'd not have made a happier choice.

Will you excuse me, but I am myself so extremely democratical that I think it a fault in your Constitution that the Governor shou'd be eligible for three years successively; it appears to me that a Government of three years, may furnish an opportunity of acquiring a very dangerous influence—but this is not the worst; Tacitus says, *plura peccantur, dum demeremur, quam dum offendimus*—a man who is fond of office and has his eye upon re-election, will be courting favour and popularity at the expense of his duty—He will give way to the popular humours of the day, let 'em be ever so pernicious—in short, his administration will be relax'd in general or partial to those whom he conceives to have the greatest interest: Whereas, were all hopes of re-election precluded 'till after the intervention of a certain number of years, he wou'd endeavour to illustrate the year of his Government by a strict rigorous and manly performance of his duty—these notions may perhaps be weak and foolish, but such as they are, I am sure you will excuse my uttering 'em.

There is a Barbarism crept in amongst us that extremely shocks me. I mean those tinsel epithets with which (I come in for my share) We are so beplaister'd—His Excellency and His Honour, The Honourable President of the Honourable Congress, or the Honourable Convention—this fulsome nauseating cant may be well enough adapted to barbarous monarchies; or to gratify the adulterated pride of the *Magnifici* in pompous Aristocracies, but in a great free manly equal Commonwealth it is quite abominable—for my own part, I wou'd as lief they wou'd put rats-bane in my mouth as the Excellency with which I am daily cramm'd—how much more true dignity was there in the simplicity of address amongst the Romans—Marcus Tullius Cicero, Decimo Bruto Imperatori, or Caio Marcello Consuli Des.; than To His Excellency Major General Noodle, or To the Honourable John Doodle—my objections are perhaps trivial and whimsical, but for my soul, I cannot help starting 'em—if therefore, I shou'd sometimes address a letter to you without the Excellency attach'd, you must not esteem it a mark of personal or official disrespect, but the reverse.

The discontent of the Troops which you mention as arising from the want of regular payment, might have been remedied by General Lewis, his warrant is undoubtedly sufficient for the Paymaster—however, I have written to that gentleman on this subject, and am in hopes that affairs for the future might be more satisfactorily conducted.

An old Rice boat which we converted the other day into a row Battery has made a considerable prize—no less than a brig with a whole Company of the Royal Highland Emigrants on board, consisting of two officers and fifty men—the Rascals altho' they saw that they were inevitably our prize had the impudence to throw their arms overboard, for which they ought to have their ears cut off, as it was contrary to all the rules of War.

I send you inclosed the State of the Enemy's Navy—I think there is no doubt of their Army having steer'd their course Northward—on this presumption I shall direct my course towards Virginia, but first must assist to regulate the military affairs of this Province in the best manner I can, tho' in fact that will be doing little, the inconveniences of this complex play we are acting of Duke and No Duke are numberless and great—the President is thought by some to be the real Commander, I am thought so by others—in short, there must be no Troops but Continental—the Council is at present employ'd in settling a more regular Post.

We have received none these eighteen days—for my own part, I conclude the mail has been intercepted and carried on board the Man of War—Seven ton and a half of powder were safely landed four days ago at Georgetown.

Adieu, Dr Sir, and believe me to be most entirely and sincerely

Yours
CHARLES LEE.

To Patrick Henry Junr
Governor of Virginia.

TO PRESIDENT RUTLEDGE.

Charlestown, July 30th 1776.

DEAR SIR,

As I hope and suppose that the Council is determin'd to establish a magazine, it wou'd be proper to furnish Colonel Kennon with a sufficient quantity of salt for the purpose. Your Excellency will therefore much oblige me in giving Orders to supply him.

I am Dear Sir, &c
CHARLES LEE.

To The President.

TO COLONEL MOULTRIE.

July the 30th, 1776.

DEAR COL.

Mr. Ferguson informs me, that he has furnished you with two hundred pair of negroe shoes: As a party is ordered on immediate service, I flatter myself you will have the kindness to spare them for the poor devils, who have so long a march before them, and are quite unshod: You will have time enough to replace them; I therefore request that you will shew your charity on this occasion—and am

Dear Colonel, Yours
CHARLES LEE.

To Col. Moultrie.

Petition, Etc.

[July 31, 1776.]

To His Excellency General Lee, Commander-in-chief, &c: The Petition of the Inhabitants of the Parish of St George, and St. Paul, including the ceded lands in the Province of Georgia, most humbly sheweth:

That your petitioners living on the frontiers of the Western parts of the Province of Georgia aforesaid, are much exposed to the barbarous attacks of the Creek Indians, and more especially from the intercourse which necessarily must subsist between them and the Indian traders, whilst an Indian trade is carried on, as it tends to bring those savages down into the settlements, and they seldom return without either committing murder or robbery, and generally both, upon the white people. That this trade is of the utmost prejudice to your petitioners, and the rest of the Province, excepting only a few men immediately concerned in it. And we would further represent to your Excellency, that at the treaty held between Sir James Wright, Bart., and John Stuart, Esq, on behalf of George the Third, and the Headmen and Warriors of the same nation, in the year 1774, the Indian traders, from self interested views, then recommended it to the said Sir James Wright and John Stuart to reject a certain offer made to them by the said Headmen and Warriors of a most valuable cession of a tract of land lying or being on Oconee River, being a fork of the Alatamaha, and by nature formed for the benefit and advantage of the inhabitants, in giving them an opportunity of sending and exporting their produce to market. And your petitioners can with truth assure your Excellency, that if the Indian trade was banished, it would be not only the means of restoring peace and tranquility to this back country, but likewise would encourage people to come and settle therein. That your petitioners submit to your Excellency's wise consideration how far prudent it might be to make an attempt to exterminate and rout those savages out of their nation, as it appears to your petitioners that a sufficient force might (with your Excellency's Assistance) now be raised against them; and in such case your petitioners will be ready, at the hazard of their lives and fortunes, to unite together for so desirable a purpose. May it, therefore, please your Excellency to take the premises into mature deliberation, and to grant such relief to your petitioners as your Excellency may think most proper. And your petitioners will ever pray.

To General James Moore.

Charlestown July 31st 1776.

Dear General,

You will oblige me extremely in consenting to the re-establishment of Lt Quinn I dare say from the manner of the man, that his misconduct must alone be ascribed to error, not to intention—if you consent, and I hope you will, and there is a vacancy in Colonel Bunkham's Regiment, he is desirous of being in it, and I understand that the Colonel is not averse—on this presumption, I enclose an order for his re-establishment.

I entreat, General, that you will provide all the North Carolina Troops with havresacks as soon as possible—inclosed is the State of the Enemy's Fleet—perhaps *en passant* They will pay you a visit—You must therefore be on your guard.

I am Dr General, Yours,
Charles Lee.

P. S. I wish you wou'd intreat the Council in my

name to have always in readiness an Express Man and Horse at Wilmington—another at Newbern and a third at Edenton; for the consequences of the irregularity and delays of the Post may be terrible.

To Brig. Gen. Moore, at Wilmington.

From Colonel Peter Muhlenberg.

July 31st 1776.

Sir,

I am very anxious to have the affair I mentioned to your Excellency this morning, settled some way or other, before We leave this place, as it may otherwise perhaps, create confusion on the march—All the Continental Troops in this place have hitherto taken rank of my officers, because they have no commissions to produce & suffer them to Rank only as Provincials. Since I mentioned this affair to your Excellency, I have received another letter from Williamsburg, which mentions that the Convention had apply'd to the General Congress to take the 7th 8th & 9th Regiments on the Continental Establishment—That the answer was, it could not be done immediately, but when those Regiments were completely mann'd & arm'd they might be taken. That the Convention had retained those three Regiments in their Service, & in consequence of this, the 7th & 9th Regts had receiv'd Provincial Pay to the 25th of June. As this is the Case, I must beg leave to say, that I should use myself ill, were I to accept a Continental Commission after this date, when other Regiments, raised long after mine, would take rank before me; I should prefer being oldest Provincial Officer before the youngest Continental. I can assure your Excellency nothing should have prompted me to mention this, did I not conceive that my Regiment had been slighted in some respects—perhaps of all the Virginia

Col^os my Connexions, and Fortune are smallest, but according to my abilities I have sacrificed perhaps as much as they. I have cheerfully given up a salary of £350, & during my stay in this place my wages are scarce half sufficient to defray my necessary Expenses. I shall not trouble your Excellency any further, only request that the Rank of the Regiment may be settled before we go, if possible.

Your Excellencys most obt. hble Servant,

PETER MUHLENBERG.

His Excellency General Lee.

FROM GENERAL ARMSTRONG.

Camp at Haddrells July 1776.

DEAR GENERAL,

I ask your pardon in not yesterday answering your last favour, nor did anything prevent but the apprehensions I had of being early favoured with another interview at Greenwich.

I thank you for your friendly regard to my health and polite liberty with respect to residence & Exercise. I hope God will prepare and direct yours for your own & the publick good—the present era brings to view the old Romans and Lacedemonians, but South Carolina presents rather the Athenian Image.

I have revolved all the hints you threw out to me of my own stay here over & over, and altho' tis a kind of maxim that a soldier must not think, yet is thinking half the design of his creation, and the human mind some have defined a thinking substance.

Now dear General permit me to say that G^l Howe has a thousand qualifications for this meridian & not a foible known to me, that will preponderate the opposite scale, and he is able to wash off all the dryness incidental as it was, with half a dozen of Madeira, or a single dance with the ladies will shake it off as we do the dust from our feet. But on the part of the Brigadier I am now serious. Can he wish a more respectable Command? It is so, from Local circumstances or in its own nature, 'tis additionally so from the talents it requires, and I think Howe a genius amongst our American best. I wish you liked his paying a visit to his N° Carolina friends for a few weeks if he chuses, then return here and take the command, when I may follow you for farther orders. What you have said of one Reg^{t} here, or now drafts are going, part of both is perfectly right. The officers in the yellow House, The men in the Barn and best of the Hutts—but I hope to-morrow or next day will bring you here—for I have not said the half on anything, please to spend a thought on the criminal sentenced to die.

Poor Thompson & Irwin, what shall be done for them? I congratulate you on the fate of Dunmore, and y^{r} letter and papers has much obliged y^{r} devoted hble Servt

John Armstrong.

General Lee.

To Colonel Muhlenberg.

Charlestown, August 1st 1776.

Dear Colonel,

What the Continental Congress can mean (if ever they so express'd themselves) by not taking your Regiment and the others on their establishment until they are compleat, is above my conception—if they mean that it was to have its full complement to a man, or that it shou'd be compleat enough for service, I am at a loss—if they meant the former, it was almost impossible that these Regiments shou'd ever be on their establishment—if they meant the latter, your Regiment certainly must have the precedency over all the Regiments on the Continent—in all the services I am acquainted with, new levies are establish'd and take rank from the time two thirds of their Regiments is rais'd. They are then suppos'd on emergencies to be fit for service—on every principle your Regiment must be considered as Continental, at least from the time you were ordered to march out of the Province. You were ordered not because I was better acquainted with your Regiment than the rest—but because you were the most compleat, the best arm'd, and in all respects the best furnish'd for service—You may depend therefore when the Congress is inform'd of the Circumstances, your Rank will not be disputed—the fact is that the Congress having no military Men in their Body are continually confounding themselves and every body else in military matters—however to do 'em justice they will bear being corrected with candour & patience—there is now a Board of War establish'd, so we have reason to flatter ourselves that things will go on with somewhat less confusion. I shall write immediately on the subject if it is necessary for your satisfaction and that of your Officers but think you need be in no pain about it. I find Colonel Sumner's is in the same predicament with yourself—I wish you wou'd inform me which Regiment was first embodied by order of its respective Convention as I apprehend your Rank must be settled accordingly.

I am Dr Colonel, Yours,

CHARLES LEE.

Colonel Muhlenberg.

TO PRESIDENT RUTLEDGE.

Charlestown August 1st 1776.

DEAR SIR,

The plan for breaking intirely up the Province of East Florida appears to me not only a wise one but indispensable for the safety of Georgia—the success will likewise make a most salutary impression on the minds of the Creeks—which is an object of the highest consideration.

The Governor of Georgia & Colonel McIntosh are of opinion that not less than a thousand men added to what force they have themselves will be requisite for the execution of the plan—but that this number will suffice—I can upon the whole muster for this occasion about six hundred including Mughlenburg's—but if it were possible to form the number wanted of your Provincials and militia it wou'd in my opinion be more for the service of this Province and for the common cause to send Mughlenburg's along with Sumpters to the other Frontiers to form a second line or Corps de reserve to the Army march'd or marching against the Cherokees—I shou'd think this East Florida Expedition wou'd suit the taste of your Militia—as they will have a chance of enriching themselves—There is nothing in the meantime to be apprehended for this Capital—Clinton will not return before Winter. I have myself thoughts of setting out for Georgia the day after tomorrow to arrange all matters relative to the projected expedition.

I am Dear Sir, Yours,
CHARLES LEE.

To His Excellency the President.

TO RICHARD PETERS.

Charlestown, August 2[d] 1776.

SIR,

I wish I had been informed how I am to address myself in writing to the Board of War, whether to the Board in general, to the first member on the List, or to the Secretary. I have ventur'd on the last mode, if it is wrong, I hope I shall be excus'd and corrected.

The irregularity and tardiness of the Post are now become a matter of very serious concern: We never receive a letter from Philadelphia in less than six or seven weeks, that from the members of the Board of War and Ordnance is only just now arrived tho' dated the 12th of June—I have been pressed by several members of the Convention of Virginia to establish a Post for this district, but am apprehensive that it might interfere with the Continental Post; however, the consequences arising from the irregularity of the Post are so very serious that all other considerations must be waved —in the meantime I am constrain'd to the necessity of putting the Continent to the expense of an express almost on every occasion.

I am extremely rejoic'd at the establishment of a Board of War; for the business of Congress was so complex and heterogeneous that it was impossible they shou'd give the necessary attention to the affairs of any one distinct department—their Regulations with respect to Returns &c shall be punctually observed.

I have ordered General Armstrong to collect the Returns from the different Corps, to digest 'em into one, and transmit 'em immediately to the Congress.

I am myself busyed in arranging matters for an expedition into East Florida.

It is much to be lamented that these Southern Colonies suffer'd the whole last Winter to pass over their heads without preparing the means either of offence or defence—not a single row galley or armed Boat was furnish'd forth by Virginia, North or South Carolina: were we provided with a moderate fleet of these sort of vessels, I think I cou'd ensure the reduction of East Florida—an object which tho' not equal with Canada, is certainly of very great importance—here the nefarious measures of the Tyrants Agents wth the Southern Indians are concerted and plann'd—their treaties negotiated and concluded—here they receive their bribes for their murderous operations, and from hence they are supplied with all the means and instruments of War; from hence they have lately made some alarming incursions into Georgia, carried off considerable number of Negroes and not less than two thousand head of cattle: they have likewise thrown up a Post on the River St Mary's which if suffer'd to remain may prove extremely troublesome to Georgia, by affording a ready asylum to Negro Deserters—from these considerations, altho' I cannot think of laying siege to Augustine, having neither boats, horses, waggons, nor any other means of conveying Cannon, ammunition or provisions for the purpose—I think it both a prudent and necessary measure to attempt breaking up the whole Province of East Florida—it will be a security to Georgia, occasion infinite distress to the Garrison of St Augustine, but above all, make a salutary impression on the minds of the Creeks who now are thought to stand wavering—They profess a good disposition towards the American cause, but if by a strong predatory expedition into the Province of the Enemy we give an idea of our prowess and superior strength they will be riveted in our interest. If I was sure Mr Clinton and his army had steer'd their course to New York as the Deserters all agree, and a Letter which was left in Long Island confirms (a copy of which is here enclos'd) I shou'd as I have nothing immediately else to do in my district, march in person with this party; but the bare possibility of his being gone to Virginia will detain me.

Every ship of the Enemy has now repass'd the Bar—it appears by this same inclos'd Letter, that they were more roughly handled than even the Deserters represented.

The Congress I make no doubt have been inform'd of the incursions made and the ravages committed by the upper and lower Cherokees—an expedition I understand is furnish'd forth by Virginia against the Upper Nations—another by this Province against the lower—the success or miscarriage is of the last consequence. I am therefore desirous of forming a second line or corps de reserve and detaching for this purpose a Regiment of Regulars, but have not as yet been able to procure waggons sufficient for two companies—It will be necessary that Congress shou'd make some regular establishment for waggons—I shou'd think one Waggon at least if not two shou'd be purchas'd and appointed to each Company of the whole Army and Regiments made responsible for theirs respectively. We shou'd then be able to march when occasion requires expedition, at present it is sometimes as much impossible to march an hundred miles, altho' the fate of a Province depended upon it, as if the soldiers wanted legs.

I hope the Congress and Board of War will excuse my giving an opinion on a subject on which it has not been ask'd, but I conceiv'd it to be my duty not to remain silent on any affairs of such moment.

I find Sir, that representations have been made that many inconveniences wou'd arise from putting the Troops of this Province on the Continental Establishment. I can assure the Congress that it is almost impossible to carry on the service if they remain on the Colonial Establishment, the difference of the Laws, the distinction of the ranks occasion much confusion—and the ridiculous farce of Duke and No Duke we are playing, (the officers not always comprehending who is their proper Commander, whether the President or Continental General) occasions very dangerous distractions, but there are other matters of more serious consideration, of which I shall not trouble you with a detail; nor do I find that the officers of this Province object to a Continental Establishment, on the contrary, all those I have convers'd with, seem desirous of it—upon the whole, I think it absolutely essential to the public Service that these Regiments shou'd immediately be put on the same footing and govern'd by the same laws with the rest, nor am I singular in opinion—the two Brigadiers—all the officers of every rank and the greater part of the gentlemen of the Country concur with me.

Colonel Mughlenburg of the 8th Battalion of Virginians has been made very uneasy by some letters He has lately receiv'd with respect to the rank of his Regiment—these Letters intimate that it was never the intention of the Congress to consider the seventh, eighth, and ninth Battalions of the Virginians on the Continental Establishment until they were entirely compleat—that his Regiment never was intirely compleat, and that consequently after having so long thought himself on the Continental Establishment, and on this presumption having march'd five hundred miles from his own province under the Command of a Continental General, he now at last finds himself only a Provincial officer. I have ventur'd to assure him and his officers who are equally uneasy that there must be some mistake in this affair—in fact, the hardship wou'd be so great that I cannot believe their apprehensions are well founded—it was (if I remember right) notify'd in April by the Committee of Safety in Virginia that they were then taken upon the Continental Establishment, and (tho' in this I may be mistaken) without the proviso of their being compleat. It happen'd at this time tho' not compleat to a man (for no Regiment ever is compleat to a man) that Mughlenburgh's Regiment was not only the most compleat of the Province, but I believe of the whole Continent—it was not only the most compleat in Numbers, but the best arm'd cloth'd, and equip'd in all respects for immediate Service—I must repeat that I cannot conceive it was ever the intention of Congress that the establishment shou'd be fill'd to a man, but that they shou'd be competent to service in or out of their Province—in most services when new levies are rais'd one half of the propos'd complement entitles 'em to establishment—Mughlenberg's Regiment wanted only forty at most—it was the strength and good condition of the Regiment that induc'd me to order it out of its own Province in preference to any other—I certainly consider'd 'em at that time as Continental Troops otherwise I cou'd have no authority to order 'em out of the Province.

I must now submit it to the consideration of the Congress if it wou'd not really be the greatest cruelty that their strength and good condition shou'd be turn'd against 'em—it was their strength and good condition which carried 'em out of their Province where had they remain'd and known that it was a necessary condition of their establishment to be compleat to a man, they certainly cou'd have accomplish'd it in three days—I do therefore most sincerely hope and confidently perswade myself that Mughlenbergs Regiment will at least date their Rank from the day I order'd 'em to march out of their Province, not only justice but policy requires it, for you will otherwise lose a most excellent Regiment.

I often represented to Congress how difficult or impossible it wou'd be to engage or retain after they were engaged any Engineers of tolerable qualification on the wretch'd pay established—The two appointed to my district have (as I expected) quitted the service—it was indeed impossible for 'em to exist. Stadler I hear has enter'd into the service of Virginia—Massenburg is retain'd by this Province at fifty four Dollars p. month, a servant, rations, and his travelling expenses —He formally begg'd his dismission from me, assur'd me (and I believe sincerely) he was zealous in the cause of America, that he wou'd willingly (if I chose it) enlist as a common soldier, but that to ride about the Continent from North to South, find horses, and appear like a gentleman was impossible. I cou'd not in conscience force him to starve, so consented to his engaging in this service—I am now without a single Engineer, and really know not how to carry on the busyness—I hope the Board will consider the necessity of supplying me.

I shall now, Sir, conclude with assuring 'em that I am with greatest respect, their most obedient humble servant

Charles Lee.

P. S. The most material event that has happen'd since I last did myself the honour of writing to the

Congress, is that, with an Old Rice Boat converted into a Row Battery we made prize of a Transport Brig with a compleat comp[a] of Royal Highland Emigrants, consisting of two officers and fifty two Privates—the Captain only escap'd. They threw their arms overboard, for which they deserve to lose their ears—seven other Prisoners were taken in a boat.

If the Congress take into their pay and immediate service any of the Maryland Troops, I beg leave to recommend to their Patronage M[r] Daniel Jenifer of that Province, who is now with me in the character of a supernumerary Aid de Camp—He is a man of spirit, zeal, activity, and sense, and there is certainly no small degree of merit in a gentleman of his age, settled way of living, and connections—to offer himself and serve as a Volunteer in a part of the world so remote from his home and generally thought favourable to few Constitutions.

The writing busyness of our Deputy Adjutant General is so heavy that he has represented the necessity of an Assistant. He cannot procure one tolerably qualified for less than twenty Dollars p. month. I have told him that I had no power to grant any allowance, but as we cannot do without such an aid, I have ventur'd to order the Paymaster General to pay this sum in hopes the Congress will approve it, if it is not approved of the Adjutant General (tho' he can ill afford it) consents it shou'd fall upon himself.

To Richard Peters, Esq[r]
Secretary to the Board of War and Ordnance.

WILLIAM FALCONER TO ANTHONY FALCONER.

[*Inclosed in the preceding letter.*]

Camp Long-Island, July 13th, 1776.

DEAR BROTHER,

With the greatest difficulty I have procured this small piece of paper to inform you of my being very well, notwithstanding the miserable situation we are in.

We have been encamped on this Island for this month past, and have lived on nothing else but salt pork and pease. We sleep upon the sea shore, nothing to shelter us from the violent rains, but our coats or miserable paltry blankets. There is nothing that grows upon this Island, it being a mere sand bank, and a few bushes which harbours millions of musketoes, a greater plague than there can be in Hell itself.

By this sloop-of-war you will have an account of an action which happened on the 28th June, between the ships and the fort on Sullivan's Island. The cannonade continued for about nine hours, and was perhaps one of the briskest known in the annals of war; we had two fifty gun ships, and five frigates from 24 to 30 guns playing on the fort, I may say without success, for they did the battery no manner of damage, and killed 15, and wounded betwixt 40 and 50. Our ships are in the most mangled situation you can conceive. The Acteon, a 30 gun frigate, run aground during the action, and it was impossible to get her off, we were obliged to burn and blow her up.

Our killed and wounded amounts to betwixt two and three hundred. Numbers die daily of their wounds.

The Commodore is wounded in two different places. His Captain lost his left arm, and right hand, and was wounded in different parts of his body; he lived but two days after the action. Captain Scott, of the Experiment of fifty guns, died of his wounds, and numbers of the other officers.

If the ships could have silenced the battery, the army was to have made an attack on the back of the Island, where they had about 1000 men entrenched up to their eyes, besides a small battery of four guns, one eighteen pounder, and three four pounders, all loaded with grape shot, so that they would have killed half of us, before we could make our landing good.

We are now expecting to embark for New York, to join Gen. Howe with the grand army. My anxiety to inform you of bad news, had well nigh made me forget to mention our passage to Cape Fear, where we arrived safely the first of May, after a voyage of three months. Though it was long, yet it was not disagreeable after we got out of the bay of Biscay, where we met with the worst weather ever known at sea, and continued in that situation for sixteen days; after that time we had very fine weather all along; sometimes we were becalmed for four or five days together, not going above ten knots a day. Upon our arrival in Cape Fear we disembarked; and were encamped in the woods until the 27th of May, when we went on board again, and sailed for this infernal place. The oldest of the officers, do not remember of ever undergoing such hardships as we have done since our arrival here.

I hope you will be so good as to watch every opportunity to let me hear from you and Mrs. Falconer, and at the same time to inform me how I shall do in case I shall be obliged to purchase my Lieutenancy. I beg you will make my excuse to my dear sister for not writing to her at this time; it is not owing to want of affection, but to the want of proper materials. I am obliged to write on the ground. You will be so good as to let Capt. Falconer know the same thing. I shall write again from New York. I am, dear Sir,

Your most affectionate brother,

WILLIAM FALCONER.

To the Hon. Anthony Falconer,
at Montrose, Scotland.

To Major White.

Fryday Night August 2nd, [1776.]

Sir,

I am extreamly concern'd that there shou'd be so great difficulty in setting your Corps in motion—I must request that you will march by break a day—You are to leave a subaltern and thirty [men] to bring up the Cattle, Tools, and ammunition—There is one circumstance I must recommend most earnestly to you and Colonel Sumner, it is to understand one another. You have distinct Corps it is true, but when you are together he commands you to all intents and purposes, and you are to march together till further orders. I mention this because, I think I see a little too much propensity to bickering amongst you Gentlemen of N. Carolina.

I am Sir, Yours
Charles Lee.

To Major White.

From Colonel Christopher Gadsden.

Light House Island, 2ᵈ Augᵗ 1776.

Sir,

In consequence of your Excellency's Permission for a detachmᵗ of my Regiment to come here—after the Enemy supposed to be at this Post.—I set off at Sundown yesterday from Fort Johnston, wᵗʰ a detachment of 120 Rank and file of my Regimt., & when we were near the Island were joined by Capt. Stone with 36 of his company. We landed about 10 o'clock last night, and as soon as we could form (in less than five minutes) after leaving 35 armed & about sixteen Boatmen to take care of the Boats, I immediately hasted along the Beach from one end of the Island to the other and when I had thoroughly investigated [it I] marched up to the Light House which we found totally deserted, & are now in possession of it. I intend to stay till to-morrow Evening, & in the mean Time I wish we could decoy or provoke the men of war & people to Land—were they to land all they have and to leave their ships at anchor without a man on board, I shou'd not doubt with the honest Fellows I have with me with God's Blessing to give your Excelly. a very good account of them. We have no pen & Ink with us—Your Excelly. may depend on everything being done in the Power of

Your obliged Hble Serv[t]

CHRIST. GADSDEN.

P. S. The ships are within a good random [shot] of a Battery that might be erected on the beach opposite to them. I believe they intend to go as soon as they can.

His Excellency Major General Lee,

Cha[s] Town.

[Upon the foregoing, which is in pencil, the following is written in ink—evidently a memorandum by General Lee intended for another document.]

The aforegoing mode of settling the temporary Rank of the two Colonels is approved, and settling the rank of Colonel Mughlenberg & Sumner until it can be ascertained, and it is ordered that they settle it according.

FROM GENERAL ARMSTRONG.

Camp at Haddrell's 3[d] August 1776.

DEAR GENERAL,

Your orders of the 1st Ins[t] to settle the Rank of the Colonels Mecklenburg & Sumner, came to hand yesterday. I thought to have held the Court at this place as of this day, but from the situation of the Members & partys found it scarcely practicable & at least to have risqued an adjournment. I have therefore appointed Monday at Ten oclock in Town where I shall attend if agreeable to you. But shou'd the thing require greater dispatch, I shall on notice attend by day or by night. Yesterday & this but little better, I have had a disagreeable swiming in my brain or headach, and thought to have thrown it off by a jant to Long Island. The Spot about one mile & quarter in length and from 40 to 60 perches wide where the Enemy Encamped is at once, Romantick & Secure, and the advanced post well enough taken, the latter however with some loss might have been cut off, had the situation been early enough known.

Yours Dear General,
JOHN ARMSTRONG.

TO COLONEL SUMNER.

Charlestown 3rd Augt 1776.

SIR,

I think you will act prudently in getting your Regiment over Ashley Ferry as soon as possible—as your men (shou'd they be inclin'd to desert) will find much greater difficulties in accomplishing it—If you are then not properly equipp'd, you may halt—send back some intelligent officer to inform me of your wants and you shall be supplied accordingly.

I am Sir, Yours,
To Colonel Sumner. CHARLES LEE.

TO COLONEL HORRY.

Charlestown Augt 3d 1776.

DEAR SIR,

I am sorry you shou'd be put to any inconveniency, but so important a concern as the preservation of the

Soldiers supercedes all considerations—I must desire therefore that you will give up Scott's house for the purpose of a convalescent Hospital—it must be done immediately, which I daresay you will most chearfully comply with as your good sense and humanity will convince you of the propriety.

I am Dr Sir, Yours,

To Colonel Horry. CHARLES LEE.

To PRESIDENT RUTLEDGE.

Charlestown August 3d 1776.

DEAR SIR,

It appears to me that your Excellency's Department and mine are not yet thoroughly ascertain'd and distinguish'd—I conceive (but I am not positive) that I have the sole Command of the Troops here both Continental and Provincial—I am just inform'd that a General Court Martial has been held at the Artillery Barracks by your Excellency's warrant—I cou'd wish before it was open'd and approv'd of that the affair might be clear'd up—I do assure you that I do not speak from an ambition of extending my authority, but to prevent confusion in future.

I find that your 1st 2nd 4th and 5th Regiments are put on the Continental Establishment. One of 'em will be order'd immediately to Georgia, but the Regiment I shou'd choose which is the 3rd still remains on the Colonial Establishment—this Regiment the most proper for an Expedition of the nature propos'd, will be the most improper to garrison a Fort—I wish therefore matters cou'd be so contrived as to send this on the expedition, and retain a better qualify'd one for the Fort.

I am Dr Sir, Yours,

CHARLES LEE.

To His Excellency the President.

To President Rutledge.

Charlestown August 6th 1776.

Dear Sir,

Governor Bullock and his Council—Col. McIntosh and his Officers are unanimously of opinion that an expedition into East Florida is necessary for the very being of Georgia and consequently of the last importance to the common cause; that not less than eleven hundred men added to what force they themselves can furnish will be adequate to the execution. The whole number of Continental Troops I can muster fit for duty, or whose time of service is not near expiring amounts to six hundred and forty. I must therefore most earnestly request your Excellency and the Council to order for this purpose a Corps of four hundred and sixty men, as likewise a Captain, two subalterns, and thirty privates of the Regiment of Artillery from the Colonial Troops of Carolina as otherwise this projected expedition (on which the very existence of a deserving sister colony, and in the success of which the whole American Community is so deeply interested) must be laid aside.

I am, Dear Sir, Yours,

Charles Lee

To The President.

To President Rutledge.

Charlestown, August 6th 1776.

Dear Sir,

The arrangement of the Troops, for the projected expedition, made by your Excellency and the Council, is, I really think, more judicious than mine—the species is better calculated for the peculiar service than what I had proposed—I am consequently pleas'd with it, and shall give orders accordingly: but I can by no means agree with your Excellency that the 1st 2nd 4th & 5th Regiments still remain Colonial—the words of the resolves of Congress on this head will in my opinion not admit of two constructions; the language is plain, explicit, and positive; the clause which restricts the Continental General from moving out of the Province without the Consent of the President and Council more than one third of the Troops unequivocally empowers him to move one third without their consent—if there is any meaning in language, this is the meaning: As to the letter of the Delegates, I do not see (if it was intelligible) that it wou'd be pertinent—it wou'd only be the comments of men in a private capacity with which (as Public officers) we have nothing to do.

As I do not chuse (in a matter of so delicate a nature) to rest entirely on my own judgment, I thought proper to call together a Council of the Officers—inclos'd is the result of their opinions—at present I shall trouble your Excellency no more on this subject, but cannot help expressing my apprehensions that great confusion and distraction will inevitably be produc'd from such a jumbled perplex'd system as now seems to be aimed at. Shou'd your Province have exceptions in its favor, shou'd the Continental General have full authority to move when and where they please the Troops of the other Provinces, whilst those of South Carolina who are to be subsisted at the common expense and enjoy equal rank with the rest, are to remain sacredly immoveable, unless by order of their own President, Council, or Assembly, it will occasion infinite discontent not only amongst the Troops but the Legislatures of the other Colonies—They will naturally ask what Title has South Carolina to these exemptions and extraordinary priviledges? another and another will claim the same, and finally, the whole become one disjointed scene of anarchy and confusion—but whatever the Congress shall determine, it is my duty chearfully to submit to. I shall now conclude with repeating that I conceive from the words of the Resolves that I have a right to move one third of these Troops out of the Province from my own authority, although I have fortunately no occasion to exert this right at present as I really think your Excellency's arrangement extremely judicious, and am D[r] Sir Yours

CHARLES LEE.

To His Excellency John Rutledge.

OPINIONS, ETC.

[*Inclosed in the foregoing letter.*]

Charlestown, August 6, 1776.

HIS Excellency Major General Lee, having thought proper to take the sense of Brigadiers-General Armstrong and Howe, and the Field Officers of the First, Second, Fourth, and Fifth Regiments of the South-Carolina forces, on a difference of opinion between his Excellency the President and General Lee, on the construction of a resolve of Congress, with respect to the above Regiments being in the Continental establishment, the following are the opinions of the above gentlemen on the subject:

Brigadiers General Armstrong and Howe are clearly of opinion, from the face of the resolves of Congress, that the above Regiments are on the Continental establishment.

The other officers, being called upon were as follows:

Colonels Gadsden and Moultrie,	Continental
Lieutenant Colonel Sumpter,	Continental
Majors Cathell and Elliot,	Continental
Lieutenant-Colonel Pinckney	not Continental
Lieutenant Colonels Motte and Robertson,	not Continental
Major Henderson,	not Continental

To the Board of War and Ordnance.

Charlestown, August 7th 1776.

Gentlemen:

As I am this instant setting out for Port Royal & Georgia, I shall only at present trouble the Board with a couple of lines which my regard for the Public Service obliges me to write; I must express my apprehensions that unless the Troops of this Province are put unconditionally and without any restrictions on the same footing with the rest—much distraction and confusion will ensue, already it has in some measure had this effect: The President and myself put two constructions diametrically opposite on the resolves of the Congress of June ye 8th. I conceive by these Resolves that I have the power of moving one third of the Troops out of the Province without consent of the President and Council, for it appears to me, if there is any meaning in language that the clause which restricts the Continental General from moving more than one third of these Troops out of the Province without the consent of the President and Council expressly gives him the power of moving one third. His Excellency the President on the other hand insists that no such power is vested in me: the officers whose opinions I have ask'd on the meaning of these Resolves are not unanimous, but the major part concur with me—inclos'd is the result of their opinions—thus already we are in a bless'd chaos of uncertainty and confusion—as near as I have been able to gather the sentiments of the officers and soldiers of the Regiments immediately interested—shou'd the President and myself have so little regard for the Public welfare as to make a tryal of our respective authority, I believe I shou'd be obey'd by three fourths, His Excellency by one; but thank God I believe we have both too much grace to make the experiment.

I hope the Congress will not think it presumption in my observing that the Clause restricting the Continental General from moving more than one third of the Troops out of the Province without the consent of the President and Council may be attended with fatal consequences—for instance, when this Capital the other day manifestly in the jaws of destruction call'd out for the assistance of her neighbours—had the General been restricted in his power, had the President and Council of North Carolina been out of the way, or had they from a timid but natural perswasion that their own Province was the real object of the Enemy, and that the Enemy's departure was only a feint in order to weaken the Province and immediately return and surprise 'em in a defenceless state—had I say, any of these circumstances prevented the Continental General from marching (and immediately marching) with more than one third of the Troops of North Carolina, Charlestown wou'd have been lost. We had an instance similar the other day, Georgia call'd out for assistance: I requested a Battalion of the Provincials from the Governor and Council and cou'd not obtain it—in short I beg leave to urge the necessity of unconditionally putting the Troops of South Carolina on the same footing with the rest; I beg leave to assure the Board and Congress that not only the two Brigadier Generals, the whole Continental officers, but nine in ten of the Provincials and of the Gentlemen of the country are firmly perswaded that their remaining on the Colonial Establishment, or half continental half provincial as they are at present, will be productive of one disjointed scene of anarchy, perplexity, and confusion—I shall beg leave before I conclude to mention one circumstance which is worthy the attention of Congress, and ought to be cleared up; Brigadier General Armstrong was order'd to be station'd at this place—he repair'd to his station according to the orders he had receiv'd, but as he had no Continental Troops with him, he was consider'd as a mere private man or Cypher: I shou'd imagine it cou'd never be the intention of Congress to order Brigadier Armstrong to ride to Charlestown for his health or merely to see the Country.

These things Gentlemen, shou'd be ascertain'd with precision as being left to the different constructions and expositions of different men will give birth to disgust, divisions and party—this at least is the conviction of Gentlemen

Your most ob[t] humble Servant
CHARLES LEE.

To The Board of War and Ordnance,
Philadelphia.

FROM THE PRESIDENT OF CONGRESS.

Philadelphia, August 8th 1776.

SIR,

The Congress having this day received a Letter from General Washington containing very important Information, I do myself the honor to enclose you a Copy of the same. You will there perceive that General Clinton, with the Troops under his Command, has joined General Howe at Staten Island, having left South Carolina soon after the Defeat he and Commodore Parker, sustained at Sullivan's Island.

In consequence of this Intelligence, the Congress are convinced, that the Enemy, by collecting their whole Force into a Point are determined to make a most vigorous Exertion at New York; and in order to ensure success in that Quarter are disposed for the present to overlook every other object. The getting possession of that City and the junction of the two Armies under Generals Howe and Burgoyne seem to be the Grand Objects they have in view, and to the attainment of which, they give up every inferior Consideration.

In this situation of our affairs, the Congress being of opinion your services in the Middle Department will be necessary, I have it it in Command to direct, that you repair as soon as possible to the City of Philadelphia there to receive such Orders as they may think proper to give you.

The attack at New York being hourly expected, and the Event of it uncertain, I am to request you will use the greatest Expedition on the Way.

With the best Wishes for your Health and Prosperity, I have the Honour to be

With the greatest Respect, Sir,

Your most obedt & very hble sert.

JOHN HANCOCK,

Presid[t]

Hon. Major General Lee.

GENERAL WASHINGTON TO THE PRESIDENT OF CONGRESS.

[*Inclosed in the preceding letter.*]

SIR,

Since closing the Letter which I had the Honour to write you this morning two Deserters have come in who left the Solebay man of War last Evening. One of them is a native of New York. Their account is, that they were in the Engagement with Col[o] Moultrie at Sullivans Island on y[e] 9th July—the particulars they give nearly correspond with the Narrative sent me by Gen[l] Lee—That they left Carolina 3 Weeks ago, as a Convoy to 45 Transports, having on board Gen[l] Clinton, L[d] Cornwallis & the whole Southern Army, consisting of about 3000 Men all of whom were landed last week on Staten Island in tolerable Health.

That on Sunday 13 Transports part of Lord Howes Fleet, & having on Board Hessians and Highlanders, came to Staten Island—That the Remainder of the Fleet which was reported to have in the whole 12000 men had parted with these Troops off the Banks of Newfoundland and were expected to come in every moment—That they were getting their heavy Carriages & Cannon on Board, had launch'd 8 Gondolas with Flat Bottoms & 2 Rafts or staps to carry Cannon. These men understand that the attack will soon be made, if the other Troops arrive—that they give out they will lay the Jersey waste with Fire and Sword—the computed strength of their Army will be 30,000 men—they farther add that when they left Carolina one Transport got on Shore so that they were not able to give her relief, upon which she surrendered with 5 Companies of Highlanders to Gen[l] Lee, who after taking everything valuable out of her burnt her—That the Admiral turn'd Gen[l] Clinton out of his Ship after the Engagement with a great deal of abuse—Great Differences between the principal naval and military Gentlemen.

That the Ships left in Carolina are now in such a weakly distressed Condition, they would fall an easy Prey.

I am Sir
With great Respect and Regard
Your most obt. & very hble Serv[t]
G[o] WASHINGTON.

Head Quarters: New York,
Aug. 7th 1776. 1 oclock, P.M.

P. S. The Ships are changing their Position, and the Men of War forming into a Line. But I still think they will wait the arrival of the remaining Hessians before any General Attack will be made—Monday's Return will shew our Strength here.

G. W.

FROM GENERAL ROBERT HOWE.

MY DEAR GENERAL,

I have detach'd the Horse agreeable to your order. I am just getting out of the Damnable Hobble in which you left me. Thompson's Detachment is march'd Also

Cattels i. e. Gadsdens, Moultrie's sets out this Evening or Tomorrow Morning when I shall take my leave of this Hotch Potch Camp and join you as fast as my Horses can carry me. I forward to you some Pacquets just received Exactly in the order they come (a new cover Excepted) Morris is well—Whiffles however as usual. Birds relicts & Nourses I shall bring along with me—they are very careless. Mrs Nourse sends her Love to the Secretary. She says her heart is with him * * *

I should be much obliged to you if you will contrive me a line to Col^o^ Bulls informing me whether I must call at Beaufort or proceed—if you are not gone on I shall certainly call myself, but the Troops unless you order otherwise will proceed the shortest way to Purisburg. Everything here is as you left it. I have nothing to add but that I long to join you and that I am with Respect & Esteem, Dear Sir,

Your most obe^t^ Serv

R. Howe.

10th August 1776.
Major General Lee,
at Beaufort Port Royal.

From General Washington.

New-York, August 12th, 1776.

My Dear Lee,

Notwithstanding I shall probably feel the effect, I do most cordially and sincerely congratulate you on *your* victory over Clinton and the British squadron at Sullivan's Island. A victory undoubtedly it is, when an enemy are drubbed, and driven from a country they were sent to conquer. Such is the case of Clinton and Sir Peter Parker, who are now with the fleet and army at Staten Island, where General Howe and the troops from Halifax have been ever since the last day of June, and Lord Howe since the twelfth of July. Some Hessians and a pretty many of the Scottish laddies have got in, and the residue of the fleet parted with off the banks of Newfoundland, hourly expected. When the whole arrive matters will soon come to a decision, every thing being prepared on both sides for the appeal, and, on ours, I hope it will be obstinate, if not successful.

The latter, it is not in the power of mortals to command; but they may endeavour to deserve it; and this I am persuaded, our troops will more than ever aim at, as I have impressed upon their minds the gallant behaviour of the brave few, who defended Sullivan's Island.

At present the enemy can bring more men to a point than we can, and when reinforced by the Hessians without number, as unless the militia (faster than heretofore) come in to our aid, their numbers, when the Hessians arrive cannot, by the best intelligence we can get, fall short of twenty-five thousand men. Ours are under twenty, very sickly, and posted on Governor's Island, Long Island, at Powlis Hook, Horn's Hook, and at the pass near King's Bridge; more militia are expected, but whether they will be in time, time only can tell, as also where the point of attack will be. An opinion prevails, countenanced by hints from some of the principal tories, and corroborated by intelligence from Staten Island, that part of the enemy's fleet and army will go into the Sound, whilst another part of it, runs up the North River, thereby cutting off all communication by water with this place, whilst their troops form a chain across the neck, and stop an intercourse with Connecticut by land: others think, they will not leave an army in their rear, whilst they have the country in their front, getting by that means between two fires, unless it is extended as a feint to withdraw our troops from the city, that they may slip in and possess themselves of it: all this is but a field of conjecture.

Our affairs in the north have been growing from bad to worse, till I hope they will mend, as one great source of the evil is in a way of being removed, I mean, the small pox; but the army have retreated from place to place, till they are now got to Ticonderoga, opposite to which on the east side of the Lake Champlain, they are about to establish a post, which they say will be invulnerable; but whether it may not be somewhat like the man who built a mill on account of a beautiful fall, and then had to consider whether it was practicable to bring water to it, remains in some measure to be determined, as it is the opinion of some, (I know nothing of the country myself,) that the enemy may pass this post and get into Lake George without receiving the least annoyance from this work. Whether they would chuse to leave a post in their rear, without establishing one themselves, sufficient to keep it in awe, is the point in question.

It gives me a very singular pleasure to hear of the gallant behaviour of your young aids, and Mr. Jenifer, as also of Colonels Moultrie and Thompson, to be the means at any time, of rewarding merit, will add greatly to my happiness; and whenever you can point out a mode that can be adopted consistently, you shall find me very ready: but you know the temper of the troops in this quarter, as well as I do, and how impracticable it is to bring in a person, let his merit be ever so great, without throwing a whole corps into confusion. This will also apply to Captain Bullet. What vacancies there may be in your department that he has his eye to, and could be appointed to with propriety, you must know better than I. That there is none here, I can undertake to say. I have no doubt but the Congress would annex the rank of colonel to his office of adjutant. I believe they have done it in the instance of Griffin, who is appointed deputy adjutant to the flying camp. If this would add any thing to his satisfaction, I should have no objection to the mention of it. With every wish for your prosperity and success, I remain with sincere regard,

Your most affectionate and obedient,

G°. WASHINGTON.

General Lee.

TO PRESIDENT RUTLEDGE.

Colonel Bull's, August 13, 1776.

D^R SIR,

We are just return'd from Port Royal which I thought it prudent to visit and inspect before we left the Province—the place has so many natural advantages for defence that few works will be necessary to put it hors d'insult—I have given directions for improving the Fort and the lines on the narrows—when the Baron has laid out the Redoubts and fleches agreed upon for Sullivan's Island, it will not be amiss if your Excellency detaches him to make a thorough survey of Port Royal and St Helena. I am told that the latter is still stronger by nature than the former, on which if two Redoubts one at Capt Joiners house and another at a Bluff about a mile below it are erected, nothing more in my opinion can be added—inclos'd I send you an account of an advantage which the Fincastle Militia have obtain'd over the Cherokees—the publication of it will give fresh encouragement to your Militia—The Congress have resolv'd the warmest thanks to Colonel Moutrie and his brave Garrison as well as to Col^l Thompson and the Corps under his command on the day of the attack—I set out tomorrow early—On my return I hope to see some of your Row Gallies on the stocks.

Adieu, Dr Sir, Yours,

CHARLES LEE.

To His Excellency John Rutledge,
President of the State of South Carolina.

FROM GEN. ANDREW LEWIS.

Williamsburg, August 13th 1776.

DR GENL

I think it highly necessary to inform you that two of our Battalions are now on their March for the Jerseys by express order of Congress to me directed. They are designed as a Reinforcement to what they call the Flying Camp opposite to Staten Island: wou'd it not appear that Congress are fully of opinion that no attempts will be made on Virginia, but upon what they found their opinion I know not. From the best accounts I can collect our Troops on both sides Hutsans River before the Enemys Camp are not less than 30,000 —the number of the Enemy not more than 10,000—If this be anything like a true state of the case it cannot be supposed our Enemies can make much impression in that Quarter. And is it not natural to suppose they will, on being informed of our condition make an attempt on this Quarter. This I mention by the bie—my Business is to obey let the consequence be as it may. The first and the third Battalions are those I have ordered North, the time for which the first and second Battalions were enlisted being nearly expired, I tho't it a favourable opportunity to attempt listing the first as the officers of that Battalion appeared extremely fond of going to the Northward, and I have succeeded so well that with the addition of 120 of the Eighth Battalion they will be compleat. This unexpected Stroke of being deprived of two Battalions has occasioned my ordering the fifth from Portsmouth where the fourth under the command of Col° Steven is Fortifying. They have 10 Cannon 24 lbers some of them mounted & will in a short time have 8 or 10 more. We have scraped out of the sand and Dirt at several Places about 30 Cannon exclusive of those at Portsmouth none of which are less than 9 lbrs and after Burning and cleaning appear to be extreamly good, such of them as we have tried prove so. Six of them I shall have in a few days mounted at York, and 3 or 4 at Gloster-Town, the Batteries will be opposite to each other. The Cannon we used against the Fleet and Camp at Gwinns Island are still at the same Batteries and think it best they shou'd remain so until circumstances make their removal necessary—I have sent an officer of the Artillery to hurry down shott from Frederick County Col° Lane having orders some months past to have them cast as we have more cannon than we expected, and the Batteries very distant from each other—I wish an augmentation of the Artillery Company, this I know you Recommended to Congress, but am not informed of any resolution on that head. The time which the Second Regiment was enlisted for are nearly expired—they refuse to inlist before they be discharged and go home to see their friends. We shall have only the fifth and sixth Regiments between the Rivers James and York—the seventh being stationed in Gloucester County and those are by sickness greatly reduced not less than 130 of a Battalion on an Average unfit for duty—It's true we have six Companies of Minute Men stationed at Hampton who are likewise very sickly and want much to go home, and two Companies at York, who are in the same bad Condition. As I said before I thought it my duty to make you acquainted with the above circumstances that you might be better be able to Guard against any stroke you might know aimed against this State. Last Wednesday Dunmore with the remains of his Fleet sailed out of our Capes where they divided. The armed Vessels and others to the number of 20 steered northwardly, and about the same number to the South. This of all he had left of 103 which cast anchor at Gwinns Island owing to various causes, the great mortality amongst both white and Black may be the chief. The number of Vessels Crippled by the Cannonade with the damage the worms did them contributed greatly to their Destruction. I hope the expedition set on foot against the Cherokees will succeed—Our Rangers in

Fincastle County have killed 25 of them at different places on Holston River without the loss of a man, and have taken a much larger number of Rifles. We have got by the arrival of a small vessel from St Eustatia 190 Half Barrels of Powder and 90 Stand of Arms—it got in the Day the Fleet went out of our Capes. The last letter I had from you is dated the 29th June which gave the pleasing Accounts of the Glorious Repulse you gave the Enemy. My Compliments to Brigadiers Armstrong and Howe.

I am Dear General

Your most Obed^t^ and very Hble Servt

ANDREW LEWIS

B^r^ Genl.

To General Lee.

FROM JOHN PAGE.

August ye 13th 1776.

MY DEAR GENERAL,

As Brigadier Lewis intends to send an Express to you, with great Propriety in my Opinion I have determined to write by it, whatever may occur to me in the few Minutes I now can snatch, for I am still pestered with Business. The Brigadier will inform you of the order from Congress to march two of your Battalions from hence to the Jerseys—I shall only observe that this added to the Indian War, and a few other circumstances will make a fine opening for Clinton to make a Push here as he can make nothing of you. However, if he should I hope it will only prove a Bait for him. I suppose before this you must have heard of our success against the Cherokees—they have received a severe check—In the several little skirmishes with them our men behaved well & have killed 25, and wounded many more without the loss of a man. We have appointed Colonel Christian, Commander on the Expedition by the request of Co^l^ Russell & the consent of Col. Lewis whom we had at first pitched upon for that Business—He will have 1450 Virginians, & 300 North Carolinians are to join him on Holston at Stalnickers—I have received a Letter this day from Col. Russel dated the 6th at Captn Shelby's near the Place of the late Skirmish from which I find nothing new has happened but that they have been informed by one Thos Price who lately escaped from the Cherokees that the Indians have large Magazines of Powder &c at a little Town called Hinwassa. Now [that] I mention Powder I must ask you whether a Sloop one Martin Commander has not brought a Quantity of Powder to Chas Town, for such a Person was to have called at Chas Town with 14000 ℔ for Virginia—this is worth enquiring after, although we have at present a tolerable good stock, having received last week from St Eustatia 8500℔—in the little Boat which brought this Powder come Passenger an Hessian Gentn who offers his service in our Army, having seen as he says a great deal of service & acted as a Lieut in the last War. He is very anxious to meet the Hessians, & does not seem to doubt that they may be all prevailed upon to come over to us. He says that he expects that a Relation of his one Christopher Howsman a Major of the Fusiliers will be amongst the Troops sent over & seems to make sure of him—however he has been 18 Months in the West Indies. He is going immediately to Phila.

There are two french Gentlemen here who were bringing in powder & Arms with Medicines, & were taken by Lord Dunmore & treated very roughly—they happened to be on Gwyn's Island when the Fleet was forced to retire & concealed themselves from the Enemy when they were flying from the Island, & by that means made their Escape & delivered themselves up to our Men—they appear to be modest sensible men—one of them who calls himself the Chevalier De St Aubin agent servie dans Le Regiment de la feronnay Dragon, says he has had the pleasure of seeing you 2 or 3 Times & thinks if he could see you again you would recollect him—he is very desirous of going to Charles Town to be examined by you, but as we expect you will shortly return here, we have advised M[r] S[t] Aubin to wait 'till we can hear from you, in the mean-time he agrees to assist in training a Troop of Horse, & says he will act as Cadet 'till he can give you Proofs of his Abilities & Right to expect some Post of Rank in the Troop. The other French Gentleman is determined to return to Martinique—I would ask you to write your opinion what we should do for these Gent[s] if I did not hope to see you soon, for I take it for granted that Clinton has left Cha[s] Town by this Time. Dunmore has at length quitted Virginia—some say he is dead, but there is no certainty of this. The Enemy endeavoured to land at Cape Henry but were repulsed with the loss of a Boat by a Party of Men Col. Stephen had sent down for that Purpose on hearing that the Fleet was coming down the Bay. For Gods sake if you do not come let us hear oftener from you—it is above a month since we rec[d] a Line from you—Present my Complts to our Friends & believe me to be

Yours Sincerely
JOHN PAGE.

To General Lee.

HENRY LAURENS TO JOHN LAURENS.

Charlestown, So Carolina 14 Aug[t] 1776.

Uncommon and exceedingly mortifying, my Dear Son, has been the late long interruption in our correspondence I find that I have not put [pen] to paper in any address to you since the 29th April and unless certain letters referred to in the subjoined list have reached you, I have no ground to hope that you have learned anything concerning me since November last—in the mean time, after long and anxious waiting I have had the pleasure of receiving your Letters of the 5th Decem. from St Augustine and of 20th March by the hand of Mr. Read, but that which you say was sent via Virginia frank'd by the Post Master came no nearer to me than Cockspur, where it was either destroyed or returned in the Packet, if Gov[r] Wright who was there had been possessed of any feelings he would have sent a Son's letter to a Father notwithstanding the opposition of their political tenets.

Once more I will attempt to present my Love to you by the hands of Mons[r] Rilliet who poor gentleman is making another effort after many disappointments to regain a footing on his native soil, you will see in the schedule of letters, he is already the bearer of several to you, which are now perhaps not worth Carriage. I have not time to review them and since they are written and packetted let them go.

I told you in my last that I was going to Georgia. I began my journey the 1st May and at Wright's Savanna Broton Island & New Hope, found Crops of Rice amounting to about 1300 Barrels which I caused to be removed to places less exposed to the threatened depredations of picaroons from St. Augustine in such places that great value still remains. I have lately learned that each Plantation is again well covered—the best Crop they say that ever was borne at Broton Island—but what of that? The whole will either be destroyed stolen or lie with the farmer to perish by time and Vermin—no small sacrifice at the shrine of Liberty, and yet very small compared with that which I am willing to make—not only Crops, but Land, Life and All must follow, in preference to sacrificing Liberty to Mammon. In such sentiments I found the people of Georgia with a few exceptions, but none more hearty than our Highland friends, the M[c]Intoshes. Lachlan is Colonel of a Battalion upon Continental establishment, two of his sons Lach, and William are subs. His brother William commands a troop of Rangers in Pay of the Colony or as I should now say the State. Jos.

Habersham is Major & John a Captain in the Battalion, in a word the Country is Military.

My negroes there all to a Man are strongly attached to me, so are all of mine in this Country; hitherto not one of them has attempted to desert, on the contrary those who are most exposed hold themselves always ready to fly from the Enemy in case of a sudden descent—many hundreds of that Colour have been stolen and decoyed by the Servants of King George the Third—Captains of British Ships of War and Noble Lords have busied themselves in such inglorious pilferage to the disgrace of their Master and disgrace of their Cause.—These Negroes were first enslaved by the English—Acts of Parliament have established the Slave Trade in favour of the home residing English and almost totally prohibited the Americans from reaping any share of it—Men of War, forts, Castles, Governors, Companies and Committees are employed and authorized by the English Parliament to protect regulate and extend the Slave Trade. Negroes are brought by Englishmen and sold as slaves to Americans—Bristol, Liverpool, Manchester, Birmingham, &c &c live upon the Slave Trade. The British Parliament now employ their Men of War to steal those Negroes from the Americans to whom they sold them, pretending to set the poor wretches free, but basely trepan and sell them into tenfold worse Slavery in the West Indies, where probably they will become the property of Englishmen again and of those who sit in Parliament; what meanness! what complicated wickedness appears in this scene! O England, how changed! how fallen!

You know, my dear Son, I abhor Slavery. I was born in a Country where Slavery had been established by British Kings and Parliaments as well as by the laws of that Country Ages before my existence, I found the Christian Religion and Slavery growing under the same authority and cultivation.—I nevertheless disliked it—in former days there was no combatting the prejudices of Men supported by Interest, the day I hope is approaching when from principles of gratitude as well as justice every Man will strive to be foremost in shewing his readiness to comply with the Golden Rule; not less than £20000 stg. would all my Negroes produce if sold at public Auction tomorrow. I am not the man who enslaved them, they are indebted to English Men for that favour, nevertheless I am devising means for manumitting many of them and for cutting off the entail of Slavery—great powers oppose me; the Laws and Customs of my Country, my own and the avarice of my countrymen—What will my Children say if I deprive them of so much Estate? these are difficulties but not insuperable. I will do as much as I can in my time and leave the rest to a better hand. I am not one of those who arrogate the peculiar care of Providence in each fortunate event, nor one of those who dare trust in Providence for defence and security of their own Liberty while they enslave and wish to continue in Slavery, thousands who are as well intitled to freedom as themselves. I perceive the work before me is great. I shall appear to many as a promoter, not only of strange but of dangerous doctrines, it will therefore be necessary to proceed with caution, you are apparently deeply interested in this affair, but as I have no doubt of your concurrence and approbation I most sincerely wish for your advice and assistance & hope to receive both in good time.

I finished my Journey, going round by Mepkin, and returned to Charles Town the 1st June half an hour after I had entered my house Intelligence was brought of a Fleet at Anchor a little to the Northward of Charles Town Bar for the History of this Fleet I refer you to Jack Wills's paper of the 2d inst. and to certain notes which I have added, his account although true in general substance is the most bungling and inaccurate of any thing I have seen from him, it would be easier to build a true and proper narrative at full length than to mend the botchery which he took a full month to compose. I wish you or somebody else would publish a fair and honest compilation from his Gazette and my papers—You know me too well to suppose I would in a tittle exaggerate or suppress. You may add as much of what follows as may appear to be necessary, but let the whole be cleverly done and introduced by such declarations of candor as these accounts are well entitled to—nothing more abhorrent to me than publications of falsehood for Truth.

Upon the tremendous range of 55 Sail of Hostile Ships before our doors and in full view, after wishing they had rather come as seekers for ffreights of Rice, I thought it my duty to add to the dignity of Vice President of the Colony (now State observe) the several offices of Engineer, Super Intendant of Works, Aid de Camp, and occasionally any other which could in the least contribute to the service of my Country then seeming to verge on a precipice and to require the support of every Man in it.—I who you know had resolved never again to mount a horse, I who thought it impossible for me to Gallop five miles a day, was seen for a month and more every day on the back of a lively Nag at ½ past 4 in the morning some times Galloping 20 Miles before breakfast and some times sitting the Horse 14 Hours in 18—& what you will say was more extraordinary I never got a tumble. But mark he was a trotting horse I will never cross a pacer again if I can avoid it—I have spoken so particularly of myself, not meaning to claim any singular or extraordinary merit, but because I know you will draw pleasing inferences of my state of health from an account of such exertions —the President was as diligent as active as a man could be & so much more useful than myself as his authority, superior abilities and advantages of youth enabled him, every Man except a few unhappy misled whom the People call Tories and a few of a worse stamp whom I call property men, was animated, discovered a Love of Country and a boldness arising from an assurance of being engaged in a just cause; Charles Town was in a a very short time inclosed by Lines, Trenches, and Redoutes—Wharves were cleared of all incumbrances, Streets strongly barricaded—retrenchments within—Batteries erected for defence at practicable Landings above the town—Thousands of Men came in from the Country, from North Carolina and Virginia and all this with a degree of celerity as amazing as our former neglect had been, much indeed are we indebted to Gen. Lee as well as to his seconds the Brigadiers Armstrong and Howe, these arrived at a critical time and we were favoured by weather which fortunately withheld the Enemy from striking a sudden blow and every moment of the interval was improved to advantage on our side.

Gen[l] Lee at first sight was exceedingly displeased with the Fort at Sullivant's wished we could save our Stores and abandon it, although he acknowledged the exterior work was impregnable; however as that could not be done, he recommended some amendments, gave advice, Orders and his presence in the beginning of the action to which if we do not altogether owe the honor of the 28 June we are certainly greatly indebted—but from the General's better knowledge of the Harbour and the vast importance of that post he must now be of a different opinion.

At the approach of the ships of war towards Sullivant's the ramparts and parapets of Fort Johnson where Col° Gadsden had chosen his command were seen covered by officers and soldiers, every one interesting himself in the fate of the sister Fortress and standing ready in case of need to second her efforts. All the Batteries round this Town were at the same time manned, Guns loaded, every article in readiness for acting in turn. Troops of regulars and Militia properly stationed for repelling all attempts to land, Engines and Men at proper stands for extinguishing Fires in the town—there was every appearance of an universal determination to give General James Grant the flat lie, it was the fortune of his old friend Will. Moultrie to speak first and he monopolized the glory of the Day.

The country Militia as well as the town continued

chearfully to do duty on this Frontier as long as one of the Enemies' Fleet remained in sight—The Active was the last, who with a tender went about ten days ago to Bull's Island the property of Captain Shubrick landed 40 White and 20 Black Men, killed by platoon firing a few head of Cattle, augmented their Black Guard by stealing six more negroes and then sailed off the coast or perhaps only a little out sight. To hear Shubrick's overseer relate the manner of their firing on the cattle and the very few of their shot which hit the mark, is droll enough and serves to raise the contempt of those who with single ball at 150 yards distance will hit the circle of an English crown.

After the attack on Sullivant's Island seconded by Ravages and murders by the Cherokee Indians on our Western frontier who probably acted in a concerted plan with the ships and troops I believe there were few men here who had not lost all inclination for renewing our former connexion with your King and his ministers. However that might have been, the great point is now settled—On the 2d. inst. a Courier arrived from Philadelphia and brought a declaration of the 4th. July by the representatives of the 13 United Colonies in Congress mét, that from thenceforward those Colonies should be "Free and Independent States." You have no doubt seen the paper or will in a few days see a Copy often repeated at full length, therefore I need not mark the particular contents, this Declaration was proclaimed in Charles Town with great solemnity on Monday the 5th Inst. attended by a Procession of President, Councils, Generals, Members of Assembly Officers Civil & Military &^{c} &^{c} amidst loud acclamations of thousands who always huzza when a proclamation is read.—To many who from the Rashness, Impolicy and Cruelty of the British Administration had foreseen this event—the scene was serious, important and awful—even at this moment I feel a Tear of affection for the good old Country and for the people in it whom in general I dearly love.—There I saw that Sword of State which I had before seen four several times unsheathed in Declarations of War against France and Spain by the Georges now unsheathed and borne in a Declaration of War against George the Third. I say even at this moment my heart is full of the lively sensations of a dutiful Son, thrust by the hand of Violence out of a Father's house into the Wide world. What I have often with truth averred in London and Westminster, I dare still aver, not a sober Man and scarcely a single Man in America wished for separation from Great Britain. Your King too, I feel for, he has been greatly deceived and abused.

Soon after the Men of War had anchored within our Bar, alarming accounts were brought of new attempts by John Stuart, Henry Stuart, Alexander Cameron and other Ministerial Agents to stir up the Savage Indians to attack our Western frontier, several Intercepted Letters from them confirmed the reports—the Indians and particularly the Cherokees had amused us by the most flattering talks, full of assurances of friendship and promises to follow our advice which always had been that they should observe a strict neutrality—but very suddenly, without any pretence to provocation those treacherous Devils in various parties headed by White Men and pushed on by those who are in employment for this cruel purpose, made an Inroad upon our settlements, burned several houses and murdered about sixty persons chiefly Women and Children. Col[l] A[w] Williamson in South, Brigadier Rutherford in North Carolina were immediately in Arms and a large Command marched from Virginia what Rutherford and the Virginia Troops have done we are not yet informed but Colonel Williamson and his parties have driven back the Savages of the lower Towns killed as many as could be come at in fight and taken some prisoners among whom are no less than 15 White men, they have also destroyed Sennecca, Keowee, Warrachy, Estatokee, Toxawa and Sugar Town together with the Crops of Corn and other grain found in fields and Barns, the only possible way of reducing the barbarians. This intelligence comes from Col° Williamson in late Letters. If the Virginians act their part well, the Cherokees will soon be reduced to the utmost distress and may possibly turn their vengeance against those hellish Instigators to this Hellish War. At the entrance of Senneca a new Town which I am told was very extensive on the Banks of Keowee, Colonel Williamson suffered from an ambuscade, his Horse by two shot was killed under him. Mr. Salvador a gentleman whose death is universally regretted was killed by his side, eight men wounded, two of whom are since dead. He nevertheless rallied his Troops, attacked the Savages beat them out and after destroying a town of near four miles long marched forward—he is undoubtedly a brave man and not a bad General—you know his deficiency in Education, what heighths might he have reached if he could have improved his Genius by Reading. If we succeed against the Cherokees the Creeks and other Indians may continue to be simple spectators of our contest with British Ships and Soldiers, otherwise we shall be attacked on all sides and greatly distressed—but men here are fearless of distress and determined to maintain their Rights, trusting in a Righteous God for a happy issue.

I told you in a former letter of the dangerous Insurrection by thousands of the back country people, these were suppressed by the vigilance and activity of Colo. Williamson in a first instance and in a second and more formidable by Colonel Richardson and troops from North Carolina—hundreds or more properly thousands were taken prisoners, informed truly of the nature of the dispute between Great Britain and the Colonies converted and sent to their habitations, about an hundred of their Colonels, Captains and other officers (from whence it appears the whole body was very large) were brought to Charlestown, these except 13 or 14 of the most tenacious soon confessed their errors united in the American Cause and also returned home —of the 13 or 14 were some sensible men particularly their chief colonel Robert Cunningham, a man of great honour, whose conscience as he said fettered him in the oath of allegiance although he admitted the injustice of taxing Americans without their own consent, & censured the British administration; he often moved me while I was President of the Council of Safety and often since the President of the Colony to accept from him and his companions an oath of Neutrality, he would not at first believe that the British Administration were so wicked as to instigate the savages to War against us—as soon therefore as he was convinced of the truth his conscience freed him from old obligations and he most heartily desired to take the oath of fidelity to the United Colonies and to have an opportunity of giving proofs of his sincerity, his fellow prisoners joined him in a petition to the President & Council, who ordered the whole to be released—they immediately repaired to Col° Williamson's Camp and offered their service, but he considering their long absence from their several homes recommended to them the care of their families—Not all however whom we have enlarged have continued faithful, some of the common fellows have quoted the example of Sir James and broke their parol—most of these are now among the Indians, some of them have again been taken prisoners and must suffer the penalty of an old law. Kirkland you may have heard made his Escape when he left his Son a child of 10 or 12 years old in Gaol—we know nothing of him since his flight—possibly this ignorant fellow may have found his way to St. James's he was confident of a hearty welcome there and of much free conversation with the Master of that House—If he was Honest, he might make a tolerable Serjeant but anything less than a Regiment will fall short of his own Mark.

The Reverend M[r] Cooper, from time to time gave offence to his Parishioners and they have dismissed him. The King's Officers, that is to say the Att^y General, Chief and Assistant Judges, Postmaster and Mr. Outerbridge are confined to the Postmaster's House the late Commander of Fort Johnson and the Collector are at large on their parol, W Wragy remains at his plantation and lately James Brisbane and some seven or eight others of our Neighbors who had signed the Association & acknowledged the Justice of the American Cause but refused to do anything which might endanger their property in case of Conquest by the other side (these and some who play a still more cunning Game are *property men*) were sent to Cheraw Goal—the success of the 28 June made some converts and those Gentlemen in particular advanced so far as to consent to bear Arms, take the Test Oath, &^{c} but still under the Air of Obedience to avail themselves of the plea of compulsion and to save property—such Men deserve no station of honor on either side. I can have no pity for these, while I sincerely commiserate the circumstances of the King's Officers and of every suffering candid man, although he may be mine Enemy.

Mrs. Stuart, the wife of the cruel Superintendent had been long confined to her House and hindered from leaving the Colony, the people had hoped that Stuart would in the case of his own have had some tender feelings for the Wives and innocent children of our friends on the Indian Frontier, but when we found that he had struck the blow, instead of retaliating as his friends ever do, the President and Privy Council ordered Mrs. Stuart to be enlarged; no valuable end could be obtained by a continuance of her suffering.

America is now well supplied with Gun Powder and Arms and every Day will probably increase our Commerce by slow steps.

The General Assembly is to meet on the 17th. September when the Declaration of Independence will be recorded among our Acts and every salutary measure pursued for the Welfare of the State. To tell you the Virginians had routed Lord Dunmore, that North Carolina is very quiet, Maryland and Philadelphia as yet unmolested, New York likely to become the seat of War for this Summer, that Boston is now secured to us by strong Fortifications, that the New England Privateers had made prizes of several Transport Ships and prisoners of many hundred Highland Soldiers would probably be to relate what you will know before this can reach you—but it may be new to you, that Gen. Lee and Gen[1] Howe went last week to Georgia, whence some expedition is intended to the Southward—the season of the year and some other circumstances are not so favorable as to give me sanguine hopes of success; and you will feel some concern when I tell you, we expect another visit by the British Ships and Troops in the Winter Months.

I have now gone through with much Intelligence such as it is, don't wonder if I tell you I write in haste. I had determined to take time by the forelock and to have saved four or five days for writing to my friends in England but some unexpected public calls and the long sickness of my good Man James I am reduced to one and I must copy for different conveyances, however I have a few words more to add.—I am now by the Will of God brought into a new World and God only knows what sort of a World it will be—what may be your particular opinion of this change I know not. You have done well to avoid writing on politics. Remember you are of full age entitled to judge for yourself. Pin not your faith upon my sleeve, but act the part which an Honest Heart after mature deliberation shall dictate and your services on the side which you may take, because you think it the right side, will be the more valuable.

I need not tell you whatever may be your determination to avoid all party disputes and to act inoffensively and circumspectly in the State where you are— I cannot rejoice in the downfall of an old friend of a parent from whose nurturing breasts I have drawn my support and strength, every Evil which befalls old

England grieves me, would to God she had listened in time to the cries of her children and had checked the Insidious Slanders of Men who call themselves the King's Servants and the King's friends, especially such of them as had been transported to America in the character of Civil Officers. If my own Interests, if my own Rights alone had been concerned I would most freely have given the whole to the demands and disposal of her Ministers in preference to a separation, but the Rights of Posterity were in question. I happened to stand as one of their Representatives and dared not betray my trust.

I am now more than ever anxious to see you, to see my Dear Harry and your Sisters, to see your Uncle and Aunt—but when and where? God direct you for the best—but pay particular attention to those friends especially to your eldest Sister and to Harry, your other Sister is at an age and has qualities to make her Foster Mother happy. I could add very much on this head—but clouds and Darkness are before me.

Remember me respectfully to each of my old friends, tell them that as an Individual I have a right to acknowledge my obligations to them and that I will take every opportunity of shewing my Regard, and although I hold my Life by a most precarious tenure yet I trust in God we shall meet again as friends, particularly inform both the M[r] Cowles's that I will when it is possible look into our accounts and adjust them—it has not been in my power to do so since my arival from England. M[r] William Cowles will do me the justice to own that 'tis not my fault those accounts were left unsettled. I had often wrote to him for them, I made one journey to Bristol for the sole purpose of settling them, and when I was leaving the Kingdom, I again took Bristol in my way to Falmouth for the same purpose I waited there to the very last hour for saving my passage in the Packet and did not receive the papers from him till I had kept the Post Chaise long in waiting at my door and in despair was just stepping into it. My friend is to blame on this score.

I am glad you continue with Mr. Bicknel and your brother with Mr. Henderson, frugality is essential to you both, consider I cannot supply you while the Sword of Britain remains unsheathed. Improve every moment of your time my dear son and continue your guidance and protection to your Brother and your Sisters, your respect and Duty to your distressed Uncle and Aunt. I feel much for them, may God protect and guide you all and may he still give Peace and mutual friendship to the divided family of Britain and promote the happiness equally of the ancient Root and of the transplanted branches.—If you do not come enquire for opportunities in Holland and in France, and write as oft as you can—& Harry too.

Adieu! My Dear, Dear Son,
HENRY LAURENS.

Why do you never say a word of M. B.

Mr. John Laurens.

LETTERS REFERRED TO.

26 Nov. and 6 Decem by Rainier from Georgia.
4th 8th & 16th January by Mr. Rilliet. Copies by Snw Mobile Capt. Smith.
22d Feburary 6 & 14 March by Mr. Rilliet. Copies by Mr. Demar viâ West Indies.
16th and 19th March by Mr. Rilliet.
26 28 and 28 March by Mr. Sandy Wright to be forwarded through St. Augustine.
29 April by Mr. Rilliet.

Endorsed: "14 August 1776 Charlestown"

To General John Armstrong.

Purisbourg, August ye 15, 1776.

Dear General,

One hundred and forty seven of Colonel Mughlenburghs Regiment with two Captains and three subalterns are left sick at Charlestown; as fast as they recover I must request you to order 'em back to Williamsburg where they are to aggregate themselves with Capt. Cochrane's Company of that Regiment—it will be politick to apprize them of their destination, for as I have reason to think that the Devil of Desertion has in some measure possess'd 'em, their being acquaint'd that they are to return home, will be the means of casting out the Dæmon—You will likewise inform Brigadier General Lewis of this step who will dispose of 'em at his discretion.

As I am told from the best authority that a prodigious quantity of powder is arrived in Virginia and Maryland, I wish you wou'd by the first opportunity send two more Tons to Georgia; write to N. Carolina to replace it, and to Virginia to replace theirs—Your letters to the Councils or Committees of those Provinces will be sufficient. I am and shall be so extremely busy^{ed} in our present expedition that you must be saddled with the detail of such matters.

I hope the Baron has already set himself to work on the Redoubts on Sullivan's Island and the Screen for the Bridge—it is my opinion that the two bridges must be preserved, and tnat in order to prevent the communication betwixt the Fort and the old bridge being cut off, a chain of small redoubts capable of containing a subaltern and thirty each with two pieces of cannon shou'd be erected in such a manner that the most distant may be commanded by its next neighbor—the second by the third, and the third by that of the fourth—I mention four at a venture, but as I am not accurately acquainted with the exact distance from the

Fort to the Bridge, perhaps five or six will be necessary —when I speak of this Chain of Redoubts being commanded each by its neighbour I mean that the face or flank presented to its neighbour sho[d] be so weak or slender that the enemy cannot make a lodgment in any one of them; as the Cannon of the next must drive 'em out shou'd they take possession of it—inclos'd is a rough sketch of my idea—without this Chain of Forts, Sullivan's Island will be a very precarious Post—It is at best a damnable one.

I beg you will present my compliments to the President and inform him that as I found Richmonds Militia falling down every day, I order'd 'em from Port Royal to their respective homes—They are a fine body of men, and it wou'd have been monstrous not to have a regard for their preservation.—My respects to Conner, and believe me D[r] General, to be entirely

Yours

CHARLES LEE.

To Brigadier Genl. Armstrong.

ORDERS TO LIEUT. BERRIAN.

Savanna Aug[t] 18th 1776.

SIR,

You are to proceed from hence to Beaufort with two Prisoners, Peter Backup and James Loftin—You are to be extremely vigilant that they do not escape, for which reason you are to keep 'em in irons at least during the Night, and place trusty Centinels over them—When you arrive at Beaufort you are to deliver them into the hands of Colonel Bull or Officer commanding the place from whom you are to demand a receipt.

CHARLES LEE

Major General

To Lieut[t] Berrian.

To Colonel Bull.

Savanna, August 18th 1776.

Sir,

Lieut[t] Berrian of the Georgian Battalion has Orders to deliver into your custody the notorious Backup, a most pernicious, active Instrument of Royal Villany. I must request that you will be extremely careful in taking necessary measures to prevent his escape—That you will detach a sufficient number of men with a trusty officer from your Corps of Militia who are to deliver him into the hands of His Excellency the President—it will be prudent to keep him at least during the Night in Irons.

I am Sir Your most ob[t] humble Serv[t]

Charles Lee

P. S. A James Loftin born in America taken by Capt. Baker and a worthy adjunct of Mr. Backup is coupled to him, of whom I must desire you will take equal care. He is one of Tonyns Lieutenants.

To Col. Bull,
Officer Commanding at Beaufort.

To President Rutledge.

Savanna, 18th August 1776.

D[r] Sir,

I ought to be asham'd of myself for a gross mistake or piece of distraction I have been guilty of; I had taken into my head that in the detachment arranged for Georgia that Thompson's Regiment was only to furnish eighty and that Capt[n] Harden's whole Company was to march—On this supposition I order'd Harden's whole Company to embark—I afterwards in looking in my

Note Book (for I had not my Note Book with me in Port Royal) perceived my mistake and I once more confess my shame for so great a one.

I have by the desire of some of the Gentlemen here order'd the notorious Backup with a worthy adjunct (as great a Rascal as himself) one Loftin (calling himself a Lieutenant of the Royal Rangers of East Florida) to Beaufort under a strong guard—from thence he will be convey'd to Charlestown where y^r^ Excellency will dispose of him according to your discretion.

Tomorrow we are to have a Council—I will inform you of the result and the measures I shall pursue in consequence of it—*en attendant*—

I am, Dr Sir, Most sincerely yours,

CHARLES LEE.

To His Exc^y^ Jno Rutledge,
President of the State of South Carolina.

CONFERENCE WITH THE GEORGIA COUNCIL OF SAFETY.

Tuesday, August 19, 1776.

GENERAL LEE waited on the Board, and proposed the following questions for their consideration:

1st Whether, as the post on St Mary's is now abandoned, and the whole country between that river and the St Johns broke up, and as there is no possibility of transporting cannon, ammunition, provisions, or collecting a sufficient number of men for the siege and reduction of Augustine, an irruption into East-Florida can be productive of so great and important advantages to the general cause, or to this state of Georgia in particular, as to compensate for the trouble and expense, and what these advantages are? What are the means of certainly supplying the troops with grain and meat? how their baggage is to be transported? whether it can be safely transported by water? if it cannot, whether wagons can pass? if the road is practicable only to horses, how pack-saddles are to be provided?

Ordered, That Messrs Jonathan Bryan and Nathan Bronson be a Committee to answer the questions proposed by General Lee.

SIR:

The Council having taken into consideration your Excellency's questions this day laid before them, are clearly of opinion that an irruption into the Province of East Florida will be attended with the most salutary consequences to this Province, and of course render service to the whole Continent.

The reasons which weigh with them are as follow:

1st That they conceive the reduction of Augustine to be a very considerable object with the Continent in general, but this Province in particular.

2^{d} They are led to hope, that if the whole country around is ravaged, the cattle on the east side of St. John's driven off, and the inhabitants obliged to evacuate their plantations and fly into the Castle, the scarcity of provisions and the want of fresh supplies of many articles from the country, will of itself oblige the garrison to submit to our arms.

3^{d} That supposing this last consequence not to happen, yet the driving our enemies so far from our country will be of infinite advantage in this, that it will be a means of preventing the loss of Negroes, either by desertion or otherwise by land.

4th That the country being in our possession, will not only, from principles of dread, attach the Indians to our interest, but also put it in our power to prevent our enemies from holding any intercourse with these savages, or having any opportunity to tamper with them, or supply or stir them up against us. And we conceive that after the Province shall be so broke up, a single troop of Horse, appointed to range on the west side of the river St. John's, will be quite sufficient to cut off all communication between the Creek Indians and the people of East Florida.

5th By carrying distress and war into the country, we incline to think the inhabitants of East-Florida will find themselves so much engaged at home as not to be able to fit out privateers against this Province till we are better prepared for them. This Province has been harassed, and they expect to be much more so, with privateers, in case some vigorous blow is not struck against East Florida; and we are inclined to think the plunder which will fall into the hands of the soldiers will compensate them for the difficulty and toil attending their march.

As to the other question, viz: What are the means of certainly supplying the troops with grain and meat? how is the baggage to be transported safely by water? —we are of opinion, that while the troops remain on this side of the river Alatamaha, there will be no occasion to do more than send a Commissary ahead to provide rice and beef at different stages, as the troops advance, the country all along abounding with provisions, after they pass this river. We think it will be necessary to send a quantity of rice in boats, with directions to meet the troops at different places; and we are informed that these boats may go with great safety, there being an excellent inland passage to a place called Picalatto Creek, less than twenty miles from St. Augustine. We imagine these boats must be procured in or about Savannah or Sunbury, and therefore we would recommend that the troops send such of their baggage as they can't conveniently carry in these boats. Some horses will certainly be necessary for troops upon their march, which, together with pack horses, we think may be got in this place. Wagons will be useless, as they cannot proceed above fifty miles from this town.

To President Rutledge.

Charlestown, August 20th 1776.

Dear Sir,

I suppose you have heard of the Enemy's having abandoned thr Post on the River St Mary and withdrawing all their stock and slaves within the River St John's wch will naturally contract the plan of our operations. We have neither cannon, ammunition, men sufficient, nor the means of transport to undertake the siege of St Augustine, so the whole will I believe conclude in an incursion of insult—tomorrow I shall fix on the number of Troops and the Officer to command the expedition. I shall then return to Charlestown, and arrange finally with you everything necessary to security against a second visit: Capt. Joiner has arm'd a small boat with swivels and a gun at the Bow which, on a larger scale will I am persuaded answer admirably for the defence of rivers. I wish the scheme may be adopted by your province in conjunction with the Gallies proposed will put you in a situation to laugh at their Tenders. You must excuse the shortness of this Letter as it is very late, so wishing you good night, I must desire you to believe me to be, Dr Sir, most sincerely yours,

Charles Lee.

To The Hon. John Rutledge.

From President Rutledge.

August 20th 1776.

Dr Sir,

I thank you for the Intelligence contained in yours of the 13th Instant. By Letters from Col. Williamson, dated the 5th we are informed that he had burned five of the Cherokee Indian Towns, laid waste their adjoining Fields which had plentiful Crops of Corn & was on his march to some other Towns higher up the Nation. The last accounts of the North Carolina Troops say they had not marched, but were to rendezvous the 13th instant at Quaker Meadows—The Congress will not agree to the Georgia Proposal for giving Presents of Cattle to the Creeks—Our delegates say that, in Consequence of my Letter to them, your Case having been mentioned to Congress, a Committee upon it had been appointed—The following is an Extract from Mr Saml Adams's Letter to me on that subject. "July 25—Your Proposal with regard to Gen. Lee coincides with my Inclination and Judgment. There is no one, more heartily disposed to gratify that Gentleman's Wishes than I am & I think to omit it in this Instance wd be hardly just—It has been moved in Congress & I have reason to believe the matter will be speedily compleated to your satisfaction." The Bearer, Rogers, has the Care of several stocks of Cattle in Georgia belonging to Mr Williamson, a Gentleman of this Town. He makes heavy Complaints of the Inattention of the Georgians, & their not taking the necessary steps to prevent the Enemy at Augustine supplying themselves wth Cattle from the Southern part of Georgia, which are now wholly exposed to their Depredations, where the Cattle are very numerous. He says a Troop of Horse was, some time ago stationed, a little beyond Sitilla River to protect the Cattle between that & St Marys—that this Troop was so negligent of their duty, that a party of 30 Men from Augustine actually came into their very Camp & carried off 6 of them Prisoners, and that they have lately removed 40 Miles to the Northward of Sitilla. They were, as formerly stationed, a very poor Cover, not being far enough to the Southward, but now there is none at all—Rogers says the Enemy have drove off near 4000 Head of Cattle, but that many of 'em being as yet only a little way over St Johns River, may be brought back, if attempts to get them are made soon. He is I believe a man of Credit, and can give you many particulars which it would be too tedious to write. Indeed Williamson suspects, & does not scruple to declare his opinion, that such strange Conduct is owing to some Scotch Folks in Georgia & in Augustine, but this *entre nous*—However * *

To the President and Council of the State of Georgia.

Savannah, August 23rd 1776.

Gentlemen,

It is certainly my duty, and I can assure you it is not less my inclination to put the Province in a State of Security—the proper means of effecting this security, I am in quality of Commander in Chief of the District to judge of. I shall never think myself under an obligation of specifying in detail my intentions—but only make requisitions of the materials which appear necessary to the end—to explain myself in particulars wou'd be inevitably to defeat my purposes. I hope, Gentlemen, therefore that I shall not be thought arrogant in confining myself to simple requisitions, but that you will consider the part I act in its proper light, that of a prudent Servant of the Public determin'd to render it all the service possible—On this principle I must request that Mr Bryant and Mr. Joyner may be supplied with the number and sort of boats they shall fix upon, and that all the Carpenters be order'd to work under their direction and not subjected to the Counter orders of any other man or set of men whatever.

I am Gentlemen &c

Charles Lee.

To His Excellency Archibald Bullock, President and the Gentlemen of the Council of the State of Georgia.

To the President of Congress.

Savannah in Georgia, 23rd Augt. 1776.

Sir,

Your letter with the thanks of the Continental Congress reach'd me at Purisburg. The approbation of the freely chosen Delegates of a free and uncorrupt people is certainly the highest honor that can be conferr'd on Mortal man.

I shall consider it as a fresh stimulus to excite my zeal and ardour in the glorious cause in which I am engaged—May the God of righteousness prosper your arms in every part of the Empire in proportion to the justice with which they were taken up—once more let me express the highest satisfaction and happiness I feel in this honorable testimony, and once more, let me assure the United States of America, that they cannot meet with a Servant (whatever may be my abilities) animated with a greater degree of ardor and enthusiasm for their safety, prosperity and glory.

The present State of this Province, its strength and weakness I shall transmit to the Board of War according to the directions I have received, and let me entreat you to be perswaded that I am, Sir, with the greatest respect

Your most obt and very humble Servt

Charles Lee.

To The Honorable John Hancock,
President of the Continental Congress.

From Francis Huger.

General Lee as Col. Huger informs Capt. Huger, is somewhat Dissatisfied with his manner of receiving some few touches on duty the General was yesterday pleased to give him—Capt. Huger confesses he was thrown into some little warmth upon being reprimanded for doing what he thought, considering the high provocation he receiv'd, his duty, even although Serjeants, as he well knew, were exempted in general from every manual chastisement, he however declares he had not yesterday or ever had the least intention to give General Lee the slightest dissatisfaction or affront either in his publick or private character; for in the first place, as a very young officer he must look cautiously before he adventures, and must of course yield to the General's so much superior Judgment, in the second, as a Gentleman, he would never offer an insult to another in his own House, and Is with respect,

His Excellency's

Most Obedt. Humb[e] Serv[t.]

FRAN[s] HUGER

Saturday 24th [August,] '76.

To His Excellency General Lee.

TO THE PRESIDENT AND COUNCIL OF THE STATE OF GEORGIA.

Savannah, August 24th 1776.

GENTLEMEN,

I am extreamly unfortunate in having so express'd myself as to have given the Council room to think that I have the least diffidence of their readiness and alacrity to cooperate in whatever is necessary for the public service.

I do assure you that I never entertain'd so injurious a thought, and give my word & honor that no person whatever has labour'd to represent the Council in an unfavorable light—the sole end and purpose of my letter was to apprize the President and Council of the method I intended to pursue, in order to obviate the imputation or suspicion of presumption and arrogance, as I know that Gentlemen not used to the short and concise method necessary in military operations are apt to misconstrue it into an inclination to bear down the civil authority—for these reasons, I must repeat that I thought it prudent to advise the President and Council of the method I intended to pursue in order to prevent their being surpris'd or shock'd at a short and simple requisition which to them must appear a novelty—and that I never myself entertain'd a suspicion, or has any officious Person endeavour'd to insinuate a want of zeal in your respectable Board.

I am, Gentlemen, with the greatest Respect,
Your most obed[t] humble Servt,
CHARLES LEE.

To his Excellency the President and Gentlemen of the Council of the State of Georgia.

TO THE BOARD OF WAR AND ORDNANCE.

Savanna, 27th August, 1776.

GENTLEMEN,

Any irregularity of Returns of the forces under my command, will not I hope be imputed to me, the extensive busyness of superintending the safety of so vast a territory as that which the Congress have committed to my charge renders it impossible for me to attend to the detail of Regiments, or in any reasonable time to collect and digest the various returns, but I have given orders to the Brigadiers to be as accurate as possible on this subject in their respective districts, and have no reason from my knowledge of the men, to think they will be deficient.

As a thorough knowledge of the present condition of this Colony, of its strength and weakness, is certainly a matter of very serious consideration, I shall lay before the Board the best and most accurate information I am able. Georgia is a state of much greater importance to the Empire of America than generally supposed, at least than what I myself imagin'd before I visited it, the variety of navigable Rivers, commodious harbours, and fine Inlets, the prodigious quantity of rice and immense stocks of Cattle on the Islands and on the main; but above all, the gentleness and salubrity of the winter seasons, with the conveniency of its situation for commerce with the West India Islands wou'd render it a most valuable possession to the enemy; the Altamaha (a very noble River) already furnishes a considerable quantity, and may in time furnish any quantity of lumber; the Garrison of St Augustine, and indeed the whole Province of East Florida draw their subsistence from Georgia—if all intercourse with her were cut off that nest of robbers and pirates wou'd probably fall to the ground, and of course the Empire of the United States become more round and entire—these circumstances summon'd up together must evince the importance of keeping Georgia or any part of it out of the hands of the Enemy—the means of doing it demands the utmost attention—I have turn'd my thoughts to the subject and shall beg leave to submit the result to the consideration of the Congress—The present State of the strength of this Colony consists of Colonel McIntosh's Battalion (a return of which is here inclosed) a Company of Independent artillery consisting of 3 officers & 23 privates with about twenty five hundred militia of all sorts, but in a very great part of these (as I learn from the authority of their own Captains) very little confidence can be placed—their principles being extreamly contaminated by a most pernicious banditti of Enemies to the common liberty—McIntosh's Battalion is really a very fine one (one of the best I think on the Continent) the Colonel himself a zealous most deserving citizen and an active understanding Officer—in short, a man whom I cou'd wish to recommend to the esteem of the Congress—but as perhaps it might appear a harsh task to insist on this Battalions acting with the necessary rigor against some of their nearest connexions and relations accused of being concerned in treasonable practices; it is my intention to remove 'em either into South or North Carolina where they can be more serviceable and have an opportunity of compleating themselves (which in this State from the dearth of men is impossible) and replace 'em with an equal or greater number from South Carolina—Such is the present condition of the strength of Georgia, very far from being adequate to its defence. My scheme for its security is, as Row gallies & arm'd boats are so well calculated for what is call'd the inland Navigation, I wou'd propose as great a number as possibly can be obtain'd; the nature of the navigation gives 'em an infinite advantage over vessels merely sailing which in these strait confin'd waters have no room for manœuvering—they will secure the Rivers against the predatory incursions of the Enemy—prevent the desertion of Negroes—sweep the Coast clear of Tenders; but above all, facilitate the means of the different States mutually assisting each other with Troops, Cannon, Provision and other requisites which is now effected with difficulty slowness and monstrous expense. Three gallies are already on the stocks in this Port, and we have arm'd and equipp'd several boats with swivels and one Gun on the Bow of each—the least of 'em capable of containing thirty men and row'd with fourteen oars—Sailors of whom we find so great a scarcity are not necessary for this species of vessels, the soldiers are competent to the busyness; besides the equipment of these gallies and boats, I propose establishing little Forts or Redoubts in certain situations on the Rivers S[t] Mary's, Satilla, Sapello and Altamaha which may enable us to make incursions from time to time (when circumstances require it) into East Florida, and render it dangerous for them to make attempts of a similar nature into Georgia. These Redoubts or little Forts will likewise serve as places of rendezvous, refreshment & retreat for Body's of Horse

Rangers which ought continually to be patroling on the Frontier—such are the best methods after having consulted the most intelligent people, which in my opinion can be devised for the defence and security of this State, unless indeed we cou'd prevail on the Province to contract their frontier by breaking up all their settlements on the other side of the Altamaha, which to me, I confess appears, a wiser and more economical measure, but this I am afraid is not to be accomplish'd. I must now beg leave to lay before the Board a matter of the highest concern, and which certainly demands the most serious attention of Congress, as unless remedied it may not only distress the circumstances of the Public, but bring a disgrace on the American Character —I mean the unconscionable advantages which individuals, Merchants Mechanics Farmers and Planters are suffer'd to take of the public necessities. If boats, horses, waggons, drugs, clothing, skins, necessaries, even little refreshments such as fruit or garden stuff are wanting for the soldiers, no price being regulated the extortion is monstrous, the expenses of the War must not only be extensively swell'd by this want of regulation, but the officers and soldiers are disgusted to the service by the toleration of such impositions; for instance the Virginians and North Caroliners are so much out of temper with Charlestown on this head, that shou'd it be again attack'd and the assistance of these Troops be again requisite, I am afraid we shall find a dangerous repugnance in them to march when order'd. I most devoutly wish therefore that the Congress will make it an object to remedy this evil—might they not recommend to or enjoin the Legislatures of the different states to appoint a Committee of Assessors from their respective bodies to fix the price of the different articles in their Provinces? whether this method is or is not proper, I cannot pretend to say, but something I must repeat, must be done.

The waste difficulty and expense arising from a want of method in provisioning the Troops when assembled in any particular spot upon an emergency are so great that magazines ought to be establish'd in every province, more particularly in those which have the greatest probability of being attack'd—by these means the Troops will not only be better fed but an immense saving to the Continent—for the Contractors not being press'd for time can at their leisure purchase every species necessary in these parts where they are best and cheapest but when a great and sudden demand is made either for Cattle, Corn, Spirits &c they are under a necessity of taking that which is next at hand and giving the sellers their own price—on this consideration in concurrence with the President and Council of South Carolina I have thought it expedient to establish some Magazines in South Carolina of Pork, Beef, Corn, &c besides straw and whiskey which in these low damp Countries is absolutely necessary; but at all events this establishment can be no loss to the Continent as the Beef and Pork at least can always with advantage be exported to the West Indies—were I at a less distance from the Congress I shou'd not take the liberty of laying out a single dollar without having obtain'd thr approbation; but at this distance I must assume such a power or let the Public affairs go to wreck and of course prove myself totally unworthy of the great trust the Congress has repos'd in me.

I am, Gentlemen, with the greatest Respect,

Your most obt. & very humble Sert.

CHARLES LEE.

To The Board of War & Ordnance.

I have in almost all my letters to Congress represented my distress from want of Engineers—I must once more entreat that I may be furnish'd with some—it is really impossible to carry on the public business without them.

To General John Armstrong.

Savannah, August y[e] 27th, '76.

My Dear General,

I agree with you entirely on the three works necessary to be effected for the defence of Charlestown, I had already pointed 'em out and given orders to the Engineer on the subject; and I hope the people and army will for a while shake off their inherent lethargy to accomplish these means, of their temporal Salvation. The People here are if possible more harum skarum than their sister Colony. They will propose anything, and after they have propos'd it, discover that they are incapable of performing the least. They have propos'd securing their Frontiers by constant patroles of horse Rangers, when the scheme is approv'd of they scratch their heads for some days, and at length inform you that there is a small difficulty in the way; that of the impossibility to procure a single horse—their next project is to keep their inland Navigation clear of Tenders by a numerous fleet of Guarda Costa arm'd boats, when this is agreed to, they recollect that they have not a single boat – Upon the whole I shou'd not be surpris'd if they were to propose mounting a body of Mermaids on Alligators—I am extreamly concern'd to hear of your indisposition, and think without flattery that every precaution shou'd be taken for the preservation of so valuable a Citizen, therefore if you are perswaded that moving Northward is necessary for your health, I only request that you will write to me a letter representing the necessity, as otherwise I do not think myself authoriz'd to grant the permission, as Congress had so positively appointed you to this department. I wish to God the Climate had agreed better with your Constitution as I know no General Officer so well suited to the

Command. You really in the vulgar phrase seem to have got the length of their foot.

Adieu, Dr General,

Yours most affectionately,

CHARLES LEE.

Brigadier General Armstrong

Make Bullit (to whom I shall write immediately) send his Returns to the Board of War.

TO THE PRESIDENT AND COUNCIL OF THE STATE OF GEORGIA.

Savanna, 28th August, 1776.

GENTLEMEN,

As I am fully perswaded that this State is of the highest importance to the common cause, and have its individual welfare very much at heart, I must beg leave to propose to his Excellency and the Council the measures which I conceive necessary for the general interest of the Continent as well as particular interest of Georgia—there is the greatest probability that the gentleness and salubrity of the winter season in this Climate, but above all, the immense stock of Cattle in your Islands have already determin'd the Enemy to make this Province their Winter Quarters—but if this last object is entirely removed, they will probably lay aside the design, and as the means of defence from a scarcity of men, are less in this Province than in any other, it is certainly our interest to divert their visit to some other Province more capable of resisting. When the Enemy are absolute masters of the sea, they of course command the islands, the leaving the Islands stock'd with cattle consequently is a very strange scheme of politics, it is literally preparing a table of invitation. I must therefore Gentlemen most earnestly conjure the Council as they regard the common cause, and the Interests of their own Province to consent to the removal of this Cattle immediately—Means may be devis'd of preventing any very heavy loss falling on the Proprietors by obliging the Commissaries to purchase this Cattle in preference to other for the use of the Army, but at any rate the measure is absolutely necessary.

I hope it will not be thought acting out of my Province, in lamenting the dangerous lenity which has been shewn to various manifested foes to the public liberty—it is in vain to march bodies of troops for the security of this Province; all schemes of defence will be ineffectual if such men as M^c^Kensey, Jolly, and others of the same stamp are suffer'd after having held a treasonable Correspondence with the Enemy, after having examin'd the strength and weakness of the Country to escape out of your hands and carry to the Enemy the most exact and minute intelligence, the places and method in which they can most advantageously attack you—I beg Gentlemen I may not be misunderstood and that you will not suppose I am taking upon me the airs of a Censor; I only lament your ill-tim'd humanity and as a servant of the United States (to whom the superintendence of the Safety of the Southern District against the attacks of the Enemy is committed), most earnestly entreat the President and Council to co-operate with my endeavours by removing at least from the particular situation where they can do mischief, not only the manifested Enemies, but even the suspected, and that for the future men who have demonstrated they are destitute of every sentiment of honour may not elude us by the ridiculous pledge of their Parole.

I am Gentlemen, with the greatest Respect

Your most ob^t^ very humble Servant

CHARLES LEE.

To his Excellency the President & Council.

To the President and Council of the State of Georgia.

Savannah, August 30th 1776.

Gentlemen,

I am extreamly flatter'd by your opinion that my recommendation of the Field Officers for the additional Battalions voted by the Congress for the defence of Georgia, will have great weight with your Convention and can assure you most solemnly, that my zeal for the Common Cause and my concern for the welfare and security of this Province in particular is so great, that no considerations or partiality cou'd influence me to recommend those who are not in my judgment, well qualifyed in the two great necessary points, that of recruiting expeditiously the Battalions, and afterwards bringing 'em expeditiously into proper order to answer the ends of soldiers—in this perswasion I venture to recommend Colonel Elbert for the first or musket battalion; indeed his own acknowledg'd merits and common justice, give him the strongest title without further recommendation. For his Lieut Colonel I wou'd propose Mr. Byrd, at present my Aid-de-Camp, but his connexion with me is so far from having influence in the recommendation, that it wou'd have a contrary effect, unless I seriously intended to render all the Service in my power to the Colony, for the experience I have of his capacity and spirit, will render his loss very considerable for it is far from being an easy matter to furnish ourselves with men capable of executing the difficult and hazardous office of Aid de Camp with coolness and distinctness. This gentleman besides from his connexion in Virginia will find the greater facility of procuring recruits—Mr. Jenefer of Maryland who has served this Campaign as Volunteer, is the gentleman I wou'd recommend for the horse or Rifle Battalions—He is a person of sense, spirit and honor, and what he undertakes, he will ardently undertake; His

Family and connexions are amongst the most considerable in Maryland, and I verily believe that through the influence and credit of his Brother, and other Relations, there is no man in that Province or the neighbouring who cou'd so soon raise a Regiment or the greater part of a Regiment—Mr. Drayton of your province I have been long acquainted with; he served in the same Regiment as myself; what his merits are as a Citizen you must be the best judges—He was always with us esteem'd a man of merit and worth, and I had myself a particular regard for him—I shou'd therefore consider it as an additional obligation to those I have already received from the Province, if he cou'd be appointed Lieut. Colonel to this Battalion. I confess I have not a little assum'd in even availing myself of the politeness of the President and Council referring matters of this moment to my opinion but must once more repeat that I have made it my principal aim to recommend in such a manner as to serve the Colony.

I must now Gentlemen return my sincerest thanks to your Body for their generous conduct towards the Continental Troops under my command—such acts of generosity and attention not only entitle you to a greater degree of alertness on the part of the soldiery, officers & men, but I hope will facilitate the means of compleating your establishment. On my part nothing shall be wanting to inculcate in their minds a proper sense of their obligation. I am Gentlemen,

Your most obt. & very hum Sert.

CHARLES LEE.

P. S. As Mr. Jenefer will set out tomorrow for Maryland, and as no time shou'd be lost the Council wou'd much oblige me in determining whether it will be more prudent to suppose him appointed for the Horse or Rifle Battalion, as his plan of recruiting must be regulated accordingly.

ORDERS ISSUED ON THE EXPEDITION TO GEORGIA, ETC.

Charlestown, Augt 7, 1776.

A Detachment of one Captain three Subalterns four Sergeants and Seventy rank and File from the 1st Battalion of South Carolina—the same number from the 2d —130 from the 3^{d} or Rangers with their common proportion of Officers to this number, and likewise 30 men from the Artillery with the proportion of officers and non-commission'd officers which Colonel Roberts shall determine to prepare themselves immediately for a march—They are to receive their Instructions from Gen^{e} Howe who will appoint two field officers to take the command of 'em.

Parole Garden. Beaufort Aug. 12th, 1776.

Colonel Hardens Company to march or sail with all possible expedition to Savanna—Capt. Joiner is to direct the mode and provide the means.

Col. Kershaw's corps to return to their respective homes as soon as possible. General Lee thanks 'em for their alacrity and zeal they have shewn.

Col. Garden will Garrison the Fort by detachments in the manner his judgment will admit.

The detachments of the Artillery from Charlestown and of Moutries Regiment to proceed immediately to Savanna in the manner Capt. Joiner directs.

Purisburg, August ye 15th 1776.

The Commanding Officers of the different Corps are immediately to send in returns of the Waggons & Horses in th^{r} respective Corps.

in consequence of the foregoing Orders.

	Horses.	Waggons.
Muhlenberg's Regiment.	11	42
Sumner's Ditto.	8	36
1 ammunition.	1	
Major White Com^{r} of the Volunteers	2	18
Col. Hugers Regiment	5	20
Total	27 :	116

Parole Fincastle. Purisburg, Augt 16, 1776.

Colonel Hugers and the Volunteers march to day to Mr Bryants where they must be at eight oclock. The acting Quarter Masters of each of these Corps to take an account of the Waggons & Geers they leave behind at Mr Bryant's.

They are to be put distinctly and mark'd that no confusion may arise at their return; a horse Guard of one subaltern two Serjeants two Corporals and thirty Privates to escort the Waggons and Horses round to Savanna.

Muhlenburg's and Sumner's to march as soon as the Boats return to Mr Bryant—they are to separate th^{r} Geers and Waggons in the same manner as directed to the other two Corps, and appoint a horse Guard to conduct th^{r} Horses to Savanna—if any Horses are lost the regiment will be responsible for 'em.

Parole Bullock. Savanna, Aug. 17, 1776.

As the different Corps are to be furnished with Powder horns and shot bags The Colonels to make out a return of the number wanting to completion.

Parole M[c]Intosh. Savanna, Aug. 18, 1776.

The Keeper of the Magazine to send in a return immediately of the Guns, ammunition and every sort of military apparatus not only in Savannah but the different Posts.

After Orders. Every Corps, the Georgian Battalion as well as the Troops lately arrived, to parade to-morrow morning at ten o'Clock, in order that th[r] arms accoutrements cloathing and Blankets may be inspected —Colonel M[c]Intosh will appoint the place of parade and inform Brigade Major Simmonds of the place appointed.

Parole Bryan. Savanna Aug[t] 20, '76.

Any Officer who refuses to obey an order delivered him by one of the General's Aid de Camps shall immediately be put under arrest let his rank be whatever it will.

Parole Sunbury. Savanna, Aug[t] 21, 1776.

Colonel Mughlenburg's Regiment to be supplied with two flints per man from the Stores—Capt. Harden's Company to furnish themselves immediately with skins for Monkeshins and leggings—powder horns and shot bags. Those who have not arms shall be furnish'd at Sunbury to which place they and Muhlenburg's are to march to-morrow morning—Hardens to have two spare Flints.

Col[o] Mughlenburg's Regiment & Capt. Harden's Company are to parade this afternoon at half past five in the rear of the Garden Battery.

Parole Elbert. Savannah, Aug[t] 22d

A Garrison Court martial to be held to morrow to

try all Prisoners brought before 'em—the necessary Witnesses to be summon'd.

A Captain & fifty men for fatigue—the Quarter master to be apply'd to for twenty Axes to cut timber for the construction of certain works thought necessary.

Parole Houston, Savanna 23^{d} Augt 1776.

The Officers of the different Corps whose soldiers are not yet supplied with Dearskins to dress for Mankaskins & Leggings are this day to apply to the Quarter Master of the Georgia Battalion who is to deliver 'em.

After Orders. As the dates of the Commissions of the Georgia Battalion commanded by Colonel McIntosh are on the first of January and as a late positive Resolve of the Continental Congress declaring the 1st & 2^{d} Battalions of South Carolina to be on the Continental establishment explicitly gives to the said Battalions rank from the fourth of November there can be no room for dispute on this subject—the two Carolina Battalions have the precedence of course.

After Orders. The Officers of the different Corps are immediately to send in a return of their convalescents & of such who are not so indispos'd but what with fresh air and attendance will in all probability speedily recover.

Parole ——. Savanna, 25 Augt 1776.

The Artillery of South Carolina agreeable to Resolve of the Continental Congress take rank from the of Novr last.

Savanna, 24 Augt 1776.

After Orders. The Party of a Captain and Sixty men which was ordered to be in readiness to march tomorrow morning to Skidaway and post themselves according to the directions of an Officer of Col. M[c]Intosh's Battalion who is to conduct and inform 'em of the nature of the Country and the duty they are to do.

Parole Fincastle. Savanna 25 Aug. 76.

Besides the party already ordered for fatigue a subaltern and thirty men of Major Mason's Detachment from Thompson's Rangers are to parade to morrow morning precisely at six o'clock.

Savanna, August y[e] 28th

2nd Lt. De la Plaine of the Georgian Battalion is appoint'd to do duty as 1st Lt. Ensign Morrison of 2d Lt. 'till the pleasure of the Congress is further known. The Court Martial of which Colonel Huger was President is approv'd of and dissolv'd—the sentence of Corporal punishment on the different Prisoners is commuted by the General into five days Confinement in the black hole—where They are to be confin'd to rice and water—They are to be convey'[d] thither tomorrow morning—a Corporal and six to mount on the place of their confinement and if it is discover'd that any other provisions are Convey'd to 'em—the Corporal will be try'd for disobedience of orders and a violation of his duty.

To the Governor at Cape Francois.

Savannah, Aug. 30th, 1776.

Sir,

It will be necessary in addressing a letter of this nature, so abruptly to your excellency, that I should inform you who the writer is. I have served as lieutenant-colonel in the English service, colonel in the Portuguese, afterwards as aid du camp to his Polish majesty, with the rank of major general. Having purchased a small estate in America, I had determined to retire, for the remainder of my days, to a peaceful asylum: when the tyranny of the ministry, and court of Great Britain, forced this continent to arms, for the preservation of their liberties, I was called, by the voice of the people, to the rank of second in command. I make no doubt of this letter's being kindly received by your Excellency, both in the character of a good Frenchman, and friend to humanity. The present conjuncture of affairs renders the interest of France and of this continent one and the same thing; every observation drawn from history must evince, that it was the exclusive commerce of these colonies, which enabled Great Britain to cope with France, gave to her a decided superiority in marine, and, of course, enabled her in the frequent wars betwixt the two nations to reduce her rival to the last extremity. This was the case, so peculiarly in the last war, that had the British ministry persevered, Heaven knows what would have been the fate of France. It follows, that if France can obtain the monopoly, or the greater part of this commerce, her opulence, strength, and prosperity, must grow to a prodigious height; and nothing can be more certain, than that if America is enabled to preserve the independence she has now declared, the greater part of this commerce, if not the monopoly, must fall to the share of France.

The imaginary plans of conquest of Lewis the Fourteenth, had they been realized, would not have established the power of that monarchy, on so solid and permanent a basis, as the simple assistance, or rather friendly intercourse with this continent, will inevitably give. Without injustice, or the colour of injustice, but, on the contrary, only assuming the patronage of the rights of mankind, France has now in her power to become not only the greatest, but the most truly glorious monarchy which has appeared on the stage of the world. In the first place, her possessions in the islands will be secured against all possibility of attack; the royal revenues immensely increased, her people eased of their present burdens, an eternal incitement be presented to their industry, and the means of increase by the facility of providing sustenance for their families multiplied. In short, there is no saying what degree of eminence, happiness, and glory, she may derive from the independence of this continent. Some visionary writers have indeed asserted, that could this country once shake off her European trammels, it would soon become more formidable alone, from the virtue and energy, natural to a young people, than Great Britain with her colonies united in a state of dependency. But the men who have built such hypotheses must be utter strangers to the manners, genius, disposition, turn of mind, and circumstances of the continent. Their disposition is manifestly to agriculture and the simple life of shepherds. As long as vast tracts of land remain unoccupied, to which they can send colonies (if I may so express it) of their offspring, they will never entertain a thought of marine or manufactures. Their ideas are solely confined to labour and to planting, for those nations, who can, on the cheapest terms, furnish them with the necessary utensils for labouring and planting, and clothes for their families; and till the whole vast extent of continent is fully stocked with people, they will never entertain another idea. This cannot be effected for ages; and what then may happen, it is out of the line of politicians to lay any stress upon: most probably, they will be employed in wars amongst themselves, before they aim at foreign conquests. In short, the apprehension is too remote to rouse the jealousy of any reasonable citizen of a foreign state. On the other hand, it is worthy your Excellency's attention to consider what will be the consequences, should Great Britain succeed in the present contest. America, it is true, will be wretched and enslaved; but a number of slaves may compose a formidable army and fleet.

The proximity of situation, with so great a force, entirely at the disposal of Great Britain, will put in her power to take possession of your islands on the first rupture. Without pretending to the spirit of prophesy, such, I can assert, will be the event of the next war; upon the whole, I must repeat, that it is for the interest, as well as glory of France, to furnish us with every means of supporting our liberties, to effect which, we only demand a constant systematic supply of the necessaries of war. We do not require any aid of men, we have numbers, and, I believe, courage sufficient to carry us triumphantly through the struggle. We require small arms, powder, field-pieces, woollen and linen to clothe our troops: also drugs, particularly bark: in return for which, every necessary provision for your islands may be expected, as rice, corn, lumber, &c. If, indeed, you could spare us a few able engineers, and artillery officers, they may depend upon an honourable reception and comfortable establishment. The Sieur de la Plain, one of your countrymen, now engaged in the cause of the United States of America will have the honour of delivering this letter to your Excellency. I have no doubt of his being received with that politeness, and kindness, to be expected from a gentleman of your rank and character.

I am, with the highest respect, your Excellency's most obedient servant,

CHARLES LEE.

To His Excellency the Governor at Cape François.

ORDERS.

September 9th [1776.]

GEN. LEE thinks it his duty before his departure to express the high sense he entertains of the conduct and behavior of the colonels and officers of the several battalions of South-Carolina, both as gentlemen and soldiers; and begs leave to assure them, that he thinks himself obliged to report their merit to the Continental Congress.

To the President of Congress.

Princeton, October 10, 1776.

Sir:

The ridiculous idea, that Lord Howe has some reasonable terms to offer, and that the Congress are desirous of their being communicated to the people, gains ground every day. This idea is strengthened by the industry of the disaffected, and does infinite mischief; I would therefore, with submission, offer it to the consideration of Congress, whether it would not be politick, in order to efface these impressions, suffer some gentlemen in the simple character of individuals who are supposed to have influence, to propose a conference with his Lordship on this subject, and demand what terms he has to offer. He most assuredly has none, but unconditional submission. His public declaration ought, it is true, to satisfy every reasonable man of this being the ultimatum; but in our present circumstances, the unreasonable and weak must be satisfied, as well as the sensible and reasonable. A committee deputed from the Congress after what has happened, would be highly improper, as it would convey an idea that they themselves did not consider independency absolutely fixed, for which reason it would be more prudent that they should suffer one or two persons in whom they can confide, to propose the conference in their private characters, who may afterwards relate, explain, and comment at large on the circumstances. I perhaps may be wrong in my conjectures, but as I am persuaded it would have a salutary effect, I cannot reconcile it to my conscience to withhold my opinion, an opinion, I can assure you, Sir, in which I am not singular, for many very sensible men, and the most active friends to the cause in this Province and the others I have passed through, concur with me. At all events, I hope the Congress will not think me impertinent, and presuming in intruding it, but impute it to my anxiety and zeal for the publick welfare.

This Province is so much weaker in numbers than I imagined in leaving Philadelphia, that the sooner the Virginia battalions march, at least as far as Brunswick, the better. You must, Sir, excuse the blots of this letter as I have not paper for a more legible copy.

I am, Sir, with the greatest respect, your most humble obedient Servant

Charles Lee.

To the President of Congress.

To the President of Congress.

Amboy, October 12, 1776.

Sir:

The Hessians who were encamped opposite this post, last night disappeared, and there is the greatest reason to think that they have quitted the island entirely, which announces some great manœuvre to be in agitation. I am confident they will not attack General Washington's lines: such a measure is too absurd for a man of Mr Howe's genius; and unless they have received flattering accounts from Burgoyne that he will be able to effectuate a junction, (which I conceive they have not) they will no longer remain kicking their heels at New York. They will put the place in a respectable state of defence, which with their command of the waters may be easily done, leave four or five thousand men, and direct their operations to a more decisive object. They will infallibly proceed either immediately up the river Delaware with their whole troops, or what is more probable, land somewhere about South

Amboy or Shrewsbury, and march straight to Trenton or Burlington. We must suppose every case. On the supposition that this will be the case, what are we to do? What force have we? What means have we to prevent their possessing themselves of Philadelphia? General Washington's army cannot possibly keep pace with them. The length of his route is not only infinitely greater, but his obstructions almost insuperable; in short, before he could cross Hudson river, they might be lodged and strongly fortified on both banks of the Delaware. I shall make no apologies to Congress for thus so freely offering my opinion; the importance of the matter is a sufficient apology. For Heaven's sake, rouse yourselves; for Heaven's sake, let ten thousand men be immediately assembled and stationed somewhere about Trenton. In my opinion your whole depends upon it. I set out immediately for Head Quarters, where I shall communicate my apprehension that such will be the next operation of the enemy, and urge the expediency of sparing a part of his army (if he has any to spare) for this object.

I am, Sir, with the greatest respect, your most obedient humble Servant

CHARLES LEE.

To the President of Congress.

To General Gates.

Fort Constitution, October ye 14th.

MY DEAR GATES,

I write this scroll in a hurry—Colonel Wood will describe the position of our Army, which in my own breast I do not approve—*inter nos* the Congress seem to stumble every step—I do not mean one or two of the Cattle, but the whole Stable—I have been very free in delivering my opinion to 'em—in my opinion General Washington is much to blame in not menacing 'em with resignation unless they refrain from unhinging the army by their absurd interference—Keep us Tionderoga; much depends upon it—We ought to have an army on the Delaware—I have roar'd it in the ears of Congress, but *carent auribus*.

Adieu, my Dr. Friend; if we do meet again, why we shall smile.

Yours, C. LEE.

To BENJAMIN RUSH.

Camp at Philipsburg Nov. ye 2nd 1776.

DR RUSH,

A Dragoon Deserter from Burgoyne's Regt. will deliver you this—He is a very intelligent fellow and I believe very honest. He is by trade a Weaver and I recommend him to your protection, by which I mean that you will put him in the best way to avail himself of his weaving talents—We are now, thank God, and the inertness of the Enemy, in a very tolerable secure condition. Mr Howe has but two moves by which He can distress us, and I flatter myself We shall be able to check-mate him in both—the various skirmishes We have had with him have been rather favorable to us than the reverse—three of the four have fallen on my division—Glover, an admirable officer acting Brigadier fairly beat 'em—a shooting match betwixt the Riflers and Hessian Chasseurs demonstrated our superiority at this time the Parties were equal in numbers, and We won the match We lost but one Man, buryed ten of theirs and took three. McDougal, it is true, in the last affair was oblig'd to retreat by the superiority of their Artillery; but He lost no credit—the loss on their side was very considerable in short He is a sensible brave Officer. When We are once fairly out of this damn'd *cul de sac* I think you will hear good accounts of us; We shall I am persuaded, harrass 'em most damnably

Our only distresses seem to me to arise from a total want of method and a little narrow dirty economy in all things relating to the Hospital and Quarter Master General departments—thrice since my arrival have We been in the Jaws of perdition from a scarcity of teams —for God's sake get some military men into your Senate, for *inter nos* all the resolves of Congress relating to Military affairs are absurd, ridiculous and ruinous. They raise the laughter and provoke the indignation of every Man of Common Sense. Where is the Cloathing so long promis'd for the Army? Why do you not make an handsome establishment for Engineers? We have three very able Foreigners in my family, and you put New-England Carpenters at the head of this important Department. Why have you not Magazines establish'd in various Provinces? It wou'd be curious œconomy in a master of a Family who kept a constant table to send every day to the Tavern for bottles of Wine rather than lay in a few pipes in his cellar. Just so you act.

As it is most probable that the operations in this part of the World will cease in three weeks or a month, I must intreat your High Mightinesses to let me return to my Southern district, as I dread the podagraferous quality of this freezing Climate. Don't you think it possible the Enemy may direct their course towards Philadelphia when They find themselves baffled here? A Corps of Observation shou'd in my opinion be station'd at Trenton or Bristol—it is late—God bless you. Good night—my love to the Lees and Bob Morris.

Yours, Dr Rush, Most Sincerely,

CHARLES LEE.

P. S. I wish you would desire little Bass to send me the bottle of Panacea.

To Doctor Benjamin Rush,
Member Continental Congress,
Philadelphia.

Gen. Schuyler to P. R. Livingston.

Albany Novr 3^{d} 1776.

Sir,

I do myself the honor to enclose you an Extract of a Letter from General Gates of the 31st ult^{o} with copy of one from Major Hoisington to him. If Sir John Johnson left Canada at the Time the Deserters mention, he has probably met with such Difficulties, as have obliged him to return, as I think he could not subsist from that Time to this in the woods. We have no less than eleven different Scoutts traversing the Country between Ticonderoga and fort Stanwix, so that I am in hopes should the Enemy attempt to penetrate to the Mohawk River, we shall have such early information as to enable us to meet him with a sufficient force. I have already ordered two Regiments from Ticonderoga to Tryon County and about one thousand of the Militia, so that our force there exclusive of the Militia of that County will amount to Two thousand men besides the Garrison of Fort Schuyler.

I wish the Convention would order the depth & Breadth of Hudson River to be carefully taken, at such places as they conceive would be most proper effectually to obstruct the Navigation. Verplanks point or Jan Canteen Hook may be proper places, perhaps the latter the most eligible of any.

I propose taking the Earliest opportunity that is afforded me to prepare everything for it—at present I cannot, as I have neither Troops nor Carpenters the latter being all employed in constructing Barracks.

I am Sir with great Respect,

Your most obedient humble Servt

Ph. Schuyler.

Peter R. Livingston, Esq. Prest.

[*Inclosed in the preceding letter.*]

TO HIS EXCELLENCY MAJOR GENERAL GATES.

Intelligence given by four Deserters from Canada, who enlisted out of Prison at Quebeck into the Royal Emigrant Regiment commanded by Col° McClean is, that on the 25th of Septr. they left Montreal and before they left the above place Sir John Johnson with the Indians and Canadians & 8th Regiment had marched to attack the Inhabitants on the Mohawk River and meet General Burgoyne at Albany who has ordered all the Forces from Chamblée & Sorell to St Johns with the Marines and train of Artillery & Sailors, to but three men in each vessel. Likewise as they passed on each side of the Lake on Sunday the 6th Instant, heard a very heavy Cannonade on the Lake, supposed to be with the Fleet.

The above Deserters were found by one of my scouts about 40 miles out, destitute of provisions and very weak. They being desirous to go to Head Quarters near New York I have passed the above Deserters for that place.

I am Sir,

Your most obedient humble Servt

JOAB HOISINGTON.

New Bury, Oct. 12th 1776.

Endorsed: Mr Hoisington with the Rank of Major Commands several Companies of Rangers embodied in Gloucester & Cumberland Counties raised to serve during the war subject to the Convention of this State and the Commander of the Northern Army.

To Dr. Benjamin Franklin.

Camp at Phillipsburg, November 6th 1776.

Dear Sir:

The gentleman who will deliver you this, was, as I understand, sent by Congress to General Washington. He was to have given specimens of his abilities as engineer, and been recommended accordingly. Whether he is a great engineer or no, I cannot pretend to say, as he has had no fair opportunity of displaying his talents. The few small works he has thrown up have been in haste, at the same time labouring under the disadvantage of not being able to explain himself to the workmen. From the little I can judge of him, he is a man of capacity and knowledge, and I am told by his countrymen, that his fort lies in surveying geographically and military a country. I know not any kind of officer more wanted in America than a military surveyor of those parts which are likely to be the scene of action. General Washington and myself have therefore concurred in opinion that he should begin with the Jerseys; and if he gives satisfactory proofs of his talents in this line, to recommend him to Congress for this important office. I must beg leave to recommend him to your protection and patronage, and request that you will furnish him with the necessary instruments. And as I am so well acquainted with your liberal way of thinking and manners, it will be unnecessary to desire you to show him all possible personal civilities.

So far for Monsieur Imbert. You will naturally expect something from me on your present situation. We have by proper positions brought Mr. Howe to his *ne plus ultra.* He has therefore apparently given [up] all hopes of taking us prisoners, as I believe he lately sanguinely promised himself. Monsieur Imbert, as you know French, will be able to explain the circumstances of both armies. The spirit of our present troops is upon the whole good, and if America is lost, it is not in my opinion owing to want of courage in your soldiers, but, pardon me, to want of prudence in your high mightinesses. Adieu! God bless you, my dear sir. Live long and make your country and friends as happy as you have rendered yourself admirable in the eyes of all good and sensible men.

Yours, most sincerely,

CHARLES LEE.

D[r] Benjamin Franklin,
Member of the Continental Congress.

FROM GENERAL WASHINGTON.

[*Instructions.*]

SIR:

The late movement of the enemy, and the probability of their having designs upon the Jerseys, confirmed by sundry accounts from deserters and prisoners, rendering it necessary to throw a body of troops over the North river, I shall immediately follow; and the command of the army which remains, after General Heath's division marches to Peekskill, devolving upon you, I have to request—

That you will be particularly attentive that all the intrenching and other tools, excepting those in immediate use, be got together and delivered to the Quartermaster General, or Major Reed, who heretofore has been intrusted with them.

That you will direct the commanding officer of Artillery to exert himself in having the Army well supplied with musket cartridges; for this purpose, a convenient place at a distance should be fixed upon that the business may go on uninterrupted.

That no troops who have been furnished with arms, accoutrements, or camp utensils, be suffered to depart the camp before they have delivered them either to the Commissary of stores or the Quartermaster General, or his assistant, as the case may be, taking receipts therefore, in exoneration of those which they have passed. In a particular manner, let the tents be taken care of, and committed to the Quartermaster General's care.

A little time now must manifest the enemy's designs, and point out to you measures proper to be pursued by that part of the Army under your command. I shall give no directions, therefore, on this head, having the most entire confidence in your judgment and military exertions. One thing, however, I will suggest, namely: that as the appearance of embarking troops for the Jerseys may be intended as a feint to weaken us, and render the strong post we now hold more vulnerable, or if they find that troops are assembled with more expedition, and in greater numbers than they expected on the Jersey shore to oppose them;—I say, as it is possible, from one or the other of these motives, they may yet pay the army under your command a visit, it will be unnecessary, I am persuaded, to recommend to you the propriety of putting this post, if you stay at it, into a proper posture of defence, and guarding against surprises. But I would recommend it to your consideration whether, under the suggestion above, your retiring to Croton Bridge and some strong post still more easterly (covering the passes through the Highlands) may not be more advisable than to run the hazard of an attack with unequal numbers. At any rate, I think all your baggage and stores, except such as are necessary for immediate use, ought to be the northward of Croton river.

In case of your removal from hence, I submit to the consideration of yourself and the general officers with you, the propriety of destroying the hay, to prevent the enemy from reaping the benefit of it.

You will consider the post at Croton's (or Pines) Bridge as under your immediate care, as also that lately occupied by General Parsons, and the other at Wright's Mill. The first I am taught to believe is of consequence; the other two can be of little use while the enemy hover about the North River, and upon our right flank.

Gen. Wooster, from the state of Connecticut, and by order of the Governour, with several regiments of Militia, are now I presume in or about Stamford. They were to receive orders from me; of course they are to do it from you. There are also some other regiments of Connecticut Militia, who came out with General Saltonstall, and annexed to General Parsons's Brigade, and others which you must dispose of as occasion and circumstances shall require; but as by the late returns, many of those regiments are reduced to little more than a large company, I recommend the discharge of all such supernumerary officers, and the others annexed to some brigade.

As the season will soon oblige the enemy to betake themselves to winter-quarters, and will not permit our troops to remain much longer in tents, it may be well to consider in time where magazines of provisions and forage should be laid in for the army on the east side Hudson's river. Peekskill, or the neighbourhood, would, I should think, be a very advantageous post for as many as can be supported there. Croton Bridge may probably be another good deposite, or somewhere more easterly, for the rest, as the Commissary, Quartermaster, &c., may assist in pointing out.

It may not be amiss to remind you, for it must (as it ought to) have some influence on your deliberations and measures, that the Massachusetts Militia stand released from their contract the 17th this instant, and that the Connecticut Militia are not engaged for any fixed period; and by what I can learn, begin to grow very impatient to return, few indeed of whom being left. If the enemy should remove the whole, or the greatest part of their force, to the west side of Hudson's river, I have no doubt of your following, with all possible despatch, leaving the Militia and invalids to cover the frontiers of Connecticut, &c. in case of need.

Given at Head-quarters, near the White Plains, this 10th November, 1776.

Go. WASHINGTON.

To Major General Lee.

TO GENERAL GREENE.

Camp at North Castle Novr ye 11th. [1776.]

MY DR GENERAL,

If you should be taken by the enemy it would be really a very serious affair, for I should have a chance of losing my horse and sulky to prevent so melancholy an event, I must request that you will send wd up to me by the Serv who will deliver you this.

I have just received a letter with the good news of the total defeat of the Cherokees I begin to think my friend Howe has lost the campaign and that his most Gracious Majesty must request a Body of Russians to reestablish order tranquillity happiness and good government amongst his deluded subjects of America. God bless you, my dr General May you live long and reap twice a year an abundant crop of laurels.

Yours most sincerely

CHARLES LEE.

FROM GENERAL WASHINGTON.

Peekskill, November 12th 1776.

DEAR SIR:

Enclosed you will find a copy of sundry resolutions of Congress, which came to hand since I left the Plains. They will discover to you their opinion as to the necessity of taking the most early measures to levy the new Army. The resolves cannot have any operation but in the instance of the Rhode Island regiments, Commissioners having come from the states of Massachusetts and Connecticut, and being on the way from Maryland. They will be superseded, too, if any have arrived from Rhode Island; therefore the resolutions are under that condition.

As it is of the last importance that the recruiting service should be begun, I must request, if the Commissioners are not arrived from Rhode Island, that you will call upon Colonel Hitchcock, who will inform you of the officers recommended to that State by General Greene, &c and give orders to them to begin their inlistments immediately, on the terms and conditions allowed by Congress. Such of them as agree to stay, and will undertake the business, will be commissioned according to the rank assigned 'em in that recommendation. I have not got it by me, having sent it away with my papers before I came from Harlem.

In respect to the militia, you will try your influence to get them to remain; perhaps the requisition from Congress for that purpose may have some effect, though I have but little expectation that it will.

The enclosed letter for Colonel Darby you will please to send in by the first flag.

I cannot conclude without reminding you of the military and other stores about your encampment and at North Castle, and to press the removal of them above Croton Bridge, or such other places of security as you may judge proper. General Howe having sent no part of his force to Jersey yet, makes the measure more necessary, as he may perhaps turn his views another way, and attempt their destruction.

I have directed Colonel Putnam to examine the passes in the Highlands eastward of this place, and to lay out such works as may be necessary to secure 'em. When you remove your present encampment, you will assign such a number of men to the several posts as you shall deem sufficient for their defence.

I hope the trial of Major Austin for burning the

houses will not be forgot; publick justice requires that it should be brought on as soon as it can.

I am, &c

Go. Washington.

To Major General Lee.

Resolves of Congress.

[*Enclosed in the foregoing letter.*]

In Congress, Nov. 4th 1776.

Whereas it is manifest, that unless effective measures are immediately taken for re-inlisting the Army, the Safety of the States may be greatly endangered.

Resolv'd, That the President be desired to write to the Commander in Chief and inform him that if upon receipt of this resolution, Commissioners from the respective States, for the purpose of appointing Officers, shall not have arrived, that then he after consulting & advising with such of his Generals, as he can conveniently call together, immediately grant warrants to such of the Officers from the respective States, who have not Commissioners present, authorized as aforesaid, as he shall think deserving of Commissions, that the Officers so appointed proceed with the utmost expedition to recruit their regiments to their full complement; that Commns be sent to Genl. Washington as soon as possible to be given to such officers as he shall appoint by Warrant, in consequence of the foregoing Resolution.

That the Commander in Chief be desired to take such steps, as he shall think most proper, for continuing the Militia now in Camp, that for this purpose, he write to such of the States as now have Militia in the government of New York, requesting their assistance in this business and that he further be directed to apply to the neighbouring States for such additional aid as he may require.

By Ord^r of Congress

JNO. HANCOCK, Prest.

TO GENERAL WASHINGTON.

Camp at Phillipsburg, November ye 12th,
nine o'clock, P.M.

DEAR GENERAL,

This instant came express from Colonel Tupper (stationed opposite to Dobb's Ferry,) one David Keech. The substance of his intelligence is as follows: That the enemy began their march at nine this morning, down the river, with their baggage, artillery, &c &c; that the man of war and two store ships had just set sail, and were making down—I mean those which came up last. The three ships still lie off Tarrytown and Sing-sing—two at the former, one at the latter. Keech says the whole army have quitted Dobbs's Ferry, and imagines the rear have by this time reached King's Bridge.

I am far from being satisfied with the conduct of our scouts. I do not think they venture far enough, for they in general bring back very lame, imperfect accounts. But I have projected a plan for breaking in at least, upon Rogers's party, and believe I shall succeed.

The sentence on Austin is that he should be reprimanded; but I have ordered a new Court Martial, with a charge of wanton, barbarous conduct, unbecoming not only an officer, but a human creature.

General Lincoln and the Massachusetts committee are using their efforts to detain the Militia. Whether they succeed, Heaven only knows. Hitchcock and Varnum do not recollect the recommendation of General Greene; but I have ordered them to give me a list of those whom they think ought to be recommended; for it is now too late to refer to Greene, as the Commissioners are expected every hour.

I wish to God you were here, as I am, in a manner, a stranger to their respective merits. When the list is made out, I shall inform myself, (as well as I can) if their recommendation is impartial, and proceed accordingly.

I am, dear General, yours, most sincerely.

CHARLES LEE.

To his Excellency General Washington.

FROM GEN. DAVID WOOSTER.

Greenwich, 12th Nov. 1776.

DEAR SR.

I this moment Recd your favor of yesterday & this will be handed you by Capt. Hills, and beg leave to acquaint you that I have posted the Regt belonging Norwalk, Stanford and Greenwich in their respective Towns for the security of them—of the other three Regts there are but four hundred and thirty yet arrived, including officers but more are expected and about ninety Light Horse We have no Tents and but about three Rounds of Powder and Ball per man—the Towns to the Eastward had furnished the Militia as they came to join the Continental Army till they were exhausted —I sent my Aid de Camp yesterday to wait on Gen Washington for an order to Draw Powder and Lead, but an order from you would serve the same purpose. I shall strictly attend your orders and am Dear Sir most respectfully

Yr very humble Servant

D. W[OOSTER]

The Honble Maj. Gen. Lee.

FROM LIEUT. COL. WILLIAM PALFREY.

Stamford Wednesday Evening, 13th Novr 1776.

MY DEAR GENERAL,

In consequence of orders I receiv'd from General Washington, I shall set off early tomorrow morning from this Place for Peek's Kill, & shall take my quarters at Captn Drake's about 2 miles on this side the *Kill*, and where I shall attend to transact the Business of my office. If circumstances would permit, I should be glad to remain here—it is ten miles nearer Head Quarters, and a well known road—but I must obey orders.

I intended to have gone to Peeks Kill this Morning, but was prevented by an alarm, which was given about ten o'clock, A. M. that the Enemy were landing a number of men from one of their ships of war at a place called Long Neck about four miles East from here. As I was the oldest officer in the place I took the Command, & mustered all the men who I could persuade to go; they consisted principally of returned Militia—Invalids stationed in the Town & a *few* of the Inhabitants to the amount of about fifty. I marched them down with all possible Expedition, crossed a small Creek in a Gondola, but before we had got to the spot the Enemy had compleated their Business & retreated—A Number of Cattle were on the Neck, they kill'd only two which they carried off, as we discovered by the Tracks of blood to the Waters Edge. There was about fifty of them, and they landed in three Boats. Shortly after we got down the Man of War weigh'd anchor, came to sail, & stood down the sound towards New York. The shore here is amazingly Expos'd and I am confident if 500 men were to land in the Night they might make themselves Masters of all the stock hereabouts.

As I have receiv'd no orders respecting the payment of the Militia—I should be exceeding glad to know whether I am to pay them or not. Unless the greatest care imaginable is taken, the Continent will be subject to the grossest impositions. It is well known that many of these Gentry have deserted—they deserve no pay & they should receive none. No warrant should be granted upon an abstract, unless it is certified to be just, by the command[g] officer of the Brigade and afterwards examined by Colonel Scammel to see if it be right Cast & the pay agreeable to the Continental Establishment.

As soon as I can get myself properly fix'd, I shall do myself the honor of waiting upon you—I must needs say I can't see the fun of going to Peek's Kill.

As a Guard will be necessary for the Security of the Continental Cash, & no Troops are station'd within two Miles of my intended Quarters, I must request the favor of you to send me an order for a sufficient Guard. If it is agreeable to you I should be glad to have Capt. Dixon of Lasher's Regiment, he is an acquaintance of mine, & an officer I can depend upon. I think, considering the risque, a Captains Guard will not be too great a one.

My Comp[ts] to Messieurs Les Francois & the Gentlemen of your Suite.

I am most Sincerely & Respectfully, My dear General, Yours,

W[M] PALFREY

I have paid your Warrant to M[r] Williams.

To Major General Lee
at North Castle
by M[r] Williams.

From General Washington.

General Greene's Quarters, November 14th 1776.

Dear Sir:

As an exchange of prisoners is likely to take effect as soon as the nature of the place will admit, and as in the course of the transaction it may possibly happen that an attempt may be made by the enemy to redeem their prisoners by men who were never engaged in our service, I must request you immediately to direct the Colonels or commanders of regiments in your division, to make out an exact list of the particular officers and privates who have been killed, taken prisoners, or are missing, in the respective regiments and companies to which they belong, specifying the names of the whole, and the time when each officer or private was killed, taken prisoner, or missing. This list, as soon as it is completed, you will transmit to Head Quarters.

I am, Sir, your most obedient Servant,

Go. Washington.

Major General Lee.

P.S. I now enclose you a copy of the recommendation of the officers for the state of Rhode Island, which was furnished by General Greene, and transmitted by me to Governour Cooke, some time since. If the Commissioners have not yet arrived from thence, you will be pleased to direct the officers therein nominated, who choose to serve, to recruit as fast as possible out of their own regiments, and agreeable to the general orders issued at the White Plains before my departure.

To the Governor of Rhode Island.

Camp North Castle Nov. y[e] 14th 1776.

Dr Sir,

There is no doubt of a considerable force being embarked or about to embark in Staten Island. They give out that S. Carolina is the place of their destination—but as it is not impossible or improbable that They may have some designs against Rhode Island, either on a pillaging scheme, or perhaps with a view of establishing winter quarters for a Part of their Troops as they find themselves straightened at N. York I think it my duty to apprise your Honour of their preparations, that you may be upon your guard—either by removing your stock—fortifying yourselves, or in short by taking such measures as your wisdom shall dictate for the welfare of America and your particular security.

I beg my respects to the Gentlemen of your Council—to the Province at large—and that you will personally be assured that I am Dr Sir, with the greatest truth,

Your most obdient humble Servt
CHARLES LEE.

[To the Hon. Nicholas Cooke Esq
Governor of the State of Rhode Island.]

FROM GEN. DAVID WOOSTER.

Sawpits, Novr 15th 1776.

D^R SIR,

I herewith send three men, who say they deserted from the Infamous Col^o Rogers's Reg^t of Rangers, one belongs to Col^o Hands Reg^t and the other two to Col. Smallwoods; they will give an account of the Situation and movements of the Enemy.

The Enemy who landed at Stanford only got two or three Cattle, and on the approach of the Militia retired on board, and made sail immediately.

I have enclosed a newspaper of a late date.

I am Sir Your very humble Servt.
DAV^D WOOSTER

The Honble Major Genl. Lee

FROM GENERAL WASHINGTON.

Gen[l] Green's Q[rs] Nov[r] 16. 1776.

DEAR SIR,

You will perceive by the inclosed Resolves that Congress have entered into some new Regulations respecting the Inlistment of the new Army and reprobating the measures adopted by the State of Massachusetts-Bay for raising their Quota of men.

As every possible exertion should be used for recruiting the Army as speedily as may be, I request that you immediately publish in orders, that an allowance of a Dollar & one third of a Dollar will be paid to the officers for every soldier they shall enlist, whether in or out of Camp. Also that it will be optional in the soldiers to enlist during the continuance of the war or for three years unless sooner discharged by Congress. In the former case they are to receive all such bounty and pay as have been heretofore mentioned in orders; Those who engaged for the latter time, that of three years, are not to receive the bounty in land.

That no mistakes may be made you will direct the recruiting Officers from your division to provide two distinct Inlisting Polls, one for those to sign who engage during the war, the other for those who enlist for Three years, if their services shall be so long required.

I am sorry to inform you, that this day about 12 o'clock, the Enemy made a General Attack upon our Lines about Fort Washington, which having carried the Garrison retired within the Fort—Co[l] Magaw finding there was no prospect of retreating across the North River, surrendered the post. We do not yet know the loss of killed and wounded on either side, but I imagine it must have been pretty considerable, as the Engagement at some parts of the Lines was of long continuance and heavy; neither do I know the terms of capitulation. The force of the Garrison before the attack was about 2000 men.

Before I left Peeks Kill I urged to Gen[l] Heath the necessity of securing the pass thro' the Highlands next to the River as well on that as this side, and to the Forts above; But as the preserving of these and others which lay more Easterly & which are equally essential is a matter of the last importance, I must beg you to turn your attention that way, and to have such measures adopted for their defence as your judgment shall suggest to be necessary.—I do not mean to advise the abandoning your present post, contrary to your own opinion, but only to mention my Ideas of the importance of those passes, and that you cannot give too much attention to their security by having works erected in the most advantageous places for that purpose.

I am D[r] Sir

Your most Obed. Serv[t]

G[o] WASHINGTON.

To Major General Lee.

P.S. I shall be obliged by your sending Gov[r] Trumbull's Letter by the first opportunity. It will be well to furnish each Col[o] in your Division with the substance of these Resolves, so far as they respect the Enlistments, to prevent any kind of mistakes.

RESOLVES OF CONGRESS.

[*Inclosed in the preceding letter.*]

In Congress, Nov. 7th, 1776.

RESOLVED, that the resolution passed the 14th of October last, That the allowance to officers of one and one-third of a dollar for enlisting soldiers be not extended or giving on the re-enlistment of the soldiers in camp, be repealed, and the same henceforth allowed.

November 12th 1776.

Resolved, As the opinion of Congress, that if the soldiers to be raised by the state of Massachusetts Bay, be inlisted on the terms offered to them, (which are more advantageous than what are offered to other soldiers serving in the same army,) it would much retard, if not totally impede, the enlistment of the latter, and produce discontent and murmur, unless Congress should equally increase the pay of these; which it is the opinion of Congress would universally be reprobated as an immoderate expence, and complained of, as a grievous burden by those who must bear it; and therefore, that the Committee from the state of Massachusetts Bay, be desired not to inlist their men on the additional pay offered by the Assembly of that state.

Upon reconsidering the Resolution of the 16th of September last, for raising eighty-eight battalions, to serve during the present war with Great Britain, Congress being of opinion, that the readiness of the inhabitants of the states to enter into the service for limited times, in defence of their invaluable privileges, on all former occasions, gives good ground to hope the same zeal for the public good will appear in future when necessity calls for their assistance; and lest the uncertain length of time which forces raised during the continuance of the present war may be compelled to serve, may prevent many from inlisting who would otherwise readily manifest their attachment to the common cause, by engaging for a limited time, therefore,

Resolved, That all non-commissioned officers and soldiers, who do not incline to engage their services during the continuance of the present war, and shall inlist to serve three years, unless sooner discharged by Congress, shall be entitled to, and receive, all such bounty and pay as are allowed to those who inlist during the continuance of the present war, except the one hundred acres of land, which land is to be granted to those only who inlist without such limitation of time.

And each recruiting officer is required to provide two distinct inlisting rolls; one for such to sign as enlist during the continuance of the war, and the other for such as inlist for three years, if their service shall be so long required.

By order of the Congress,

JOHN HANCOCK, Pres.

ADDRESS TO THE MILITIA FROM MASSACHUSETTS.

[November 16, 1776.]

GENERAL LEE most earnestly entreats and conjures the Officers and Soldiers of the Massachusetts Militia as they regard the sacred cause in which They are engag'd—as they respect the property of their fellow citizens the security of their Fellow Soldiers and their own honour that they will continue in their present Posts a few days longer—Thursday shall be the utmost—The General cannot specify the reasons of his being so earnest in his entreaties, but can assure 'em that it is of the last importance—from all the movements of the Enemies Troops there is the greatest reason to assure ourselves that their abominable designs are already totally defeated. Nay We have reason to believe that They themselves have abandoned all thoughts of success, and that nothing but a base and wicked defect of zeal and spirit in our soldiers and officers can revive their hopes and it must be allowed that the refusing at such a crisis as this to remain under arms for the few days requested is not only a scandalous but wicked defect in zeal virtue and spirit. The General is himself persuaded that the Men if left to themselves are not capable of so flagitious a conduct —but that some few of their officers who unhappily have been elected to stations their characters disgrace have laboured to dissuade the soldiers from a resolution which honour duty and religion demand of them—these officers are already known and shall be hung out to the public notice as enemies and Pests to their Country. Once more therefore the General earnestly recommends to the officers and the men at large to follow their own virtuous natural dispositions and comply with the request he has made—tho' at the same time he perhaps ought to make an apology to 'em for making use of so earnest and energetick terms in requesting what in fact is so trifling an exertion of fortitude and self denial as to remain only four days longer under arms.

To Colonel Reed.

Camp, November 16th 1776.

My Dear Reed,

Whether it is owing to my ignorance of certain circumstances, or what reason, I can't pretend to say, but from the time the great Stores were secured, and the impossibility of preventing the Enemy from passing up and down the River ascertain'd, I confess I cannot conceive what circumstances give to Fort Washington so great a degree of value and importance as to counterbalance the probability or almost certainty of losing 1400 of our best Troops. In this perswasion, I cannot help expressing my concern that General Greene has reinforced it. I shou'd have been rather pleas'd had he called off a considerable part of the Garrison—in my opinion the Enemy will not besiege it so much from an Idea of its intrinsic value as with a view of saving their honour & figuring in the foreign papers. You recommend to me some movements in order to distract—You must be too well acquainted with the natural strength of the Ground, not to see the facility of circumvallating themselves *hors d'insulte*.

Yesterday I detach'd a Party of Eleven hundred

under Sullivan in hopes of surprising Rogers and his neighbouring Brigade, but they had intelligence and fled—The Militia leave us tomorrow—Our numbers will be small to protect so large a tract of Country from the depredations of the Enemy, which is really an important point considering their circumstances, I wish not to cede another inch and hope to effect it. You may assure the General, that I will act offensively to the utmost of my power.

Adieu, my D[r] Reed. My respects to the General.

Yours Affectionately
C. LEE.

Col Reed.

From an apprehension that the original shou'd miscarry I send a copy by Peeks Kill.

FROM COLONEL REED.

Fort Lee, Nov. 16, 1776.

D[R] GENERAL,

This Morning the Attack was made upon Mount Washington by the whole of Gen. Howes Army in three Divisions—our Troops kept the Lines as long as could have been expected but were at length obliged to yield to superior Numbers—They retired under the Guns of the Fort which stopp'd the Approach of the Enemy—soon after this a Flag went in from the Enemy & since that there appears such an Intercourse that we suppose the Fort has or will soon capitulate. The General has thought it proper you should have the earliest Advice of this Event that you may regulate yourself accordingly.

The General has directed me to suggest to your Consideration the Use or Propriety of retaining your present Post under all Circumstances & would be glad to hear from you on the subject.

I am with much Regard
Yours
J. Reed,
A. G.

To Major General Lee,
Camp near White Plains.

To Colonel Reed.

Novem. 17, 1776.

Dear Reed,

I received yours yesterday, and at the same time a Note from Blodget Green's Secretary with the account of the capitulation of Fort Washington—I have only time to reply to the propriety of retaining our present post—concisely 'tis my opinion and the opinion of the General Officers that we ought for manifold reasons * * *

[The copy of the letter ends thus imperfectly with page 18 in a fragment of one of General Lee's letter-books containing pages 3–18 inclusive.]

General Washington to William Palfrey.

Hackensack, Nov[r] 18, 1776.

I just now Receiv[d] the favor of your Letter of the 17th. I confess I did not expect that any Warrants would have been presented to You for Payment except those which I signed myself. The inconveniences which might arise if several Persons in the same Army were allowed to draw are obvious, and such as might produce great uneasiness and injustice to the Publick. All that applied to me were told, that the Abstracts were to be deposited with you, and sent down in order to be signed by me at once, or that they would be compleated by my signature, if brought at different times. I cannot allow double pay to Major Lee or any other officer. It is expressly against the Resolves of Congress. The Militia will be payed on making out proper abstracts, and such as are satisfactory to you, as other Troops are. You must inform their officers, that they should be very particular in not charging for a longer time than the men were in actual service & the abstracts should be Certified by their Brig^r or Col^s Commandants.

As I cannot conceive it will be for the Public good, that Warrants should be drawn by different Officers, and to prevent further mistakes on that account, I request that you will remove your office near my Head Quarters, and pay no Warrants hereafter but such as come from me, giving notice of your removal.

I shall mention to Congress the demands that will be on you, desiring that provision may be made for the same.

I am, Sir,
Y^r most Obed^t Servt
G^o WASHINGTON.

[To Lieut. Col. William Palfrey,
Paymaster General.]

TO GENERAL JOHN SULLIVAN.

Head Quarters, North Castle,
19th November, 1776.

SIR,

I am directed by General Lee to request (as he is going this morning to the Saw pits,) that you will act in his stead till he returns, and give the necessary orders for your division.

In any thing respecting Tories, that you will act according to your own discretion.

I am, Sir, Respectfully yours,

JOHN S. EUSTACE

A. D. Camp.

Major General Sullivan.

TO GENERAL WASHINGTON.

Camp, November 19th 1776.

DEAR GENERAL:

The recommendation of General Greene which you transmitted to me, threw the officers to whom I communicated it into so great a flame of discontent, that I ventured, notwithstanding your orders, to hesitate. They accused him of partiality to his connections and townsmen, to the prejudice of men of manifestly superiour merit; indeed it appears from the concurrent testimony of unbiassed persons, that some of the subjects he recommended were wretched; in short, I was so stunned with their clamour that I delayed till the arrival of the committee; for which I ought to ask your pardon, but at the same time think the delay has been salutary.

My objections to moving from our present post are, as I observed before, that it would give us the air of being frightened; it would expose a fine fertile country to their ravages; and, I must add, that we are as secure as we could be in any position whatever. We are pretty well disencumbered of our impediments, which I propose depositing on or about Crumb Pond, which, (though I confess I have not reconnoitered the place,) from its situation, must be full as safe, and is much more centrical than Peekskill. If on further examination it has any material disadvantages, we can easily move from thence. As to ourselves, (light as we are) several retreats present themselves. In short, if we keep a good look out, we are in no danger; but I must entreat your Excellency to enjoin the officers posted at Fort Lee to give us the quickest intelligence if they observe any embarkations of troops in the North River.

Our scouts are of late grown more vigilant, and make prisoners. The Militia, according to their laudable custom, would not stay a moment beyond their usual time. Oh, General, why would you be over-persuaded by men of inferiour judgment to your own? It was a cursed affair.

Yours, most affectionately,

CHARLES LEE.

To His Excellency General Washington,
Hackensack.

P. S. The returns of the soldiers of the different regiments, now in the hands of the enemy, according to the mode you require, are not yet made out, but will soon, and shall be sent.

To BENJAMIN RUSH.

Camp, November 20th, 1776.

MY DEAR RUSH:

The affair at Fort Washington cannot surprise you at Philadelphia more than it amazed and stunned me. I must entreat that you will keep what I say to yourself; but I foresaw, predicted, all that has happened; and urged the necessity of abandoning it; for could we have kept it, it was of little or no use. Let these few lines be thrown into the fire, and in your conversations only acquit me of any share of the misfortune—for my last words to the General were—draw off the garrison, or they will be lost. You say I ought to desire the General to press the Congress for the necessary articles. I have done it a thousand times, and the men are now starving for the want of blankets. I confess your apathy amazes me. You make me mad—You have numbers—your soldiers do not want courage—but such a total want of sense pervades all your counsels that Heaven alone can save you. Inclosed are some hints. I could say many things—let me talk vainly—had I the powers I could do you much good—might I but dictate one week—but I am sure you will never give any man the necessary power—did none of the Congress ever read the Roman History? Adieu, my dear Rush,

Yours most sincerely,

CHARLES LEE.

1st. You must have an army—this army cannot be had on the terms proposed—give 'em the full bounty and list 'em only for a year and a half—in short you have so bungled your affairs that you must come into any terms.

2d. Put some military man at the head of the Board of War.

3d. Strip even yourselves of blankets.

FROM WILLIAM GRAYSON.

Hackensack, November 20th 1776.

SIR,

His Excellency has directed me to write to you, and acquaint you with the late movements of the enemy. They landed this morning between Dobb's Ferry and Fort Lee, as it is imagined, at a place called Closter Dock, nearly opposite to Phillips's House, and (as the General has been informed) in great numbers, and an advanced party of them have proceeded as far as a hill two miles above the liberty pole, about a mile and a half above General Greene's quarters, where I left his Excellency. The road leading from thence to the bridge above Hackensack, as well as the bridge, is open for our troops to retreat; and from present appearances, it is expected they may be got off without the loss of many of them. What their object is cannot at present be clearly ascertained; but it is imagined the getting possession of Fort Lee is one part of their design; however, it is possible, and perhaps probable, they may have other and more capital views.

His Excellency thinks it would be advisable in you to remove the troops under your command on this side of the North River, and there wait for further orders.

I am, Sir, with the greatest respect, your most obedient Servant

W. Grayson.

To General Heath.

Nov. 20. [21st, 1776.]

Dear General,

I yesterday received your Note for which I thank you, but had before received the intelligence of the Enemys having landed in the Jersey. Colonel Reed has written me a short Billet, that I do not well understand. I shall be obliged to you for some account of the condition and progress of your Barracks, and what number of Men they are or will be capable of lodging, and what is the state of your defences shou'd you be attack'd; as likewise your numbers and how they are station'd, if you have any sketch of the country be so kind as to favor me with it, and am Dr General

Yours most Sincerely

C. L.

To General Heath, Peekskill.

To General Heath.

Novem^r 21st 1776.

DR General,

I have just received a Recommendation not a positive order, from the General, to move the Corps under my Command to the other side of the River. This recommendation was I imagine on the presumption that I had already moved nearer the Peekskills, there is no possibility of crossing over Dobb's Ferry, or at any place lower than Kings Ferry, which to us, would be such an immense round, that we cou'd never answer any purpose. I must therefore desire and request, that you will order two thousand of your Corps, under a B^r General to cross the River, apprize the General, & wait his farther Orders. As soon as we have finish'd a necessary Jobb, I will replace the number from hence which Jobb will I believe be finished tomorrow.

I am Dr General, Yours

Charles Lee.

To James Bowdoin.

Camp at Philipsburg, November 21, 1776.

Dear Sir:

Before the unfortunate affair of Fort Washington, it was my opinion that the two armies—that on the east and that on the west side of North River—must rest each on its own bottom; that the idea of detaching and reinforcing from one side to the other, on every motion of the enemy, was chimerical; but to harbour such a thought in our present circumstances is absolute insanity. In this invasion, should the enemy alter the present direction of their operations, and attempt to open the passage of the Highlands, or enter New-England, I should never entertain a thought of being succoured from the western army. I know it is impossible. We must therefore depend upon ourselves. To Connecticut and Massachusetts, I shall look for assistance. The time of service of the men who compose the little Corps under my command is near expiring. The enemys troops are well clad for a winter campaign. Should they attempt when the winter sets in to open the communication of the Highlands, or enter New-England, I know not what we have to oppose 'em. Some means must be devised to raise your regular battalions, for as to your Militia, they are grown more detestable than ever, not from the bad quality of the men, for they are certainly good, but from the wretched character of the officers, particularly the lower sort, who want every attribute of soldiers and citizens. They want spirit, patience, constitution, integrity, and publick virtue of course. If your men run away you may be assured that the way is led by the officers. There are, notwithstanding, some worthy subjects amongst 'em, but the bad preponderates so enormously that little confidence can be placed in your Militia. I must repeat, therefore, that I hope not only the legislative body, but the whole Gentlemen of the New-England Provinces, will exert themselves to forward the completion of the Continental regiments. For Heaven's sake, Sir, contrive to send us some blankets, otherwise we must dissolve away before the time of our natural death. I hope the cursed job of Fort Washington will occasion no dejection: the place itself was of no value. For my own part I am persuaded that if we only act with common sense, spirit, and decision, the day must be our own.

Adieu, dear Sir, and believe me to be, most respect fully, yours

CHARLES LEE.

To the President of the
Council of Massachusetts.

From Colonel Reed.

Hackensack, Nov. 21, 1776.

Dr General:

The Letter you will receive with this contains my Sentiments with Respect to your present Station: But besides this I have some additional Reasons for most earnestly wishing to have you where the principal Scene of Action is laid. I do not mean to flatter, nor praise you at the Expence of any other, but I confess I do think that it is entirely owing to you that this Army & the Liberties of America so far as they are dependant on it are not totally cut off. You have Decision, a Quality often wanting in Minds otherwise valuable & I ascribe to this our Escape from York Island—from Kingsbridge & the Plains—& I have no Doubt had you been here the Garrison at Mount Washington would now have composed a Part of this Army. Under all these Circumstances I confess I ardently wish to see you removed from a Place where I think there will be little Call for your Judgment & Experience to the Place where they are like to be so necessary. Nor am I singular in my Opinion—every Gentleman of the Family the Officers & soldiers generally have a Confidence in you—the Enemy constantly inquire where you are, & seem to me to be less confident when you are present.

Col. Cadwallader, thro a special Indulgence on Acc[t] of some Civilities shewn by his Family to Gen. Prescot has been liberated from New-York without any Parole—he informs, that the Enemy have a Southern Expedition in View—that they hold us very cheap in Consequence of the late Affair at Mount Washington where both the Plan of Defence & Execution were contemptible—if a real Defence of the Lines was intended the Number was too few, if the Fort only, the Garrison was too numerous by half.—General Washington's own Judgment seconded by Representations from us, would I believe have saved the Men & their Arms but unluckily, General Greene's Judg[t] was contrary this kept the Generals Mind in a State of Suspence till the Stroke was struck—Oh! General—an indecisive Mind is one of the greatest Misfortunes that can befall an Army—how often have I lamented it this Campaign.

All Circumstances considered we are in a very awful & alarming State one that requires the utmost Wisdom & Firmness of Mind—as soon as the Season will admit I think yourself & some others should go to Congress & form the Plan of the new Army—point out their Defects to them & if possible prevail on them to bind their whole Attention to this great Object—even to the Exclusion of every other—If they will not or cannot do this, I fear all our Exertions will be vain in this Part of the World. Foreign Assistance is solliciting but we cannot expect they will fight the whole Battle—but Artillery & Artillerists must be had, if possible.—

I intended to have said more but the Express is waiting—& I must conclude with my clear & explicit Opinion that your Presence is of the last Importance—

I am with much Affection & Regard
Your very Affec.
Hbbl Ser
J Reed

To Major Gen. Lee,
White Plains.

From General Washington.

Hackinsac, Nov[r] 21st 1776.

Dear General,

It must be painful to you as well as to us, to have

no news to send you, but of a melancholy nature. Yesterday morning, the Enemy landed a large body of troops, below Dobbs Ferry, and advanced very rapidly to the fort call'd by your name; I immediately went over, & as the fort was not tenable on this side, & we in a narrow neck of land, the passes out of which, the enemy were attempting to seize, directed the troops consisting of Beal's, Heard's the remainder of Erving's brigades, & some other parts of broken regiments, to move over to the West side of Hackensac river; a considerable quantity of stores, and some artillery have fall'n into their hands; we have no accounts of their movements this morning; but as this country is almost a dead flatt, we have not an intrenching tool, & not above 3000 men, & they much broken & dispirited not only with our ill success, but the loss of their tents and baggage, I have resolved to avoid any attack, tho' by so doing, I must leave a very fine country open to their ravages, or a plentiful store house, from which they will draw voluntary supplies.

Your favour of the 19th[th] is just come to hand. I approve of your step with respect to the Rhode Island officers, as I am unacquainted with their merits. I was obliged to leave the determination of this matter much to Gen[l] Green, hoping I confess that he would make an arrangement acceptable to his Country men; however I am well satisfied with what you have done, & must leave it on that footing.

With respect to your situation, I am very much at a loss, which now to determine. There is such a change of circumstances since the date of your letter, as seems to call for a change of measures; your post will undoubtedly answer some important purposes, but whether so many or so great as your removal is well worthy of consideration. You observe, it prevents a fine fertile country affording them supplies; but now they have one much more so and more contiguous; They have traversed a part of that Country, leaving little behind them; is it probable they will return? if not, the distance must be too great in winter time, to render it effectually serviceable; Upon the whole, therefore, I am of opinion, and the gentlemen about me concur in it, that the public interest requires your coming over to this side with the Continental Troops, leaving Fellows's & Wadsworth's brigades to take care of the stores during their short stay, at the expiration of which I suppose they will set out home.

My reasons for this measure & which I think must have weight with you, are, that the Enemy are evidently changing the seat of War to this side of the North river—That this Country therefore will expect the Continental Army to give what support they can, or failing in this, will cease to depend upon or support a force, from which no protection is giv'n to them. It is therefore of the utmost importance, that at least an appearance of force should be made to keep this Province in the connection with the others; if that should not continue, it is much to be feared, that its influence on Pensylvania would be very considerable, and more & more endanger our publick interests; Unless therefore some new event should occur, or some more cogent reason present itself, I would have you move over, by the easiest and best passage; I am sensible your numbers will not be large, & that perhaps it may not be agreeable to the troops: As to the first, report will exaggerate them, & present the appearance of an army, which at least will have an effect to encourage the desponding here; and, as to the other you will doubtless represent to them that in duty and gratitude, their service is due wherever the Enemy make the greatest impression or seem to intend so to do.

The stores at North Castle, Croton bridge, & King's Ferry, are to be removed to Peek's-Kill so as to be under Gen[l] Heath's eye; this, we hope, there will be time & means to do.

Coll. Putnam who has been surveying the Country, thinks the bridge at Croton river a very important place; and that troops would be necessary there: you will please to regard it accordingly by leaving, or ordering one Regiment there.

I am Sir, With great regard,

Yr most obt. Servt,

Go Washington

To The Honble. Major Genl. Lee,
at the White Plains.

From General Heath.

Peeks Kill Nov. 21st 1776.

Dr General,

I have just received your favor of this Days Date—I Imagine that you have ere this received an account of cur loss of ordnance, stores, Provisions, Tents &c on the West Side of Hudsons River which is rumored here, and I fear is but too true.

As to the state of the Barracks in this Quarter, it is not many days since I arrived here, during which I have been pushing the Works & Buildings as far as Possible. Barracks are propos'd to be built in & near this place for about 3,500 men, and at the north entrance of the Highlands for about 2000. I am informed that at the latter place several are in Good forwardness, at this place those sufficient
14 or 1500 men are in a Pretty Good way.

I have here upwards of 4000 men
the Garrisons of Fort Montgomery
and Independence, I have disposed
the following manner, vizt Two
the West side of Hudson River
of the mountains near Siduny
River—a Brigade
Peeks-Kill Landing &
Gorge of the mountains
beyond Robinson's Bridge, which is the Principal Pass

on the East side of the River—works and barracks are constructing at each of those posts. The Ground by nature Exceedingly strong, but being very rocky the works require a large Proportion of , which we cannot make being almost Entirely destitute of Bill Hooks, and altho our Engineer has repeatedly wrote in pressing terms for them, few have as yet been obtained, and at the same time numbers of them as I informed are in the stores below entirely useless.

Colonel Putnam acquaints me that there is another pass through the Highlands about Eleven Miles East of this, but rather Inconsiderable, but that Nine miles further he is informed there is a very Good one. He rides tomorrow or next Day
view it carefully—I have not as yet
of the country round this Place, Colonel
is preparing one, but it is not as yet

I think we shall suffer
as to grain I think there will

I am Dr General

Y

General Lee.

P. S. Some of our Batteries on the River are very good on the water side, we are endeavouring to secure them as fast as possible in the Rear—Attempts have been made to fix a chain a Cross the River which has twice broke. A Committee from the Convention of the State of New York assisted by some officers Here have been sounding the River through the Highlands, and have found it in one or two places favorable to be obstructed.

Yours,

W. H.

From General Heath.

Peekskill, November 21, 1776
10 oclock at night.

Dear General:

I am now to acknowledge the receipt of your favours of this day's date, the former of which I had answered early in the evening. With respect to the latter, upon having recourse to my instructions, I find they are such as not to admit of moving any part of the troops from the posts assigned to me, unless it be by express orders from his Excellency or to support you in case you are attacked. My instructions, among other things, are as follows:

"Your division, with such troops as are now at Forts Montgomery, Independence, and Constitution, are to be under your command, and remain in this quarter, for the security of the above posts and the passes through the Highlands from this place and the one on the west side of Hudson's River—Unnecessary it is for me to say anything to evince the importance of securing the land and water communication through these passes, or to prove the indispensable necessity of using every exertion in your power to have such works erected for the defence of them as your own judgment, assisted by that of your Brigadiers and Engineer, may show the expediency of. You will not only keep in view the importance of securing these passes, but the necessity of doing it without delay, not only from the probability of the enemy's attempting to seize them, but from the advanced season, which will not admit of any spade work after the frost (which may be daily expected) sets in. Lose not a moment therefore in choosing the grounds on the east and west side of the river, on which your intended works are to be erected. Let your men for each post be speedily allotted," &c

After instructions so positive and pressing, you will readily agree, that it would be very improper in me to order any of the troops from posts to which they are so expressly assigned, and from business which in his Excellency's view is so very important. Add to this, their present disposition is such that to collect anything near the number you mention would occasion as great delay, and cause many of them to march nearly as far, as if sent immediately from your quarter.

I am, dear General, with esteem,
Yours respectfully,
W. Heath

General Lee.

To Meshech Weare.

General Lee's Quarters, November 21, 1776.

May it please your Excellency: Hurry of business at present prevents the General from writing himself. He has desired me to apologize for the same, and to inform your Excellency that there is the greatest probability of the enemy's paying you a visit very soon, a deserter having just come from the enemy, who declares 'twas in orders they should embark this day. Their design is, we imagine, to obtain secure winter quarters for themselves and shipping. Yesterday they landed, by the best intelligence we can get, about five thousand, in the Jerseys, four miles from Dobbs's Ferry. The particulars, since they landed, we have not learned. This manœuvre don't look like embarking, but the deserter appears so confident in his assertion that the General thought proper to acquaint your Excellency of it immediately.

I am, Sir, with respect, your obedient, humble Servant
William Bradford,
Aid-de-Camp to General Lee
By General Lee's orders.

To President Weare of New Hampshire.

[The same to Gov. Nich. Cooke of Rhode Island.]

To Colonel Reed.

Camp Nov'r ye 21st 1776.

Dr Sir—

I have just receiv'd your letter dated Hackensac by Cornelius Cooper—his Excellency recommends it to me to move with the Troops under my command to the other side the River—I apprehend that this advice is founded on the presumption either that We have the means of crossing at or nearer Dobbs Ferry, or that my Corps is mov'd up the Country near to Kings Ferry. There are no means of passing Dobbs Ferry—and as We remain where you left us, the round by Kings Ferry wou'd be so great that We cou'd not be there in time to answer any purpose—I have therefore order'd General Heath who is close to the only Ferry which can be pass'd, to detach two thoushand men—to apprize his Excellency, and wait his further orders a mode which I flatter myself will answer better what I conceive to be the spirit of the orders than shou'd I move the Corps from hence—withdrawing our Troops from hence, would be attended with some very serious consequences which at present wou'd be tedious to enumerate—as to myself, I hope to set out to-morrow.

I am, my Dr Sir, Yours—

Charles Lee.

Colonel Reed, Adjutant General
of the Continental Forces, Hackensack, P Express.

The bearer Mr. Cornelious Cooper is Express to His Excellency Genl Washington.

Instructions to Gen. Nixon.

Camp, November 22d 1776.

Sir,

You are to proceed with the two Brigades and Party of Light Horse under your Command to Phillips's house—but previously you are to detach some able Scouts who are to reconnoitre well the Ground, and observe if there is no Body of the Enemy in or near the place superior to your own. You are to subdivide a sufficient number of your men into small parties who beginning at Phillips's house are to collect all the stout able horses—all the Cattle fat and lean—all the sheep and hogs, leaving only some milch Cows and a few hogs requisite for the immediate subsistence of the Families. You are to oblige the People to deliver up all their Blankets and Coverlings reserving only one to each Person. You are to give Certificates to the families for every article taken, and upon your return deliver to the Commissary General all the fat Cattle—to the Quarter Master General all the Blankets and Coverings, the lean horses and cattle, taking receipts for the same—if it should happen to rain before you arrive at the point order'd I wou'd by no means have you expose your men to the Wet—but lodge 'em in the barns & houses as well as you can taking care to place proper Guards and Centinels to secure you against Surprises—above all it is strictly enjoin'd you not to suffer your soldiers and officers to pillage plunder or insult the wretch'd people.

CHARLES LEE.

To Brig[r] Genl. Nixon. Major Gen'l.

ADDITIONS. During the night flanking Parties wou'd only occasion confusion—You are therefore to have none —as soon as the day appears you are to detach the sixth part from each Corps. Your own judgment will direct and the nature of the ground point out on which flank They are to or whether it will be necessary that both sides should be flanked. I must particularly request that you have a strong Advanced Party of a field officer and an hundred and fifty men—that Capt. Lewis with fivety scouts advance before them at least a mile and a half in front. Your light horse in advancing ought to bring up the rear at an hundred yards distance in retreating the same I once more repeat that if it rains you will lodge your men as well as you can. Above all let the strictest silence be observed. When you return these orders are to be re-delivered to me.

Endorsed: N° 31. Nov. 22d. '76. Gen. Nixon's Instructions with a return of the Cattle, Sheep, Hogs, Horses &c. taken off Philips Manor.

To the President of the Massachusetts Council.

Camp near Phillipsbourg, 22[d] November, 1776.

Sir:

Indecision bids fair for tumbling down the goodly fabrick of American freedom, and, with it, the rights of mankind. 'Twas indecision of Congress prevented our having a noble army, and on an excellent footing. 'Twas indecision in our military councils which cost us the garrison of Fort Washington, the consequence of which must be fatal, unless remedied in time by a contrary spirit. Enclosed I send you an extract of a letter from the General, on which you will make your comments; and I have no doubt but that you will concur with me in the necessity of raising immediately an army to save us from perdition. Affairs appear in so important a crisis, that I think even the resolves of the Congress must no longer too nicely weigh with us. We must save the community in spite of the ordinances of the Legislature. There are times when we must commit treason against the laws of the State for the salvation of the State. The present crisis demands this brave, virtuous kind of treason. For my own part (and I flatter myself that my way of thinking is congenial with that of Mr. Bowdoin's) I will stake my head and reputation on the propriety of the measure. To come to the point: I request and conjure you, therefore, to waive all formalities, and devise some means of completing not only your regiments prescribed to the Province, but add, if possible, four companies to each regiment. We must not only have a force sufficient to cover your Province and these fertile districts from the insults and irruptions of the tyrant's troops, but sufficient to drive 'em out of all their quarters in the Jerseys, or all is lost. Disaffection is daily increasing in Pennsylvania, which must be checked by a tremendous superiority. In the meantime send up a formidable body of Militia to supply the place of the Continental troops, which I am ordered to convey over the river. Let your people be well supplied with blankets and warm clothes as I am determined by the help of God to unnest 'em even in the dead of winter. Let me hear from you soon.

Yours most affectionately and respectfully

CHARLES LEE.

For Heaven's sake lose no time in sending up the Militia, and a number of shoes, stockings, and blankets, for the army. If Massachusetts and Connecticut do not now exert themselves, they must, and indeed ought to be, enslaved; but if they act with the necessary vigour and virtue, I will answer for their success.

To General Heath.

Camp, November 23d 1776.

Sir:

By your mode of reasoning, the General's injunctions are so binding that not a tittle must be broke through for the salvation of the General and the Army. I have ordered Glover's brigade to march up towards the Peeks Kills to put the passage of the Highlands out of danger; but I intended to take two thousand from your division with me into the Jerseys; so I must desire that you will have that number in readiness by the day after tomorrow, when I shall be with you early in the forenoon; and am, Sir, your most obedient Servant

CHARLES LEE.

Major-General Heath.

From General Heath.

Peekskill, November 24th 1776.

Sir:

Be my mode of reasoning as it may, I conceive it to be my duty to obey my instructions, especially those which are positive and poignant; and that to deviate from them, even in extreme cases, would be an errour; though perhaps an errour on the right side.

I can assure you, Sir, that I have the salvation of the General and Army so much at heart that the least recommendation from him, to march my division, or any part of them, over the river, should have been instantly obeyed, without waiting for a positive order.

My conduct must be approved or censured, as I adhere to, or depart from, my orders; and as it is my duty, I shall strictly abide by them, until they are countermanded in such manner, as will justify a deviation from them, to him who instructed me, and to the world.

I shall be happy in being honoured with your company to-morrow;

And am, with respect and esteem,

Your obedient humble servant,

W. Heath.

General Lee.

To Colonel Reed.

Camp, Nov'r ye 24th 1776.

My Dr. Reed

I receiv'd your most obliging flattering letter—lament with you that fatal indecision of mind which in war is a much greater disqualification than stupidity or even want of personal courage—accident may put a decisive Blunderer in the right—but eternal defeat and miscarriage must attend the man of the best parts if curs'd with indecision. The General recommends in so pressing a manner as almost to amount to an order to bring over the Continental Troops under my command—which recommendation or order throws me into the greatest dilemma from sev'ral considerations—Part of the troops are so ill furnish'd with shoes and stockings blankets &cc that They must inevitably perish in this wretched weather—part of 'em are to be dismissed on Saturday next and this part is the best accoutred for service—What shelter We are to find on the other side the river is a serious consideration: but these considerations shou'd not sway me; my reason for not having march'd already—is that We have just receiv'd intelligence that Rogers's Corps, the L. Horse, part of the Highlanders and another Brigade lye in so expos'd a situation as to give the fairest opportunity of being carried off. I shou'd have attempted it last night but the rain was too violent, and when our pieces are wet you know our Troops are *hors de combat*—This night I hope will be better—if We succeed We shall be well compensated for the delay—We shall likewise be able in our return to clear the Country of all the articles wanted by the Enemy—in evry view therefore the expedition must answer—I have just receiv'd a most flattering letter from Don Louis Venzaga, Governor of N. Orleans—He gives me the title of *General de los estados unidos Americanos*, which is a tolerable step towards declaring himself our ally in positive terms—the substance is that He is sensible of the vast advantages which must result from the separation to his Master and Nation—that He cannot positive enter into a regular system of commerce without consulting his Master but in the meantime He will render us all the service in his Power—I only wait myself for this busyness I mention of Rogers & Co being over—shall then fly to you—for to confess a truth I really think our Chief will do better with me than without me—

I am D[r] Reed yours most sincerely

CHARLES LEE.

Inclos'd is a petition from [some] of the poor sufferers from Austin's expedition—I beg the General will forward it to Congress.

Colonel Reed—

To General Washington.

Camp, Nove[r] 24th, 1776.

Dear General,

I have received your Orders and shall endeavour to put 'em in execution, but question much whether I shall be able to carry wth me any considerable number, not so much from a want of zeal in the men, as from their wretched condition with respect to shoes, stockings, blankets, &[c] which the present bad weather renders more intolerable I sent Heath orders to transport two thousand men across the River, apprize the General and wait for further orders, but that great man (as I might have expected) intrench'd himself within the Letter of his Instructions and refused to part with a single file, tho' I undertook to replace 'em with a part of my own. I shou'd march this day with Glovers Brigade, but have just received intelligence that Roger's Corps, a part of the Light Horse, and another Brigade lye in so exposed a situation as to present us the fairest opportunity of carry[g] 'em off—if we succeed, it will have a great effect, and amply compensate for two days delay.

I am D[r] General Yours most Sincerely

Charles Lee.

To His Excellency General Washington.

To the Commissioners from Massachusetts.

Camp, Novem[r] y[e] 24th 1776.

Gentlemen:

As I flatter myself that I have given reasons to the Continent of America that I am above all jobbs and partiality, that I would not recommend my twin Brother unless I thought him capable of filling the Station with dignity; I hope that what I now venture to say will not be taken in a wrong sense, but that you will attribute it to the real motive, my love and zeal for America. It is the sole principle that actuates me—for Heavens sake, Gentlemen, as you regard the honour and safety of your Country, as you regard the liberties of Posterity and the particular reputation of your Province let all consideration of connexions or personal interests be waved for the present. Your Liberties stand on the verge of perdition, they depend on the quality and character of your Army, and the character and quality of your Army depend on the choice of your officers—in this conviction, I must be free to say that your appointment of Colonel Henshaw to a Regiment must have bad consequences. He is from what I have seen totally unfit for such a station, such an election will cast a damp on the really deserving. They will begin to think that valour, industry, and activity will be of no importance, and that Connexions or personal Interest are to carry all before 'em; of course they will no longer labour to qualify themselves essentially for their Country's service Your soldiers are brave, and your arms have been duly disgraced by the incompetency of your officers—it is time to remedy the evil—if partiality is at this crisis to bear down all before it, your Cause must be despair'd of. You have many capable Officers amongst you; for God's sake, therefore, Gentlemen, look about you, and chuse some fitter subject. I most earnestly entreat your pardon for the liberty I take; but am sure that on reflection you will not only excuse but thank me for the admonition rough and presuming as it may appear to be, that God Almighty may inspire us all, civil and military, with the pure and sole desire of serving America, in this tremendous crisis is the prayer of, Gentlemen,

Your most obed^{t} Servant
CHARLES LEE.

To The Hon^{o} The Commissioners
from the State of Massachusetts Bay.

FROM GENERAL WASHINGTON.

Newark, Novr 24th 1776.

DEAR SIR,

By the negligent and infamous conduct of the post rider, the Eastern Mail of Friday was brought to Hackensac and there stopped to fall into the hands of the Enemy. Supposing it may have contained some letters from you of a public nature, I have thought it proper to give you the earliest notice, that you may guard against any advantages the Enemy may expect to derive from the accident.

I perceive by your letter to Col^{o} Reed, that you have entirely mistaken my views in ordering Troops from Gen. Heath's Division to this Quarter. The posts and passes in the Highlands are of such infinite importance that they should not be subjected to the least possible degree of risk. Col. Reed's second letter will have sufficiently explained my intention upon this subject, and pointed out to you that it was your division which I wanted & wish to march. As the Enemy have possessed themselves of the usual route of Dobbs Ferry and Hackensac it will be necessary for you to choose some back way in which you and your Troops may come secure. I doubt not they will try to intercept you, if this precaution is not used, and therefore have been induced to mention it. I would also mention the necessity of my hearing frequently from you in the course of your march, in order to a due regulation of matters, and that I may know how to conduct myself.

I am Dr Sir,

Your most ob^{t} Servt

G^{o} Washington.

P. S. I have received your favor of the 20th and feel with you for the distresses of the Army for want of necessary cloathing and covering. I have pointed this out to Congress several times. How to remedy it, I know not. From the number of prizes taken at the Eastward, I should suppose the Troops from thence could have been much better provided with necessaries than from the more southern States, where they have not the same advantages of an open Navigation.

The Honble Major Genl. Lee.

From General Washington.

Newark, November 24th 1776.

Dear Sir,

I wrote you this morning of the probability that some of your letters to me had fallen with the mail into the enemy's hands. My apprehensions on that head have been since confirmed by direct intelligence from their camp. I am informed that a letter from you is confidently said to have come to their hands, and that measures are undertaken to intercept your march. To prevent them from effecting this object, I have judged it proper to acquaint you of this accident, and of their design; at the same time I must request that you will take every precaution to come by a safe and secure route. I am told by those who have an intimate knowledge of the country, that after you leave Haverstraw the western Road by Kakiate will be proper for you to take. But I will not undertake to prescribe any one in particular, only observing, that you will by all means keep between the enemy and the mountains.

Before I conclude, I would wish you to leave under the care of General Heath, the two twelve-pounders on travelling carriages. They will be safe with him at Peekskill. The brass twenty four I would have you bring, provided it can be done without great inconvenience.

I need not urge the necessity of your gaining intelligence of the enemy's situation in the course of your march; I will be silent on that head; nor need I mention the propriety of your sending frequent expresses, to advise of your approaches. Hoping and trusting that your arrival will be safe and happy,

I am, dear sir, your most obedient servant

G°. WASHINGTON.

To Major General Lee.

P. S. The expresses should come by the western road otherwise they may fall in with the enemy. Enclosed you will receive a copy of sundry resolves of Congress, which you will publish in orders.

TO THE COMMISSIONERS FROM MASSACHUSETTS.

Camp, Novem[r] 25th 1776.

GENTLEMEN,

Colonels Varnum & Hitchcock will deliver you this Note. I am more confirm'd in the propriety of what I took the liberty to recommend yesterday. I entreat and conjure you to retain Colonel Little, if possible, and to discard all thoughts of Henshaw—the prejudice will be infinite from such a strange election

I once more request your Pardons for the liberty I take, and assure you that I am Gentlemen

Yours most faithfully

CHARLES LEE.

To the Hon°. The Committee
of Massachusetts Bay

TO JAMES BOWDOIN.

Camp at Phillipsburg, November ye 25th

DEAR SIR,

Would it not be prudent to order all the Continental stores to a more centrical place than Boston? Worcester, for instance, I should think would be a convenient place. There is another reason for this measure: should the enemy take it into their heads to send a fleet before Boston, in the confusion, when every man is attentive to his own affairs, the publick is totally neglected. The small arms should likewise be moved. For Heaven's sake, Sir, devise some means of furnishing us with blankets. Can no method be found of putting a stop to the enormous and impious extortion of the merchants on the soldiers?

I am, dear Sir, your most obedient Servant

CHARLES LEE.

The Honourable James Bowdoin,
President of the Council of Massachusetts.

FROM GENERAL JOHN SULLIVAN.

$Novem^r$ 26th, 1776.

DEAR GENERAL,

Col. Scammell ordered a Party of thirty Men from my Division to relieve a Party of Glover's stationed at Dobbs Ferry they marched by way of Tarry Town and were met since dark by a Party of Horse about twelve or fifteen in Number about three Miles on this side of Tarry Town. The Party of Horse upon discovering our people halted in the road and were hailed by our party but made no answer, but rode off near half a mile and halted again. Our party came up with them hailed a second time and received no answer. The Horse retreated about the same Distance and there halted until our People came up, upon hailing them a third time and receiving no answer our Party fired, upon which the Horse retreated again. The officer dispatched a Messenger to me and pursued. I have ordered out a hundred and fifty men to cover our Party if any thing further is necessary you will please to let me know.

I am with much Respect
Your Excellency's most obt. hble Servt
JNO. SULLIVAN.

FROM GENERAL JOHN SULLIVAN.

Tuesday Evening, [Nov. 26. 1776.]

D[R] GEN[L]

The Party fired upon by our People turned out to be a number of Tories which I learn by a second Message from L[t] Rust I have therefore dismissed the Party I ordered out

I am, Dear Gen[l]., Yours &[c]
JNO. SULLIVAN.

His Excellency Genl. Lee.

TO GENERAL HEATH.

Camp, Philipsbourg Novem[r] 26th 1776.

SIR,

I perceive that you have formed an opinion to yourself that shou'd General Washington remove to the streights of Magellan, the instructions he left with you upon a particular occasion, have to all intents and purposes invested you with a command separate from, and independent of any other superior. That General Heath & General Lee are merely two Major Generals, who perhaps ought to hold a friendly intercourse with each other, and when this humour or fancied Interests prompts, may afford mutual assistance; but that General Heath is by no means to consider himself obliged to obey any Orders of the Second in Command—this Idea of yours, Sir, may not only be prejudicial to yourself but to the Public. I cou'd wish Sir, before things go any further you wou'd correct the notion. I enjoin'd you to send two thousand men over the River and inform'd you that I wou'd replace 'em with an equal number, this was the only mode in my power of complying with the intentions of the General, but it seems your danger was so imminent and your instructions so positive that instead of taking a step which both duty & Common sense dictated, you are so kind as to advise me to send the Troops from hence—the two Days march from here to Peekskill and the Want of Waggons with the badness of the road making no sort of difference. But I must Inform you, Sir, that we cou'd not have been (such are our circumstances) in less than five days at Peeks Kill, and that five days may turn the fate of an Empire. If any misfortune shou'd happen from this refusal, you must answer for it. If any misfortune had happen'd to your present post by the detachment of these two thousand men from your Corps, the blame wou'd have fallen upon me—But enough on this subject, I shall therefore Conclude, that the Commander in Chief is now separated from us, that I of course command on this side the Water, that for the future I must & will be obey'd.

I am Sir, Yr. Hum. Serv[t.]

CHARLES LEE.

To Major General Heath.

To General Washington.

Camp, Philipsbourg Novemb^{r} ye 26, 1776.

Dear General,

It never was my Idea to leave the Highlands unguarded, but only for expedition's sake that Heath should detach two thousand of his corps immediately over the River, and to replace these two thousand by the same number the most lightly accoutred from this Body here 'till the Main Body with their Baggage, Cannon, &c, cou'd move. I conceived this movement cou'd be attended with no risk, as he has now nothing to guard but the Western Passages—for there is no possibility of their approaching by the Eastern, having as I can learn, no vessels on the Eastern River to transport their cannon—and the Road from Kingsbridge by Land is now almost impracticable—the want of Carriages and this disappointment with respect to Heath, but above all the alarms, we have been thrown into by the activity of the Tories, and the important consideration of leaving this Country in a tolerable state of security on my departure, have still detained me here. The Enemy kept a very considerable part of their Force on this side of Kings Bridge 'till yesterday—so considerable indeed that from what we saw, we conceived the numbers transported to the Jerseys not near so great as you were taught to think. This and the apprehension of their gleaning all the forage of this district, contributed to the other considerations I have mention'd have detain'd me so much longer than I cou'd have wish'd. Yesterday they drew themselves in, and at the same time we made a sweep of the Country from Philips's house—part of the Army have moved on—I set out tomorrow. No militia are come in to cover the Country. I have wrote most pressing Letters on this subject to Trumbull & hope they will have effect. I have been equally urgent with Mr Bowdoin for Blankets, Shoes, &^{c} indeed our Soldiers are not in a moving condition but seem well disposed and engage themselves beyond expectation, but we are in great want of money for bounty. I have been under the necessity without authority to draw for this purpose—several deserters come out to day inform us that a considerable embarkation is made for Amboy—I shall take care to obey y[r] Excellency's orders in regard to my march as exactly as possible, and am

D[r] General, Yours,
CHARLES LEE.

His Excellency General Washington,
Newark.

TO SIR WILLIAM HOWE.

[November 26th, 1776.]

SIR,

Inclos'd is a letter from the Widow of General Montgomery to Lady Ranelagh, with another addressed to Colonel Darby, which I have no doubt of being transmitted—there are two circumstances I beg leave to mention to your excellency which mutual interest and humanity require to be ascertained—the first is the sacredness of Hospitals. I conceive that in all parts of the modern world Hospitals are or ought never to be disturbed. Unless some regulation of this kind takes place the sick and wounded on both sides may suffer in a manner which I am persuaded is repugnant to your generous way of thinking, and I flatter myself that you will believe is not less disagreeable to mine—an instance of this kind fell out the other day—Two Hessian Chasseurs were taken Prisoners, one of whom was very much wounded. I left a surgeon's mate to attend and his unhurt comrade to nurse him. Some of your L. Horse broke into the house and most inhumanly murdered the wretch'd mate—the natural consequence of such a procedure will be the massacre of those who shall hereafter unfortunately be wounded and taken. I wou'd propose, sir, therefore that every Hospital should be sacred from insults, that the Surgeons and Attendants shou'd not be considered as lawful Prisoners—that in order to distinguish the Hospitals from Common houses, a White flag should be hoisted on the Top and the title inscribed on the door—if any abuses shou'd be made of this regulation the infamy must redound on the heads of the Generals of either Party—the other circumstance I have to mention is the treatment and maintenance of Prisoners—those of yours who fall into our hands, have the full liberty of the Towns or villages allotted to 'em and credit for a comfortable and ample subsistence—on the contrary the Americans whom Chance has thrown into your hands, are as we are assur'd confin'd closely in prison and by short allowance and harsh usage almost directly forced to inlist—if this mode can be approv'd of by Mr Howe He is strangely alter'd—it is neither consonant to humanity nor the eternal rules of justice—perhaps, and I most willingly believe the fact is exaggerated—but be that as it may. My proposal with respect to Prisoners is that the Privates of the American Army in your hands shou'd have the full allowance of soldiers according to the rule observ'd by us towards yours—that the officers on both sides should have a decent stipend in proportion to their respective ranks, and that a current account shou'd be kept and the bills negotiated by the mutual arrangement of both Parties—I refer your Excellency to the mode establish'd by the Continental Congress which has been publish'd and presume if it's approv'd of you will consent to adopt the same.

I remain what I ever have been with the greatest esteem for your excellent personal qualities, most truly and devotedly Yours

Charles Lee.

I take the liberty of sending some letters for different prisoners.

Endorsed: Letter from Gen. Lee to Gen. Howe p. Flagg of Truce, Novr 26th, 1776. N° 45.

From General Washington.

Newark, November 27th 1776

Dear Sir:

I last night received the favor of your letter of the 25th. My former letters were so full and explicit, as to the necessity of your marching as early as possible, that it is unnecessary to add more on that head. I confess I expected you would have been sooner in motion. The force here, when joined by yours, will not be adequate to any great opposition; at present it is weak, and it has been more owing to the badness of the weather that the enemy's progress has been checked, than any resistance we could make. They are now pushing this way; part of 'em have passed the Passaic. Their plan is not entirely unfolded, but I shall not be surprised if Philadelphia should turn out the object of their movement. The distress of the troops for want of clothes I feel much; but what can I do? Having formed an enterprise against Rogers, &c., I wish you may have succeeded.

I am, dear sir, with great esteem, your most obedient servant

Go. Washington.

To Major General Lee.

To the New England Governors.

Camp Philipsbourg, 27th November, 1776.

Sir,

As the whole fate of America depends on the speedy completion of the new Army—all considerations ought undoubtedly to be postpon'd to this object.

The officers, and indeed it must necessarily be so, are of my opinion that nothing impedes the recruiting of the Army so much as the present rage of Privateering that unless this is in some measure check'd, it is in vain to expect any success. I wou'd therefore humbly refer to your Consideration whether it is not expedient to lay a temporary embargo on Privateers until the Regiments of each state are completed. Our situation is so delicate and alarming, and the absolute necessity of the Army's being rais'd without delay so obvious, that you will at least excuse the liberty I take in proposing the only mode which occurs to me.

I am Sir, With the greatest respect,

Your most obt. humble Servt.

CHARLES LEE.

Endorsed : Copy of Letters sent to Governors Trumbull, & Cook & Mr. Bowdoin, & the President of the Council of New Hampshire. N° 35.

FROM GENERAL WASHINGTON.

Brunswick, Nov[r] 29th 1776.

DEAR SIR,

I this morning received your favor of the 26th Your Letters to Gov[r] Trumbull for a reinforcement of militia, were exceedingly proper, though I doubt much whether they can be obtained, having suffered many inconveniences in the course of the present Campaign; nor was the application to M[r]. Bowdoin for cloaths for the soldiery less necessary. I am happy to hear the men discover so much readiness to engage in the service, and that there may be no objection for want of bounty money, I have directed the paymaster to advance it to the Col[s] appointed and who agree to continue again.

I imagine you have settled with the Commissary a Plan for being supplied with provisions on your march, that will be highly expedient; If you have not, I shall on information use my exertions to have you furnish'd in the best manner that circumstances will admit of. We left Newark yesterday morning and arrived here to day, in a little time after our departure the enemy entered. Whether they mean to push farther or have any Capital object in view, I suppose will be discovered in a few days, their impressing a number of waggons on Staten Island and other circumstances Indicate their movements.

I am Dr Sir
Your affect. H. Servt
G^o WASHINGTON.

To Major General Lee.

GENERAL WASHINGTON TO GENERAL HEATH.

Head Quarters Brunswic Nov. 29, 1776.

DEAR SIR,

Yours of the 26th overtook me a few Miles from this Place where I arrived this day at noon. The Enemy gave us not the Least Interruption upon our March. I am glad to hear that the Stores that Were at Tapan and Stotts Landing have all got safely up. I hope you will have the same good Luck with the Flour.

I approve of the steps you have taken to keep the Tories, in the neighbourhood of your Post, in order, and also of your offers of assistance to the state of New York in obstructing the passage of the North River above Constitution, it is an object of so much Consideration, that I think too much attention cannot be paid to it.

I hope you will be able to prevail upon Scott's Brigade to remain with you some Little time beyond their Engagements, if the recruiting service goes on with tolerable success their number will soon be replaced by that means. I am led to expect considerable Reinforcements from Pennsylvania and this state. I shall be in Want of them as the Time of the flying Camp from Jersey & Maryland expires Tomorrow, and I fear few will be induced to stay longer. If the Reinforcements are equal to my Expectations, I hope I shall at least be able to prevent a further Penetration of the Enemy Who have already got too great a Footing in this part of the Country.

Mr. Palfrey has orders to advance to the Colonels who are appointed and have agreed to remain in the Service, such sums of money as are necessary for the Bounties of the new enlisted men. I am Sir

Your most humble serv[t]

G[o] Washington.

General Heath.

Orders.

Line of March on supposition that the reserved Picquets are detached against the Enemy.

The Detachment from Nixon's Brigade must furnish the Advance Guard of a subaltern and thirty—Sullivan's Division the rear Guard of a Cop[y] of fifty—The other Corps must furnish the flanking Parties, composed of a sixth Part of their respective Numbers to march in an indian file with a proper proportion of Officers. These flankers to be disposed according to the discretion of the Commanding General of the Detachment, either on the right left or both Flanks as shall be judged prudent—As a line of two deep in files has consequently an insufferable long Rear, The Line of march is to be doubled into four. The left half of each Brigade doubling behind the right as was practiced yesterday—Small intervals of about fifteen Paces to be observed between the Head of each Division and the rear of the preceeding into which Intervals the Flankers may be called in when occasion requires. It is recommended to the Officer who leads the Column to march slow and to the whole to keep their files well closed. If there should appear any Danger of being outflanked, or the Genl. Commanding thinks right to engage in a line of two deep—the following method is to be observed—Glover's Brigade is to draw out of the Line immediately into the Rear about one hundred yards, if the Ground will admit —consider itself as a Corps De Reserve, and act accordingly, that is sustain & reinforce, as circumstances require. This Manœuvre will give room for the rear Ranks of the rest to develop into two deep.

Above all a most strict silence is to be observed.

To General Washington.

Peekskill, November ye 30th 1776.

Dear General:

I received yours last night, dated the 27th, from Newark. You complain of my not being in motion sooner. I do assure you that I have done all in my power, and shall explain my difficulties when we have both leisure. I did not succeed with Rogers, and merely owing to the timidity or caution of the enemy, who contracted themselves into a compact body very suddenly. I am in hopes I shall be able to render you more service than had I moved sooner. I think I shall enter the Province of Jersey with four thousand firm and willing troops, who will make a very important diversion. Had I stirred sooner, I should have only led an inferior number of unwilling. The day after tomorrow we shall pass the river, when I shall be glad to receive your instructions; but I could wish you would bind me as little as possible, not from any opinion, I do assure you, of my own parts, but from a persuasion that detached Generals cannot have too great latitude, unless they are very incompetent indeed.

Adieu, my dear Sir. Yours, most affectionately,

Charles Lee.

His Excellency General Washington,
Elizabeth-Town.

P.S. I have just been speaking with General Heath,

the strictness of whose instructions a good deal distress me. I could have replaced the few I require, by men who are able to do stationary duty, but not to make expeditious marches. My numbers will in consequence be fewer than I promised.

To James Bowdoin.

Camp Croton Pond, November 30, 1776.

Dear Sir:

The affairs of America are in a more alarming situation every day. The enemy have passed the Passaic; unless, therefore, the New-England Provinces exert themselves not only vigorously, but essentially, we are lost. General Washington has ordered me with the Continental troops over the river. This measure may be necessary for the safety of the Jerseys, or perhaps even for Philadelphia, but the hardships that the men must encounter at this season of the year will, I apprehend, prevent very considerably, if not entirely, the recruiting the new army; and unless an army is formed, and immediately, you must submit to the yoke prepared. If this army cannot be formed in the mode proposed, by volunteers, which at best is a very bad mode, it follows that some other must be adopted. The scheme that I would propose is what ought to have pointed itself out at first; it is that which all countries have adopted; for when the soldiers of a community are composed of volunteers, war becomes quite a distinct profession. The arms of a Republic get into the hands of its worst members. Volunteers being composed in general of the most idle, vicious, and dissolute part of every society, the usual catastrophe is, that they become the tools of some General, more artful than the rest, and finally turn the arms put into their hands for the defence of their country, against their country's bosom. This has and must be the fate of every people who have not wisdom enough to make, and virtue enough to submit to, laws which oblige every citizen to serve in his turn as a soldier. It may be answered that your Militia is established on this principle. But your Militia from the incompetency of their officers, or some other vice in its constitution, manifestly does not answer the purposes. I would therefore take the liberty to propose, as the Army will probably not be raised by volunteers, and as an Army so composed is at best a very dangerous remedy, that you should fill your regiments by drafts from your Militia. Let every seventh man be obliged to serve in the regular regiments for one year, and you will have an Army immediately, excellent in all respects, formidable against the external enemy, and less dangerous to their fellow-citizens.

I hope to God your Governments have energy sufficient to accomplish the point; and I hope your gentlemen of the first distinction and property have patriotism to lead the way in submitting to so necessary and wholesome a regulation. If you have not, there are only two things left to your choice: either to call in the troops of France and Spain, or submit unconditionally to the tyranny of Britain. If your gentlemen lead the way in cheerfully obeying the summons of their country, I am myself persuaded the people will cheerfully follow. For God's sake, Sir, convince them of the necessity. Suffer not a spark of whatever virtue amongst you to be latent. Now is the time to call it all into action.

In this pious work, that God Almighty may assist you, is the most fervent prayer of one who is, dear Sir, most truly yours,

CHARLES LEE.

To the Honorable James Bowdoin.

N.B. Our want of blankets and stores is every day more crying. I would be much obliged to you, as this scheme will be applicable to New-Hampshire, to send them a copy.

From Governor Trumbull.

Hartford, November 30, 1776.

Sir:

Your favours of the 21st and 22nd instant, were duly received, and now answer, that for the reasons and events you mention, do fully concur in the sentiment, that we must very much, if not altogether, depend upon ourselves on this side the river for preventing the enemy from penetrating this way. In this view of the matter, the assembly have ordered four battalions for march as soon as possible, properly equipped and furnished to continue till the 15th of March next; in meantime our quota of regulars will be raising and forwarding. The most effectual measures have been taken to engage officers of the stamp you mention; much certainly depends upon it, and flatter myself there will be no further cause of complaint upon that head. The forming of officers, as well as men, is a work of time.

We have the highest sense of your zeal, vigilance and labor, for our common safety and prosperity; and in turn assure you of every reasonable exertion to aid your endeavours; we have consequently ordered a considerable supply of clothing, blankets, &c immediately to be forwarded, and are determined, with a due dependence upon the divine Disposer of events, notwithstanding our late disappointments, and the additional loss of the fort by your name, to maintain our cause to the last extremity.

I am, with great esteem and regard, your most obedient, humble Servant

Jonth. Trumbull

The Honorable Major General Lee.

To General Heath.

Peeks Kill, December 1st 1776.

For the satisfaction of Gen. Heath, and at his request, I do certify, that I am commanding officer, at this present writing, in this post, and that I have, in that capacity, ordered Prescott's and Wyllis's regiments to march.

Charles Lee, Maj. Gen.

From General Washington.

Brunswick, December 1st 1776.

Dear Sir:

The enemy are advancing, and have got as far as Woodbridge and Amboy, and from information not to be doubted, mean to push to Philadelphia. The force I have with me is infinitely inferiour in number, and such as cannot give or promise the least successful opposition. It is greatly reduced by the departure of the Maryland Flying-Camp men, and sundry other causes. I must entreat you to hasten your march as much as possible, or your arrival may be too late to answer any valuable purpose. Your route, and the place to join me, I cannot particularize; in these instances you must be governed by circumstances, and the intelligence you receive. Let the former be secure. I hope to meet a considerable reinforcement of Pennsylvania Associators; it is said they seem spirited upon this occasion.

I am, dear sir, yours, &c.

G°. Washington.

To Major General Lee.

FROM DR. JOHN MORGAN.

Ramapough, Decr 2nd, 1776.

DR GENERAL,

I think it my Duty to give you every piece of Information in my power to procure, leaving you to judge how far it is to be regarded.

I have seen a very intelligent Person at Sufferings who came last night from Hoppers Tavern, 10 Miles on this side Hackensack. He says that there are not more than a thousand Hessians and Waldeckers at Hackensack, & none of the British Troops; the Enemy having pushed on to Newark & Elizabeth Town: That three Armaments have sailed from N. York, & in fact that they have left no great Body of Troops in that place: Those which are there being posted chiefly at Kingsbridge. The precipitate Retreat of our Troops from Hackensack has made thousands of Tories: Several friends to the cause of Liberty think a good stroke might be struck by a brigade or two marching suddenly and surprising those left at Hackensack, which might occasion some delay in their march towards the Southward, and allow time for succours to arrive to General Washington.

My informer says the Tories declare openly that whenever G. Washington makes a stand, a body of the British Troops will be sent this way to prevent a junction of that part of the Army under your command with Genl. Washington. He says that one of the three Armaments, and that the largest is intended up the Delaware to favour the operations of the Troops now at Elizabeth Town on their way to Philadelphia. I make no comment on this information, but think it my duty to relate matters as I hear them; perhaps you have more authentic Intelligence.

I remain Dr General, Your most ob^{t} hble Servt.

JOHN MORGAN.

Major Genl. Lee,
at his Quarters near Peekskyll.

To General Joseph Spencer.

Peeks Kill, Decr ye 2^{d} 1776.

DR General,

If you have reason to think that any considerable Corps of the Militia will join you in a few days, you may venture to keep the Post you at present occupy, but if there is no prospect of such a junction I wou'd by no means have you remain, as you might with your few numbers, in a position which demands a considerable Force, be expos'd to insult or surprise. In this case you should retire to the hill where two companies of Fellows' Brigade are posted to cover the stores, it is strong by nature and requires but little labor to be rendered very respectable. I wish to God the militia may join you soon so as to enable you to keep your present Post, as it is in my opinion very important—it protects a fine country of forage much wanted by the enemy—it covers the frontiers of Connecticut, and keeps the large bodies of Tories in order, who without some such check wou'd probably take an active part I hope you have detach'd the four hundred men to Heath or his heart will break. He is confident that all the movements of the Enemy in every part of the continent are only feints, that they only mean to weaken him, and that when He is taken all is lost—the fact is so many men of the Party I march'd off from White Plains are so fatigu'd that without taking two Regiments from Heath I cou'd not march in force sufficient to the Jerseys, and perhaps the fate of America depends on the competency of my force—this number ordered from you is to replace the two Regts.

Adieu Dr General. Let me hear from you on every occasion.

Yours

Charles Lee.

From General Washington.

Trenton, December 3d, 1776.

Dear Sir :

I was just now favored with your letter of the 30th ultimo. Having wrote you fully both yesterday and to day of my situation, it is unnecessary for me to add much at this time. You will readily agree that I have sufficient cause for my anxiety, and to wish for your arrival as early as possible. In respect to instructions on your route, you must be governed by circumstances. This has been the language of all my letters since I had occasion to call for your aid. The sooner you can join me with your division, the sooner the service will be benefitted. As to bringing any of the troops under General Heath, I cannot consent to it. The posts they are at, and the passes through the Highlands, being of the utmost importance, they must be guarded by good men. I would have you to give me frequent advices of your approach. Upon proper information in this instance, much may depend.

I am &c

G°. Washington

To Major General Lee.

To General Washington.

Haverstraw, December ye 4th 1776.

Dear General :

I have received your pressing letter; since which intelligence was sent to me that you had quitted Brunswick, so that it is impossible to know where I can join you. But although I should not be able to join you at all, the service which I can render you will, I hope, be full as efficacious. The Northern Army has already advanced nearer Morristown than I am. Shall put myself at their head tomorrow. We shall upon the whole compose an army of five thousand good troops in spirits. I should imagine, dear General, that it may be of service to communicate this to the corps immediately under your command. It may encourage them, and startle the enemy; in fact, their confidence must be risen to a prodigious height if they pursue you, with so formidable a body hanging on their flanks or rear. I shall clothe my people at the expense of the Tories which has a double good effect—it puts them in spirits and comfort, and is a correction of the iniquity of the foes of liberty. It is paltry to think of our personal affairs, when the whole is at stake; but I entreat you to order some of your suite to take out of the way of danger my favourite mare, which is at Hunt Wilson's, three miles the other side of Princeton.

I am, dear General, Yours

CHARLES LEE.

His Excellency General Washington.

To General Heath.

Haverstraw, 4th December, 1776.

Sir,

The troops here are so distressed for rum this rainy weather, that I must request you'll immediately forward ten hogsheads of rum down to Colonel Hay's landing in Haverstraw Creek.

I am, sir, yours,

CHARLES LEE,
Major General.

To Major General Heath.

To General Heath.

Ringwood Iron-works 6th December, 1776.

Sir,

I am directed by General Lee to inform you he has had the misfortune to lose three of his best camp horses, and begs the favor you'll have some inquiry made amongst the soldiery under your command. One is a black, with a nag tail, fifteen hands high; a brown bay, with a switch tail, fourteen-and-a-half hands; and a sorrel mare, with a blaze-face and a switch tail, about fourteen hands and an inch.

The General offers three guineas reward, or a guinea for each.

I am, Sir, your very obedient, humble servant

Joseph Nourse, Secretary.

Honourable Major-General Heath, Peekskill

To Gov. Nicholas Cooke.

Pompton, 7th December, 1776.

Dear Sir,

As there is now no doubt of the enemy's directing a considerable force towards your island, my duty to the publick, and my regard for the welfare of your Colony in particular, urge me to every expedient which may be serviceable to you; and I must entreat you not to impute the freedom with which I shall offer my thoughts upon this occasion to a petulance of disposition, but to the most pure and disinterested zeal. I have, sir, from what I have observed of the New England troops, the highest confidence in the valor of your men and common run of your officers, particularly those who are of the younger part. They have activity and fire, and in general more knowledge than those advanced in years, who are not only destitute of knowledge, but incapable, from a certain rustiness of mind and temper, of acquiring any. In fact, the only advantage of years in any profession is, that it enables us to add to our stock of knowledge. But if we do not avail ourselves of the days which nature has made a present of to us for this purpose, the more years have passed over our heads, the more disqualified are we for the profession of a soldier of any rank. Now it unfortunately happens in New England, that to the most disqualified the highest trusts are committed. To speak directly, the appointments of Generals in your Provinces threaten destruction; but in fact it is impossible that you should have men equal to this arduous task. Theory joined to practice, or a heaven-born genius, can alone constitute a General. As to the latter, God Almighty indulges the modern world very rarely with the spectacle; and I do not know, from what I have seen, that he has been more profuse of this ethereal spirit to the Americans than to other nations. But to come to the point: Rhode Island will probably be, attacked; your men and younger-officers are good, but I am persuaded you have no man with you capable of conducting an army; no man who has sufficient knowledge as an Engineer. I have therefore resolved to send a gentleman, with whose great talents, activity, and zeal I am well acquainted. His name is Malmedie, a Frenchman. I entreat, if you cannot give him the entire command, to be directed by his counsels. You must excuse his heat of temper at times, as it is derived from a noble source of enthusiasm for your cause. Procure for him an able interpreter; and treat him, as I am sure you will, with all the respect and attention he deserves. God bless you, Sir. Believe me to be, most devotedly, yours

Charles Lee

Governour Cooke.

P. S. I believe I shall send you Colonel Varnum, but I hope you will continue to give Mr. Malmedie high Colonial rank, which will lead him to Continental.

FROM WILLIAM KENNON.

North Carolina, Halifax, December 7, 1776.

SIR:

The magazines you ordered are accordingly formed, and from a conversation of yours with Mr Southerland, my agent at Cross Creek, and your letter to General Moore, I judged it to be your wish that I should form magazines in Georgia, North-Carolina and Virginia. I immediately prepared for doing so, in such manner as I thought best from so imperfect a knowledge of your desires, and found occasion often to regret that you had not sent for me from Cross Creek to have met you on the road, or have wrote me a line; however, I have done what I believe will answer your design, and in such a way as must meet your approbation, since the Continent will be at no expense unless the provisions should be used; for things are laid in on such terms as to produce more than prime cost and charges, either by shipping to the West Indies or selling to the merchant exporters.

I am just returned from the southern line of Georgia, and have formed magazines on the Altamahaw, on the head of Ocgechey, at Augusta, and about forty miles above Savannah. In this state I've formed them so as to answer the service here, or transport to Virginia, at an easy rate, according to orders. Such provisions as I've laid in for Virginia and North-Carolina will, by a circumstance worth the attention of the Congress, be very dear, which is the vast number of commissaries, contractors, or purchasers, appointed by the imprudence of the Virginians, and the want of integrity of the North Carolinians; for they, in order to enhance the price of provisions, by raising of which most in this Colony live, appointed by so many competitors in the purchase that I am now paying double at least to what I did a few days ago; for there are now nine Commissaries in this state, of separate interests, with a number from Virginia, and the people here are combining to advance it to a most exorbitant height; and unless there is a single purchaser appointed for your district, which must chiefly be furnished from North Carolina with pork and beef, the Continent will suffer one hundred per cent, in all the meat used by the troops. This, Sir, I hope will deserve your particular attention, and that I shall hear from you as soon as your arduous situation will admit. I am not courting the place of Commissary General of your district, though it would be acceptable to me, but it is my duty to lay before you, Sir, this extraordinary and improper expense, as I wish the business done by me should be in a way the least burthensome to the State. There are variety of reasons which might be urged against the measure of so great a number of Commissaries; but one good reason is enough for Government: the exorbitant increase in the price of provisions by thirty or forty purchasing competitors. Would any private gentleman of the Congress, having occasion for twenty thousand barrels of beef and pork, to be bought up at one certain market, employ a single factor or agent to execute that trust; or would he order thirty different agents to purchase up the provisions, maintain each of them as bidders on each other at vendue and risk beside the want of their knowledge and integrity? Too many fingers in the publick purse will endanger the State of North-Carolina, and the Congress, as far as in them lays, should prevent it.

This will be delivered to you by Captain Allen, who can explain this, and every other matter, to your satisfaction. These Commissaries are now insisting to march to Charles-Town with their different regiments; and I need not tell you, Sir, what an effect such a competition will have at that market, already the highest on the globe; but can be lowered by the quantity of provisions in this State, provided the purchase is left to one upright, industrious, deserving man.

Your letter to Mr Harrison, Paymaster in Virginia,

was forwarded in a few days after date express by me, but no answer received. I am this day sending for the hundred thousand dollars mentioned therein, which I hope to receive. If I do not, Captain Allen will inform you, and you will order it from Philadelphia by immediate express, as I am in great want, having borrowed large sums from private people, who have sometime expected payment. It would be also necessary for me to have a further credit on the Continental Treasury, and I am ready to enter into any security, if any should be required; and as to the hundred thousand, if it is necessary, I will give security for that sum also before it is paid me at Charlestown; in which case, it may be sent to the Commanding officer, with direction as to the security. I have the fullest confidence that should M[r] Harrison decline sending this hundred thousand dollars you will order it, so that I shall receive at least that sum in two months from this date. In the meantime, I shall borrow on the credit of this expectation. I have purchased a quantity of rum and osnabrigs, the latter of which the nakedness of the soldiers induced me to do. I have devoted my whole time to the service of you and your district, and shall on all occasions prove to you my desire of being serviceable to the Continent; but I wish not to be interrupted by injurious competitions, which can answer no other purpose but increase the price of provision to an intolerable height, and introduce confusion in the camp by a variety of agents.

I sometime ago wrote by post from Wilmington, and lately sent you two letters, one from M[r] Bryan and the other from Hispaniola, which I hope you have received.

I have the honor to be, Sir, with all duty and respect,

Your most obedient Servant,

WILL. KENNON.

From General Heath.

Peekskill, December 8th 1776.

Dear General:

Yesterday afternoon Lieutenant Colonel Vose arrived at this place from Albany, with Greaton's, Bond's, and Porter's regiments, making in the whole between five and six hundred men. I have advised them not to lose a moment's time, but to follow you immediately. I am furnishing them with provisions, tents, &c. and they will begin their march this day.

Captain Williams, of Greaton's informs me this morning that General Gates had sent forward orders for the troops to rendezvous at Goshen. He had not received your letter until he heard from you that they might know what route to take.

I have advised the troops here to proceed, as it is most probable General Gates who is to be at Goshen this night, will join them on the road.

I submit it to you, sir, if it would not be best to send an express back, with such directions as you may think proper, either to halt them on the road from Goshen, until General Gates comes up, or march forward and join you without loss of time.

I am, dear General, your most humble servant

W. Heath.

Major General Lee.

P.S. General Gates has with him Paterson's, Stark's, Read's & Poor's regiments.

To General Washington.

Morris-Town, December ye 8th, 1776.

Dear General:

Colonel Humpton will give you a return of the Militia already assembled, and of those (if it can be called a return) expected. The whole will, as it is said, make by tomorrow morning one thousand. My corps that passed the North River will amount (for we are considerably diminished) to seven and twenty hundred; in fact our Army may be estimated at four thousand. If I was not taught to think that your army was considerably reinforced, I should immediately join you; but as I am assured you are very strong, I should imagine we can make a better impression by hanging on their rear; for which purpose, a good post at Chatham seems the best calculated. It is at a happy distance from Newark, Elizabethtown, Woodbridge, and Boundbrook. It will annoy, distract, and consequently weaken 'em. As to your Excellency's idea of surprising Brunswick, the post I propose taking offers the greatest probability of success. But we are so ill shod and destitute of light-horse that this desultory war is hard upon the poor soldiers; but must do 'em the justice to say that they have noble spirits and will, I have no doubt, render great service to their country.

God bless you, General,

Yours, most sincerely

CHARLES LEE.

His Excellency General Washington,
Trenton.

TO GENERAL WASHINGTON.

Chatham, December ye 8th 1776.

DEAR GENERAL:

Major Hoops has just delivered to me your Excellency's letter. I am certainly shocked to hear that your force is so inadequate to the necessity of your situation, as I had been taught to think you had been considerably reinforced. Your last letters proposing a plan of surprises and forced marches convinced me that there was no danger of your being obliged to pass the Delaware; in consequence of which proposals I have put myself in a position the most convenient to coöperate with you by attacking their rear.

I cannot persuade myself that Philadelphia is their object at present, as it is almost certain that their whole troops lately embarked have directed their course to the Eastern provinces; for Spencer writes me word that half of it has passed the sound, and the other half turned the south western end of Long Island and steered eastward. I detached Colonel Varnum and Mons. Malmedie to take the direction of the Rhode Island Troops, who are without even the figure of a General. It will be difficult, I am afraid, to join you; but cannot I do you more service by attacking their rear? I shall look about me tomorrow, and inform you further.

I am, dear General, Yours

CHARLES LEE.

To His Excellency General Washington.

TO A COMMITTEE OF CONGRESS.

Morris-Town, December 8th 1776.

GENTLEMEN:

Enclosed is a return of the Militia already assembled. More are expected in. The whole will, it is said, make by to morrow morning one thousand. My corps that passed the North River will amount (for we are considerably diminished) to seven and twenty hundred; in fact our Army may be estimated at four thousand. If I was not taught to think that the army with General Washington had been considerably reinforced, I should immediately join him; but as I am assured he is very strong, I should imagine we can make a better impression by beating up and harassing their detached parties in their rear, for which purpose a good post at Chatham seems the best calculated. It is at a happy distance from Newark, Elizabethtown Woodbridge and Boundbrook. We shall, I expect, annoy, distract, and consequently weaken them in a desultory war; but we are so ill shod and destitute of light horse, that the troops are in a bad condition for this species of service. I must do 'em the justice to say, that they have noble spirits, and will, I have no doubt, render great service to their country.

I am, Gentlemen, with the greatest respect, your most obedient, humble servant,

CHARLES LEE.

To the Honorable
Richard Henry Lee and
Benjamin Rush,
Committee of Congress.

FROM THE MASSACHUSETTS ASSEMBLY.

Boston December 8, 1776.

SIR:

The General Court have received your favors of the 21st 22nd 27th and 30th November last, and gratefully acknowledge your care in favouring us with all necessary intelligence. With pain we read the disasters that have befallen us, but yet are not dispirited. Immediately on receipt of your first letter, we forwarded to the camp supplies, in addition to what we had sent before, of shoes stockings, and blankets. Are now exerting, and shall continue to exert, ourselves for affording to the army every species of clothing in our power. We had issued orders for raising a part of all our able bodied effective men at home when your first letter was received, and we have pursued every means we could devise for expediting their march, and hope they will all seasonably arrive in camp, to support our common cause, and that their number will not fall short of six thousand men. We are now contemplating the most effectual measures for raising with vigour our quota of the Continental Army, and are determined to call into action every power and strain every nerve in support of our liberties. We earnestly request your frequent correspondence, which will give us great pleasure. The alarming accounts we have for four or five days successively received, of a large naval force near New-Port, though it may embarrass our proceedings, yet will not divert us from our purposes. Our ardent wish is, that you may be succeeded in your exertions in the common cause, in which we shall not fail to coöperate with you.

To General Lee.

P. S. The General Court have just laid a general embargo on all shipping.

To General Heath.

Chatham, December ye 9th 1776.

Dear General:

I am very much obliged to you for your welcome tidings, and have only to beg that you will direct the regiments you speak of to march without loss of time to Morris-Town. I sent an express to you last night from the General, ordering your division over the river, which I confess for my own part, I am heartily sorry for, as I think we shall be strong enough without you, and New England, with your district, will be too bare of troops. I am in hopes here to reconquer (if I may so express myself) the Jerseys. It was really in the hands of the enemy before my arrival.

Adieu, dear sir,

Charles Lee.

To Major General Heath

Peekskill.

From General Washington.

Trenton Falls, December 10th 1776.

Dear Sir:

I last night received your favor by Colonel Humpton; and were it not for the weak and feeble state of the force I have, I should highly approve of your hanging on the rear of the enemy and establishing the post you mention. But when my situation is directly opposite to what you suppose it to be, and when General Howe is pressing forward with the whole of his army except the troops that were lately embarked, and a few besides left at New York, to possess himself of Philadelphia, I cannot but request and entreat you, and this too by the advice of all the General officers with me, to march and join me with all your whole force with all possible expedition. The utmost exertions that can be made will not be more than sufficient to save Philadelphia. Without the aid of your force, I think there is but little, if any, prospect of doing it. I refer you to the route Major Hoops would inform you of. The enemy are now extended along the Delaware at several places. By a prisoner who was taken last night, I am told that at Pennytown there are two battalions of Infantry, three of Grenadiers, the Hessian Grenadiers, Forty-second of Highlanders, and two others. Their object, doubtless, is to pass the river above us, or to prevent your joining me. I mention this that you may avail yourself of the information. Do come on. Your arrival may be happy; and if it can be effected without delay, may be the means of preserving a city whose loss must prove of the most fatal consequences to the cause of America.

I am, &c°

G°. Washington.

To Major General Lee.

P. S. Pray exert your influence and bring with you all the Jersey Militia you possibly can, Let them not suppose their State is lost, or in any danger, because the enemy are pushing through it. If you think General St. Clair or General Maxwell would be of service to command 'em, I would send either.

From M. Malmedy.

Providence, 10th December, 1776.

My General:

I could not arrive till the 6th. owing to the difficulty I met with in some places to procure horses. As soon as I arrived, I sent the letter with which you intrusted me, to the Governour. Accept, Sir, my warmest thanks for the recommendation with which you have honored me, and be assured I shall exert my utmost endeavours to render myself worthy the opinion and goodness you have expressed in my behalf.

The Governour desired me to view the lines of circumvallation, which were opened on the right bank of the river by Mr Crow. They are drawn on that side quite around the town. They appeared to me to be at too great a distance from the town, and too extensive; and from the difficulty of defending them, on a sudden emergency, and by reason of the great number of men requisite for their defence—you know, my General, how dangerous such lines are. They have heretofore been found useless in many places, although traced out with great judgment. I proposed to the gentlemen to draw others within them. I perceived they were satisfied with the utility of this, and agreed to it. I changed the defences, and brought the posts nearer; and possibly, my General, when they are finished, you will think them capable of being defended. They were desired by the people to quiet their fears. I asked last night for orders to see Holan's Ferry, which you particularly recommended to me. This morning I wait for instructions.

I cannot give you a true idea of the distribution and arrangement of the troops; they are not yet settled. I always view with pleasure the great number of beautiful towns, which every moment present themselves to view. I can never believe the enemy will be able to overrun this country, without great difficulty. You have doubtless an account of their numbers and positions.

You were pleased, my General, to request these gentlemen to give me the rank of a Colonel; which they immediately granted to me. It is very flattering to me to owe my promotion to you. The qualities you possess, and the deserved reputation which you enjoy, render this infinitely precious to me.

It is of great importance, my General, to me, to be commissioned by Congress, if you desired it, before the first of January, in order to be older in rank than a number of others. Permit me this morning, I beseech you, to beg the favor of you to make this demand for me as soon as possible. My acknowledgements for the favour shall equal the respect with which I am, my General,

Your most humble and obedient Servant

MALMEDY.

FROM GENERAL WASHINGTON.

Trenton Falls, December 11th 1776.

DEAR SIR:

Your favour of the 8th instant, by the Light Horseman, reached me last night. Having wrote you fully respecting my situation just before it came to hand, it is unnecessary to add much now. I shall only say that Philadelphia, beyond all question, is the object of the enemy's movements, and that nothing less than our utmost exertions will be sufficient to prevent General Howe from possessing it. The force I have is weak and entirely incompetent to that end. I must therefore entreat you to push on with every possible succour you can bring. Your aid may give a more favorable complexion to our affairs. You know the importance of the city of Philadelphia, and the fatal consequences that must attend the loss of it.

I am, &c.

To Major General Lee. G°. WASHINGTON.

TO GENERAL HEATH.

Morris-Town, December y[e] 11th 1776.

SIR,

I would recommend to you, if you are at Ramapouch or Pompton, to take your route either by the Great or Little Falls; if by the Great Falls, you may come by Hachquacknock. If by the Little Falls you may inquire for Newark Mountains, and come a route at a small distance from the river; but had better send an express to Springfield, seven miles west of Elizabeth-Town, where about one thousand Militia are collected to watch the motions of the enemy. Their subsequent motions must be directed according to circumstances.

CHARLES LEE, Major General.

P.S. The gentlemen to whom you are to address yourself for intelligence are Colonel Ford, at or near Springfield, or the Rev. James Caldwell, near Chatham.

TO GENERAL HEATH.

Head-Quarters, Morris-Town, December 11th, 1776.

MUCH RESPECTED SIR:

By order of General Lee, I beg leave to inform you that we have no rum for the soldiery, and but very little flour. As the Army is continually increasing, I am apprehensive that the Army must suffer. General Lee therefore recommends that you order a large quantity of the above-mentioned articles on after the Army.

Your most obedient and very humble servant,

ALEX. SCAMMELL, D. A. G'L.

Major-General Heath.

TO GENERAL WASHINGTON.

Morristown, December ye 11th, 1776.

We have three thousand men here at present; but they are so ill-shod that we have been obliged to halt these two days for want of shoes. Seven regiments of Gates's corps are on their march, but where they actually are, is not certain. General Lee has sent two officers this day; one to inform him where the Delaware can be crossed above Trenton; the other to examine the road towards Burlington, as General Lee thinks he can, without great risk, cross the great Brunswick post road, and by a forced night's march, make his way to the ferry below Burlington. Boats should be sent up from Philadelphia to receive him. But this scheme he only proposes, if the head of the enemy's column actually pass the river. The Militia in this part of the Province seem sanguine. If they could be sure of an army remaining amongst 'em, I believe they would raise a very considerable number.

To ———.

Morristown Decr ye 11th 1776

Dr Sir

Capt Gibson's merit in so cheerfully encountering the fatigues and dangers of an expedition to New Orleans for the service of his country will I am perswaded sufficiently recommend him to the Congress I shall only add that he is a man qualifyed to render still greater services and that they cannot too greatly encourage such merit—

I am, Sir, with the greatest respect.

Your most obt Humble Servt

Charles Lee.

From the Rev. James Caldwell.

Turkey, December 12, 1776.

Dear Sir:

I thank you for your favour from Baskenridge of this morning, and intended to do myself the honor to wait upon you, and set out for that purpose, but found my horse would not perform the journey with sufficient expedition, and cannot procure another here. And indeed I find this the best place to observe the enemy's motions. From sundry persons who have been upon the road between Brunswick and Princeton, I learn the army has very generally marched forward; indeed, all except guards of the several posts. Yesterday they sent a reinforcement to Elizabethtown from Amboy, of near one thousand. Some say the whole at Elizabethtown are about one thousand; others say fifteen hundred. They are carrying off the hay from Elizabethtown to New York. At New York there are but about five hundred men left at Fort Lee; it is said a battalion of the Scotch. At Hackensack, and from thence to Elizabethtown, none. I believe Elizabethtown is their strongest post, as they were afraid of our Militia, who have taken off many of the most active Tories, made some prisoners, and, among others, shot their English Forage-master, so that he is mortally or very illy wounded. A company of our Militia went last night to Woodbridge, and brought off the drove of stock the enemy had collected there, consisting of about four hundred cattle and two hundred sheep. Most of those cattle are only fit for stock. Colonel Ford begs your directions what to do with them. I advised that those not fit to kill should be sold, recording the marks, that Whig owners might receive the money for which they sell respectively. It will cost more than the value of them to keep them in a flock. They are driven up the country to be out of the enemy's way, and the Colonel will follow your directions as to the disposition of them.

At a council of the Field Officers this morning, a majority of them advised to remove the brigade of Militia back again to Chatham, for which they assigned these reasons: Many of the Militia, rather fond of plunder and adventure, kept a continual scouting which kept out so many detached parties that the body was weakened; and the enemy being now stronger at Elizabethtown than they are, they thought they would better serve the cause by lying at Chatham till the expected army approaches for their support.

Colonel Ford also desires your directions with respect to the arms, horses, or other property taken with any of the enemy. The parties who take them think themselves entitled to these things.

I enclose you some examinations. Colonel Ford thinks, from the circumstances of the wagons taken up at Brunswick to go empty to Trenton, that the enemy intended to retreat. I hope their retreat will be guarded against. I have very much suspected as soon as our whole Army is over the river they will return to reduce this Province, leaving only part of their Army at the river to prevent ours returning, till they have plundered us at their pleasure.

With every kind wish for your prosperity, dear sir, your unfeigned friend and most obedient and humble servant

James Caldwell

The Honorable General Lee

P. S. I have sent you Jacob Vincent and two or three more Light-Horse, in whom you can depend.

To General Gates.

Basking Ridge, Dec'r ye 1^{2}_{3}th 1776.

My Dr Gates:

The ingenious manœuvre of Fort Washington has unhing'd the goodly fabrick We had been building—there never was so damn'd a stroke—*entre nous*, a certain great man is most damnably deficient—He has thrown me into a situation where I have my choice of difficulties—if I stay in this Province I risk myself and Army and if I do not stay the Province is lost for ever—I have neither guides Cavalry Medicines Money Shoes or Stockings—I must act with the greatest circumspection—Tories are in my front rear and on my flanks—the Mass of the People is strangely contaminated—in short unless something which I do not expect turns up We are lost—our Counsels have been weak to the last degree—as to what relates to yourself if you think you can be in time to aid the General I wou'd have you by all means go You will at least save your army—it is said that the Whigs are determin'd to set fire to Philadelphia if They strike this decisive stroke the day will be our own—but unless it is done all chance of Liberty in any part of the Globe is forever vanish'd—Adieu, my Dr Friend—God bless you.

Charles Lee.

From General Washington.

Head Quarters at Keith's December 14th 1776.

Dear Sir:

I last night received your letter of the 11th instant by Major DeHart. I am much surprised that you should be in any doubt respecting the route you should take, after the information you have had upon that head, as well by letter as from Major Hoops, who was despatched for the purpose. A large number of boats *was procured and is still retained at Tinnicum under a* strong guard, to facilitate your passage across the Delaware. I have so frequently mentioned our situation and the necessity of your aid, that it is painful to me to add a word on the subject. Let me once more request and entreat you to march immediately for Pitt's Town, which lies on the route that has been pointed out, and is about eleven miles from Tinnicum Ferry. That is more on the flank of the enemy than where you are. Advise me of the time you will arrive there, that a letter may be sent you about your further destination, and such other movements as may be necessary.

The enclosed for Generals Gates and Arnold you will forward by an officer without delay. The former I have requested to come on with the regiments he has, with all possible expedition; the latter to go to the eastward on the intelligence received from Governour Trumbull. Part of the enemy have advanced as far as Burlington, and their main body, from the best information, is in the neighbourhood of Trenton and at Penny-Town.

The Congress have adjourned from Philadelphia to meet at Baltimore on the 20th instant, and sensible of the importance of the former, have directed it to be defended to the utmost extremity, to prevent the enemy from possessing it. The fatal consequences that must attend its loss are but too obvious to every one. Your arrival may be the means of saving it; nothing but a respectable force, I am certain, from melancholy experience, can induce the Militia to come in and give their aid. The Roebuck and a sloop of war have arrived in Delaware Bay, and from the last advices were laying not far within the Capes. I have wrote to General Heath to proceed with his troops with all possible despatch to Pitt's-Town, where I hope to hear of the arrival of General Gates with the regiments that are with him in a short time, if my information is true.

I am, dear sir, yours, &c

G°. Washington.

P. S. The letters for Generals Gates and Arnold I have sent by another conveyance.

From M. Malmedy.

Providence, 20th December, 1776.

My General:

I had in your orders on the 1st that I should go to Holan's Ferry, which you particularly recommended to me. The gentlemen of the Committee imagined that Warwick Neck was more important, since the enemy are in Rhode-Island. I returned the same evening. I have traversed all near to the point of Connecticut, all the neck of Warwick. I cannot perceive in all that part the possibility of hindering the enemy from making a descent. The banks throughout are easy of access, and the vessels can come close to the land. There is, however, an advantageous situation for a camp upon the high ground, from whence we can hinder the enemy from forming, and withdrawing themselves from the fire of their cannon. It might serve as a camp of observation. On my return I gave a particular account of this matter.

You know, my General, the situation of the town of Warwick. It is mere folly to attempt to defend it, in case the enemy makes a descent in its neighborhood. I there found some works begun. I thought it my duty not to oppose the desire of the commandant. We have therefore continued and prolonged them, with some regularity, adapted to the ground. The same night I returned to Providence, and gave an account to the Governour of the difficulty of defending that town, and that the post ought to be evacuated. I have sent him an order of retreat for the detachment with the outguards, and requested him to drive from Patuxet a great number of cattle and forage, which are on the neck. I cannot doubt but from its situation, that is the place where the enemy will make their descent, if they land. I think, my General, that after making efforts at Patuxet, and all along the river, we ought to defend Providence, and there engage them. I presented to the Governour four reasons to support this determination. I believe the place where I am will, in a month, be out of danger of a *coup de main.* In that case, the General who shall command the forces, supporting his left and extending obliquely on the right, will cover Boston, and that Province; and I do not believe the enemy dare enter Connecticut, and by that means separate themselves from their vessels, which is their place of arms; nor are they so numerous as to render themselves masters of the river. I beg pardon, my General, for giving you this account of arrangements, especially in a country where you are much better acquainted with. Allow me the indulgence granted to a scholar, who makes essays on your pieces, and whose feeble observations you can easily rectify.

The County of Patuxet is, and will always be, interesting. I pray you to assemble some troops there, and to order a number of fascines, which can be readily found at hand, where occasion requires.

The Governour appears to approve my opinion, and has requested me to continue to give it on all military matters. The little disposition I have seen in this town, relative to troops, in this time of perplexity and danger, when all ought to be in a state of activity, has determined me to present a regular distribution of regiments, and an order of service. I thought it necessary to send them accompanied with letters, and some sentiments in honour of this country. I here enclose you a copy of my first letter, and the order of service.

The gentlemen here are polite. I cannot but think myself honoured with the testimonies they have given of satisfaction on my conduct, and I am particularly flattered with the rank they have given me. But, my General, I do not see that they have done the smallest thing in the matter I proposed to them, nor even in those things which ought not to be deferred a moment. Be pleased to put a favourable interpretation on what I have the honour to say, and believe I give this detail only from the desire I have to see proper dispositions made for the defence of this country. Notwithstanding the proximity of the enemies, and the ease with which they may land, I do not see above six or seven hundred men at Warwick, one thousand or eleven hundred here, four hundred citizens at the most ready to take arms, and only one company of Artillery. The Colonels of the regiments do not know where to rendezvous in case of alarm. I see no posts established; I see no artillery in motion, nor any preparations for that purpose; no exercise at cannon, notwithstanding the great want of instruction. In the meantime the enemy are ten thousand. They do not make any general movement; but they can in one tide embark in flat bottomed boats and land at Warwick-Neck, and arrive at Providence in four hours. That town is worth such an attempt at this moment. It is very important on account of the great quantity of merchandise and ships in its port. I cannot account for the conduct of the English Generals, if they have good intelligence. The people here give themselves up to a lethargick idea, because they are not numerous, and because they serve as a defensive post to Rhode-Island. The Americans ought to fear the illusion; for these two months past it has been very destructive. General Lincoln arrived here the evening before last. I hope he will put things in order. The next day, at ten o'clock, he set out for Bristol and Holan's Ferry, without my knowing of his journey. I am sensibly affected with the disappointment, not having yet a lodging or a horse. I waited on the Committee. My interpreter informed them of my sensibility of not knowing of the departure of General Lincoln, and that I had not yet taken a view of what I proposed. They answered me with the same politeness as usual, that he desired me to see the place, and proposed to make the tour with me, and that he desired Mr Varnum to inform me of this. However, I was not informed as to what I proposed; they were absorbed in business. It is a misfortune in a Government, when military affairs are in the hands of the legislative authority. These are related, but ought in their particular execution, to be independent of each other. I have been well satisfied as to a lodging, but I cannot be supplied with horses. I thought it my duty, sir, to give you a particular account. You have sent me with letters of business and confidence. You have perhaps informed Congress, and have possibly a reliance on my zeal and good will. I will be very unfortunate if in the execution of what I am charged with, I find them useless; and this cannot but appear by the actual situation of things. I fear I shall not hereafter be thought worthy of any confidence, and I am particularly jealous of losing yours and that of the Congress. I beg you will inform Congress of the true situation of affairs. If, my General, I have expressed too great a degree of sensibility in this portrait, I know the goodness with which you have honoured me, and I beg you will correct any thing amiss, or which may displease. "*Honi soit qui mal y pense.*"

I cannot too often repeat, my General, the civilities I have received from these gentlemen. I owe them all my services, and they are but a small mark of my gratitude. I do not know how I shall be employed here. I beg you to recollect the expressions in your letter and your pleasure when you sent me here. I have not yet had a word of orders. To-day Mr. Lincoln is arrived. M[r] Varnum is a Brigadier General. I have rank of him in this Province. I should be very glad to know the line of service to which I ought particularly to be destined. I am no engineer by profession. I have some knowledge and some little abilities. I will finish the open lines with diligence, because they are useful, and because there is but one man here who knows that kind of work. I shall apply myself to everything that depends upon me in this country; but I beg you will not confine me to that profession; I can execute another with more advantage. Be so kind, my General, as to consult Congress, and inform me what is your and their intention respecting my services, and inform the Governour, to whom you have recommended me here. In whatever manner you dispose of me, I will not neglect any of the duties which my condition, emulation, and honour prescribe. These are the pretensions, these the reasons to which I resign myself.

I should go to day to Bristol and Holan's Ferry, but it snows to such a degree that there is no travelling. I should be glad to be under your immediate orders, if there is any operations this spring. I am told half of the fleet is in Virginia; perhaps you are there. I am sorry to be at such a distance from you.

I am, &c

MALMEDY.

FROM M. MALMEDY.

Providence, December 20th 1776.

MY GENERAL:

Upon my arrival here, I sent your letter to the Governour, and offered them my services, without asking any rank. The Assembly of this Province immediately granted me that of Colonel, with which I was flattered and well satisfied. Two hours after, the Assembly having read your letter a second time more attentively, and being determined by some other circumstances, gave me the rank of Brigadier General, which I acknowledge I have not yet deserved.

Ought I not to fear, my General, that this promotion, which is an act of favour, will be a kind of disgrace to me, and that these gentlemen, by loading me with favors, have only prepared me for humiliation, if the Continental Congress should hesitate? Is there not a probability of my not keeping this rank? If I do my duty, it would seem somewhat unjust. That promotion was entirely unsolicited by me. I hope the Congress will attend to these observations, and I beg you would set them in the strongest point of view.

I am, with respect, my General,

MALMEDY.

To His Excellency General Lee, at the Army of the United States of America, in the Jerseys or elsewhere.

FROM JAMES M. VARNUM.

Providence, 23d. December, 1776.

SIR,

I have but one moment to inform you that the enemy, between five and six thousand men, are in possession of Rhode Island. Their menaces are directed against Providence; but as the New England states are forming a plan for its effectual security, the enemy must I think, desist from their plan.

The immense prize ship has just arrived at New Bedford, which occasions my immediate departure into that quarter, to prevent any manœuvres of General Clinton to take it. This makes it impossible for me to give you a full account.

The state have honoured me with the command of their troops.

I am, sir, your very humble servant

J. M. VARNUM.

To General Lee.

To Captain Primrose Kennedy.

Sir:

The fortune of war, the activity of Colonel Harcourt, and the rascality of my own troops, have made me your prisoner. I submit to my fate, and I hope that whatever may be my destiny, I shall meet it with becoming fortitude; but I have the consolation of thinking, amidst all my distresses, that I was engaged in the noblest cause that ever interested mankind. It would seem that Providence had determined that not one freeman should be left upon earth; and the success of your arms more than foretell one universal system of slavery. Imagine not, however, that I lament my fortune, or mean to deprecate the malice of my enemies; if any sorrow can at present affect me, it is that of a great continent apparently destined for empire, frustrated in the honest ambition of being free, and enslaved by men, whom unfortunately I call my countrymen.

To Colonel Harcourt's activity every commendation is due; had I commanded such men, I had this day been free; but my ill-fortune has prevailed, and you behold me no longer hostile to England, but contemptible and a prisoner!

I have not time to add more, but let me assure you, that no vicissitudes have been able to alter my sentiments; and that as I have long supported those sentiments in all difficulties and dangers, I will never depart from them but with life.

C. Lee.

From General Washington.

Newtown, 29th December, 1776.

Dear Sir:

I have the pleasure of enclosing you a letter from your friend Robert Morris, Esq., with a draft on Major Small for £116. 9. 3. sterling.

It will afford me the highest satisfaction to receive a line from you, informing me of the state of your health and your situation, in both of which I hope you are as happy as a person under your circumstances can possibly be.

Such further supplies as you may have occasion for, shall be from time to time remitted to you.

I am, dear Sir, yours, &c

Go Washington.

To Major General Lee,
Prisoner.

To Robert Morris.

N. York, Jany ye 28. [1777.]

My Dr Sir,

I am extremely obliged to you for your kindness and attention—the money for the bill I am told I shall get to-day—I have nothing to request at present but that you will write to Mr Nourse to take care of what belongs to me—and if that my servant Guiseppe is well enough you will send him and desire him to bring the Dogs with him as I am much in want of their Company—God bless you

My respects to Mrs Morris

Yours sincerely

C. Lee.

To Robt Morris, Esq, Phila.

To General Washington.

New York 9th Febry. 1777.

My Dear Sir,

As Lord & General Howe have given me permission to send the Inclosed to the Congress, and the contents are of the last importance to me, and perhaps not less to the Community I most earnestly entreat my dear General that you will Dispatch it immediately & order the Express to be as expeditious as possible, they have likewise Indulged me with the Permission of sending for one of my Aids de Camps—I must therefore request that you will consent to either Bradford or Eustace returning with the Flag of Truce—he will have leave to stay here a day & safe Conduct back, my reason for this request is, that I have many things material with respect to my private affairs which can be settled better by conference than letter. I am likewise extreamly desirous that my Dogs should be brought as I never stood in greater need of their Company than at present. God bless you, my dear Sir, and send you Long Life and Happiness.

Yours most affectionately,

C. Lee.

His Excellency General Washington.

To the President of Congress.

New York 10th Febry 1777.

Sir,

As it is of the Greatest consequence to me, & I think of no less to the Public, I am persuaded that the Congress will comply with the request I am going to make, it is, that they will permit two or three gentlemen to repair to New York to whom I may communicate what so deeply interests myself & in my opinion The Community—the most Salutary Effects may & I am convinced will result from it & as Lord & General Howe will grant a safe Conduct to the Gentlemen Deputed it can possibly have no ill consequences unless the Fatigue & Inconveniency to the particular Gentlemen who are appointed—to Lighten which and save time which in the present situation of Affairs is a matter of the most material consideration, I cannot help expressing my wishes, that some of those gentlemen who at present compose the Committee at Phil[a] might be nominated but this must be referred to your better judgment. If my own interests were alone at stake I flatter myself that the Congress would not hesitate a single moment in acquiescing with my request; but this is far from the case, the Interests of the Public are equally concerned; at least in the opinion of one, who is, and ever shall be most sincerely attached to their welfare.

I am Sir, with the greatest Resp[t.]

Your most obt Humble Sevt

C. Lee

P. S. The Gentlemen Deputed, must pass thro' General Washingtons Camp, where passports will be ready for them.

To General Washington.

New York, Feb. 26, 1777.

My dear Sir,

I am extremely glad Morris is so far recovered that there is a probability of his leaving Philadelphia, where I left him (as I thought) in a very bad way from the effects of his Southern Expedition. I have the sincerest love and affection for him, his excellent qualities, his good sense and integrity must endear him to everybody who knows him. Eustace I consider as my adopted son, considering the circumstances of his being taken out of other hands & his affection for me, I ought to look upon him in this light—in short should any accident happen to me, it has long been my resolution to leave everything I possess on this side the water between these two young men. You will much oblige me therefore by sending Morris to New York the instant he joins you. General Howe will I make no doubt transmit a passport for him by the same flag of truce with this letter as likewise for the gentlemen whom I impatiently expect from the Congress. Eustace, if he comes up in consequence of the enclosed letter will I dare say have the same indulgence—Adieu my dear friend —God preserve and protect you

Yours most sincerely

Gen. Washington. CHARLES LEE.

P.S. You will, I request, shew this note to Morris and his father if he is with you.

TO THE PRESIDENT OF CONGRESS.

N. York March y[e] 19th 1777.

SIR,

In the letter which sometime ago I did myself the honor of addressing to the Congress, altho my own interests were deeply concerned, they were not simply so; I conceived those of America in general to be equally at stake. I am confident that had not some difficulties, which a man in my situation must be unacquainted with, prevented it, you would have comply[d] with my request or favoured me with the reasons of my disappointment, I most earnestly conjure you therefore Sir, that as Lord and General Howe will grant 'em safe passports two or three Gentlemen may be deputed to converse with me on subjects of so great importance not only to myself but the Community I so sincerely love—to prevent delay I have commissioned M[r] Morris to deliver this letter and flatter myself that I shall not be thought indecently pressing when I request that the Gentlemen may without loss of time be deputed or that the inexpediency of the measure may be signify'd to me by letter.

I am, Sir, with the greatest respect,

Your Most Obedient humble Serv[t],

CHARLES LEE.

The Honbl[e] John Hancock.

Scheme for Putting an End to the War, Submitted to the Royal Commissioners, 29th March, 1777.

The following document was first published in Mr. George H. Moore's "*Treason of Charles Lee*"—a paper read before the New York Historical Society, on the 22nd of June, 1858. It had been preserved among the papers of the Secretary to the Royal Commissioners, afterwards Sir Henry Strachey, Bart., M.P., &c. With other interesting papers, it was brought to New York, where, being offered for sale, a portion of the collection was purchased by Mr. Moore.

In order to put on record, not only a proof of the authenticity of this important document, but the fact that the MSS. of which it was one were neither disposed of by the honored family from whose archives they were taken, nor obtained in any improper manner by their present possessor, we are authorized to print the following statement by Sir Edward Strachey, Bart., with reference to such of these papers as have come into the possession of Mr. Moore:

"These Papers were obtained by undue means from Sutton Court, but "having fallen into honourable hands, the retention of them is sanctioned "by the present representative of the Strachey family.

"E. Strachey."

"Sutton Court,
"15 June, 1860."

As on the one hand it appears to me that by the continuance of the War America has no chance of obtaining the ends She proposes to herself; that altho by struggling She may put the Mother Country to very serious expence both in blood and Money, yet She must in the end, after great desolation havock and slaughter, be reduc'd to submit to terms much harder than might probably be granted at present—and as on the other hand Great Britain tho' ultimately victorious, must suffer very heavily even in the process of her victories, evry life lost and evry guinea spent being in fact worse than thrown away: it is only wasting her own property, shedding her own blood and destroying her own strength; and as I am not only perswaded from the high opinion I have of the humanity and good sense of Lord and General Howe that the terms of accommodation will be as moderate as their powers will admit, but that their powers are more ample than their

Successors (shoud any accident happen) wou'd be vested with, I think myself not only justifiable but bound in conscience to furnish all the lights, I can, to enable 'em to bring matters to a conclusion in the most compendious manner and consequently the least expensive to both Parties—I do this with the more readiness as I know the most generous use will be made of it in all respects—their humanity will incline 'em to have consideration for Individuals who have acted from Principle and their good sense will tell 'em that the more moderate are the general conditions; the more solid and permanent will be the union, for if the conditions were extremely repugnant to the general way of thinking, it wou'd be only the mere patchwork of a day which the first breath of wind will discompose and the first symptoms of a rupture betwixt the Bourbon Powers and Great Britain absolutely overturn—but I really have no apprehensions of this kind whilst Lord and General Howe have the direction of affairs, and flatter myself that under their auspices an accommodation may be built on so solid a foundation as not to be shaken by any such incident—in this perswasion and on these principles I shall most sincerely and zealously contribute all in my power to so desirable an end, and if no untoward accidents fall out which no human foresight can guard against I will answer with my life for the success.

From my present situation and ignorance of certain facts, I am sensible that I hazard proposing things which cannot without difficulties be comply'd with; I can only act from surmise, therefore hope allowances will be made for my circumstances. I will suppose then that (exclusive of the Troops requisite for the security of Rhode Island and N. York) General Howe's Army (comprehending every species, British, Hessians and Provincials) amounts to twenty thoushand men capable to take the field and act offensively; by which I mean to move to any part of the Continent where occasion requires—I will suppose that the General's design with his force is to clear the Jersey's and take possession of Philadelphia—but in my opinion the taking possession of Philadelphia will not have any decisive consequences—the Congress and People adhering to the Congress have already made up their minds for the event; already They have turn'd their eyes to other places where They can fix their seat of residence, carry on in some measure their Government; in short expecting this event They have devis'd measures for protracting the War in hopes of some favourable turn of affairs in Europe—the taking possession therefore of Philadelphia or any one or two Towns more, which the General may have in view, will not be decisive—to bring matters to a conclusion, it is necessary to unhinge or dissolve, if I may so express myself, the whole system or machine of resistance, or in other terms, Congress Government—this system or machine, as affairs now stand, depends entirely on the circumstances and disposition of the People of Maryland Virginia and Pensylvania—if the Province of Maryland or the greater part of it is reduc'd or submits, and the People of Virginia are prevented or intimidated from marching aid to the Pensylvania Army the whole machine is dissolv'd and a period put to the War, to accomplish which, is, the object of the scheme which I now take the liberty of offering to the consideration of his Lordship and the General, and if it is adopted in full I am so confident of the success that I wou'd stake my life on the issue—I have at the same time the comfort to reflect, that in pointing out measures which I know to be the most effectual I point out those which will be attended with no bloodshed or desolation to the Colonies. As the difficulty of passing and of re-passing the North River and the apprehensions from General Carlton's Army will I am confident keep the New Englanders at home, or at least confine 'em to the East side the River; and as their Provinces are at present neither the seat of Government strength nor Politicks I cannot see that any offensive operations against these Provinces wou'd answer any sort of Purpose—to secure N. York and Rhode Island against their attacks will be sufficient. On the supposition then, that General Howe's Army (including every species of Troops) amounts to twenty or even eighteen thoushand men at liberty to move to any part of the Continent; as fourteen thoushand will be more than sufficient to clear the Jersey's and take possession of Philadelphia, I wou'd propose that four thoushand men be immediately embark'd in transports, one half of which shou'd proceed up the Patomac and take post at Alexandria, the other half up Chesepeak Bay and possess themselves of Annapolis. They will most probably meet with no opposition in taking possession of these Posts, and when possess'd they are so very strong by nature that a few hours work and some trifling artillery will secure them against the attacks of a much greater force than can possibly be brought down against them—their communication with the shipping will be constant and sure—for at Alexandria Vessels of a very considerable burthen (of five or six hundred Tons for instance) can lie in close to the shore, and at Annapolis within musket shot—all the necessaries and refreshments for an Army are near at hand, and in the greatest abundance—Kent Island will supply that of Annapolis and every part on both banks of the Patomac that of Alexandria. These Posts may with ease support each other, as it is but two easy days march from one to the other, and if occasion requires by a single days march, They may join [A] and conjunctly carry on their operations wherever it shall be thought eligible to direct 'em; whether to take possession of Baltimore or post themselves on some spot on the Westward bank of the Susquehanna which is a point of the utmost importance—but here I must beg leave to observe that there is a measure which if the General assents to and adopts will be attended with momentous and the most happy consequences—I mean that from these Posts proclamations of pardon shou'd be issued to all those who come in at a given day, and I will answer for it with my life

—that all the Inhabitants of that great tract southward of the Patapsico and lying betwixt the Patomac and Chesepeak Bay and those on the eastern Shore of Maryland will immediately lay down their arms—but this is not all, I am much mistaken if those potent and populous German districts, Frederic County in Maryland and York in Pensylvania do not follow their example—These Germans are extremely numerous, and to a Man have hitherto been the most staunch Assertors of the American cause; but at the same time are so remarkably tenacious of their property and apprehensive of the least injury being done to their fine farms that I have no doubt when They see a probability of their Country becoming the seat of War They will give up all opposition but if contrary to my expectations a force should be assembled at Alexandria sufficient to prevent the Corps detach'd thither from taking possession immediately of the place, it will make no disadvantageous alteration, but rather the reverse—a variety of spots near Alexandria on either bank of the Patomac may be chosen for Posts equally well calculated for all the great purposes I have mention'd—viz—for the reduction or compulsion to submission of the whole Province of Maryland for the preventing or intimidating Virginia from sending aids to Pensylvania—for in fact if any force is assembled at Alexandria sufficient to oppose the Troops sent against it, getting possession of it, it must be at the expence of the more Northern Army, as they must be compos'd of those Troops which were otherwise destin'd for Pensylvania—to say all in a word, it will unhinge and dissolve the whole system of defence. I am so confident of the event that I will venture to assert with the penalty of my life if the plan is fully adopted, and no accidents (such as a rupture betwixt the Powers of Europe) intervenes that in less than in two months from the date of the proclamation not a spark of this desolating war remains unextinguished in any part of the Continent.

ᴬ On the Road from Annapolis to Queen Ann there is one considerable River to be pass'd, but as the ships boats can easily be brought round from the Bay to the usual place of passage or Ferry, this is no impediment if the Two Corps chuse to unite They may by a single days march either at Queen Anns or Malbrough.

Endorsed (in the handwriting of Henry Strachey, Secretary to the Royal Commissioners, Lord and Sir William Howe) "Mr. Lee's Plan—29th March, 1777."

From General Washington.

Morristown, 1 April, 1777.

Dear Sir,

I am to inform you, that Congress, not perceiving that any advantage would be derived, either to yourself or the public interest, from an interview between you and a part of their members, could not consider themselves at liberty to comply with your request. At the same time I am to assure you, that every means will be pursued to provide for your safety, and the attainment of your liberty. This I had in charge when Major Morris was permitted to visit you; but I thought proper to defer the communication of it, for reasons which you would deem satisfactory. The enclosed letters came when Congress transmitted the result of your applications. That from Mʳ Morris contains sundry bills of exchange, the detention of which I hope has not subjected you to the least possible inconvenience.

I am, dear Sir, with great regard and esteem,

Your most obedient Servant,

G° Washington.

To Major General Lee,

Prisoner.

To Robert Morris.

N. York April ye 4th 1777.

My Dr Sir,

I have received your most friendly letter & the bills which if not paid shall be deposited in the manner you direct that of £50 has been already paid by Mr Chamier, it is much to be lamented for my own sake as well as that of the Public that the Congress have not thought proper to comply with my request—as their Persons wou'd have indubitably been safe it cou'd not possibly have been attended with any bad consequences and might with good ones. I never before the receipt of your letter heard a syllable of my being sent to England, and as the intentions of Lord and General Howe are kept remarkably secret, I imagine your Informant cou'd only advise you of this from conjecture—but as it possibly may happen—my anxiety for having my servant with me, and some cloaths is great—I therefore request My Dr Friend that you will forward him to me immediately if his health permits—his establishment hereafter depends on his compliance—Adieu my Dr Morris and my respects to your wife—

Yours most sincerely

C. Lee.

Robert Morris, Esq.

I once more entreat you will send Guiseppe immediately and furnish him with the necessary money.

To Guiseppi Minghini.

N York April 4th 1777.

Guiseppi

If your health permits I desire you will without a moments delay set out for this place—your establishment] & fortune depend on your compliance—bring with you as many summer cloaths as you can—silk stockings, linnen wastecoats and breeches tights, boots and a new hat—some books likewise particularly Ainsworth's Dictionary & the six french books, l'histoire politique—if any of the Dogs are with you bring them. Mr. Robt Morris will furnish you with the necessary money.

Addio—come immediately

CHARLES LEE.

To Guiseppi Minghini,
General Lee's Servt
Philadelphia.

TO GENERAL WASHINGTON.

N York, April ye 5th [1777.]

MY DEAR SIR:

It is a most unfortunate circumstance for myself, and I think not less so for the Publick, that the Congress have not thought proper to comply with my request—it cou'd not possibly have been attended with any ill consequences, and might with good ones at least it was an indulgence which I thought my situation entitled me to—but I am unfortunate in all things, and this stroke is the severest I have yet experienced. God send you a different fate. Adieu, My Dr General

Yours most truly and affectionately

CHARLES LEE.

P.S. The enclosed for Philadelphia—I beg you will forward—and that if my servant comes up you will dispatch him immediately.

General Washington.

JACOB MORRIS TO GEN. WASHINGTON.

Philadelphia April 10th 1777.

SIR,

I find by several Gentlemen lately from camp, that I am much censured for not accepting the Commission offer'd by the State of New York, & I am greatly concerned to hear that some people have been ill-natured and ungenerous enough to impute my refusal to General Lee's persuation—this is a reflection upon both that Gentleman's Character & my own that distresses me exceedingly; & I will venture to declare that no friend to him, me or his Country would sport such a cruel sentiment, however I must allow that my refusing immediately after my return from N. Y. was rather untimely and left room for ill-natured suggestions. I only repent therefore that I had not done it previous to my going in.

I am informed that your Excellency apprehended I had already received the Commission & thought it a little extraordinary that I did not send or give in my reasons for declining at Head Quarters—but as that was not the case, I considered it unnecessary—however as I wish, Sir, that you shou'd be perfectly acquainted with my objections to entering into that Corps, I shall inform you.

It has ever been my ambition & ever will be, shou'd my Country or your Excellency think proper to honour me with any military employment, to acquire, if possible, in that station, some small degree of reputation—but being chose to so important an office as Major in a Regiment where the Corps of officers are men of very low Births and no educations, men who I am very conscious are totally ignorant in military affairs, who have not sufficient abilities to improve & who I should be suspicious in time of action might desert me & thereby leave both my life & Character to be sacrificed, are to me capital objections. After this let me be impertinent enough to ask whether Your Excellency can suppose I shou'd be able to bring that Regiment to any order or perfection—their deficiency in which wou'd fall entirely upon my Shoulders, as the most active officer in the Regiment those ostensible reasons among several others too tedious to trouble your Exce^lly with at present deterred me from accepting it.

When I was informed by one of the members of the Convention that they had thought proper to make me that appointment & requested to know whether I would take it, I made some inquiry & was led to believe that it was one of the oldest Regiments on the new establishment of that State & returned them answer that I was very thankful for the honor they had conferred on me & wou'd with pleasure accept but I have since discovered that it is the youngest in the State, where there are four Majors above me, therefore a less probability of my rising—however I do not mean to offer this as a reason for my refusing—

I must beg your Excellency's pardon when I tell you that when I consider the length of time I have been in service & the rank I before held in the army, I think something more than a majority in the youngest Regiment perhaps on the Continent is due me—I claim no other merit than the length of time & rank I have held in the army.

Your Excellency may rely on my wishing for nothing more ardently than to be able to remove that censure so unjustly bestowed on me by my Countrymen—as the Gentleman who promised to carry this goes off this instant—must conclude by subscribing myself

Your Excellency's very humble Servant

JACOB MORRIS.

His Excell^y Genl Washington.

To Robert Morris.

N. York, May ye 19th 1777.

My Dr Sir,

I have just received your letter of the 18 of April—it is very unfortunate that the Congress shou'd have conceiv'd that the Conference which the Gentlemen who were deputed were to have had with me was to have been in the presence of a British Officer—but as I had no notion that they wou'd entertain such an idea it never enter'd my head to assure 'em of the contrary—it would for several reasons have been highly improper to have open'd the business by letter—which if I have the pleasure of seeing you you will be convinc'd of—the two small bills remain as yet unpaid but I have no occasion for money at present as my table is very handsomely kept by the General, who has indeed treated me in all respects with kindness generosity and tenderness. My love to Byrd to Mrs Morris and all my other particular friends—and believe me to be, Dr Sir,

Your most obdt humble servt and Sincere Friend,

Charles Lee.

Robert Morris, Esq.

To General Washington.

Centurion, June 9th, 1777.

My Dear Sir:

Multiplicity of business, the miscarriage of letters or some accident has prevented you from doing what really is in my opinion an act of justice—I mean clearing up to the world the charge brought against Lord Drummond for a breach of Parole; after having read all the Papers relative to this subject, his letters to you, yours to him, Capt Vanderput's, and the Parole, I declare solemnly that it does not appear to me that there is any one thing in his Lordship's conduct which merited even the shadow of censure. The intention of the Parole in restraining him from going on board any of the King's ships was certainly to prevent intelligence being given of the state of the Continent. As this was manifestly the intention I could almost say that if even he had gone on board the Asia voluntarily altho' the terms of the Parole would not have been literally adhered to, the spirit would not have been violated, as it cannot possibly be supposed that he could give any intelligence which would have been new to Cap[t] Vanderput; to and from whose ship people were passing and repassing every day—but Capt. Vanderput's evidence puts it beyond all doubt that his Lordship did not go voluntarily but was compelled on board.

A public charge from persons we esteem sinks deep in the mind of a man of sentiment and feeling. I really believe Lord Drummond to be such, and have reason to think that he has an esteem for you, at least from all I can learn he has ever spoken of you in the handsomest terms. Now, as it appears to me that there can be no doubt from the concurrence of every testimony of his having adhered as scrupulously as possible to the spirit of the Parole, as the affair is of so delicate a nature, as I am acquainted with your way of thinking, I repeat that I must ascribe it rather to a miscarriage of his letters than to any other cause that you have not done him that justice which, had you received them, I am persuaded you must have thought his due. I can perceive he is very much hurt at the charge, and his sensibility I confess, increases the good opinion I before had of him. Not only therefore justice to him but let me add My Dear General, a regard for you obliges me to wish that this affair may be cleared up in some manner satisfactory to the party I think injured; it is a duty which I know if omitted cannot fail of giving much uneasiness hereafter to a man of your rectitude and humanity. I must observe in addition that I cannot imagine his Lordship's return after an absence of three months could administer any reasons for suspicion, for he must either have remained in the West Indies or have returned to some port in North America, as he was prevented by the spirit of the Parole from going to England, indeed the terms of the Parole implied an obligation to return to New York. His long absence likewise from the Continent rendered it impossible for him to furnish any intelligence of the situation of affairs. Should it be asked, why a man in my present situation should interest myself so warmly in this business with which I myself had no concern? I must answer that not only my love of justice, my duty as a Gentleman, and my regard for you enjoin the task, but that I really feel myself personally obliged to Lord Drummond, for since my confinement he has shown a most generous, humane and disinterested attention to me. In the course of conversation this business was accidentally brought on the carpet. As I was a stranger to the circumstances, I was anxious to be made acquainted with them. He submitted the papers to my perusal—I really thought him injured; assured him that it must have proceeded from mistake or the miscarriage of his letters, and offered myself as a volunteer instrument to obtain some reparation. Let me hear from you My Dear General, as soon as possible, and on this subject.

God preserve and bless you and send you every possible felicity is the prayer of one who is most

Truly and affectionately yours

CHARLES LEE.

As I would not unnecessarily swell the packet I have been contented with sending the letters to and from Cap[t] Vanderput—which I think sufficient. This I do on the supposition that those sent have miscarried.

From General Washington.

Head Quarters Morris Town July 4th 1777.

Dear Sir

I received your favor of the 7th June, in which you enter into a consideration of the breach of parole imputed to Lord Drummond, and give it as your opinion, that his conduct has not been such as to justify the imputation.

It can answer no valuable purpose to enter into a discussion of the particulars of this affair, which would probably end as it began and leave his Lordship and myself in the same way of thinking respecting it, which we now entertain. I shall only observe, that at the time the matter happened, it was clearly my sentiment and that of every Gentleman with whom I conversed on the subject, that his Lordship had acted in an exceptionable manner, irreconcileable to the true spirit of his parole. No circumstance, that has since come to my knowledge, appears to me to be of sufficient weight to remove the suspicion, and from any thing I know, I must still retain the same idea of his conduct that I had at first.

I should be sorry to injure his Lordship or any other Gentleman, in so delicate a point, but I do not think justice requires me, either to retract or extenuate what I have said. He may perhaps have acted as he did through misconception; but whatever was the cause, the conclusion I draw was fully authorised by appearances.

You cannot but be sensible, My dear Sir, that the omission of trifling circumstances, or a small difference in representing the same, is capable of altering the complexion of a fact and making it appear in a light very opposite to that in which it ought really to stand, and this will suggest the propriety of not being hasty in fixing your judgment as to the true nature of his Lordship's proceeding in this affair.

I am with much regard and esteem
Dear Sir, Your most Obd[t] Serv[t]
G[o] WASHINGTON.

To Major General Lee,
Prisoner.

To MISS SIDNEY LEE.

New York, Dec[r] y[e] 15, 1777.

MY D[R] SISTER,

This note will I believe, be del'd to you by Capt[n] Rutherford, a very particular friend of mine. He will inform you that my health & spirits are much better than I had reason to expect, for the transition from great and constant exercise to restraint is trying. Our Friend Butler is always the same man he was; and I need not say more to his honor. He tells me that you are tolerably well: keep up your spirits, for mine are good. How do the Townshends? My love to 'em all, to the Manwarrings, Faulkners, Hinks's and Hunts.

Adieu, God bless you,
Your most affectionate Brother
C. LEE.

PAROLE.

I CHARLES LEE of London in the County of Middlesex in England having Leave from his Excellency General Sir Henry Clinton to be out on Parole, do hereby pledge my Faith and Word of Honor, that I will not depart from the House I am placed in by the Commissary for Prisoners, and that I will not go beyond the Limits of this City, and that I will not do so or say any Thing contrary to the Interest of his Majesty or his Government, and that whenever required so to do, I will repair to whatever Place any of his Majesty's Commanders in Chief shall judge expedient to order me.

Given under my Hand in New York *this* 27*th of December* 1777.

CHARLES LEE.

Witness, J. WEMYSS

A true Copy
JOHN WINSLOW,
D. Com. Prisoners.

TO GENERAL WASHINGTON.

New York December ye 30th 1777.

DR. GENERAL

As I have the strongest reason to flatter myself that You interest yourself in whatever concerns my comfort and welfare I think it my duty to inform you that my condition is much better'd—it is now four or five days that I am on my parole, have the full liberty of the City and its limits, have horses at my command furnished by Sr Henry Clinton and General Robinson—am lodg'd with two of the oldest and warmest Friends I have in the world—Colonel Butler and Major Disney of ye 38th Regt with the former I was bred up from the age of nine years at school—the latter is a Commilito from the time I enter'd the service in the 44th Regt.—in short my situation is rendered as easy, comfortable and pleasant as possible for a man who is in any sort a Prisoner—I have nothing left to sigh for but that some circumstance may arise which may make it convenient for both Parties that a general exchange may take place, and I amongst the rest reap the advantage. I have or can have no request at present, my Dr General to make but that you will commission some proper Person to recommend the care of my Farm and affairs to Mr Nourse and to Mr White of Winchester to give my love to all my Friends, particularly to Green, Mifflin, Reed and Moyland and to be persuaded that I am most sincerely and devotedly

Yours
CHARLES LEE.

To His Excellency General Washington.

JACOB MORRIS TO GENERAL WASHINGTON.

Princeton, January 21st 1778.

SIR

Major Williams who will deliver your Excellency this Packet handed me the inclosed papers from my Friend Genl Lee this morning. His being in some measure relieved from his confinement is an event upon which I most sincerely congratulate your Excellency.

As I shall wait your Excellency's instructions how to proceed with regard to the several applications contained in the Genls letters, the honour of a few lines from Head Quarters as speedily as possible on that subject will make me very happy.

Those Letters directed to myself and such other papers which are inclosed, as shall be thought proper, I must submit to your Excellency's pleasure to return with the answer to this.

I remain with Great Respect
Your Excellency's
Most obedient humble Servant,
JACOB MORRIS.

His Excellency General Washington.
Major Williams.

From General Washington.

Valley Forge, 27 January, 1778.

Dear Sir,

I last night received your favor of the 30th ultimo. It gave me great pleasure to hear that you were released from your confined situation, and permitted so many indulgences. You may rest assured, that I feel myself very much interested in your welfare, and that every exertion has been used on my part to effect your exchange. This I have not been able to accomplish. However, from the letters, which have lately passed between Sir William Howe and myself upon the subject of prisoners, I am authorized to expect, that you will return in a few days to your friends on parole, as Major-General Prescott will be sent in on the same terms for that purpose. Indeed, till I saw Major Williams last night, I supposed that he had arrived either at New York or Rhode Island, having directed his releasement as soon as I was at liberty to do it. I will take the earliest opportunity to recommend to your friends, Mr Nourse and Mr White, the care of your farm.

Your request to Major Morris, in favor of Mrs. Battier, reached me only last night. I wish I had been informed of it sooner. I have enclosed a passport for her to Major Morris, and I doubt not but he will do everything in his power to accommodate a lady, from whose husband you have received so many civilities.

I am, dear Sir, with great esteem and regard &c.

G^o^ Washington.

From Dr. Matthew Powell.

Jamaica 1st March 1778.

Dear General,

Going into the Coffee House at Kingston, I heard that a Ship was to sail for New York, and hearing that you were there, the thought struck me, to enquire how my friend fared in these troublesome times. As a *friend* I have often sympathized with you, tho' perhaps I have not coincided with you in opinion. I have often, and still regret that so great and good talents were not employed for that Country & that Constitution so deservedly held in Veneration over all the World, yet I still flatter myself that an accommodation will take place, & reinstate everything in its proper Channel.

I am now & have been settled in this Island four years—a married man, & father of a fine Girl—a Physician practising the healing art, and proprietor of a Sugar Plantation—All which I believe will plant me here for some years. I shall be much pleased to hear how you do—and should be happy if any chance should bring you to this Island, to testify the esteem I have for you. I am told it would not be right to Seal my letter. I shall comply with what is right, but nothing can Seal my mouth from assuring you with how much regard I have the honor to be, Dear General,

Your most obt. & most humble Servant,

MATT POWELL.

(my address) Physician in Spanish Town.

JOSHUA LORING TO COL. SAMUEL B. WEBB.

New York, March 15th 1778.

DEAR SIR,

I yesterday made application to General Robertson for your proposal, and had I met the same Encouragement from the Commodore every thing had been settled to your Wishes, but I apprehend it will now not be worth your attention, as I have this Morn'g: received a letter from Mr Boudinott with Genl Washington's leave to go to Phila & I am to take Genl Lee with me, and expect a general Exchange will immediately take place if I can be of any Service to you command me and am Sir

Your Most Obed^{t} Humble Servt
Jos^{A} Loring,
Commiss^{y} Pris^{rs}

Col. Webb.

Joshua Loring to Elias Boudinot.

New York, March 18th 1778.

Sir,

I am to acknowledge the receipt of yours of 8th Ins^{t} inclosing a Pass for Major Williams & myself to go to Phil^{a} with General Lee, for which I think myself much obliged. I have sent over to Long Island for a very particular acc^{t} of all the Monies due to the Inhabtants for your Officers board, and have directed Mr. Winslow to forward it to You, as it will be impossible to get it in time for me to bring, as we set out the 20th but for your Government I have made a rough Estimate and think it will take about £10,000, N. Y. Curr^{y} to discharge the whole. They went over to the Island 20th Jany 1777 & We have never had less than 250 there one time with another, they were on board Ship but 12 days. I have only to add my wishes for a speedy & final Settlement of our business, and that in future there may be a better Understanding. You shall hear from me the moment I arrive at Phil^{a}

I am Sir
Your Most Obd^{t} Humble Servt
Jos^{A} Loring.

Elias Boudinott, Esq.

Receipt.

Received from Colonel William Butler, Eight

pounds Eleven & Six pence, str. being in full for Eight Dozen port Wine sold General Lee—

New York, 21st March, 1778.

ROBERT [SECOR]

£8: 11: 6. stg.

JACOB MORRIS TO GENERAL WASHINGTON.

Bristol 26th March 1778.

SIR,

It makes me very happy to have it in my power to transmit a piece of information which I am sure will be highly pleasing to Your Excellency.

I parted with Genl Lee yesterday at the Enemy's Lines near Philadelphia in good health & spirits—he acquainted me by a note before I left the picket that as soon as Col. Campbell & the Hessian officers arrive Sir Wm Howe had informed Mr. Loring that he should be permitted to come out.

Inclosed is a letter for Mr. Boudinot.

I am with great respect

Your Excellys most ob. humble Sert

JACOB MORRIS.

His Excelly Genl Washington.

ALEX. HAMILTON TO GENERAL GREENE.

DR GENERAL,

We have to request you will order a couple of very good teams to be got ready to proceed to the enemy's lines for General Lee's baggage. He is to come out on parole on Sunday morning. You will judge when they ought to set out from here—suppose to-morrow noon, so as to get in the neighborhood of Vandeering's mill by to-morrow night. When they are ready to set out to-morrow let them make report to Head Quarters and passports will be given.

Yr. hum. Serv.
A. HAMILTON, A. D. C.

Head Quarters
April 3. [1778.]

PAROLE.

I CHARLES LEE Major General do hereby acknowledge myself a Prisoner of War to the Kings Army, and do pledge my Faith & Sacred Honor that I will not directly, nor indirectly give any intelligence to the King's Enemies, nor say nor do anything contrary to the interest of his Majesty or his government, but in all things will conduct myself as a Prisoner of War ought to do, and that whenever required, I will immediately repair to whatever place His Excellency the Commander in Chief of his Majesty's army in North America shall please to order

Given under my hand this 5th *Day of April at* Phila 1778.

CHARLES LEE.

In Presence of
CHAs O'HARA.
JOSa LORING.

TO GENERAL WASHINGTON.

York April ye 13th 1778.

DR GENERAL

I have reason to hope that the Congress will unembarrass the negotiation of the Commissioners with respect to a general exchange of Prisoners, of all matter which I think foreign to the purpose and that I shall soon be at liberty to take an active part—but I could wish that they would be a little more expeditious tho we cannot expect expedition from democratic councils—it is a curse annexed to the blessing—I perhaps ought to make an apology to you for a liberty I have taken, but if it is viewed in a proper point of view, I am in hopes it can neither be considered a step of indelicacy towards you, nor by General Howe as any violation of the parole I have given. You must know that it has long been the object of my studies, how to form an army in the most simple manner possible—I once wrote a treatise tho I did not publish it, for the use of the Militia of England. By reading Machiavel's institutions and Martial Saxe I have taken it into my head that I understand it better than almost any man living—in short I am mounted on a hobby horse of my own training and it runs away with me indeed I am so infatuated with it that I cannot forbear boasting its excellencies on all occasions, to Friends or Enemies—You must excuse me therefore if I could not refrain from recommending the Beast to some members of the Congress.

God bless you, My D[r] General, and make you happy —for I am most sincerely and affectionately yours

CHARLES LEE.

Inclosed are two notes—for two of my particular friends—which I entreat you will forward by the first Flag of Truce.

PLAN OF AN ARMY, ETC.

A Plan for the Formation of the American Army in the least Expensive Manner possible, and at the same Time for rendering their Manœuvres so little complex that all the Essentials may be learnt, and practised in a few Weeks.

It is allowed by all sensible Soldiers that the Formation Arrangement, and Exercise of the Infantry in

Europe are extremely deficient in Point of Simplicity, that nothing taught is practicable in Action, and it is to be lamented that America has servilely copied these Defects: the Romans, who undoubtedly were the greatest Masters of Tactics were remarkably simple to so great a Degree Indeed that four days of what they called *de Versis*, or we call drilling were only thought requisite —Martial Saxe saw this, and made a public Jest of the Arrangement of Modern Armies, it is true the Invention of Fire Arms has made some Difference; but the Principles of Tactics continue, and ever will continue the same so far as relates to Division, and Subdivisions, charging the Front, advancing, rallying and retreating without Confusion—Colours, Colours he repeats it are the Life and Soul of Manœuvring, and if ever Simplicity was necessary it certainly is for the Americans, who are drawn from their Ploughs have little Time for dressing, and are called forth immediately to actual service—I will venture to pronounce that if the Americans are servilely kept to the European Plan, they will make an Aukward Figure, be laugh'd at as a bad Army by their Enemy, and defeated in every Rencontre which depends on Manœuvres: and I will on the other hand Venture to pronounce that if the Plan propos'd is adopted they will be superior to the Enemy in Every Affair which depends on Manœuvres—It is so simple, Plain, and obvious to every Man who has Common Sense, that if the Officers have only common Discretion, and can at all judge of Distances, they cannot be thrown into Confusion; that they will with Ease change their Front, retire, advance, or rally—

The King of Prussia was ask'd by Martial Saxe why he continued to adhere to a System so obviously barbarous, he acknowledged it was barbarous, but as long as he beat his Enemies who were equally in a State of Barbarism, he thought it absurd to change it, for the Barbarism itself was an advantage to him, as long as other Powers were so kind were so kind as to tread in the same steps. His Troops were continually exercised, and by dint of Exercise what was complex to other Troops to an Extreme Degree, were rendered in some Measure Simple, and easy to his: but if once other Powers ădopted a system more simple he should certainly be obliged to do the same; but what in this way of Reasoning may be sensible in a German Prince would be to the highest Degree absurd in the Americans who ought to make it their Study to come to the Essential Point at once—In this Persuasion the following Plan is offer'd—

Resolv[d]—That

1st Each Regiment to consist of two Battalions.

2[d] Each Battalion to consist of four Companies, Centuries or Grand Division.

3[d] Each Company, Century, or Grand Division to consist of one Captain, 1 Capt[n] Lt., 2 Lieu[ts], 1 Ensign, or Standard Bearer—8 or at least 6 Sergeants, and the same number of Corporals—One Hundred and 20 Privates which is Sixty four Files, two Deep—two Drummers, or horn Sounders.

4th A Colour or Standard to every Grand Division, Company or District One L[t] Colonel, Major, Adjutant, Sergeant Major, Drum Major, Horn Sounder, Major to each Battalion—

The Regimentary Officers to be one Colonel, one Regimental Colour Bearer or Ensign Major with an Orderly Horseman to attend the Colonel—the Ensign Major to have the rank of Lieut—so that Every Regiment will consist of—1 Colonel, 2 L[t] Col[s], 2 Majors, 8 Captains, 8 Capt[n] L[ts], 16 Lieu[ts], 1 Ensign Major, 8 Ensigns, 56 or 64 Sergeants or Corporals, 2 Serg[t] Majors, 2 Drum Majors, 16 Drummers, or horn Sounders, 1024 Privates.

Thus the Battalions will be compleatly and distinctly Officer'd, and the Expence less than that of any European Establishment.

It may be said that the Proportion of Officers is still too great, that Economy dictates a further Diminution the same argument might serve for Arming the Men with sticks instead of Muskets; but in the formation of Armies, the great Point to be considered is how to render 'em serviceable and fit for Action—if the Officers are well chosen there cannot be too great a Number—

Every Man who has seen Service complains of the paucity of Officers—there Certainly ought to be as great a Number of Officers in the Day of Action in the Rear, as in the Front of a Battalion—Many Battles have been lost from this defect, it is true if the Officers, are not well chosen, they are Encumbrance, and Useless Expence, but for this the Appointees must answer—

As the preposterous Number of General Officers are not only Expensive, and a great Disadvantage in the Exchange of Prisoners—but a Depreciation of the Dignity of the American Service—

I would propose that every Brigade should consist of four Regiments or Eight Battalions, that a Major General's Division should be eight Regiments, 16 Battalions; if it should be at any Time necessary, (as it must be) to divide a Brigade; the Eldest of the four Colonels may act as an Occasional Brigadier.—I know not what is the State of the Field Artillery; if there are Guns Sufficient two should be appointed to each Regiment; but I could wish to recommend four or Eight Rifled Barrel'd Amaretts [amusettes] of Four Ounce Calibre, mounted on Light Carriages—I think they would do more Execution on the whole than Field Pieces—

As to Cavalry (but I speak it with the utmost Difficulty, as I am not or cannot be much acquainted with the service) it appears to me, that digesting it with one Corps, and appointing one General as it is called of Horse to command and controul it will rather be disadvantageous, than advantageous to the service—He must be a bold man that will undertake it a Cavalry Officer is not to be form'd in a Day, a Week a Year, or five Years—he must be bred to it from his Youth—With all their Pains there are not five tolerable Cavalry Officers in Europe—The Detail, and combinations are infinite; and if ever any Officer is appointed to command the whole, the consequence will probably be that to cloak his own Insufficiency which is inevitable: he will only check the Ardor (by absurd Restriction) of those who as the head of their respective States may in the Spirit of Partisans render Essential Services—Upon the whole, I could wish that the Spirit of Hussary might be encouraged, that every Young Gentleman, who can raise a Troop might be allowed to exercise his Genius and Industry with as few Restrictions as are consistent with the general Rules of Subordination; that they may have full Play for their Valour, Industry, and Enterprise—Pulaski's Scheme of dressing, arming, and Manœuvring his Legion appears to me admirable—I sincerely wish that Congress may double the Number of his Legion, as I am persuaded from his Principle that he will render them most essential services—A Company of Five Negroes were annext to every Regiment to act as Pioneers they would be Extremely serviceable—

It is said that a Design is Entertained of laying aside Entirely the Office of Colonel, this in my opinion would be Wrong—as the more degrees of Rank there are in an Army the more spurs there are to military ardor, and ambition—The Romans had at least fifty different Ranks of officers in their Legion: but if the Expence is objected to four Battalions may be thrown into a Regiment, and two Regiments form a Brigade—I have heard it has been likewise proposed to take the Staff that is the Aid de Camps and Brigade Majors out of the Line, as is the Practice of the British Army; if this Plan is adopted it will in my opinion ruin the Army. Of the many defects in the British Military Establishment, this is universally Exclaimed against as the greatest; it is the Eternal subject of complaint, Discontent, and Murmuring: for God's sake let us not copy their defects—a Regimental Colour is necessary for every Regiment, by which all their manœuvres must be regulated—Although I object to a General of Horse:

I think an Inspector to Examine their state and condition absolutely necessary—

There is little Probability of America being so superior in Force with their Manifest Inferiority in other Respects as to make an Offensive War: to say that the Americans are so equal to the British in Discipline Officers, and even Ardor or Numbers, as that a Decisive Action in fair Ground may be risqued is talking Nonsense—to hold this Language to the common Soldiers may be prudent enough; but to try the Experiment would be Insanity: a plan of Defense, harassing and impeding can alone Succeed; And in consequence a General Scheme should be laid out—The Enemy will certainly act offensively; and their Plan must be one of these three; to attack, and Cut off Gen[l] Washington, to carry on a Wasting War; or to make themselves masters of certain Districts or Posts, which will give them a greater Extent of Country; occasion Defection amongst the People from Intimidation; and of Course add to their Numbers by American Recruits; if the first is their Plan no Rules can be prescribed; the Issue must certainly depend on General Washington's Force and conduct; if the Second a large Body of Light Troops both horse and foot commanded by Vigilant Judicious, and active Officers can alone defeat and baffle 'em—but if the last is their Project our Preparations are more Simple it is most probable that General Howe will endeavor to make himself master of Lancaster, and give himself Possession of that Rich Country—to prevent which the following Measures are necessary—As it is a Standing Maxim in War to begin with securing our Rear, and providing for a Retreat: all the Fords of Susquehanna from the mouth of Juniata to the Bay ought thoroughly to be Examined only two left open and these two most conveniently chosen, relative to the Position of the covering army; both banks of these two ought to be Strongly redoubted; but as Fords are at best but a precarious Communication—the whole Boats of the River ought to be collected to the most Convenient Point, and protected in the same manner as both Banks by Redoubts: when the Rear Retreat, and Command are thus Secured, able Field Engineers ought to be Employed to chuse proper Positions to cover Lancaster—If Conestoga Creek is well reconnoitrd, I am mistaken if many Excellent Posts may not be discovered—Where Strong Redoubts or rather Forts ought to be constructed but in such a manner that a Retreat (if there is occasion to withdraw the Troops which occupy 'em) may be not precarious—It is far from impossible that if these Precautions are made known to the Enemy—but that they may attempt to turn the Susquehanna by Embarquing their Troops, landing them at Baltimore, or somewhere to the Westward of the mouth—Baltimore ought therefore to be put in a state of Defence—and the Ablest Surveying Field Engineers be immediately detached to Examine the whole tract from Baltimore along the Western Bank quite to York, and chuse Positions that may be taken if occasion requires, and mark out at least if not construct Forts or Redoubts at proper Passes—

Endorsed, (in the handwriting of Charles Thomson, Secretary of Congress) "Genl Lee's plan of an Army, & thoughts on the mode of conducting Operations for the Campaign—1778."

To the President of Congress.

McAlasters, April ye 17th, 1778.

Dr Sir,

As the Congress have shewn a solicitude to procure my exchange (which does me infinite honour) I beg leave to submit to their judgment a mode which I think wou'd infallibly succeed—it is this, that General Burgoyne shou'd be liberated from all obligation not to act on condition I am put at entire liberty—but as He is of higher rank any other General Officer or two Field Officers shou'd be thrown with me into the bargain—as to Mr. Prescott They set not the least value upon him—and tho' General Howe may perhaps in his own heart, be entirely indifferent, or rather wish that Burgoyne may not be at liberty—a point of delicacy will in my opinion oblige him to accede to the proposal—whether I am an object of this importance or not They are the best judges but to speak plainly and perhaps vainly I am really convinc'd as things are circumstanc'd, I am of more consequence to you than General Burgoine is to the other Party I am far from clear that his being liberated will not be advantageous to America, as He certainly is not on the best terms with the Commander in Chief. I am well and hope always shall be well with General Washington—and to speak again vainly I am perswaded (considering how he is surrounded) that he cannot do without me. I ought, I confess, to have propos'd this when I was with you, but the odd humour in which I found some of the members almost frightened me from giving my opinion on any subject. I intreat, my dr. Sir, that you will make this motion, or if you think it improper, as President—to put the affair into the hands of some of my particular Friends, Mr Lee, Mr Carrol, or Mr Chase—if Burgoine is not yet gone it will certainly succeed—and if he is gone it will in all probability. I have many reasons to think it will, but at least it is worth the experiment.

God bless you, Sir, let me hear from you as soon as possible

Yours most sincerely and affectionately,

CHARLES LEE.

Endorsed (in the handwriting of President Laurens) "Major Genl. Lee 17th April, 1778. Recd 21st at night."

FROM GENERAL WASHINGTON.

Valley Forge, 22 April, 1778.

DEAR SIR,

Mr Boudinot, at Commissary Loring's request, met him at Germantown yesterday; from whence he is just returned, after having agreed on a final exchange of yourself and other officers, with that gentleman. That delay may not produce danger, I shall send in a flag tomorrow for your parole; and, when obtained, I shall most cordially and sincerely congratulate you on your restoration to your country and to the army. I could not however refrain, till the happy event should take place, from rejoicing with you on the probability of it, nor from expressing my wish of seeing you in camp, as soon as you can possibly make it convenient to yourself, after you are perfectly at liberty to take an active part with us; of which I shall not delay giving you the earliest notice. I have received your favor of the 13th instant from Yorktown. The contents shall be the subject of conversation, when I have the pleasure of seeing you in circumstances to mount your hobby-horse, which will not, I hope, on trial be found quite so limping a jade, as the one on which you set out for York.

I am, &c
G° Washington.

To Major General Lee.

To General Washington.

Prato Verde April ye 28th 1778.

My Dr General

You may better imagine than I can express the happiness which your letter gave me, tho at the time I received it which was the night before last, there was some little drawback on my happiness—viz a small attack of the gout with indications of its being a severe fit, but by three doses of what Lord Chatham calls the great American Panacea, I find myself so much better and the indications so much weaker that I hope to set out tomorrow or the next day at furthest—but you may be assur'd that I will not defer my departure a single moment.

I have read the Papers, and all I shall say on the subject is that nothing can equal the impudence of North and his Colleagues but the patience or rather stupid forbearance of the People in not tearing the Scoundrels to pieces.

Adieu My Dr General till I have the pleasure of seeing you.

CHARLES LEE.

His Excellency General Washington,
Head Quarters.

TO THE PRESIDENT OF CONGRESS.

York Town May 13th 1778

SIR,

When I first engaged myself in the cause of America, I was a Major General of six years standing in the Polish service, and Lt Colonel in the English which last I should not have retained, if the half pay annexed to it had not been too considerable a sum to throw wantonly away, or had it been incompatible with my higher rank—General Ward to whom, for certain reasons, precedence of me was given, and to which I acquiesced for these reasons, afterwards resigned, and I of course became second in command.

Since the first establishment of the American army a very great and rapid promotion has been made of General Officers, All the Brigadiers, a multitude of Colonels, and some even below that rank are now in the same rank with myself, in short whilst others are advanced several steps, I remain stationary—I hope I shall not be thought to speak invidiously when I remark that there is no officer in your service of any degree whatever, who held the same rank in Europe that

I did, and that had I chosen to have remained in the Polish or Portuguese service or entered into the Russian, I should at this day have been a Lieut. General. I must humbly therefore refer it to the consideration and justice of the Congress whether it is reasonable that I should be kept in the same station not only with those who have never had rank in other services, but with those who entered into the American, in so much a lower capacity than myself, I must beg leave to add that before I had the misfortune of being taken prisoner, and upon the first great promotion of Brigadiers to the rank of Major Generals, my remaining stationary appeared so unreasonable to his Excellency Gen Washington that he attributed it merely to inadvertency and seemed to make no doubt, but that on the first application, the Congress would assent to my promotion.

I am Sir with the greatest respect,

Your most Ob[t] Hum[bl] Servt.

CHARLES LEE.

The Hon[ble] Mr. Laurens.

CHARLES PETTIT TO COL. THOMAS BRADFORD.

Moore Hall, 19 May 1778.

DEAR SIR,

General Lee has signified his Expectation of being in camp to morrow, and His Excellency has desired me to provide Quarters for him on the Right of the Army. I have sent an Officer round and can find no tolerable Prospect of accommodating him unless you and your Brother will be kind enough to remove from the Quarters you are in; in such Case other good Quarters shall be assigned you. Col. Biddle mentions to me Mr. Moses Coates's about a mile from hence, just back of his Quarters, where there is a good House and agreeable Family with every convenient Accommodation, and will probably suit you both at least equally well with your present Situation. The Necessity of providing Quarters in that Neighbourhood for Gen[l] Lee obliges me to make this Request, and as it will so much tend to accomodate the Army and oblige Gen[l] Greene and myself, I cannot doubt the ready Compliance both of your Brother (to whom my Compliments) and yourself.

I am Sir
Your most obed[t] hum[e] Serv[t]
CHAS. PETTIT A. Q. M. Gen[l]

Col. Thomas Bradford,
D. Com[y] of Prisoners.

MEMORANDUM.

[May 1778.]

I have the strongest reason to think (my reasons shall be given hereafter) that it is not General Howe's intention to direct his operations against Boston, but that his views are to establish himself in the Middle Colonies. I may be mistaken but the reasons for my surmise are very strong—I have the strongest reasons to persuade myself that He will not endeavour to force his way in a direct rout towards the Susquehannah but that he will endeavour to deceive Gen: Washington by appearances and turn his flank either by transporting some part of his Troops in ships to the head of Chesapeake Bay or by forced marches and Pontoons, crossing the Susquehannah and taking Post on the Western bank of that River for which reason I cou'd wish at least that there was a corps of observation somewhere on that Bank. I shou'd think Gunpowder River well calculated for that purpose—I have the strongest reason to think that the Enemy have an idea (I know they had the last year) to make a grand foraging party (if I may so express it) in order to collect and seize all the

Tobacco near the great navigable waters of Maryland; for which reason I cou'd wish that the stores of Tobacco near the navigable waters were remov'd back and secur'd—the grounds of this idea are that considering the high price Tobacco bears They should be the (*sic*) able to indemnify themselves for the expenses of a Campaign or at least enrich the Captors, which to them is a Capital object. I have likewise the strongest reason to think that they flatter themselves that by establishing themselves about Annapolis, Baltimore, or even Alexandria—They shall be able to augment considerably their army with convict and indented servants —it therefore behoves the Congress and General to take such measures as will secure this suspected class of men, I own I wish that Annapolis, Baltimore, Alexandria, and the avenues from these places to York were put in a State of defence—at least the precaution can be attended with no inconvenience If General Burgoine and his troops can consistently with honor and good faith be retain'd for some months, the advantages will be prodigious. I think it may be done the Tories now on their parole may be reclaim'd and I believe will not answer the Summons.

Endorsed (in the handwriting of General Washington) "From Major Gen. Lee, 1778."

From Otway Byrd.

Nesting, June 1st 1778.

My Dear General,

As your enlargement is now reduced to a certainty, I shall beg leave most heartily to congratulate you; and give you every affectionate assurance of the satisfaction I enjoy on the happy event: and must be permitted to inform you that very few circumstances either private or public could afford me more real pleasure than is occasioned by this instance of your good fortune—I was as far as Fredericksburg on my way to Berkeley in hopes of having the indulgence of giving you these tokens of attachment in person, but was extremely disappointed, when I was made acquainted with your return to Camp.

Had I not from many substantial reasons been induced to quit the Military life, I should have thought myself exceedingly happy to have had the honor of once more attending my worthy General in the Field, and I am vain enough to flatter myself from the many instances I have experienced of his friendship I shouldn't have been a disagreeable one in the number of his retinue. If you are not provided with Gentlemen to act in the capacity of Aid-de-Camps, I would take the liberty to recommend a Captain Page of Col. Baylor's Regiment, a young Gentleman with whom I am connected, and one whom I have the highest opinion of. As I may succeed in my recommendation, I think it necessary to give you a hint of his being a Virginia[n], and a person possessed of that degree [of] laziness you so justly observed is natural to us who are unlucky enough to be born under so hot a meridian. As I know you would rather write than be idle, I am in great hopes I shall now & then be favoured with an epistle—My Mother, Sister Farley, and the fat Squire insist on presenting their Love to you.

I am My Dear Gen[l]

Yours truly Affectionate

OTWAY BYRD.

Major General Lee

Head Quarters Valley Forge Camp

To Benjamin Rush.

Camp at Valley forge June ye 4th 1778.

My DR Rush,

Tho I had no occasion for fresh assurances of your Friendship, I cannot help being much pleased with the warmth which your letter, deliver'd to me by Mr. Hale, breathes, and I hope it is unnecessary to assure you that my sentiments with respect to you, are correspondent—You would think it odd that I shou'd seem to be an Apologist for General Howe. I know not how it happens, but when I have taken prejudices in favor or against a Man, I find a difficulty in shaking them off—From my first acquaintance with Mr Howe I lik'd him I thought him friendly candid good natur'd brave and rather sensible than the reverse. I believe still that he is naturally so, but a corrupt or more properly speaking no education, the fashion of the times, the reigning idolatry amongst the English (particularly the soldiery) for every scepter'd Calf, Wolf, Hog, or Ass, have so totally perverted his understanding and heart, that private friendship has not force sufficient to keep a door open for the admittance of mercy towards political Hereticks. He was besides perswaded that I was doubly criminal both as Traitor and Deserter—in short so totally was He inebriated with this idea that I am convinced He wou'd have thought himself both politically and morally damn'd had he acted any other part than what He did—He is besides the most indolent of Mortals, never took farther pains to examine the merits or demerits of the Cause in which He was engaged than merely to recollect that Great Britain was said to be the Mother Country, George the Third King of Great Britain, that the Parliament was call'd the representatives of G. Britain, that the King and Parliament form'd the Supreme Power, that a Supreme Power is absolute and uncontrollable, that all resistance must consequently be rebellion, but above all that

He was a Soldier, and bound to obey in all cases whatsoever—these are his notions, and this his logic, but through these absurdities I cou'd distinguish when He was left to himself rays of Friendship and good nature breaking out—it is true he was seldom left to himself, for never poor Mortal thrust into high stations, was surrounded by such fools and scoundrels—M^c^Kensey, Balfour, Galoway were his Councillors—They urg'd him to all his acts of harshness. They were his Scribes; all the damn'd stuff which was issued to the astonish'd World was theirs—I believe he scarcely ever read the letters He sign'd—You will scarcely believe it, but I can assure you as a fact, that He never read that curious proclamation issued at the head of Elk, till three days after it was publish'd—You will say that I am drawing my Friend Howe in more ridiculous colours than He has yet been represent'd in—but this is his real character—He is naturally good humour'd and complacent, but illiterate and indolent to the last degree unless as an executive Soldier, in which capacity He is all fire and activity, brave and cool as Julius Cæsar—his understanding is, as I observ'd before rather good than otherwise, but was totally confounded and stupefy'd by the immensity of the task impos'd upon him—He shut his eyes, fought his battles, drank his bottle, had his little Whore, advis'd with his Counsellors, receiv'd his orders from North and Germain, one more absurd than the other, took Galoways opinion, shut his eyes, fought again, and is now I suppose to be call'd to Account for acting according to instructions; but I believe his eyes are now open'd. He sees that He has been an instrument of wickedness and folly—indeed when I observ'd it to him, He not only took patiently the observation, but indirectly assented to the truth of it—He made at the same time as far as his *mauvaise honte* wou'd permit an apology for his treatment of me—Thus far with regard to Mr Howe—You are struck with the great events, changes and new characters which have appear'd on the stage since I saw you last—but

I am more struck with the admirable efficacy of Blunder—it seem'd to be a tryal of skill which Party shou'd outdoe the other, and it is hard to say which play'd the deepest strokes—but it was a capital one of ours which certainly gave the happy turn which affairs have taken. Upon my Soul it was time for fortune to interpose or We were inevitably lost—but this We will talk over another time—I suppose we shall see one another at Philadelphia very soon—*én attendant*—God bless you

Yours affectionately
C. LEE.

My love to Mrs Rush.

To GENERAL WASHINGTON.

Camp, June ye 15th 1778.

DR GENERAL,

As your time must necessarily be taken up by more and a greater variety of business than perhaps ever was impos'd on the shoulders of any one Mortal, the most clear simple and agreeable method of communicating my sentiments on any matter of importance must certainly be throwing 'em on paper—you will have more leisure to weigh and consider the strength or weakness of my arguments and I flatter myself that what I now or I hope shall at any time, offer will not be imputed to presumption impertinence or a spirit of criticism, but to my zeal for the public service. You will pardon me then when I express freely my thoughts on the present arrangement with respect to the command of the General Officers which I cannot help thinking not only extremely defective but that it may be productive of the worst consequences. We are, it seems, to have the superintendence of one division in the present situation of affairs (that is as long as We remain tranquil and undisturb'd), but the instant our tranquility is disturb'd and a movement is to be made We are to quit this division and abruptly to take the command of another—by these means We are put out of all possibility of becoming acquainted with the names, faces and characters of the officers who are to execute the orders We give, and the Soldiers who are to look up to us in the hour of tryal must be Strangers to our voices and persons. They cannot, consequently, have that confidence in us which is so necessary and which habit and acquaintance usually inspire—indeed it appears to me not only repugnant to the rules of war, but of common prudence to introduce, for the first time, a General to his officers and soldiers in the moment of attack.—I must intreat pardon, therefore, in urging the expediency of affixing, without loss of time, the respective Generals to the wings or divisions which They are to command in real actions so that the Commanders and Commanded may not fall into the mistakes, blunders and distractions which otherwise from their being Strangers to each other must inevitably ensue.

Yesterday and the day before I had some conversation with Mr Budenot. He is from many circumstances fully persuaded that it is not the Enemy's intention to pass through the Jerseys to N. York. I have myself from the beginning been inclined to the same opinion and on the supposition that this is not their design We ought to consider with ourselves what They most probably will do—my opinion is that (if they are in a capacity to act offensively) They will either immediately from Philadelphia or by a feint in descending the River as far as New Castle, and then, turning to the right march directly and rapidly towards Lancaster, by which means They will draw us out of our present position and oblige us to fight on terms perhaps very disadvantageous or that They will leave Lancaster and this Army wide on the right, endeavour to take Post on the lower parts of the Susquehanna and by securing a communication with their Ships sent round into the Bay for this purpose, be furnished with the means of encouraging and feeding the Indian War broke out on the Western Frontier—this last plan I mention as a possibility but as less probable than the former.

If they are not in a capacity to act offensively but are still determined to keep footing on the continent, there are strong reasons to think that They will not shut themselves up in Towns, but take possession of some tract of Country which will afford 'em elbow room and sustenance and which is so situated as to be the most effectually protected by their command of the Waters—and I have particular reasons to think that They have cast their eyes for this purpose, on the lower Counties of Delawar and some of the Maryland Counties of the Eastern Shore, that They have had thoughts of adopting this measure some time ago I learnt from Mr Willin when They entertain'd an idea of offering or assenting to, if proposed, a cessation of hostilities—as to any apprehensions from the unwholesomeness of the climate, they laugh at it—if They are resolved on this plan it certainly will be very difficult to prevent 'em or remove 'em afterwards as their Shipping will give 'em such mighty advantages. Whether They do or do not adopt any one of these plans there can no inconvenience arise from considering the subject, nor from devising means of defeating their purposes on the supposition that They will—in short I think it wou'd be proper to put these queries to ourselves shou'd They march directly towards Lancaster and the Susquehanna or indirectly from N. Castle, what are We to do? shou'd They (tho' it is less probable) leave this Army and even Lancaster wide on the right and endeavour to establish themselves on the lower parts of the Susquehanna, what are We to do? and shou'd they act only on the defensive and attempt to secure to themselves some such tract of country as I have mention'd what measures are we to pursue? these are matters I really think worthy of consideration. We have many and I believe able Field Engineers in the camp or at York; why cannot They be employ'd in some essentials in surveying well the Country on both sides the Susquehanna—determining on the most proper Fords for our army if on any occasion They shou'd be oblig'd to ford it, in examining well all the best positions which may be taken betwixt the head of Elk and the Delawar, as, also, betwixt Philadelphia, Wilmington and Lancaster—what use may be made of Conestoga Creek if We are oblig'd to cover Lancaster and (to extend their task further), how Baltimore may be put in a more defensive state and what passes and defiles there are in one line of direction from Baltimore to York and in another line from that part of the lower Susquehanna where it is most probable the Enemy would chuse for their landing place, to York—but I am swelling out my paper to a most insufferable bulk—and intreat D[r] General that you will excuse not only it's length but whatever You find illtimed or impertinent in the contents as I am, most sincerely and devotedly,

Yours

CHARLES LEE.

P. S. Mr. Welford tells me that the officers at Philadelphia publickly express their surprise at their General's stupidity in not marching strait to Lancaster which They say must indubitably force us out of our present position, or cover us with disgrace by laying waste the finest part of America under our noses—this evidences still stronger the necessity of examining well and immediately Conestoga Creek, where if I am not mistaken, a fine position may be taken. He says their Cavalry now amounts to 2500 Men—that the bulk of their Force is still at Philadelphia.

FROM GENERAL WASHINGTON.

Head Quarters, 15 June, 1778.

DEAR SIR,

I have received your letter of this date, and thank you, as I shall any officer, over whom I have the honor to be placed, for his opinion and advice in matters of importance; especially when they proceed from the fountain of candor, and not from a captious spirit, or an itch for criticism.

No man can be more sensible of the defects of our present arrangement, than I am; no man more sensible of the advantage of having the commander and commanded of every corps well known to each other, and the army properly organized. Heaven and my own letters to Congress can witness, on the one hand, how ardently I have labored to effect these points during the past winter and spring; the army, on the other, bears witness to the effect. Suspended between the old and new establishments, I could govern myself by neither with propriety; and the hourly expectation of a committee, for the purposes of reducing some regiments and changing the establishment of all, rendered a mere temporary alteration unnecessary, which from its uncertainty and shortness could effect no valuable end. That I had a *power* to shift regiments and alter brigades every day, if I chose to do it, I never entertained a doubt; but the *efficacy* of the measure I have very much questioned, as frequent changes, without apparent causes, are rather ascribed to caprice and whim, than to stability and judgment.

The mode of shifting the major-generals from the command of a division, in the present tranquil state of affairs, to a more important one in action and other capital movements of the whole army, is not less disagreeable to my ideas, than repugnant to yours, but is the result of necessity. For, having recommended to Congress the appointment of Lieutenant Generals for the discharge of the latter duties, and they having neither approved nor disapproved the measure, I am hung in suspense; and being unwilling, on the one hand, to give up the benefits resulting from the command of lieutenant-generals in the cases above mentioned, or to deprive the divisions of their major-generals for ordinary duty on the other, I have been led to adopt a kind of medium course, which, though not perfect in itself, is in my judgment the best that circumstances will admit of, till Congress shall have decided upon the proposition before them. Your remark upon the disadvantages of an officer's being suddenly removed from the command of a division to a wing, though not without foundation, as I have before acknowledged, does not apply so forcibly in the present case, as you seem to think. There is no major-general in this army, that is not pretty well known, and who may not, if he chooses, soon become acquainted with such officers as may be serviceable to him. Their commands being announced in general orders, and the army prepared for their reception, a major-general may go with the same ease to the command of a wing consisting of five brigades, as to a division composed of two, and will be received with as little confusion, since the brigades remain perfect and no changes have happened in them.

Mr Boudinot's conjecture of the enemy's intention, although it does not coincide with mine, is nevertheless worthy of attention; and the evils of the measure have been guarded against, as far as it has been in my power, by removing the stores and provisions as fast as possible from the Head of Elk and the Susquehanna, and by exploring the country, surveying the roads, and marking the defiles and strong grounds; an engineer and three surveyors have been employed in this work nearly a month, though their report is not yet come in. Boats are also prepared on the Susquehanna for the transportation of our troops, in case we should find it necessary to move that way. But nevertheless it gives me real pleasure to find you have turned your thoughts that way, and are revolving the questions contained in your letter; and here let me again assure you, that I shall be always happy in a free communication of your sentiments upon any important subject relative to the service, and only beg that they may come directly to myself. The custom, which many officers have, of speaking freely of things and reprobating measures, which upon investigation may be found to be unavoidable, is never productive of good, but often of very mischievous consequences.

I am, &c

G^o WASHINGTON.

To Major General Charles Lee.

FROM GEORGE JOHNSON.

Philadelphia, June 17th, 1778.

DEAR SIR,

I heartily thank you for your letter, and regret that I cannot have the pleasure of meeting you; the great wish of my life is to see peace between two countries I almost equally love, while it is a question whether this or an inexterminable war is to take place. I meant in words I had learnt from you, to set before you the many and mutual advantages both would derive from an agreement; and as the terms now offered are more for the interest of your favorite America than you ever hoped to obtain, I should have made no scruple to ask your good offices, and to engage my own, to remove any obstacles that might obstruct the peace.

I should think it a greater honor to contribute in the smallest degree to this, than to have the greatest share in bringing about victory: these, to a thinking man like you, who has many friends on both sides, subject him to a double regret.

I may not find another occasion of meeting you easily, but I would travel far to have the pleasure of embracing you, as a fellow subject of the same empire, and a friend. You will see by some speeches in the House of Commons, that others whom you value have the same wish. A celebrated poem, just published, says,

"By virtue, captive Lee is doubly blest."

A pamphlet wrote by Governor Johnstone's brother

is much applauded by the nation, where a spirit prevails like that between tender relations who are more disposed to love and respect, after a quarrel has convinced both of the advantage and value of friendship. I send you the pamphlet.

You do Sir H. Clinton great justice in believing him incapable of an inhuman or illiberal measure; you may, with great confidence, assert, that he had no share in the havock you say has embittered people's minds to a degree of madness. Your letter to me is the only notice he has, of the burnings you mention. If any other houses besides magazines were destroyed, it must have been by the wantonness of Soldiers; as the officer who formed the plan for destroying the preparations for the invasion of the island, confined it to this object. The destruction of houses was no part of his project; otherwise he would have mentioned the success of it, which he has not done. I will deliver the messages you give me, and will ever seek every occasion to shew that I am with regard,

Dear Sir,

Your most affectionate friend

and humble Servant

Geo. Johnson.

P. S. Sir Henry Clinton bids me thank you for your letter, and charges me to enclose one he has received for you, from England.

Major Gen. Lee.

From General Washington.

Head-Quarters, 30 May, 1778.

Sir,

Poor's, Varnum's, and Huntington's brigades are to march in one division under your command to the North River. The quartermaster-general will give you the route, encampment, and halting days, to which you will conform as strictly as possible, to prevent interfering with other troops, and that I may know precisely your situation every day. Leave as few sick and lame on the road as possible. Such as are absolutely incapable of marching with you are to be committed to the care of proper officers, with directions to follow as fast as their condition will allow.

Be strict in your discipline, suffer no rambling, keep the men in their ranks and the officers with their divisions, avoid pressing horses as much as possible, and punish severely every officer or soldier, who shall presume to press without proper authority. Prohibit the burning of fences. In a word you are to protect the persons and property of the inhabitants from every kind of insult and abuse.

Begin your march at four o'clock in the morning at the latest, that it may be over before the heat of the day, and that the soldiers may have time to cook, refresh, and prepare for the ensuing day—I am &c.

G° WASHINGTON.

P. S. June 18th.—The foregoing instructions may serve you for general directions, but circumstances have varied since they were written. You are to halt on the first strong ground after passing the Delaware at Coryell's Ferry, till further orders, unless you should receive authentic intelligence, that the enemy have proceeded by a direct route to South Amboy, or still lower. In this case you will continue your march to the North River, agreeably to former orders, and by the route already given you. If my memory does not deceive me, there is an advantageous spot of ground at the ferry to the right of the road leading from the water.

ORDER OF MARCH AND ROUTE OF THE ARMY FROM CAMP VALLEY FORGE TO NEWBURG ON THE NORTH RIVER OPPOSITE FISHKILL.

Brigades	Division	Commander	Crossing
Poor Varnum Huntington	1st	Lee	Coryells
1st Penns[a] 2d Ditto late Conway	2nd	Mifflin	Sherard
Woodford Scott No. Carolina	3d	Marquis	Coryells
Glover Patterson Learned	4	deKalb	Easton
Weedon Muhlenberg 1st Maryld 2d Ditto	5	Stirling	Coryells

The Detachm[t] under Col[o] Jackson to move to and take possession of Philadelphia and prevent plundering & any abuse of Persons. Van Scoicks Regiment to replace the 8th Pennsylvania Reg[t] in the Pennsylvania Brigade—The 2d State Regm[t] of Virginia to replace the 13th Regiment in Scott's Brigade—Park of Artillery to be attached to the Several Divisions Equally and march with them.

The 1st and 2d Divisions to move the morning after Intelligence is received of the Enemy's Evacuation of the City.

The 3rd & 4th Divisions the morning after these, & the 5th Division the morning succeeding—every day's march to begin at 4 o'clock, A.M. at furthest.

G[o]. WASHINGTON.

1st 3rd & 5th Divisions by Coryell's Ferry & thro the Clove by Smiths.

To Coryell's & Cross	3 Days
Halt	1
White House	1
3 miles beyond the Cross Roads	1
4 do beyond Morristown	1
Halt	1
Pompton Bridge	1
Sufferans	1
near Smith's Tavern	1
Halt if necessary	1
Newborough	1
	— 13

2d Division by Sherard's Ferry and Sussex Court House.

To Sherard's Ferry and Cross	3
Halt	1
Union Iron Works	1
Halket's Town	1
Sussex Court House	1
Halt	1
4 M. beyond Col. Martins	1
Warwick	1
5 M. beyond Chester	1
Halt if necessary	1
Newborough	1
	— 13

4th Division by Easton & Sussex Court House

To Easton	3
Halt	1
Crossing	1
6 miles beyond Carrs	1
Sussex Court House	1
Halt	1
Then as in 2d Division	5
	— 13

Regard to be had to the convenience of Water as well as Distance.

ORDERS RELATIVE TO THE MARCH FROM VALLEY FORGE JUNE 1778, AFTER GEN. LEE'S AND GEN. MIFFLIN'S DIVIS[NS] HAD MARCHED.

The Army is to March to Morrow & till further Orders in the following Order.

The Marquis De La Fyatte is to lead with	Woodford's Scott's North Carolina	Brigades.
The Baron de Kalb next with	Glovers Pattersons Learneds	Brigades

The Artillery Park and spare Ammunition.

Lord Sterling with	Weedons Muhlenbergs 1st Maryland 2d Maryland

The disposition for the Baggage of the Army to be as follows:

The Commander in Chief's Baggage is to march in the front of the column of Waggons—The Adjutant General's, Paymaster Generals Engineers Muster Master General Auditor of Accounts The Baggage of the Marquis de la Fyattes De Kalbs Division the Baggage of Lord Stirlings Division & then the Waggons of the Quarter Master General's department Flying Hospital & lastly the Com^y & Forage Master General's Waggons—The whole Baggage to fall in the Rear of the Column of Troops. The Genl officers commanding the Grand Divisions to appoint such guards upon the baggage as shall be necessary for the Security thereof—They will also, appoint a party of Pioneers to move in front of the Columns, to assist the Artificers in repairing Bridges and bad places in the roads.

There will be a party of Artificers to go in front & rear of the whole, to mend Bridges and repair the Broken Carriages; which will take their Orders from the Q. M. Gen[l].

The sub Inspectors are to assist the Quarter Master General in regulating the order of March, encampment and planting of Guards & to accompany and follow his Directions accordingly.

G[o] WASHINGTON.

Note, the Light Horse is to March in front and upon the Right flank a days and encamp in the Rear of the Troops o Nights.

The new guards will form the advanced guards of the army and the old guards the rear guard. Each regiment will send out a flank guard on the right flank in the proportion of a serjeant and 12 men to every 200 men.

TO GENERAL WASHINGTON.

Camp, June ye 22[d] [1778.]

D[R] GENERAL,

About eleven miles from Head Quarters and eight miles from this Camp is a most admirable position for the whole Army either in two or one line—it's left is cover'd by Stony Brook it's front Clear, excepting to the front of the right where is a strong wood and mill dam where it will be proper to throw a Brigade—a strong Brigade or two shou'd occupy likewise a Wood on the right—it's situation is high and commanding—the ground dry and good—it is well watered having besides Stoney Brook on the left—a large Rivulet in the front—another in the rear—it commands likewise both the roads to Princeton that by Pennyton and that inclining to Hopewell meeting house.

I am D[r] Sir, Yours,

C. LEE.

Wou'd it not be proper to hint your intention to Gov[r] Livingston—his letter which Colonel Scammel will deliver to you shews the necessity.

His Excellency General Washington.

From Gov. William Livingston.

Princeton, 22[d] June, 1778.

Dear General

Last night I had from General Dickinson the following account—That he had been below and was just returned, that is to Bordentown. That the Enemy had made no movements yesterday except bringing up their rear which was the cause he believes of their halting at Holley. That they were expected to march early this morning—That he had three detachments of Militia on their lines who were briskly engaged in obstructing the different roads, & will be prepared to skirmish when they advance & that the Enemy had lost near 500 men by desertion since they left Philadelphia.

I do not see upon what principles we retard their progress except that of the grand army engaging them —If that is not in contemplation, I think for the good they do, we ought rather to hang on their rear, & drive the rascals thro' the State as soon as possible.

Believe me to be with great respect

Your most humble Ser[t]

Wil: Livingston.

Major General Lee.

Disposition of the Militia belonging to the State of New Jersey, made by Major Gen[l]. Dickinson, Viz[t].

Head Quarters, Chamber's Tavern
June 25, 1778.

Colonels Furman, Haight & Holmes, with their respective Battalions, are ordered to gain the Enemies Right Flank & join Col. Morgan's detachment, who are to annoy the Enemy in that Quarter as much as in their power. They will consist of 3 Col—1 Lt. Col—3 Maj—7 Cap—15 Subs—13 Serj[t]—12 Corp—163 Priv.

Colonels Neilson & Webster with their Battalions will take post in Front of the Enemy, throw every possible obstruction in their Rout, impede their march & harass them, whenever opportunity present. This Detachment will consist of 2 Col—1 Lt Col—1 Maj—6 Capt.—16 Subs—19 Serj'[ts]—13 Corps—218 Privates.

Capt. Lane & 25 of his Company of axmen to attend Col. Neilson.

Col. Scudder with his Battalion will join Brig'[r] Gen[l] Scott on the left flank of the Enemy consisting of 150 Privates.

The whole of the remaining Militia, are to be equally divided & to do duty on the lines alternately, Officers as well as privates.

General Washington to General Lafayette.

Instructions.

Sir,

You are immediately to proceed with the detachment commanded by General Poor, and form a junction, as expeditiously as possible, with that under command of General Scott. You are to use the most effectual means for gaining the enemy's left flank and rear, and giving them every degree of annoyance. All continental parties that are already on the lines, will be under your command, and you will take such measures, in concert with General Dickinson, as will cause the enemy the greatest impediment and loss in their march. For these purposes you will attack them as occasion may require, by detachment, and if a proper opening should be given, by operating against them with the whole force of your command. You will naturally take such precautions as will secure you against surprise, and maintain your communication with this army.

Given at Kingston, this 25th day of June, 1778.

G° WASHINGTON.

GENERAL LAFAYETTE TO GENERAL WASHINGTON.

Cranberry, half-past nine o'clock,
[25th] June 1778.

DEAR GENERAL,

Inclosed I have the honor to send you a letter which Colonel Hamilton was going to send me from this place when I arrived with the detachment, and which may give you an idea of the position of the enemy. I will try to meet and collect as soon as possible our forces, tho' I am sorry to find the enemy so far down that way. We will be obliged to march pretty fast, if we want to attack them. It is for that I am particularly concerned about provisions. I send back immediately for the purpose, and beg you would give orders to have them forwarded as speedily as possible, and directed to march fast, for I believe we must set out early to-morrow morning. The detachment is in a wood, covered by Cranberry Creek, and I believe extremely safe. We want to be very well furnished with spirits as a long and quick march may be found necessary, and if

Gen. Scott's detachment is not provided, it should be furnished also with liquor; but the provisions of this detachment are the most necessary to be sent as soon as possible, as we expect them to march.

If anything new comes to my knowledge, I will immediately write to your Excellency, and I will send an express in the morning.

I have the honor to be, &c.

LAFAYETTE.

I wish also we could get some axes, but it should not stop the so important affairs of provisions.

COLONEL HAMILTON TO GENERAL LAFAYETTE.

25 June, 1778.

SIR,

We find, on our arrival here that the intelligence received on the road is true. The enemy have all filed off from Allen Town, on the Monmouth Road. Their rear is said to be a mile westward of Lawrence Taylor's tavern, six miles from Allen Town. General Maxwell is at Hyde's Town, about three miles from this place. General Dickinson is said to be on the enemy's right flank; but where, cannot be told. We can hear nothing certain of General Scott; but, from circumstances he is probably at Allen Town. We shall, agreeably to your request, consider and appoint some proper place of rendezvous for the union of our force, which we shall communicate to Generals Maxwell and Scott, and to yourself. In the meantime I would recommend to you to move toward this place as soon as the convenience of your men will permit. I am told that Colonel Morgan is on the enemy's right flank. We had a slight skirmish with their rear this forenoon, at Robert Montgomery's, on the Monmouth Road, leading from Allen Town. We shall see General Maxwell immediately, and you will hear from us again. Send this to the General after reading it.

I am your ob't Serv't
ALEX. HAMILTON.

Doctor Stile's House, Cranberry Town
9 o'clock.

We are just informed that General Scott passed by Hooper's tavern, five miles from Allen Town, this afternoon at five o'clock.

M. De Lafayette.

COLONEL HAMILTON TO GENERAL SCOTT.

SIR,

This part of the troops marches instantly—We are to join in the Monmouth road one mile this side of Taylor's Tavern. You will govern yourself accordingly. If you can find Morgan let him be desired again to keep close to the enemy and attack when we attack.

I am Sir, Y[r]. Obed Serv
ALEX HAMILTON
Aide De Camp

You will endeavour to keep up a communication of intelligence.

GENERAL LAFAYETTE TO GENERAL WASHINGTON.

At Cranberry, 5 o'clock, June [26th] 1778.

DEAR GENERAL,

I have received your orders for marching as just as I could and I have marched without waiting for the provisions tho' we want them extremely. Gen. Forman and Col. Hamilton sat out last night to meet the other troops and we shall be together at Hidestown or somewhat lower. Gen. Forman is firmly of opinion that we may overtake the enemy,—for my part I am not so quiet upon the subject as he is, but his sentiment is of great weight on account of his knowledge of the country. It is highly pleasant to me to be followed and countenanced by the army that if we stop the enemy and meet with some advantage they may push it with vigor. I have no doubt but if we overtake them we possess a very happy chance. However, I would not have the army quite so near as not to be quite master of its motions, but a very little distance may do it. I have heard nothing of the enemy this morning. An officer of militia says, that after they had pitched their tents yesterday night, they struck them again. But I am inclined to believe they did not go farther, and that the man who brought the intelligence was mistaken. I expect some at Hidestown which I will immediately forward to you. I beg when your Excellency will write to me, that you could let me know the place you have reached, that I might govern myself accordingly.

With the highest respect I have the honor to be, &c.

LAFAYETTE.

TO GENERAL WASHINGTON.

Camp, at Kingston, 25 June, 1778.

DEAR GENERAL,

When I first assented to the Marquis de Lafayette's taking the command of the present detachment, I confess I viewed it in a very different light from that in which I view it at present. I considered it as a more proper business of a young, volunteering general, than of the second in command in the army; but I find it is considered in a different manner. They say that a corps consisting of six thousand men, the greater part chosen, is undoubtedly the most honorable command next to the Commander-in-chief; that my ceding it would of course have an odd appearance. I must entreat, therefore, after making a thousand apologies for the trouble my rash assent has occasioned you, that, if this detachment does march, I may have the command of it. So far personally; but, to speak as an officer, I do not think that this detachment ought to march at all, until at least the head of the enemy's right column has passed Cranberry; then, if it is necessary to march the whole army, I cannot see any impropriety in the Marquis's commanding this detachment, or a greater, as an advanced guard of the army; but if this detachment, with Maxwell's corps, Scott's, Morgan's, and Jackson's, is to be considered as a separate, chosen, active corps, and put under the Marquis's command until the enemy leave the Jerseys, both myself and Lord Stirling will be disgraced.

I am, dear General, Yours, &c

CHARLES LEE.

GENERAL LAFAYETTE TO GENERAL WASHINGTON.

[Hightstown] 26th June, 1778,
at a quarter after Seven.

DEAR GENERAL,

I hope you have received my letter from Cranberry, where I acquaint you that I am going to Hight's Town, though we are short of provisions. When I got there, I was sorry to hear that Mr. Hamilton, who had been riding all the night, had not been able to find anybody who could give him certain intelligence; but by a party who came back, I hear the enemy are in motion, and their rear about one mile off the place they had occupied last night, which is seven or eight miles from here. I immediately put Generals Maxwell and Wayne's brigades in motion, and I will fall lower down, with General Scott's, with Jackson's regiment, and some militia. I should be very happy if we could attack them before they halt, for I have no notion of taking one other moment but this of the march. If I cannot overtake them, we could lay at some distance, and attack tomorrow morning, provided they don't escape in the night, which I much fear, as our intelligences are not the best ones. I have sent some parties out, and I will get some more light by them.

I fancy your excellency will move down with the army, and if we are at a convenient distance from you, I have nothing to fear in striking a blow if opportunity is offered. I believe that, in our present strength, provided they do not escape, we may do something.

General Forman says that, on account of the nature of the country, it is impossible for me to be turned by the right or left, but that I shall not quite depend upon.

An officer, just from the lines, confirms the account of the enemy moving. An intelligence from General Dickinson says that they hear a very heavy fire in the front of the enemy's column. I apprehend it is Morgan, who had not received my letter, but it will have the good effect of stopping them, and if we attack, he may begin again.

Sir, I want to repeat you, in writing, what I have told to you, which is, that, if you believe it, or if it is believed necessary or useful to the good of the service and the honour of General Lee, to send him down with a couple of thousand men, or any greater force; I will cheerfully obey and serve him, not only out of duty, but out of what I owe to that gentleman's character.

I hope to receive soon your orders as to what I am to do this day or to-morrow, to know where you are and what you intend, and would be very happy to furnish you with the opportunity of completing some little advantage of ours.

LAFAYETTE.

P. S. The road I understand the enemy are moving by is the straight road to Monmouth.

Colonel Hamilton to General Washington.

Robins's Tavern, 8 miles from Allen Town,
12 o'clock, June 26, 1778.

Sir :

We have halted the troops at this place. The enemy, by our last reports, were four miles from this (that is, their rear), and had passed the road which turns off toward South Amboy, which determines their route toward Shrewsbury. Our reason for halting, is the extreme distress of the troops for want of provisions. General Wayne's detachment is almost starving, and seems both unwilling and unable to march further till they are supplied. If we do not receive an immediate supply, the whole purpose of our detachment must be frustrated.

This morning we missed doing anything, from a deficiency of intelligence. On my arrival at Cranberry yester-evening, I proceeded by desire of the Marquis, immediately to Hightstown and Allen Town, to take measures for co-operating with the different parts of the detachment, and to find what was doing to procure intelligence. I found every precaution was neglected; no horse was near the enemy, or could be heard of till late in the morning, so that before we could send out parties and get the necessary information, they were in full march, and as they have marched pretty expeditiously we should not be able to come up with them during the march of the day, if we did not suffer the impediment we do, on the score of provisions. We are entirely at a loss where the army is, which is no inconsiderable check to our enterprize. If the army is wholly out of supporting distance, we risk the total loss of the detachment in making an attack.

If the army will countenance us, we may do something clever. We feel our personal honor, as well as the honor of the army, and the good of the service, interested; and are heartily desirous to attempt whatever the disposition of our men will second, and prudence authorize. It is evident the enemy wish to avoid, not to engage us.

Desertions, I imagine, have been pretty considerable today. I have seen eight or ten deserters, and have heard of many more. We have had some little skirmishing by detached parties: one attacked their rear guard with a degree of success, killed a few, and took seven prisoners.

I am with great respect and regard, Sir,
Your obedient Servant,
A. Hamilton.

His Excellency General Washington.

P. S. The Marquis and General Dickinson send their compliments. My writing renders theirs unnecessary.

An officer just comes in, who informs us that he left the enemy's rear five miles off, still in march, about half an hour ago. To ascertain still more fully their route, I have ordered a fresh party on their left, toward the head of their column. They have three brigades in rear of their baggage.

From General Washington.

Cranberry, 26 June, 1778.

Dear Sir,

Your uneasiness on account of the command of yesterday's detachment fills me with concern, as it is not in my power fully to remove it without wounding the feelings of the Marquis de Lafayette. I have thought of an expedient, which though not quite equal to the views of either of you, may in some measure answer both; and that is, to make another detachment from this army for the purpose of aiding and supporting the several detachments now under the command of the Marquis, and giving you the command of the whole, under certain restrictions; which the circumstances arising from your own conduct yesterday render almost unavoidable.

The expedient I would propose, is for you to march towards the Marquis with Scott's and Varnum's brigades. Give him notice, that you are advancing to support him, and that you are to have command of the whole advanced body; but, as he may have formed some enterprise with the advice of the officers commanding the several corps under his command, which will not admit of delay or alteration, you will give him every assistance and countenance in your power. This, as I observed before, is not quite the thing; but may possibly answer, in some degree, the views of both. That it may do so, and the public service receive benefit from the measure, is the sincere wish of, dear Sir,

Your most obedient servant.

G° WASHINGTON.

GENERAL WASHINGTON TO GENERAL LAFAYETTE.

Cranberry, 26th June 1778.

MY DEAR MARQUIS,

General Lee's uneasiness, on account of yesterday's transaction, rather increasing than abating, and your politeness in wishing to ease him of it, have induced me to detach him from this army with a part of it, to reinforce, or at least cover, the several detachments at present under your command. At the same time, that I felt for General Lee's distress of mind, I have had an eye to your wishes and the delicacy of your situation; and have, therefore, obtained a promise from him, that when he gives you notice of his approach and command, he will request you to prosecute any plan you may have already concerted for the purpose of attacking, or otherwise annoying the enemy; this is the only expedient I could think of to answer the views of both. General Lee seems satisfied with the measure, and I wish it may prove agreeable to you, as I am with the warmest wishes for your honour and glory, and with the sincerest esteem and affection. Yours, &c

G° Washington.

General Lafayette to General Washington.

At Robins's Tavern, half past four,
26 June, 1778.

Dear General,—

I have received your excellency's favor notifying your arrival at Cranberry, and am glad to have anticipated your orders in not going too far. I have felt the unhappy effects of the want of provisions, for I dare say if we had not been stopped by it, as we were already within three miles of the enemy's rear, we would very easily have overtaken them and fought with advantage.

I have consulted the general officers of the detachment, and the general opinions seems to be that I should march in the night near them, so as to attack the rear guard when on the march. We have also spoken of a night attack. The latter seems dangerous. The former will perhaps give them time of escaping, as it is impossible I would move quite close by them, at least nearer than three miles.—Col. Morgan is towards the right flank, Gen. Dickinson is a little upon the left, Gens. Scott and Maxwell have insisted upon going further down than we are now; for Wayne's and Jackson's corps they have not had provisions at all but will be able to march in the night. I beg you would let me know your intention and your opinion of the matter, my motions depend much upon what the army will do for countenancing them. I beg you would be very particular upon what you think proper to be done and what your excellency will do. I wish indeed you would anticipate the different cases which may happen according to the place where the enemy lays—Gen. Wayne, Col. Hamilton and several officers have gone to reconnoitre it. I fancy they will lay about seven or eight miles from here. Your Excellency knows that by the direct road you are only three miles further from Monmouth than we are in this place.

The enemy is said to march since this morning, with a great confusion and fright. Some prisoners have been made, and deserters come amazingly fast. I believe an happy blow would have the happiest effect, and I always regret the time we have lost by want of provisions.

I beg you would answer to me immediately, and with the highest respect I have the honor to be &c

LAFAYETTE.

COLONEL HAMILTON TO GENERAL WASHINGTON.

[June 26th, 1778, Evening.]

SIR:

The result of what I have seen and heard, concerning the enemy, is, that they have encamped with their van a little beyond Monmouth Court House, and their rear at Manalapan's river, about seven miles from this place. Their march to day has been very judiciously conducted;—their baggage in front, and their flying army in the rear, with a rear guard of one thousand men about four hundred paces from the main body. To attack them in this situation, without being supported by the whole army, would be folly in the extreme. If it should be thought advisable to give the necessary support, the army can move to some position near the enemy's left flank, which would put them in a very awkward situation, with so respectable a body in their rear; and it would put it out of their power to turn either flank, should they be so disposed. Their left is strongly posted, and I am told their right also.

By some accounts, one part of their army lies on the road leading from the Monmouth road to South Amboy. It is not improbable that South Amboy may be the object.

I had written thus far when your letter to the Marquis arrived. This puts the matter on a totally different footing. The detachment will march to-morrow morning at three o'clock to English Town.

I am with great regard and esteem,

Your obedient Servant,

A. Hamilton.

His Excellency Gen. Washington.

General Lafayette to General Washington.

Half past ten, [P. M. 26th] June, 1778.

Dear General,

Your orders have reached me so late and found me in such a situation that it will be impossible to follow them as soon as I could wish. It is not on account of any other motive than the impossibility of moving the troops and making such a march immediately, for in receiving your letter I have given up the project of attacking the enemy, and I only wish to join Gen. Lee —I was even going to set out, but all the Brigadiers, Officers, &c. have represented that there was a material impossibility of moving troops in the situation where ours find themselves—I do not believe Gen. Lee is to make any attack to-morrow, for then I would have been directed to fall immediately upon them, without making 11 miles entirely out of the way. I am here as near as I will be at English Town. To morrow at two o'clock I will set off for that place.

I do not know if Morgan's corps, the militia, &c. must be brought along with the other part of the detachment. Gen. Forman who don't approve much of that motion, says that our right flank must be secured, unless to incur the most fatal consequences for the whole army.

I beg your pardon Sir, if my letter is so badly written, but I want to send it soon and to rest one or two hours.

I have the honor to be, &c.

LAFAYETTE.

Be so good as to send a speedy answer of what you think proper to order me.

To GENERAL WASHINGTON.

Near Englishtown June ye 27th 7 o'clock.

DR GENERAL

I did not receive your order to halt until the head of the Detachment was within a mile of English Town Creek—I immediately halted on the receipt—indeed it was not my intention to proceed further than the first brook or water—I have taken a tolerable strong Post in the wood where I shall wait for further orders—unless the expediency of making some movement is so forcible as to oblige me—the enemy certainly lay at Monmouth, last night—at least the rear of 'em, but whether They mov'd or no this morning is uncertain. The People here are inconceivably stupid. I have sent two lively young footmen (for they have no horses) to reconnoitre.

I am Dr Sir, Yours—

C. LEE.

P. S. I wish Your Excellcy woud order me some axes—a little spirits for the men and two or three (if they can be spared) active well mounted light Horsemen.

His Excellency General Washington.

General Washington to the President of Congress.

Englishtown six miles from Monmouth,
June 28, 1778, half after 11 A.M.

Sir,

I was duly honored with your favor of the 20th inst, with the report to which it referred, and trust my situation will apologize for my not answering it before. I am now here with the main body of the army and pressing hard to come up with the enemy. They encamped yesterday at Monmouth Court House having almost the whole of their front, particularly their left wing, secured by a marsh and thick wood and their rear by a very difficult defile, from whence they moved very early this morning. Our advance, from the rainy weather, and the intense heat when it was fair (though these have been equally disadvantageous to them) has been greatly delayed. Several of our men have fallen sick from these causes, and a few unfortunately have fainted and died in a little time after. We have a select and strong detachment more forward, under the command of Maj. Gen. Lee, with orders to attack their rear, if possible. Whether the detachment be able to come up with it is a matter of a question, especially, before they get into strong grounds. Besides this Morgan with his corps and some bodies of militia are on their flanks. I cannot determine yet at what place they intend to embark—some think they will push for Sandy Hook, whilst others suppose they mean to go to Shoal Harbor. The latter opinion seems to be founded in the greater probability, as from intelligence several vessels and crafts are lying off that place. We have made a few prisoners, and they have lost a good many men by desertion—I cannot ascertain their numbers, as they came into our advanced parties and pushed immediately into the country I think five or six hundred is the least number that have come in the whole—they are chiefly foreigners.

I have the honor to be with great respect

Sir, your most obt. servant

G° Washington

The Hon. Henry Laurens, Esq.
President of Congress.

General Washington to the President of Congress.

Fields near Monmouth C[t] House,
June 29th 1778.

Sir,

I have the honor to inform you that about seven o'clock on yesterday morning both armies advanced on each other. About 12 oclock they met on the grounds near Monmouth Court House, when an action commenced we forced the enemy from the field and encamped on the ground. They took a strong post on our front, secured on both flanks by morasses and thick woods, where they remained till about 12 at night and then retreated. I cannot at this time go into a detail of matters; when opportunity will permit I shall take the liberty of transmitting to Congress a more particular account of the proceedings of the Day.

I have the honor to be, with g[t] resp[t]

Sir, your most obt. servt

G° Washington

To Hon. Henry Laurens Esq.
&c. &c.

ROBERT TROUP TO CHIEF JUSTICE JAY.

Peekskill, June 29, 1778
½ after 9 oclock P.M.

MY DEAR SIR

By a letter received a few hours ago from Major Armstrong, we learn that our army were the night before last at English town, in New Jersey between six and seven miles from Monmouth Court House, where the main Body of the Enemy were posted—that they were marching, it is presumed in order to cut off their Communication entirely with South Amboy, & the other possible places of Embarcation—That Gen Lee Commanded 4,000 men which were constantly harassing their Flanks—that the militia of N. Jersey were in the highest spirits, and almost to a man in arms—That 500 British & German Soldiers had deserted, & more were hourly coming.

We shall move at 2 oclock in the morning for the White Plains—Our object is to make a shew of attacking N. York to prevent their throwing a force into N. Jersey to operate in favour of Sir Henry Clinton. We have a pretty respectable army.

I am sorry that we can't grant Miss Bayard's Requests, and the more so because you have applied for her. But my dear Sir, we shall be Putnamized, to all Intents and Purposes, if we suffer any person to go into New York. This consideration induced me to prevail upon the General, to shut the Door, immediately after I left you at Fishkill. I do not think that a single Flag will be granted, during the whole Campaign, unless for Public Purposes.

When I receive any further Intelligence that may be depended upon I shall communicate it to you without delay.

My best Respects to all my Friends at Poughkeepsie In the greatest hurry,

I am, My Dear Sir, Your obliged Humble Ser.

ROB. TROUP.

Hon. Judge Jay.

[To Richard Henry Lee.]

Englishtown, June 28th [29th,] 1778.

* * What the devil brought us into this level country (the very element of the enemy) or what interest we can have (in our present circumstances) to hazard an action, somebody else must tell you, for I cannot. I was yesterday ordered (for it was against my opinion and inclination) to engage. I did, with my division, which consisted of about four thousand men. The troops, both men and officers, showed the greatest valour: the artillery did wonders; but we were outnumbered; particularly in cavalry, which was, at twenty different times, on the point of turning completely our flanks. This consideration naturally obliged us to retreat; but the retreat did us, I will venture to say, great honour. It was performed with all the order and coolness which can be seen on a common field day. Not a man or officer hastened his step, but one regiment regularly filed off from the front to the rear of the other. The thanks I received from his Excellency were of a singular nature. I can demonstrate that had I not acted as I did, this army, and perhaps America, would have been ruined. * *

Colonel John Laurens to Henry Laurens.

Head Quarters, English Town, 30th June, 1778.

My Dear Father:

I was exceedingly chagrined that public business prevented my writing to you from the field of battle, when the General sent his dispatches to Congress. The delay, however, will be attended with this advantage, that I shall be better able to give you an account of the enemy's loss; tho' I must now content myself with a very succinct relation of this affair. The situation of the two armies on Sunday was as follows: Gen[l] Washington, with the main body of our army, was at 4 miles distance from English Town. Gen[l] Lee, with a chosen advanced corps, was *at* that town. The enemy were retreating down the road which leads to Middle Town; their flying army composed (as it was said), of 2 battalions of British grenadiers, 1 Hessian grend[rs], 1 battalion of light infantry, 1 regiment of guards, 2 brigades of foot, 1 reg[t] of dragoons and a number of mounted and dismounted Jagers. The enemy's rear was preparing to leave Monmouth village, which is 6 miles from this place, when our advanced corps was marching towards them. The militia of the country kept up a random running fire with the Hessian Jagers; no mischief was done on either side. I was with a small party of horse, reconnoitring the enemy, in an open space before Monmouth, when I perceived two parties of the enemy advancing by files in the woods on our right and left, with a view as I imagined, of enveloping our small party or preparing a way for a skirmish of their horse. I immediately wrote an account of what I had seen to the General, and expressed my anxiety on account of the languid appearance of the continental troops under Gen[l] Lee.

Some person in the meantime reported to Gen[l] Lee that the enemy were advancing upon us in two columns, and I was informed that he had, in consequence, ordered Varnum's brigade, which was in front, to repass a bridge which it had passed. I went myself, and assured him of the real state of the case; his reply to me was, that his accounts had been so contradictory, that he was utterly at a loss what part to take. I repeated my account to him in positive distinct terms, and returned to make farther discoveries. I found that the two parties had been withdrawn from the wood, and that the enemy were preparing to leave Monmouth. I wrote a second time to Gen[l] Washington. Gen[l] Lee at length gave orders to advance. The enemy were forming themselves on the Middle Town road, with their light infantry in front, and cavalry on the left flank, while a scattering, distant fire was commenced between our flanking parties and theirs. I was impatient and uneasy at seeing that no disposition was made, and endeavored to find out Gen[l] Lee to inform him of what was doing, and know what was his disposition. He told me that he was going to order some troops to march below the enemy and cut off their retreat. Two pieces of artillery were posted on our right without a single foot soldier to support them. Our men were formed piecemeal in front of the enemy, and there appeared to be no general plan or disposition calculated on that of the enemy; the nature of the ground, or any of the other principles which generally govern in these cases.

The enemy began a cannonade from two parts of their line; their whole body of horse made a furious charge upon a small party of our cavalry and dissipated them, and drove them till the appearance of our infantry and a judicious discharge or two of artillery made them retire precipitately. Three regiments of ours that had advanced in a plain open country towards the enemy's left flank, were ordered by Gen[l] Lee to retire and occupy the village of Monmouth. They were no sooner formed there, than they were ordered to quit that post and gain the woods. One order succeeded another with a rapidity and indecision calculated to ruin us. The enemy had changed their front and were advancing in full march towards us; our men were fatigued with the excessive heat. The artillery horses were not in condition to make a brisk retreat. A new position was ordered, but not generally communicated, for part of the troops were forming on the right of the ground, while others were marching away, and all the artillery driving off. The enemy, after a short halt, resumed their pursuit; no cannon was left to check their progress. A regiment was ordered to form behind a fence, and as speedily commanded to retire. All this disgraceful retreating, passed without the firing of a musket, over ground which might have been disputed inch by inch. We passed a defile and arrived at an eminence beyond, which was defended on one hand by an impracticable fen, on the other by thick woods where our men would have fought to advantage. | Here, fortunately for the honour of the army, and the welfare of America, Gen[l] Washington met the troops retreating in disorder, and without any plan to make an opposition. He ordered some pieces of artillery to be brought up to defend the pass, and some troops to form and defend the pieces. The artillery was too distant to be brought up readily, so that there was but little opposition given here. A few shot though, and a little skirmishing in the wood checked the enemy's career. The Gen[l] expressed his astonishment at this unaccountable retreat. M[r]. Lee indecently replied that the attack was contrary to his advice and opinion in council. We were obliged to retire to a position, which, though hastily reconnoitred, proved an excellent one. Two regiments were formed behind a fence in front of the position. The enemy's horse advanced in full charge with admirable bravery to the distance of forty paces, when a general discharge from these two regiments did great execution among them, and made them fly with the greatest precipitation. The grenadiers succeeded to the attack. At this time my horse was killed under me. In this spot the action was hottest, and there was considerable slaughter of British grenadiers. The General ordered Woodford's brigade with some artillery to take possession of an eminence on the enemy's left and cannonade from thence. This produced an excellent effect. The enemy were prevented from advancing on us, and confined themselves to cannonade with a show of turning our left flank. Our artillery answered theirs with the greatest vigour. The General seeing that our left flank was secure, as the ground was open and commanded by it, so that the enemy could not attempt to turn it without exposing their own flank to a heavy fire from our artillery, and causing to pass in review before us, the force employed for turning us. In the meantime, Gen[l] Lee continued retreating. Baron Steuben was order'd to form the broken troops in the rear. The cannonade was incessant and the General ordered parties to advance from time to time and engage the British grenadiers and guards. The horse shewed themselves no more. The grenadiers shewed their backs and retreated every where with precipitation. They returned, however again to the charge, and were again repulsed. They finally retreated and got over the strong pass, where, as I mentioned before, Gen[l] Washington first rallied the troops. We advanced in force and continued masters of the ground; the standards of liberty were planted in triumph on the field of battle. We remained looking at each other, with the defile between us, till dark, and they stole off in silence at midnight. We have buried of the enemy's slain, 233, principally grenadiers; forty odd of their wounded whom they left at Monmouth, fell into our hands. Several officers are our prisoners. Among their killed are Co[l] Moncton, a captain of the guards, and several captains of grenadiers. We have taken but a very inconsiderable number of prisoners, for want of a good body of horse. Deserters are coming in as usual. Our officers and men behaved with that bravery which becomes freemen, and have convinced the world that they can beat British grenadiers. To name any one in particular w[d] be a kind of injustice to the rest. There are some, however, who came more immediately under my view, whom I will mention that you may know them. B. Gen[l] Wayne, Col. Barber, Col. Stewart, Col. Livingston, Col. Oswald of the artillery, Cap[t] Doughty deserve well of their country, and distinguished themselves nobly.

The enemy buried many of their dead that are not accounted for above, and carried off a great number of wounded. I have written diffusely, and yet I have not told you all. Gen[l] Lee, I think, must be tried for misconduct. However, as this is a matter not generally known, tho' it seems almost universally wished for, I would beg you, my dear father, to say nothing of it.

You will oblige me much by excusing me to M[r] Drayton for not writing to him. I congratulate you, my dear father, upon this seasonable victory, and am ever,

Your most dutiful and affectionate,
JOHN LAURENS.

The Honble Henry Laurens, Esq[r].

We have no returns of our loss as yet. The proportion on the field of battle appeared but small. We have many good officers wounded.

TO GENERAL WASHINGTON.

Camp, English Town, July 1st [30th June] 1778.

SIR,

From the knowledge I have of your Excellency's character, I must conclude, that nothing but the misinformation of some very stupid, or misrepresentation of some very wicked person, could have occasioned your making use of such very singular expressions as you did, on my coming up to the ground where you had taken post: they imply'd, that I was guilty either of disobedience of orders, of want of conduct, or want of courage. Your Excellency will therefore infinitely oblige me, by letting me know, on which of these three articles you ground your charge, that I may prepare for my justification; which I have the happiness to be confident I can do, to the Army, to the Congress, to

America, and to the World in general. Your Excellency must give me leave to observe, that neither yourself, nor those about your person, cou'd, from your situation, be in the least judges of the merits or demerits of our manœuvres; and, to speak with a becoming pride, I can assert, that to these manœuvres the success of the day was entirely owing. I can boldly say, that had we remained on the first ground, or had we advanc'd, or had the retreat been conducted in a manner different from what it was, this whole army, and the interest of America, would have risk'd being sacrificed. I ever had, (and I hope ever shall have,) the greatest respect and veneration for General Washington; I think him endow'd with many great and good qualities; but in this instance, I must pronounce, that he has been guilty of an act of cruel injustice towards a man who certainly has some pretensions to the regard of ev'ry servant of this country; and, I think, Sir, I have a right to demand some reparation for the injury committed; and unless I can obtain it, I must, in justice to myself, when this campaign is closed, (which I believe will close the war,) retire from a service, at the head of which is placed a man capable of offering such injuries:—but, at this same time, in justice to you, I must repeat that I from my soul believe, that it was not a motion of your own breast, but instigated by some of those dirty earwigs who will for ever insinuate themselves near persons in high office; for I really am convinced, that when General Washington acts from himself, no man in his army will have reason to complain of injustice or indecorum.

I am, Sir, and hope I ever shall have reason to continue, your most sincerely devoted humble Servant,

Charles Lee.

His Excellency General Washington.

From General Washington.

Head Quarters, English-Town, June 30th 1778.

Sir:

I received your letter, (dated, through mistake, the 1st of July) expressed, as I conceive, in terms highly improper. I am not conscious of having made use of any very singular expressions at the time of my meeting you, as you intimate. What I recollect to have said, was dictated by duty, and warranted by the occasion. As soon as circumstances will permit, you shall have an opportunity either of justifying yourself to the army, to Congress, to America, and to the world in general; or of convincing them that you were guilty of a breach of orders, and of misbehaviour before the enemy, on the 28th inst., in not attacking them as you had been directed, and in making an unnecessary, disorderly, and shameful retreat.

I am Sir, your most obedient Servant,

G° Washington.

Major General Lee.

To General Washington.

Camp, June 28th [30th,] 1778.

Sir,

I beg your Excellency's pardon for the inaccuracy in mis-dating my letter. You cannot afford me greater pleasure than in giving me the opportunity of shewing to America, the sufficiency of her respective servants. I trust, that the temporary power of office, and the tinsel dignity attending it, will not be able, by all the mists they can raise, to offiscate the bright rays of truth.

In the mean time, your Excellency can have no objection to my retiring from the army. I am, Sir,

Your most obedient Humble Servant,

CHARLES LEE.

General Washington.

TO GEN. WASHINGTON.

Camp, June 30th, 1778.

SIR,

Since I had the honour of addressing my letter by Colonel Fitzgerald to your Excellency, I have reflected on both your situation and mine; and beg leave to observe, that it will be for our mutual convenience, that a Court of Enquiry should be immediately ordered; but I could wish it might be a Court Martial: for, if the affair is drawn into length, it may be difficult to collect the necessary evidences, and perhaps might bring on a paper war betwixt the adherents to both parties, which may occasion some disagreeable feuds on the Continent; for all are not my friends, nor all your admirers. I must entreat, therefore, from your love of justice, that you will immediately exhibit your charge; and that on the first halt, I may be brought to a tryal, and am, Sir,

Your most obedient Humble Servant,

CHARLES LEE.

His Excellency Gen. Washington.

GENERALS WAYNE AND SCOTT TO GEN. WASHINGTON.

Englishtown, 30th June, 1778.

SIR,

We esteem it a duty, which we owe to our country, ourselves, and the officers and soldiers under our command, to state the following facts to your Excellency.

On the 28th instant, at five o'clock in the morning, we received orders to march with the following detachments, namely, Scott's and Varnum's brigades, Colonels Butler and Jackson in front, amounting to seventeen hundred men; Colonels Wesson, Livingston, and Stewart, with one thousand men, commanded by General Wayne; a select detachment of fourteen hundred men, rank and file, under General Scott, with ten pieces of artillery properly distributed among the whole.

About eight o'clock, the van under Colonel Butler arrived on the left of Monmouth Court-House, on the rear of the left flank of the enemy, who were in full march, moving in great haste and confusion. At this time our main body, under General Lee, were formed at the edge of a wood about half a mile distant from the Court-House. General Wayne, who was in front reconnoitring the enemy, perceiving that they had made a halt, and were preparing to push Colonel Butler with their horse and a few foot, gave direction for him to form and receive them, and at the same time sent Major Byles to General Lee, requesting that those troops might be advanced to support those in front, and for the whole to form on the edge of a deep morass, which extends from the east of the Court-House on the right a very considerable distance to the left. The troops did arrive in about an hour after the requisition, and were generally formed in this position.

About the same time, General Scott's detachment had passed the morass on the left, and the enemy's horse and foot that had charged Colonel Butler, were repulsed. The number of the enemy now in view might be near two thousand, though at first not more than five hundred, exclusive of their horse. The ground we now occupied was the best formed by nature for defence of any, perhaps in this country. The enemy advanced with caution, keeping at a considerable distance in front. General Scott, having viewed the position of the enemy, as well as the ground where about twenty-five hundred of our troops were formed, repassed the morass and took post on the left, in a fine open wood, covered by said morass in front.

Whilst this was doing, General Wayne, perceiving that the troops on the right, from the wood to the Court House, were retreating, sent Major Fishbourn to General Lee, requesting that the troops might return to support him. In the interim General Wayne repassed the morass, leaving Colonel Butler's regiment to keep post on the right flank of the enemy. Generals Scott and Wayne then went together along the morass to the Court House, when Major Fishbourn returned, and said that General Lee gave no other answer, than that he would see General Wayne himself, which he never did. The enemy having now an opening on the right of General Scott began to move on, when General Wayne and General Scott sent to General Lee to request him at least to form, to favor General Scott's retreat; but this requisition met with the same fate as the last. The troops kept still retreating, when General Scott perceiving that he would not be supported, filed off by the left. General Wayne ordered Colonel Butler to fall back also. Thus were these several select detachments unaccountably drawn off without being suffered to come to action, although we had the most pleasing prospect from our numbers and position, of obtaining the most glorious and decisive victory. After this, we fortunately fell in with your Excellency. You ordered us to form part of those troops, whose conduct and bravery kept the enemy in play, until you had restored order.

We have taken the liberty of stating these facts, in order to convince the world that our retreat from the Court House was not occasioned by the want of numbers, position, or wishes of both officers and men to maintain that post. We also beg leave to mention, that that no plan of attack was ever communicated to us, or notice of a retreat, until it had taken place in our rear, as we supposed by General Lee's order.

We are, &c

Anthony Wayne,
Charles Scott.

General Washington to the President of Congress.

Englishtown, July 1, 1778.

Sir,

I embrace this first moment of leisure to give Congress a more full and particular account of the movements of the army under my command since its passing the Delaware, than the situation of our affairs would heretofore permit.

I had the honor to advise them that on the appearance of the enemy's intentions to march through Jersey becoming serious, I had detached Gen. Maxwell's brigade in conjunction with the militia of that State, to interrupt and impede their progress by every obstruction in their power, so as to give time to the army under my command to come up with them, and take advantage of any favorable circumstances that might present themselves. The army having proceeded to Coryell's ferry and crossed the Delaware at that place, I immediately detached Col. Morgan, with a select corps of 600 men to reinforce Gen. Maxwell, and marched with the main body towards Princeton.

The slow advance of the enemy had greatly the air of design, and led me with others to suspect that Gen. Clinton, desirous of a general action, was endeavouring to draw us down into the lower country, in order by a rapid movement to gain our right and take possession of the strong grounds above us. This consideration and to give the troops time to repose and refresh themselves from the fatigues they had experienced from rainy and excessively hot weather, determined me to halt at Hopewell Township, about five miles from Princeton, where we remained till the morning of the 25th. On the preceding day I made a second detachment of 1500 chosen troops, under Brig. Gen. Scott, to reinforce those already in the vicinity of the enemy and more effectually to annoy and delay their march. The next day the army moved to Kingston, and having received intelligence that the enemy were prosecuting their route towards Monmouth Court House, I despatched 1000 select men under Brig[r] Gen Wayne and sent to the Marquis De la Fayette to take the command of the whole advanced corps, including Maxwell's brigade, and Morgan's light infantry, with orders to take the first fair opportunity of attacking the enemy's rear. In the evening of the same day the whole army marched from Kingston, where our baggage was left, with intention to preserve a proper distance for supporting the advanced corps, and arrived at Cranberry early the next morning. The intense heat of the weather and a heavy storm unluckily coming on, made it impossible to resume our march that day without great inconvenience and injury to the troops. Our advanced corps being differently circumstanced, moved from the position it had held the night before, and took post in the evening on the Monmouth road, about 5 miles from the enemy's rear, in expectation of attacking them next morning on their march. The main body having remained at Cranberry, the advanced corps was found to be too remote, and too far upon the right to be supported either in case of an attack upon or from the enemy, which induced me to send orders to the Marquis to file off by his left, towards Englishtown, which he accordingly executed early in the morning of the 27th.

The enemy in marching from Allen-Town had changed their disposition, and placed their best troops in the rear, consisting of all the Grenadiers Light Infantry and Chasseurs of the line. This alteration made it necessary to increase the number of our advanced corps; in consequence of which I detached Major Gen. Lee, with two brigades, to join the Marquis at Englishtown, on whom of course the command of the whole devolved, amounting to about 5000 men. The main body marched the same day, and encamped within three miles of that place. Morgan's corps was left hovering on the enemy's right flank, and the Jersey Militia amounting at this time to about 7 or 800 men, under Gen. Dickinson, on their left.

The enemy were now encamped in a strong position, with their right extending about a mile and a half beyond the Court House, to the parting of the roads leading to Shrewsbury and Middletown and their left along the road from Allentown to Monmouth, about three miles on this side of the Court House. Their right flank lay on the skirt of a small wood, while their left was secured by a very thick one—a morass running towards their rear, and their whole front covered by a wood, and for a considerable extent towards the left with a morass. In this situation they halted till the morning of the 28th.

Matters being thus situated, and having had the best information, that if the enemy were once arrived at the heights of Middletown, ten or twelve miles from where they were, it would be impossible to attempt anything against them with prospect of success, I determined to attack their rear the moment they should get in motion from their present ground. I communicated my intention to Gen. Lee, and ordered him to make his disposition for the attack, and to keep his troops constantly lying upon their arms to be in readiness at the shortest notice. This was done with respect to the troops under my immediate command.

About 5 in the morning Gen. Dickinson sent an express, informing that the front of the enemy had begun their march. I instantly put the army in motion, and sent orders by one of my aids de camp to Gen. Lee, to move on and attack them unless there should be very powerful reasons to the contrary; acquainting him at the same time that I was marching to support him, and for doing it with the greater expedition and convenience, should make the men disencumber themselves of their packs and blankets.

After marching above five miles, to my great surprise and mortification, I met the whole advanced corps retreating, and as I was told, by General Lee's orders, without having made any opposition except one fire given by the party under the command of Col. Butler, on their being charged by the enemy's cavalry, who were repulsed. I proceeded immediately to the rear of the corps, which I found closely pressed by the enemy, and gave directions for forming part of the retreating troops, who by the brave and spirited conduct of the officers aided by some pieces of well-served artillery, checked the enemy's advance, and gave time to make a disposition of the left wing and second line of the army upon an eminence, and in a wood a little in the rear, covered by a morass in front, on this were placed some batteries of cannon by L[d]. Stirling, who commanded the left wing, which played upon the enemy with great effect, and seconded by parties of infantry, detached to oppose them, effectually put a stop to their advance.

Gen. Lee being detached with the advanced corps, the command of the right wing, for the occasion, was given to Gen. Greene. For the expedition of the march and to counteract any attempt to turn our right, I had ordered him to file off by the new Church, two miles from Englishtown and fall into the Monmouth road, a small distance in the rear of the Court House while the rest of the column moved directly on towards the Court-house. On intelligence of the retreat, he marched up, and took a very advantageous position on the right.

The enemy by this time finding themselves warmly opposed in front, made an attempt to turn our left flank, but they were bravely repulsed and driven back by detached parties of infantry. They also made a movement to our right, with as little success, Gen. Greene having advanced a body of troops, with artillery, to a commanding piece of ground, which not only disappointed their design of turning our right, but severely enfiladed those in front of the left wing. In addition to this Gen. Wayne advanced with a body of troops and kept up so severe and well directed a fire, that the enemy were soon compelled to retire behind the defile, where the first stand in the beginning of the action had been made. In this situation the enemy had both their flanks secured by thick woods and morasses while their front could only be approached through a narrow pass. I resolved nevertheless to attack them, and for that purpose ordered Gen. Poor, with his own and the Carolina Brigade to move round upon their right and Gen. Woodford upon their left, and the artillery to gall them in front; but the impediments in their way prevented their getting within reach before it was dark. They remained upon the ground they had been directed to occupy during the night, with the intention to begin the attack early the next morning, and the army continued lying upon their arms in the field of action to be in readiness to support them. In the meantime the enemy were employed in removing their wounded, and about twelve o'clock at night marched away in such silence, that though Gen. Poor lay extremely near them they effected their retreat without his knowledge. They carried off all their wounded, except four officers and about forty privates whose wounds were too dangerous to permit their removal.

The extreme heat of the weather, the fatigue of the men from their march through a deep sandy country, almost entirely destitute of water—and the distance the enemy had gained by marching in the night made a pursuit impracticable and fruitless. It would have answered no valuable purpose, and would have been fatal to numbers of our men, several of whom died the preceding day with heat.

Were I to conclude my account of this day's transactions without expressing my obligations to the officers of the Army in general, I should do injustice to their merit, and violence to my own feelings. They seemed to vie with each other in manifesting their zeal and bravery. The catalogue of those who distinguished themselves is too long to admit of particularizing individuals. I cannot however forbear mentioning Brig^{r} Gen Wayne, whose good conduct and bravery thro' the whole action deserves particular commendation.

The behaviour of the troops in general after they recovered from the first surprise, occasioned by the retreat of the advanced corps, was such as could not be surpassed.

All the artillery both officers and men that were engaged, distinguished themselves in a remarkable manner.

Inclosed Congress will be pleased to receive a return of our killed, wounded, and missing. Among the first were Lieut. Col. Bonner, of Penn[a]. and Major Dickinson of Virginia, both officers of distinguished merit and much to be regretted. The enemy's slain left on the field and buried by us, according to the return of the persons assigned to that duty, were four officers, and two hundred and forty five privates. In the former number was the Hon. Col. Monckton. Exclusive of these they buried some themselves, as there were several new graves near the field of battle. How many men they may have had wounded cannot be determined—but from the usual proportion, the number must have been considerable. There were a few prisoners taken.

The peculiar situation of Gen. Lee at this time requires that I should say nothing of his conduct. He is now in arrest. The charges against him, with such sentence as the Court Martial may decree in his case, shall be transmitted for the approbation or disapprobation of Congress, as soon as it shall be passed.

Being fully convinced by the gentlemen of this country that the enemy cannot be hurt or injured in their embarkation at Sandy Hook, the place to which they are going, and unwilling to get too far removed from the North River, I put the troops in motion early this morning and shall proceed that way, leaving the Jersey Brigade, Morgan's Corps, and other light parties (the militia being all dismissed) to hover about them—to countenance desertion, and to prevent their depredations as far as possible. After they embark the former will take post in the neighborhood of Elizabethtown—the latter rejoin the corps from which they were detached.

I have the honor to be with great respect,

Sir, Your most Obedient Servant,

G[o] Washington.

To the Hon. Henry Laurens Esq &[c] &[c]

Return of the killed wounded and missing of the American Army in the battle of Monmouth, on the 28th of June, 1778.

Killed: 1 Lieut. Col. 1 Major, 3 Captains, 2 Lieuts. 1 serjeant, 52 rank and file.

Wounded: 2 Cols. 8 Captns, 4 First Lieuts, 2 Second Lieutenants, 1 Ensign, 1 Adjutant, 8 serjeants, 1 Drum. 120 rank and file.

Missing: 5 serjeants, 126 rank & file. Many of the missing dropped through fatigue and have since come in.

Artillery: Killed. 1 First Lieut. 7 Matrosses, 1 Bombadier.

Wounded: 1 Capt. 2 serjeants, 1 Corporal, 1 gunner, 10 Matrosses.

Missing: 1 Matross

Six horses killed and two wounded.

A Report of the British & American Troops, Fallen in the Action Near Monmouth & Buried under Care of Col.l Van Dyck. By Different Officers, viz.t

	British.	Americans.
Capt. Graham..	28	7
Capt. Kirkwood..	19	5
Capt. Frie	25	3
Capt. Beebe	24	3
Lieut. V. Valkenburgh	8	3
Lieut. Bruff	21	3
Lieut. Reeves	11	2
Ensign Wolford	23	0
Lieut. Ferrit	7	3
Lieut. Colgate	12	0
Serg.t Jones	3	0
Serg.t Brown	5	0
Serg.t of 12 Virginia B.t	4	0
By the different Inhabitants..	27	0
Totals	217	29

Cornelius Van Dyck, Ltt. Col.

Endorsed (in the handwriting of General Washington,) "A Report of the No. of Slain, buried in the Field of Battle near Monmouth Court H°. 29th June 1778. Note.—Those buried by the Enemy not included in these reports."

General Wayne to his Wife.

Spotts Wood, 1st July, 1778.

Dear Polly,

On Sunday the 28th June our flying Army came in view of the Enemy about Eight O'Clock in the Morning, when I was Ordered to Advance and Attack them with a few men—the Remainder of the Army under Genl *Lee* was to have Supported me—we accordingly Advanced—and Received a Charge from the British horse and Infantry, which we soon [Repulsed]—however our Genl thought Proper [to Retreat] in place of Advancing—without our firing a Single Shot—the Enemy following in force—which Rendered it very Difficult for the small force I had to gain the main body, being often hard pushed and frequently Surrounded—after falling back about a Mile we met His Excellency, who Surprised at our Retreat, knowing that Officers as well as men were in high Spirits and wished for Nothing more than to be faced about and meet the British fire—he Accordingly Ordered me to keep post where he met us with Stewarts & Livingstons Regiments and a Virginia Regt then under my Command with two pieces of Artillery and to keep [the Enemy] in play until he had an [opportunity] of forming the Remainder of the Army and Restoring Order—We had but just taken post when the Enemy began their attack with Horse, foot, & Artillery, the fire of their whole united force Obliged us after a Severe Conflict to give way—when a Most tremendious Cannonade Commenced on both Sides, and Continued near four Hours without Ceasing—during this time every possible Exertion was made use of by His Excellency and the Other Generals to Spirit up the Troops and to prepare them for an Other tryal—the

Enemy began to Advance again in a heavy [Column], against which I ordered some & advanced with some of my to meet them—the Action was Exceedingly warm and well Maintained on each Side for a Considerable time—at Length Victory Declared for us—the British Courage failed, and was forced to give place to American Valour.

We Encamped on the field of Battle where we found among the Dead and Wounded a number of the first Officers of the British Army—we have taken a great many prisoners—and their men are coming into us by Hundreds of a Day—

In this affair I lost Eight brave field Officers killed and wounded, with many other Officers and men—on the part of the Enemy—the Slaughter has been great and on their Grand[rs], Infantry, and Guards—their Loss is not less than twelve or fifteen Hundred men killed & wounded.

Every General & other officer (one excepted) did Everything that could be expected on this Great Occation, but Penns[a] shewed the Road to Victory—Adieu, Dear Polly—Send this to my poor old Mother—& tell her that I am safe & Well—kiss our Little People for me. ANT[Y] WAYNE.

COL. JOHN LAURENS TO HENRY LAURENS.

Head Quarters (on the lovely banks of the Raritan, opposite New Brunswick), 2d July, 1778.

MY DEAR FATHER:

I had the pleasure of writing to you the day before yesterday, from English Town, but through some mistake my letter was not delivered to the express, altho it was written in a hurry. I recollect no circumstance in it relative to our late engagement, which farther inquiry and consideration do not confirm. From a second view of the ground, as well as the accounts I have since had of the enemy's strength and designs, it is evident to me that Mr Clinton's whole flying army would have fallen into our hands, but for a defect of abilities or good will in the commanding officer of our advanced corps. His precipitate retreat spread a baneful influence everywhere. The most sanguine hope scarcely extended farther, when the Commander in chief rallied his troops, than to an orderly retreat; but by his intrepidity and presence of mind, a firm line of troops was formed on a good position, from whence he cannonaded with advantage, and detached light parties in front, who drove the enemy from the field. Genl Clinton and Lord Cornwallis were both present at the action.

The reason for not pursuing them farther with the main body of our army was, that people well acquainted with the country said that the strength of the ground would render it impracticable for us to injure them essentially; and that the sandy, parched soil, together with the heat of the sun, would probably occasion us considerable loss. From the specimen of yesterday's march we have reason to think it fortunate that we took the part we have done; the heat of the weather, thirsty soil, and heavy sand, reduced us to the necessity of bringing on many of our weaker men in waggons.

We are now arrived in a delightful country where we shall halt and refresh ourselves. Bathing in the Raritan, and the good living of the country will speedily refresh us. I wish, my dear father, that you could ride along the banks of this delightful river. Your zeal for the public service will not at this time permit it. But the inward satisfaction which you must feel from a patriotic discharge of your duty, is infinitely superior to the delights of retirement and ease. I admire your constant virtue, and will imitate your example.

Your most affectionate

JOHN LAURENS.

Col. Morgan writes this day, that the rear of the

enemy is a mile below Middle Town; that he has had a skirmish with several of their light parties, which has cost them some lives. He had only one man wounded. Desertions continue, and I suppose will be very considerable at the moment of embarkation.

I have seen the General much embarrassed this day, on the subject of those who distinguished themselves in the battle of Monmouth. To name a few, and be silent with regard to many of equal merit w[d] be an injustice to the latter; to pass the whole over unnoticed w[d] be an unpardonable slight; indiscriminate praise of the whole w[d] be an unfair distribution of rewards; and yet, when men generally conducted themselves so well as our officers did, this matter is allowable and is eligible, because least liable to give offence.

The merit of restoring the day, is due to the General; and his conduct was such throughout the affair as has greatly increased my love and esteem for him. My three brother aids gained themselves great applause by their activity and bravery, while the three secretaries acted as military men on this occasion, and proved themselves as worthy to wield the sword as the pen.

Gen[l] Steuben, his aids and your son, narrowly escaped being surrounded by the British horse, early on the morning of the action. We reconnoitred them rather too nearly, and L[d] Cornwallis sent the dragoons of his guard to make us prisoners. Gen[l] Clinton saw* the Baron's star, and the whole pursuit was directed at him; but we all escaped, the dragoons fearing an ambuscade of infantry.

We have buried Col. Moncton with the honours of war.

The Honble Henry Laurens, Esq[r]

President of Congress, Philadelphia.

* A dragoon deserter from the enemy just informs us of this. He says three others came off with him, and that the Hessians are deserting amazingly.

To Isaac Collins.

[*New Jersey Gazette Nº* 31, *Vol. I.*, *July* 8, 1778.]

Brunswick, July 3d, 1778.

Sir,

Not satisfied with robbing me and the brave men under my command of the credit due to us with respect to the affair of the 28th, such an atrocious attack has been made on my conduct, and so gross are the injuries I have received, that I have demanded a Court-martial, which is to be held tomorrow. The reason that I address this note to you, is, that a most invidious, dishonest, and false relation has appeared in your paper of July the 1st—I must therefore, entreat as you are an honest man, that you will desire your readers to consider the aforesaid relation as a fiction. Before long they shall have a minute, just, and faithful account—In the meantime I beg you will print this note —and am, Sir,

Your most obedient Servant,
Charles Lee.

Mr. Isaac Collins.

July 3d, 1778.

Sir,

I desire you will consider this as a postscript to the note I have already addressed to you, and that you will request whatever printer is your correspondent at Philadelphia, to insert the note and postscript in his paper. To call the affair a complete victory would be a dishonorable gasconade—It was indeed a very handsome check, which did the Americans honor. No affair can be more convincing of what they are equal to; in a retrograde manœuvre of near four miles, no confusion was observable but what arose, and ever will arise from a monstrous abuse, which, if tolerated, will be one day fatal—I mean the liberty which individuals, without authority, take to direct and give their opinions. The behaviour of the whole, both men and officers, was so equally good that it would be unjust to make distinctions; tho' I confess it is difficult to refrain from paying compliments to the artillery, from General Knox and Colonel Oswald down to the very driver. It is difficult to say which was the decisive point—it was a battle in pieces, and by dint of fighting in a variety of places—in the plain and in the woods—by advancing and retreating, the enemy were at last fairly worn down.

I am, Sir, Yours,

CHARLES LEE.

ACCOUNT OF THE BATTLE OF MONMOUTH.

Referred to in the foregoing letter.

[*New Jersey Gazette, Vol. I., No.* 30, *June* 24, 1778. No. 29 is dated June 17. No. 31 is dated July 8. The publication was probably interrupted by the military movements, &c.]

TRENTON, *July* 1. His Excellency General Washington, having early intelligence of the intended movement of the enemy from Philadelphia, detached a considerable body of troops under the command of Major General Lee, in order to support General Maxwell's Brigade of Continental troops already in this state, and the militia under Generals Dickinson and Heard. These troops were intended to harrass the enemy on their march through this state to Amboy, and to retard them till General Washington, with the main body, could get up. In the mean time several small skirmishes happened between the enemy and General Maxwell's troops, joined by the militia, but without any considerable execution on either side.

The march of the enemy being by this means impeded, and the main army having crossed the Delaware at Coryell's ferry on the 20th and 21st ult°, proceeded by the way of Hopewell, Rocky Hill, Kingston and Cranberry, and on the 27th overtook the enemy at Monmouth Court House, whither they retired from Allentown on the approach of our troops, leaving their intended route to Amboy.

It having been previously determined to attack the enemy on their march, a suitable disposition was made the same evening. General Lee, with a detachment of pick'd men, consisting of about 1500, and reinforced by a strong body of Jersey militia, advanced to English Town (about six miles from Monmouth Court House) the militia then proceeded to the meeting house; the main army under General Washington being about four miles in the rear of English Town. In this position the whole halted until advice could be received of the enemy's motion.—At three o'clock on Sunday morning their first division under General Knyphausen, began their march, of which we had intelligence in about two hours, when General Lee received orders to advance and begin the attack, the main army at the same time advancing to support him. About half a mile beyond the Court House, General Lee began his attack, and drove the enemy for some time; when they being reinforced, he was obliged to retreat in turn, 'till met by General Washington with the main army, which formed on the first advantageous ground—In the meantime two field pieces covered by two regiments of the detachment and commanded by Colonels Livingston and Stewart, were advanced to check the enemy's approach, which they performed with great spirit and with considerable loss on both sides. This service being performed, they retired with the pieces to the front line, then completely formed, when the severest cannonade began that it is thought ever happened in America. In the mean time strong detachments marched and attacked the enemy with small arms, with various success—The enemy were finally obliged to give way, and we took possession of the field, covered with dead and wounded. The intense heat of the weather, and the preceding fatigue of the troops, made it necessary to halt them to rest for some time. The enemy in the mean time presenting a front about one mile advanced beyond the seat of action—as soon as the troops had recovered breath, General Washington ordered two brigades to advance upon each of their flanks, intending to move on in front at a proper time to support them, but before they could reach their destination night came on, and made any further movements impracticable.

They left on the field the honorable Col. Monckton, with several other officers and a great number of privates, which cannot yet be ascertained with precision.—About 12 o'clock on Sunday night they moved off with great precipitation towards Middletown, leaving at the Courthouse five wounded officers and above forty privates. They began the attack with their veteran grenadiers and light infantry, which renders their loss still more important. On our side Lieut. Col. Bonner, of Pennsylvania, and Major Dickinson of Virginia, are slain—Col. Barber, of this State, is wounded by a musket ball, which passed thro' the right of his body, but it is hoped will not prove mortal. Our troops behaved with the greatest bravery, and opposed the flower of the British army—Our artillery was well served, and did amazing execution. Before, during, and after the action, deserters came over in great numbers, and still continue so to do. Of the enemy's dead many have been found without any wound, but being heavily cloathed, they sunk under the heat and fatigue. We are well assured that the Hessians absolutely refused to engage, declaring it was too hot. Their line of march from the Court House was strew'd with dead, with arms, knapsacks, and accoutrements, which they dropt on their retreat. They had the day before taken about fifteen prisoners, whom in their haste they left behind. Had we been possessed of a powerful body of cavalry on the field, there is no doubt the success would have been much more compleat, but they had been so much employed in harassing the enemy during the march, and were so detached, as to give the enemy a great superiority in number, much to their advantage. Our success, under heaven, is to be wholly ascribed to the good disposition made by his Excellency, supported by the firmness and bravery of both officers and men, who were emulous to distinguish themselves on this occasion. The great advance of the enemy on their way, their possession of the strong grounds at Middletown, added to the exhausted state of our troops, made an immediate pursuit ineligible; and our army now remains about one mile advanced from the field of battle, having been since employed in collecting the dead and wounded, and burying the former.

Thus (says a correspondent) the enemy have had two campaigns to march from New York to Philadelphia, and back again, with the diminution of at least half their army. How much cheaper might his Britannic Majesty, buy sheep and oxen in England, in the usual manner, than he now gets them, by employing an army to steal them in America!

The enemy, on their way through Burlington county, wantonly destroyed a very valuable merchant-mill near Bordentown,* the iron works at Mount Holly, and the dwelling houses, out houses, &c. of Peter Tallman, Esq., and Col. Shreve.

Previous to the evacuation of Philadelphia, the enemy plundered the inhabitants of most of the waggons and horses in and near the city, and totally destroyed some and greatly injured many very valuable buildings, especially such as were situated about the suburbs of the town and near the lines. A number of the active tory inhabitants, being conscious of their guilt, and dreading the vengeance of their countrymen, went off with the enemy.

Monday last twenty seven British prisoners, chiefly grenadiers, who were taken by surprise on Saturday

[* See advertisement of the ruins, &c., in N. J. Gazette: Oct. 14, 1778.]

last near Monmouth Court house, were brought to this town. The same day thirty six more arrived at Princeton, part of those taken in the late engagement, and many more are on their way.

By the best accounts we have received, upwards of 500 of the British Army, chiefly Hessians, have deserted and returned to Philadelphia since the enemy left that city; and a considerable number have come in to other places.

We hear that several British transports have been lately taken on their passage from Philadelphia to New York, one of which had five refugee families with their furniture, &c° on board.

To Robert Morris.

Brunswick, July ye 3rd 1778.

My Dr Sir,

To use the words of my Lord Chatham, have we not a gracious Prince on the Throne? is he not still the same? I trust he is; but there is something rotten betwixt him and his People—not content with robbing me and the brave men under my command of the honor due to us—a most hellish plan has been formed (and I may say at least not discourag'd by Head Quarters) to destroy for ever my honour and reputation—I have demanded a Court Martial which has fortunately been granted—if I had been let alone, I should with patience have suffered 'em to pick up the laurels which I had shaken down and lay'd at their feet; but the outrageous attacks made are enough to drive patience itself to madness—I shall not trouble you at present with a detail of the action, but by all that's sacred Genl. Washington had scarcely any more to do in it than to strip the dead—by want of proper intelligence we were ordered to attack the covering party supposed to consist only of fifteen hundred men—Our intelligence as usual was false—it proved to be the whole flower of the British Army, Grenadiers, L. Infantry Cavalry and Artillery amounting in the whole to Seven thousand men—by the temerity, folly, and contempt of orders of General Wain we found ourselves engaged in the most extensive plain in America—separated from our main body the distance of eight miles—The force we cou'd bring to action not more than three thousand men—in danger every moment of having our flanks turn'd by their Cavalry—it required the utmost presence of mind and courage to extricate ourselves out of this dangerous situation, and on this occasion it is no crime to do justice to myself. Upon my Soul I feel I know the whole Army saw and must acknowledge that I did exhibit great presence of mind and not less address—altho' my orders were perpetually counteracted I manœuvred my antagonists from their advantageous ground into as disadvantageous a one—no confusion was seen, the Battalions and artillery supported and were supported by each other through a plain of four miles, without losing a single gun, a single color, or sacrificing a single Battalion until I led 'em totally exhausted into the ground where the general was posted, who had as I observ'd before nothing to do but to strip their dead—it is true they cannonaded each other for some time but the Enemy were so completely worn down that they cou'd never attempt the least impression—The General has the madness to charge me with making a shameful retreat—I never retreated in fact (for 'till I join'd him it was not a retreat but a necessary and I may say in my own defence masterly manœuvre) I say I never retreated but by his positive order who invidiously sent me out of the field when the victory was assur'd—Such is my recompense for having sacrificed my Friends, my connexions, and perhaps my fortune for having twice extricated this man and his whole army out of perdition, and now having given him the only victory he ever tasted. Do not my D[r] Friend, imagine I talk in this heated manner to every man—to you I venture to pour out my indignation—but I give you my word I am so sensible of my ticklish situation that I am with others perfectly moderate and guarded—the cool parts of this letter I wish you wou'd read to Richard Henry Lee and Duar, to what others you think prudent

I am most sincerely and affectionately Yours

C. Lee.

Hon. Robert Morris.

Gen. Washington to John Augustine Washington.

Brunswic, 4 July, 1778.

Dear Brother,

Before this will have reached you, the account of the battle of Monmouth will probably get to Virginia; which, from an unfortunate and bad beginning, turned out a glorious and happy day. The enemy evacuated Philadelphia on the 18th instant. At ten o'clock that day I got intelligence of it, and by two o'clock, or soon after, had six brigades on their march for the Jerseys, and followed with the whole army next morning. On the 21st we completed our passage over the Delaware at Coryell's Ferry, about thirty-three miles above Philadelphia, and distant from Valley Forge about forty miles. From this Ferry we moved down towards the enemy, and on the 27th got within six miles of them.

General Lee, having the command of the van of the army, consisting of full five thousand chosen men, was ordered to begin the attack next morning, so soon as the enemy began their march; to be supported by me; but, strange to tell! when he came up with the enemy, a retreat commenced; whether by his order, or from other causes, is now the subject of inquiry, and consequently improper to be descanted upon, as he is in arrest, and a court-martial is sitting for his trial. A retreat, however, was the fact, be the causes what they may; and the disorder arising from it would have proved fatal to the army, had not that bountiful Providence, which has never failed us in the hour of distress, enabled me to form a regiment or two (of those that were retreating) in the face of the enemy and under their fire; by which means a stand was made long enough (the place through which the enemy were pursuing being narrow) to form the troops, that were advancing, upon an advantageous piece of ground in the rear. Here our affairs took a favorable turn, and, from being pursued, we drove the enemy back over the ground they had followed, and recovered the field of battle, and possessed ourselves of their dead. But as they retreated behind a morass very difficult to pass, and had both flanks secured with thick woods, it was found impracticable with our men, fainting with fatigue, heat, and want of water, to do anything more that night. In the morning we expected to renew the action, when, behold, the enemy had stolen off silently in the night, after having sent away their wounded. Getting a night's march of us, and having but ten miles to a strong post, it was judged expedient not to follow them any further, but to move towards the North River, lest they should have any design upon our posts there.

I observe what you say respecting voluntary enlistments, or rather your scheme for raising two thousand volunteers; and I candidly own to you, that I have no opinion of it. These measures only tend to burthen the public with a number of officers, without adding one jot to our strength, but greatly to confusion and disorder. If the several States would but fall upon some vigorous measures to fill up their respective regiments, nothing more need be asked of them. But while these are neglected, or in other words ineffectually and feebly attended to, and these succedaneums tried, we can never have an army to be depended upon.

The enemy's whole force marched through the Jerseys, excepting the regiment of Anspach, which, it is said, they were afraid to trust, and therefore sent them round to New York by water with the Commissioners. I do not learn that they have received much of a reinforcement as yet; nor do I think they have a prospect of any worth speaking of, as I believe they stand very critically with respect to France. As the post waits, I shall only add my love to my sister and the family, and strong assurances of being, with the sincerest regard and love.

Your most affectionate brother,

G° WASHINGTON.

LIEUT.-GEN. SIR HENRY CLINTON, K.B., TO LORD GEO. GERMAINE.

New York, July 5, 1778.

MY LORD,

I have the honor to inform your Lordship, that pursuant to his Majesty's instructions I evacuated Phil[a] on the 18th June, at three oclock in the morning, and proceeded to Gloucester Point, without being followed by the enemy. Every thing being from thence passed in safety across the Delaware through the excellent disposition made by the Admiral to secure our passage the army marched at 10 oclock and reached Haddonfield the same day. A strong corps of the enemy having, upon our approach, abandoned the difficult pass of Mount-Holly the army proceeded without any interruption from them, excepting what was occasioned by their having destroyed every bridge on our road. As the country is much intersected with marshy rivulets, the obstructions we met with were frequent, and the excessive heat of the season rendered the labour of repairing the bridges severely felt.

The advanced parties of our light troops arriving unexpectedly at Crosswicks on the 23rd, after a trifling skirmish, prevented the enemy from destroying the bridge over a large creek at that village, and the army passed it the next morning. One column, under the command of his Excellency Lieut Gen. Knyphausen, halted near Emlay's-town, and as the provision train and heavy artillery were stationed in that division the other column, under Lieut. Gen. Earl Cornwallis took a position at Allen's town, which covered the other encampment.

Thus far, my Lord, my march pointed equally towards the Hudson's River and Staten Island by the Raritan. I was now at the juncture when it was necessary to decide ultimately what course to pursue. Encumbered as I was by an enormous provision train, &c to which impediment the probability of obstructions and length of my march obliged me to submit, I was led to wish for a route less liable to obstacles than those above mentioned.

I had received intelligence that Gens Washington and Lee had passed the Delaware with their army, had assembled a numerous militia from all the neighbouring provinces; and that Gates with an army from the northward, was advancing to join them on the Raritan. As I could not hope that after having always hitherto so studiously avoided a general action Gen. Washington would now give into it against every dictate of policy: I could only suppose that his views were directed against my baggage &c, in which part I was indeed vulnerable. This circumstance alone would have tempted me to avoid the passage of the Raritan, but when I reflected that from Sandy Hook I should be able, with more expedition [and greater secrecy] to carry his Majesty's further orders into execution, I did not hesitate to order the army into the road which leads through Freehold to the Neversink. The approach of the enemy's army being indicated by the frequent appearance of their light troops on our rear, I requested his Excellency Lieut General Knyphausen to take the baggage of the whole army under the charge of his division, consisting of the troops mentioned in the margin.* Under the head of baggage was comprised, not only the wheel carriages of every department, but also the bat horses, a train, which as the country admitted but of one route for carriages, extended near twelve miles. The indispensible necessity I was under of securing these, is obvious, and the difficulty of doing it, in a most woody country, against an army far superior in numbers, will, I trust, be no less so.

I desired Lieut. Gen. Knyphausen to move at day break on the 28th and that I might not press upon him in the first part of the march, in which we had but one route, I did not follow with the other division † till near eight o'clock. Soon after I had marched, reconnoitering parties of the enemy appeared on our left flank. The Queen's rangers fell in with and dispersed some detachments among the woods in the same quarter. Our rear guard having descended from the heights above Freehold, into a plain near three miles in length, and about one mile in breadth; several columns of the enemy appeared likewise descending into the plain, and about ten o'clock they began to cannonade our rear. Intelligence was at this moment brought me, that the enemy were discovered marching in force on both our flanks. I was convinced that our baggage was their object; but it being in this juncture engaged in defiles, which continued for some miles, no means occurred of parrying the blow, but attending the corps which harrassed our rear, and pressing it so hard as to oblige the detachments to return from our flanks to its assistance.

I had good information that Gen. Washington was up with his whole army, estimated at about 20,000, but as I knew there were two defiles between him and the corps which I meant to strike, I judged that he

* 17th light dragoons, 2d battalion of light infantry, Hessian Yagers, 1st & 2[d] Brigades British, Sterne's and Loo's brigades of Hessians, Penn[a] Loyalists, West Jersey Volunteers, Maryland Loyalists.

† 16th light dragoons, 1st battalion of British Grenadiers, 2[d] ditto, 1st battalion of light infantry, Hessian grenadiers, guards, 3[d] 4th 5th brigades, British.

could not have passed them with a greater force than what Lord Cornwallis's division was well able to engage; and had I even met his whole army in the passage of those defiles, I had little to apprehend, but his situation might have been critical.

The enemy's cavalry, commanded it is said by M. La Fayette, having approached within our reach, they were charged with great spirit by the Queen's light dragoons. They did not wait the shock, but fell back in confusion, upon their own infantry.

Thinking it possible that the event might draw a general action, I sent for a brigade of British and the 17th light dragoons from Lieut. Gen. Knyphausen's division, and having directed them on their arrival to take a position effectually covering our right flank, of which I was most jealous, I made a disposition of attack on the plain, but before I could advance, the enemy fell back and took a strong position on the heights above Freehold Court House. The heat of the weather was intense, and our men already suffered from fatigue. But our circumstances obliged us to make a vigorous exertion. The British Grenadiers with their left to the village of Freehold, and the Guards on the right of the Grenadiers began the attack with such spirit, that the enemy gave way immediately. The second line of the enemy stood the attack, with greater obstinacy, but were likewise completely routed. They then took a third position, with a marshy hollow in front, over which it would have been scarcely possible to have attacked them. However part of the second line made a movement to the front, occupied some ground on the enemy's left flank, and the light infantry and Queen's Rangers turned their left.

By this time our men were so overpowered with fatigue, that I could press the affair no further; especially as I was confident the end was gained for which the attack been made. I ordered the light infantry to rejoin me; but a strong detachment of the enemy having possessed themselves of a post, which would have annoyed them in their retreat, the 33rd Regiment made a movement towards the enemy, which, with a similar one made by the first grenadiers, immediately dispersed them.

I took the position from whence the enemy had been first driven, after they had quitted the plain, and having reposed the troops till ten at night, to avoid the excessive heat in the day, I took advantage of the moonlight to rejoin Lieut-Gen. Knyphausen, who had advanced to Nut-swamp, near Middletown.

Our baggage had been intercepted by some of the enemy's light troops, who were repulsed by the good dispositions made by Lieut Gen. Knyphausen and Major Gen Grant, and the good countenance of the 40th Regt whose pickets alone were attacked, and one troop of the 17th light dragoons. The two corps which had marched against it, (being as I since learn a brigade on each flank) were recalled, as I had suspected, at the beginning of the action.

It would be sufficient honour to the troops, barely to say, that they had forced a corps, as I am informed of near 12,000 men, from two strong positions; but it will, I doubt not, be considered as doubly creditable when I mention that they did it under such disadvantages of heat and fatigue, that a great part of those we lost fell dead as they advanced, without a wound.

Fearing that my first order had miscarried, before I quitted this ground, I sent a second for a brigade of infantry, the 17th light dragoons, and 2d battalion of light infantry to meet me on the march, with which additional force, had General Washington shewn himself the next day, I was determined to attack him, but there not being the least appearance of an enemy, I suspected he might have pushed a considerable corps to a strong position near Middletown; I therefore left the rear guard on its march, and detached Major Gen. Grant to take post there, which was effected on the 29th. The whole army marched to this position the next day, and then fell back to another near Neversink, where I awaited two days, in the hope, that Mr. Washington might have been tempted to have advanced to the position near Middletown, which we had quitted; in which case I might have attacked him to advantage.

During this time the sick and wounded were embarked, and preparations made for passing to Sandy Hook Island by a bridge, which by the extraordinary efforts of the navy was soon completed, and over which the whole army passed in about two hours time; the horses and cattle having been previously transported.

Your Lordship will receive herewith a return of the killed, wounded, missing, &c. of his Majesty's troops on the 28th of last month: That of the enemy is supposed to have been more considerable, especially in killed.

The loss of Lieut-Col. Monckton, who commanded the 2d battalion of grenadiers is much to be lamented.

I am much indebted to Ld. Cornwallis for his zealous services on every occasion; and I found great support from the activity of Major Gen. Grey, Brigadier General Matthew, Leslie, and Sir William Erskine.

I beg leave to refer your Lordship, for any other particulars which you may wish to be informed of, to Col. Patterson, who will have the honor of delivering these dispatches, and whose services in this country, entitle him to every mark of your Lordships favor.

I have the honor to be, &c.

H. Clinton.

Return of the killed, wounded, missing, &c. of the troops under the command of Gen. Sir Henry Clinton in an engagement with the rebel army on the heights of Freehold, C[o] of Monmouth, New Jersey, the 28th of June, 1778.

Total British:

1 Lieut. Col. 1 Captain, 2 Lieuts. 4 serjeants, 56 rank and file, killed; 3 serjeants, 45 rank and file, died

with fatigue; 1 Col. 1 Lieut Col. 1 Major, 7 Captains, 5 Lieuts. 7 serjeants, 137 rank and file, wounded; 3 serjeants, 61 rank and file, missing.

Total German:

1 rank and file killed; 11 rank and file, died with fatigue; 11 rank and file, wounded.

General Total:

1 Lieut. Col. 1 Cap^{n} 2 Lieuts. 4 serjeants, 57 rank and file killed; 3 serjeants, 56 rank and file, died with fatigue; 1 Col. 1 Lieut Col. 1 Major, 7 Captains, 5 Lieuts. 7 serjeants, 148 rank and file, wounded; 3 serjeants, 61 rank and file, missing.

Colonel Hamilton to Elias Boudinot.

My dear Sir,

You will by this time imagine that I have forgotten my promise of writing to you, as I have been so long silent on an occasion, which most people will be fond of celebrating to their friends. The truth is I have no passion for scribbling and I know you will be at no loss for the fullest information. But that you may not have a right to accuse me of negligence, I will impose upon myself the drudgery of saying something about the transactions of the 28th, in which the American arms gained very signal advantages; and might have gained much more signal ones.

Indeed, I can hardly persuade myself to be in good humour with success so far inferior to what we, in all probability should have had, had not the finest opportunity America ever possessed been fooled away by a man, in whom she has placed a large share of the most ill-judged confidence. You will have heard enough to know that I mean General Lee. This man is either a driveler in the business of soldiership or something much worse. To let you fully into the silly and pitiful game he has been playing, I will take the tale up from the beginning; expecting you will consider what I say, as in the most perfect confidence.

When we came to Hopewell Township, the General unluckily called a council of War, the result of which would have done honor to the most honorable society of midwives, and to them only. The purport was, that we should keep at a comfortable distance from the enemy, and keep up a vain parade of annoying them by detachment. In pursuance of this idea, a detachment of 1500 men was sent off under General Scott to join the other troops near the enemy's lines. General Lee was *primum mobile* of this sage plan; and was even opposed to sending so considerable a force. The General, on mature reconsideration of what had been resolved on, determined to pursue a different line of conduct at all hazards. With this view, he marched the army the next morning towards Kingston and there made another detachment of 1000 men under General Wayne; and formed all the detached troops into an advanced corps under the command of the Marquis De la Fayette. The project was, that this advanced corps should take the first opportunity to attack the enemy's rear on the march, to be supported or covered as circumstances should require by the whole army.

General Lee's conduct with respect to the command of this corps was truly childish. According to the incorrect notions of our army his seniority would have entitled him to the command of the advanced corps; but he in the first instance declined it, in favour of the Marquis. Some of his friends having blamed him for doing it, and Lord Stirling having shown a disposition to interpose his claim, General Lee very inconsistently reasserted his pretensions. The matter was a second time accommodated; General Lee and Lord Stirling agreed to let the Marquis command. General Lee a little time after, recanted again and became very importunate. The General, who had all along observed the greatest candor in the matter, grew tired of such fickle behaviour and ordered the Marquis to proceed.

The enemy in marching from Allen Town had changed their disposition and thrown all their best troops in the rear; this made it necessary to strike a stroke with propriety, to reinforce the advanced corps. Two brigades were detached for this purpose, and the General willing to accommodate General Lee, sent him with them to take command of the whole advanced corps, which rendezvoused the forenoon of the 27th at English Town, consisting of at least 5000 rank & file, most of them select troops. General Lee's orders were, the moment he received intelligence of the enemy's march to pursue them and to attack their rear.

This intelligence was received about five o'clock the morning of the 28th, and General Lee put his troops in motion accordingly. The main body did the same. The advanced corps came up with the enemy's rear a mile or two beyond the Court House; I saw the enemy drawn up, and am persuaded there were not a thousand men—their front from different accounts was then ten miles off. However favorable this situation may seem for an attack it was not made; but after changing their position two or three times by retrograde movements our advanced corps got into a general confused retreat, and even rout would hardly be too strong an expression. Not a word of all this was officially communicated to the General; as we approached the supposed place of action we heard some flying rumours of what had happened, in consequence of which the General rode forward and found the troops retiring in the greatest disorder and the enemy pressing upon their rear. I never saw the General to so much advantage. His coolness and firmness were admirable. He instantly took measures for checking the enemy's advance, and giving time to the army, which was very near, to form and make a proper disposition. He then rode back and had the troops formed on a very advantageous piece of ground;—in which and in other transactions of the day General Greene and Lord Stirling rendered very essential service, and did themselves great honor. The sequel is, we beat the enemy and killed and wounded at least a thousand of their best troops. America owes a great deal to General Washington for this day's work. A general rout dismay and disgrace would have attended the whole army in any other hands but his. By his own good sense and fortitude he turned the fate of the day. Other officers have great merit in performing their parts well; but he directed the whole with the skill of a Master Workman. He did not hug himself at a distance and leave an Arnold to win laurels for him; but by his own presence, he brought order out of confusion, animated his troops, and led them to success.

A great number of our officers distinguished themselves this day. General Wayne was always foremost in danger. Col. Stewart & L[t]. Col. Ramsay were with him among the first to oppose the enemy. Lt. Col. Olney at the head of Varnum's Brigade made the next stand. I was with him, got my horse wounded and myself much hurt by a fall in consequence. Col. Livingston behaved very handsomely. Our old friend Barber was remarkably active; towards the close of the day, he received a ball through his side—which the doctors think will not be fatal. Col. Silly & Lt. Col. Parker were particularly useful on the left—Col. Craig, with General Wayne on the right. The Artillery acquitted themselves most charmingly. I was Spectator to Lt. Col. Oswald's behaviour, who kept up a gallant fire from some pieces commanded by him, uncovered and unsupported. In short one can hardly name particulars without doing injustice to the rest. The behaviour of the officers and men in general was such as could not easily be surpassed. Our troops, after the first impulse from mismanagement, behaved with more spirit & moved with greater order than the British troops. You know my way of thinking about our army, & that I am not apt to flatter it. I assure you I never was pleased with them before this day.

What part our family acted let others say. I hope you will not suspect me of vanity when I tell you that one of them Fitzgerald, had a slight contusion with a musket-ball; another, Laurens had a slight contusion also—and his horse killed—a third, Hamilton had his horse wounded, in the first part of the action with a musket ball. If the rest escaped, it is only to be ascribed to better fortune, not more prudence in keeping out of the way. That Congress is not troubled with any messenger aids to give swords & other pretty toys to, let them ascribe to the good sense of the Commander in Chief, & to a certain turn of thinking in those about him which put them above such shifts.

What think you now of General Lee? You will be ready to join me in condemning him. And yet, I fear, a Court Martial will not do it. A certain preconceived & preposterous opinion of his being a very great man will operate in his favour. Some people are very industrious in making interest for him. Whatever a Court Martial may decide, I shall continue to believe and say—his conduct was monstrous and unpardonable.

I am Dr Sir

Y^rs^ affect^y^,

ALEX. HAMILTON.

Brunswick, July 5th 78.

One wing of the Army marched this morning towards the North River, another goes tomorrow—The enemy by our last accounts were embarking their luggage—They are three miles below Middletown. French importunity cannot be resisted—I have given two Frenchmen letters to you. I am very serious about Mr. Toussard—and as far as a Majority in some corps, Armand's, Pulaski's or such like, would wish you to interest yourself for him. The Marquis De Vienne, I am so far in earnest concerning, that if his pretensions are moderate and he can be gratified I should be glad of it—but I fear they will be pretty high

---

PRESIDENT LAURENS TO COL. JOHN LAURENS.

Philadelphia, 6th J[uly, 1778.]

MY DEAR SON,

I have
favors of the 30th ult° & 2d
-jects for the exercise of a gratefi
God for the deliverance of our great & good
-er in Chief & of our Army, from the Snare which had been set for them, for the escape of you my Dear fellow citizen from the dangers to which your duty had necessarily exposed you—& while I bless God for the providential interposition in our favor I congratulate with my Country Men on the partial victory gained over our Enemies on the 28th June at Monmouth.

Repair your particular loss immediately by purchasing one of the very best Horses you can meet with & more than one or two if needful, draw on me for the amount or tell me how I may remit a sufficient sum.

The term Snare shews the present sentiments of my mind, that my former jealousies respecting the conversation with an old friend at the lines, the reception & lodging Doctr W. were not groundless—these circumstances will naturally recur to your own—but antecedently to either of these, a conversation at York-town, tête a tête, which, if the Gentleman had ever been sincere, discovered [a cha]nge,
some ungracious hints applied to an
love, had alarmed me.—You
were grounds for my suspicions
his pretences to leave Philadelphia, at
the justness of my observation that the whole
conduct in this City carried the face of Stratagem
not subsisted, a concerted Plan by which our Army was

to have been disgraced, perhaps ruined: he would not have himself to the fatigue & hazards of loss by various nd March, or if necessity had obliged him Army would have been far enough urs—whatever is is best—I now indebted to the Man I suspected as Judas . whose example in all cases ought to be fo[llo]wed by Men of his disposition.

Certainly for my country's sake, I rejoice at the late happy event, certainly for your sake, but I have a feeling of joy respecting your General which, uncommon as such impressions are in my mind, stronger for an Individual than a general good, for an Individual stronger than for one so very nearly bound to my heart, seems to overbound all other joy—there are rational grounds for this apparent excess which shall be explained to your Conviction and satisfaction whenever I am so happy as to take you into my Arms.

I thank you very much, my dear son, for the minute account of the transactions at Monmouth, such intelligence enables me to make acceptable transmissions to my friends at home, & without such I should be very barren, for * * *

I now live in a house & in a stile somewhat better than which I had patiently humbled myself in, from the 28th September to the 27th June at York Town—somewhat below the rank of my Overseers. I have now a Bed for a friend & Board for a half a dozen or more every day. Come see for a fortnight how I live & let me tell you, you will feel it, whether you come or do not come.

Adieu My Dear Son persevere in your Duty, God will bless you and make your Father happy

HENRY LAURENS

Your General transmits his despatches by a common messenger—I love and reverence him * * *

Col° John Laurens.

ELIAS BOUDINOT TO COLONEL HAMILTON.

Philadelphia, July 8, 1778.

MY DEAR SIR,

I had concluded your Laurels had produced a forgetfulness of your old friend, but am now rejoicing in my disappointment having your obliging & very entertaining favour of the 5th Inst. just handed me. With the utmost sincerity I congratulate you and my Country on the kind interposition of Heaven in our favour on the 28th ultimo. It seems to me as if on every occasion we are to be convinced that our political salvation is to be as through the fire. I scarcely know whether I am more distressed that any Person engaged in the cause of America & to whom she has entrusted her safety could be capable of betraying her Interest in the critical moment of decision, or more really gratified & pleased that the Supreme Disposer of human events is continually baffling not only the formidable & open force of our enemies, but also the more dangerous & secret efforts of false or lukewarm friends.—The General I always revered & loved ever since I knew him, but in this instance he rose superior to himself—Every lip dwells on his praise, for even his pretended friends (for none dare to acknowledge themselves his enemies) are obliged to croak it forth. The share that his family (for whom I retain a real friendship) has in the honors of the day afforded me real pleasure and among the rest none more than that of your Lordship.

The Congress have not made a House till yesterday —I am afraid I shall have my hands full here—and am not greatly elated at the prospect.

We have undoubted intelligence of the sailing of a French fleet for this country, under the command of Vice Admiral Count de Estaing consisting of 12 ships of the Line, 6 Frigates & two Xebeques.—I have reason to believe the French Ambassador is on board—An English fleet lay at S[t] Helena ready to follow them, consisting of Eleven Ships—1 of 90—9 of 74, and one of 64 guns.

I am sorry to inform you that there is also intelligence of the settlement of Wyoming being cut off by Coll. Butler with about 1000 Indians Tories & British Troops. It is supposed that Carlisle will soon be the frontier of this State as the inhabitants are flying in from all quarters. About 200 inhabitants were scalped.

I must beg the favour of your presenting my most respectful Compliments of Congratulation to his Excellency and the family, especially my worthy friend Harrison. I am, D[r] Sir, With great regard,

Faithfully your friend,

ELIAS BOUDINOT

Coll. Hamilton.

FROM GENERAL REED.

Fleming Town July 1778.

DEAR SIR,

I did not receive your Letter of the 3d. Inst. till yesterday & then it came accompanied with the News Paper from Trenton containing your Note to the Printer respecting the Publication in his preceding Paper. I cannot but feel myself exceedingly hurt by the Manner in which you have treated this Matter while you supposed me the Author of the whole Publication. The Terms of your Letter to say nothing of the Publication seem to me to be such a Deviation not only from the line of Friendship but even of Civility which I might have expected from you as can only be excused by the Embarrassments and Anxiety of your Situation. But while I truly regret the Occasion I cannot discover the Prudence or Wisdom of diminishing the Number of your Friends at such a time,—& especially those who have Seats in Congress where alone you can expect to have those "enormous Injuries" redress'd of which you complain. The Additions & Corrections I made to the

Acc[t] received from Gov. Livingston by the Printer were made in such Haste that I did not pay so much Attention to the Performance as I have since done; but now upon a careful Perusal I am totally at a Loss to discover where there is the least disrespectful Mention of you or a Fact related from which a censorious Enemy would have extracted an unfavorable Idea of your Conduct I am very sure so far as my Pen was concerned nothing of that kind was intended but the reverse. Tho' not a soldier by Profession I have seen enough of Armies to caution me against forming hasty Judgments of Men or Actions from mere Report—tho' I heard much therefore on that Day I suspended any opinion, and if you will read the Paper with Attention, which I cannot think you yet have done, I am sure you will see a favourable Construction put on every Part of your Conduct. When compared with the official Account since published by Congress it must appear even to yourself to contain Matter of Praise & Approbation—It says that you did attack & drive the Enemy for some Time & at last only retired toward the main Army on Account of the Enemy's great Superiority of Force—it made your Numbers short I believe of the Reality but therefore more favourable to your Conduct. —What does the Acc[t] sanctified by public Authority say, that you had 5000 instead of 1500 Men, that you retreated without making any Opposition except by a small Party under Col. Butler which was successful & in short that your Conduct was Matter of Surprize and Mortification to the Commander in Chief.—It is admirable to every Person I have conversed with & will be so to the whole world First, In what circumstance the first Publication was unfavorable to you— & secondly, Why you should attempt to destroy the Veracity of that Account and thereby fully establish the Credit of one which must wound your Feelings so sensibly.—Upon the whole I cannot admit that the Epithets you have applied to it as invidious, dishonest & false are by any Means proper & as you have only made a general Charge without pointing out wherein it is false & dishonest I cannot tell how much of this unhandsome Language I am to take to myself or whether any. But this I can and shall say that the Additions and Alterations I made were strictly true & founded chiefly upon my own Observation—& you will excuse me for differing entirely with you in supposing I could possibly know nothing of the principal Part of the Action as that I believe will be allowed to have been after I met you from which Time till the Close of the Affair I was with the General at his Desire or reconnoitering in Front but chiefly the former where all Intelligence came & from whence the Movements were directed.—I am at a Loss to know what Individuals you mean whom you censure as directing & giving Opinions without Authority if you had any Reference to Gen. Cadwallader & myself I shall not hesitate to say the Charge is unwarrantable—as we gave no Directions nor did we on any Occasion offer an Opinion but when requested by the Commander in Chief. As Gentlemen of the Country we had a Right to attend the Army as Volunteers & as Friends to the General to attend him at his Desire without being liable to Censure for either.—That I entertained a very high Opinion of your Talents and Abilities in common with my Countrymen & that they were displayed much to the Advantage of this Country & your own Honour during our Retreat from Kingsbridge to Peeks Kiln in 1776 are Sentiments which I have on every occasion express'd—& that in the Affair of Fort Washington, Gen[l] W. manifested an Indecision of Mind which if uncorrected would shade the brighter Parts of his Character are Facts equally true: but I can easily conceive that more Experience & happier Arrangements may have given him greater Confidence in his Troops as well as on his own Judgment for a long acquaintance

[*The rest of this draft is lost*]

To General Reed.

North Castle, July ye 22d, 1778.

Dr. Reed,

Tho' it may appear somewhat paradoxical I must say that your letter has fill'd me with astonishment, anger, and pleasure—I am astonish'd that a Man of your clear understanding shou'd have confus'd matters so strangely as you seem to have done on the subject of my letters to the Printer at Trenton, and to yourself. I am pleas'd in your having confirm'd me in the opinion I had entertain'd of your regard and friendship, and I am angry that you shou'd suppose me for a single moment, capable of availing myself of some expressions You had made use of in a confidential letter, to embroil you with a man that the publick interest certainly and perhaps your personal concerns render it necessary You shou'd be on good terms with—You suppose I was fermented to an unusual warmth when I wrote these two letters—but if you had consider'd yourself cooly all circumstances, I am inclined to think you wou'd have reason'd very differently—the fact is this—at a moment when a most atrocious attack was made on my fame and fortunes, a printed letter was put into my hands, containing (what I still assert to be) an invidious, false, and dishonest relation of the affair of the 28th—stung to the quick, and knowing enough of the nature of mankind, that when rightly or wrongly They are deeply prepossess'd, their pride or obstinacy renders 'em loath to be undeceiv'd, I thought it prudent and incumbent to address this note, which it seems has given such dreadfull offence, to Mr Collins—this step may, for aught I know, have been hasty and imprudent but I declare were it undone, I shou'd on the coolest deliberation do it—after I had wrote and seal'd this note, I was told by several persons that you were the Author—I wou'd not or cou'd not give credit to the report—but however such was the uneasiness that the bare possibility of its being a fact created in me that I cou'd not rest without taking the most expeditious means of clearing up the point—for to my own honour I must say it, that nothing equally shocks my nature with the idea that those of whom I have once form'd a high opinion, whose friendship I have courted and flatter'd myself to have obtain'd, whose talents I respect, and whose qualities I love, shou'd turn out the reverse of what I thought 'em—and I think you have no reason to doubt that you stood in this state of relation to me—in this, if I may so express it, friendly agitation of uneasiness I wrote to you, and believe sent it by the same hand as I did that to the Printer—When I met you near Morris Town, you cleared up the point infinitely to my satisfaction, and if anything further is necessary to be said on the subject I most sincerely ask both you and myself pardon for having for a single instant harbour'd so offensive a notion. You tell me I am much sunk in the public esteem and confidence—all I can say in reply is, that if a Community for whom I have sacrific'd everything can so rashly form conclusions they and not I are the immediate objects of compassion—You tell me this is a time I have occasion for friends—as a Man of society I wish, and ever shall wish, for a number of Friends; the greater number, the more the honour and pleasure—but if you mean Friends to support my cause on the present occasion—I despise the thought—I ask only for common justice—I know, I am conscious that nothing but cabal artifice, power, and iniquity can tarnish my name for a moment—but if They are to prevail, woe on the community as to myself—*impavidum ferient ruinæ.* No attack it seems can be made on Gen. Washington, but it must recoil on the assailant—I never entertained the most distant wish or intention of attacking Gen. Washington, I have ever honour'd and respected him as a Man and as a Citizen—but if the Circle which surrounds him chuse to erect him into an infallible Divinity, I shall certainly prove a Heretick, and if great as He is, he can be perswaded to attempt wounding evry thing I ought to hold dear, He must thank his Priests, if his Deityship gets scratch'd in the scuffle—When you say that I have now put it out of the power of my Friends in and out of Congress to offer a word in my defense upon my honour I know not what you mean. I can only surmise from it that my particular Friends have suffered their minds to be carried away in the general torrent of delusion, raised by all the wicked arts that Hell can prompt to its ministers. I repeat I demand nothing from the Public but justice—that I have been grossly villainously dealt with—and the dread of no power on earth shall prevent me from exposing the wickedness of my Persecutors. I wish not to attack, but must, it is my duty, to defend—and if this is thought dangerous I must observe, that the blood and treasure expended in this war has been expended in vain—as North and Mansfield had they succeeded cou'd not possibly have established a more odious Despotism—As to you My Dr. Reed I still have all the reason possible to rank you as I have ever done, one of the first in my esteem and affection—and I flatter myself that when you are better inform'd that good opinion you had of me will rather be augmented than diminish'd.

C. Lee.

PUBLICATION FUND.

NEW-YORK HISTORICAL SOCIETY.

FOUNDED 1804.

THE PUBLICATION FUND.

THE NEW-YORK HISTORICAL SOCIETY has established a fund for the regular publication of its transactions and Collections in American History. Publication is very justly regarded as one of the main instruments of usefulness in such institutions, and the amount and value of what they contribute to the general sum of human knowledge through this agency, as a just criterion of their success.

To effect its object, the Society proposed to issue One Thousand Scrip shares of TWENTY-FIVE DOLLARS each. Each share is transferable on the books of the Fund, in the hands of the Treasurer, and entitled the holder, his heirs, administrators or assigns, to receive:

I. INTEREST—Until the Fund was complete, or sufficient, in the opinion of the Trustees, to enable the publications to commence without impairing the principal thereof, interest on the par value of his share or shares at the rate of five per cent. per annum.

II. PUBLICATIONS—One copy of each and every publication made at the expense of the Fund, amounting to not less than one Octavo Volume of five hundred pages per annum.

The number of copies of these publications is strictly limited to TWELVE HUNDRED and FIFTY—of which the Society receives for corresponding Societies and exchanges for the increase of the Library, TWO HUNDRED and FIFTY copies—but no copies are offered for sale or disposition in any other manner by the Society.

The conditions of subscription included a pledge on the part of the Society that the moneys received should be applied for these purposes, and no other, and be invested solely in stocks of the United States, the City and State of New-York, or on bond and mortgage, and be held forever by the President, Recording Secretary, and Treasurer of the Society, as Trustees (ex-officio) of the Publication Fund.

The first proposals for the establishment of this Fund were issued in 1858. Received with much less interest on the part of the members than was expected, its total amount up to 1865 was so small as to suggest the necessity of abandoning the scheme and returning the amount of subscriptions and interest to the subscribers. An earnest effort, however, in that year brought up the amount to a point which gave the assurance of ultimate and not distant success.

Admonished by the universal change of values, which has taken place within the past few years, and the necessity of increasing the amount of the Fund, the Society determined to terminate the issue of shares at the original price, and to double the price of the remaining shares. Other measures are in view which promise to enhance the value of the shares without failure in the full discharge of every obligation to the shareholders, who will receive all its benefits without any additional contribution to the increased Fund.

Under the authority and direction of the Executive Committee, the series of publications began with the volume for the year 1868.

Interest still due upon any shares to January 1, 1868, will be paid to shareholders on application to the Secretary to the Trustees at the Library of the Society, Second Avenue, corner of Eleventh Street, where the volume for the current year is also ready for distribution.

THOMAS DE WITT,
ANDREW WARNER,
BENJAMIN H. FIELD,
Trustees.

GEORGE H. MOORE,
Secretary to the Trustees.

*** Any person desiring to procure these publications, may purchase a share in the Publication Fund, by enclosing a check or draft for FIFTY DOLLARS, payable to the order of BENJAMIN H. FIELD, Treasurer of the New-York Historical Society, for which the certificate will be immediately transmitted, *with the volumes already published*, as the purchaser may direct.

☞ Address GEORGE H. MOORE, Librarian of the Historical Society, Second Avenue, corner of Eleventh St., New-York City.

NEW-YORK, *December*, 1872.

ORIGINAL SUBSCRIBERS TO THE FUND.

SHARE		
1.	James Lenox,	*N. Y. City.*
2.	Same,	"
3.	Same,	"
4.	Same,	"
5.	Same,	"
6.	Same,	"
7.	Same,	"
8.	Same,	"
9.	Same,	"
10.	Same,	"
11.	John B. Moreau,	"
12.	Henry T. Drowne,	"
13.	Benjamin H. Field,	"
14.	Thomas W. C. Moore,	"
15.	George Bancroft,	"
16.	William Chauncey,	"
17.	Charles H. Ward,	"
18.	William Menzies,	"
19.	J. Watts de Peyster,	"
20.	Edwin Croswell,	"
21.	Edward Everett,	*Boston, Mass.*
22.	Horace Binney,	*Phila., Pa.*
23.	Frederic de Peyster,	*N. Y. City.*
24.	Augustus Schell,	"
25.	Andrew Warner,	"
26.	Gouverneur M. Wilkins,	"
27.	Erastus C. Benedict,	"
28.	James Savage,	*Boston, Mass.*
29.	S. Alofsen,	*N. Y. City.*
30.	Albert A. Martin,	"
31.	William B. Campbell,	"
32.	John Alstyne,	"
33.	John Armstrong,	"
34.	Wm. L. Chamberlain,	"

SHARE		
35.	William B. Crosby,	*N. Y. City*
36.	Horatio S. Brown,	"
37.	John A. Hardenbergh,	"
38.	William P. Powers,	"
39.	Samuel Marsh,	"
40.	William H. H. Moore,	"
41.	C. V. S. Roosevelt,	"
42.	Robert Townsend,	*Albany.*
43.	David Thompson,	*N. Y. City.*
44.	James Stokes,	"
45.	George C. Peters,	"
46.	George T. Trimble,	"
47.	William Curtis Noyes,	"
48.	Thomas Suffern,	"
49.	Richard H. Bowne,	"
50.	George H. Purser,	"
51.	John H. Chambers,	"
52.	George W. Pratt,	"
53.	Henry A. Hurlbut,	"
54.	August Belmont,	"
55.	George R. Jackson,	"
56.	Cleayton Newbold,	"
57.	George Bruce,	"
58.	F. A. Palmer,	"
59.	John Ward,	"
60.	Samuel Jaudon,	"
61.	Thomas T. Sturges,	"
62.	John Reid,	"
63.	Gustavus Swan,	"
64.	Matthew Clarkson,	"
65.	William A. White, Jr.,	"
66.	Wm. M. Halstead,	"
67.	Thomas DeWitt,	"
68.	Charles P. Kirkland,	"

SHARE
69. H. G. Lawrence, *N. Y. City.*
70. Edward F. De Lancey, "
71. Cyrus Curtiss, "
72. Shepherd Knapp, "
73. Edward DeWitt, "
74. D. B. Fayerweather, "
75. Mark Hoyt, "
76. Charles M. Connolly, "
77. Cornelius DuBois, "
78. L. C. Clark, "
79. Thomas Lawrence, "
80. David T. Valentine, "
81. H'y Russell Drowne, "
82. John Fowler, Jr., "
83. William Bowne, "
84. Henry T. Drowne, "
85. Nehemiah Knight, *Brooklyn.*
86. William S Thorne, *N. Y. City.*
87. Alex'r McL. Agnew, "
88. Robert C. Goodhue, "
89. George F. Nesbitt, "
90. John E. Wool, *Troy.*
91. John P. Treadwell, *New Milford, Conn.*
92. Isaac Fryer, *N. Y. City.*
93. Charles J. Martin, "
94. Franklin F. Randolph, "
95. Samuel Coulter, "
96. David Van Nostrand, "
97. Addison G. Bickford, "
98. Jonas G. Dudley, "
99. Theodorus B. Taylor, "
100. William Scott, "
101. David Sloane, "
102. Joseph G. Harrison, "
103. Same, "
104. Same, "
105. Same, "
106. Edward Walker, "
107. John C. Hewitt, "
108. Charles I. Bushnell, "
109. Giles F. Bushnell, "
110. John C. Calhoun, "
111. Thomas J. Lee, *Boston, Mass.*

SHARE
112. S. Whitney Phœnix, *N. Y. City.*
113. Same, "
114. Same, "
115. Same, "
116. Same, "
117. Same, "
118. Same, "
119. Same, "
120. Same, "
121. Same, "
122. Same, "
123. Same, "
124. J. B. Bright, *Waltham, Mass.*
125. Robert L. Stuart, *N. Y. City.*
126. Same, "
127. Alexander Stuart, "
128. Same, "
129. George T. Jackson, "
130. John A. Anderson, "
131. Charles P. Daly, "
132. Evert A. Duyckinck, "
133. Henry C. Carter, "
134. Andrew J. Smith, "
135. Mathias Bloodgood, "
136. J. Romeyn Brodhead, "
137. Jno. A. McAllister, *Phila., Pa.*
138. Nath. W. Hunt, *N. Y. City.*
139. Theo. S. Parker, *Hoboken, N. J.*
140. William M. Brown, *N. Y. City.*
141. And. Brown, *Middletown, N. J.*
142. Joseph B. Varnum, *N. Y. City.*
143. Charles B. Cotten, "
144. Alvin A. Alvord, "
145. Wm. Henry Arnoux, "
146. Same, "
147. Same, "
148. Same, "
149. Albert Smith, *New Rochelle.*
150. M. C. Morgan, *N. Y. City.*
151. S. Howland Robbins, "
152. Francis Bacon, "
153. A. Spiers Brown, "
154. George C. Colburn, "
155. John Calvin Smith, *Manlius.*

SHARE
156. W. B. Eager, Jr., *N. Y. City.*
157. Isaac J. Greenwood, "
158. Frederic R. Fowler, "
159. Anthony Dey, Jr., "
160. Seymour J. Strong, "
161. Ebenezer J. Hyde, "
162. William B. Taylor, "
163. Ferd. J. Dreer, *Phila., Pa.*
164. Aug. Toetdeberg, *Brooklyn.*
165. Charles C. Moreau, *N. Y. City.*
166. Charles H. Hart, *Phila., Pa.*
167. Henry Phillips, Jr., "
168. Francis B. Hayes, *Boston, Mass.*
169. T. Stafford Drowne, *Brooklyn.*
170. Cortlandt De Peyster Field, *N. Y. City.*
171. John S. Craig, *N. Y. City.*
172. Charles H. Rogers, "
173. Maurice Hilger, "
174. E. A. Benedict, "
175. William Everdell, "
176. Geo. R. Drowne, *Boston, Mass.*
177. J. Watts de Peyster, *N. Y. City.*
178. James B. Andrews, *N. Y. City.*
179. Constant A. Andrews, "
180. Loring Andrews, Jr., "
181. Walter S. Andrews, "
182. Clarence Andrews, "
183. William L. Andrews, "
184. Same, "
185. John Armstrong, "
186. Paul K. Weizel, *B'klyn, N. Y.*
187. John F. McCoy, *N. Y. City.*
188. Joseph B. Hoyt, "
189. James Benedict, "
190. J. Nelson Tappan "
191. Francis Wigand, "
192. C. H. Isham, "
193. D. B. Fayerweather, "
194. John A. Hardenbergh, "
195. J. W. Weidmeyer, "
196. Edwin Faxon, *Boston, Mass.*
197. F. A. Gale, *N. Y. City.*

SHARE
198. John Caswell, *N. Y. City*
199. William C. Dornin, "
200. William P. Cooledge, "
201. John R. Ford, "
202. Israel Corse, "
203. Daniel Morison, "
204. John Bridge, "
205. Wilson G. Hunt, "
206. Charles H. Smith, "
207. John P. Crosby, "
208. Erastus Corning, *Albany.*
209. Same, "
210. James B. Colgate, *N. Y. City*
211. Samuel Marsh, "
212. Edwin Parsons, "
213. Robert J. Hubbard, "
214. J. Watts de Peyster, "
215. James A. Raynor, "
216. Robert J. Livingston, "
217. John C. Barron, "
218. Henry K. Brewer, "
219. John A. Nexsen, "
220. Marshall O. Roberts, "
221. William N. Blakeman, "
222. Herman C. Adams, "
223. Thomas B. Gunning, "
224. Abraham Bogardus, "
225. John E. Lauer, "
226. E. M. Crawford, "
227. James C. Holden, "
228. Samuel Colgate, "
229. William B. Ross, "
230. William K. Hinman, "
231. John W. Quincy, "
232. James M. Bruce, "
233. Miss Annie Moreau, "
234. Lewis Hallock, "
235. The Library of the City of Amsterdam, *Amsterdam, Netherlands.*
236. Mrs. Anna Boynton, *N. Y. City.*
237. Rufus D. Case, *N. Y. City.*
238. Cyrus Butler, "

SHARE

239. Richard S. Field, *Princeton, N. J.*
240. A. O. Zabriskie, *Jersey City, N. J.*
241. Michael Lienau, *Jersey City, N. J.*
242. William A. Whitehead, *Newark, N. J.*
243. Simeon Draper, *N. Y. City.*
244. Freeman M. Josselyn, *Boston, Mass.*
245. Theodore W. Riley, *N. Y. City.*
246. John Boyd, Jr., "
247. George K. Sistare, "
248. J. Warren S. Dey, "
249. William H. Bridgman, "
250. Anson Phelps Stokes, "
251. William C. Martin, "
252. A. Robertson Walsh, "
253. Joseph A. Sprague, "
254. Charles A. Peabody, "
255. William H. Morrell, "
256. John V. L. Pruyn, *Albany, N. Y.*
257. Frederick James de Peyster, *N. Y. City.*
258. William H. Macy, *N. Y. City.*
259. Thomas Paton, "
260. David Stewart, "
261. David Stewart, Jr., "
262. John E. Williams, "
263. John P. Townsend, "
264. William H. Morrell, "
265. Homer Morgan, "
266. John Armstrong, "
267. Same, "
268. Same, "
269. Same, "
270. N. Norris Halstead, *Harrison, Hudson Co., N. J.*
271. Wm. C. Tallmadge, *N. Y. City.*
272. Howard Crosby, "
273. Mrs. Mary E. Brooks, "
274. Edward Hodges, "
275. Robert W. Rodman, "

SHARE

276. John L. Riker, *N. Y. City.*
277. Walter R. T. Jones, "
278. Claudius L. Monell, "
279. Byam K. Stevens, Jr., "
280. Francis Many, "
281. Henry M. Taber, "
282. T. M. Peters, "
283. John B. Cornell, "
284. S. Alofsen, "
285. Same, "
286. Robert B. Minturn, Jr., "
287. George Tugnot, "
288. Rufus S. Bergen, *Green Point.*
289. Benj'n W. Bonney, *N. Y. City.*
290. Benj'n W. Bonney, Jr., "
291. John S. H. Fogg, *Boston, Mass.*
292. John H. Wright, "
293. William Wood, *N. Y. City.*
294. F. G. Van Woert, "
295. Alex'r T. Stewart, "
296. John B. Cronin, "
297. Georgf D. Morgan, "
298. Homer Tilton, "
299. Samuel Frost, "
300. Same, "
301. James H. Pinkney, "
302. William T. Pinkney, "
303. Charles H. Phillips, "
304. James Eager, "
305. William Underhill, "
306. John D. Clute, "
307. Abraham B. Embury, "
308. Charles L. Richards, "
309. William Beard, "
310. James H. Welles, "
311. John Gallier, "
312. Charles Le Boutillier, "
313. Thomas Le Boutillier, "
314. John G. Lamberson, "
315. Russell C. Root, "
316. Clarkson Crolius, "
317. William Murphy, *Chappaqua.*
318. Daniel T. Willets, *N. Y. City*
319. Charles Gould, "

SHARE

320. John B. Bartlett, *N. Y. City.*
321. Mathias Clark, "
322. Robert M. Roberts, "
323. *Jas. Hasbrouck Sahler,* "
324. Frederic de Peyster, "
325. Same, "
326. Same, "
327. John J. Latting, "
328. David Buffum, "
329. F. H. Parker, "
330. George W. Thompson, "
331. Thomas F. Youngs, "
332. Oliver G. Barton, "
333. Abram E. Cutter, *Charlestown, Mass.*
334. William E. Lewis, *N. Y. City.*
335. John H. Johnston "
336. William B. Clerke, "
337. John C. Connor, "
338. Henry T. Morgan, "
339. Abram A. Leggett, "
340. James Davett, "
341. Erastus S. Brown, "
342. Asher Taylor, "
343. Edward Bill, "
344. William H. Tuthill, *Tipton, Cedar Co., Iowa.*
345. Henry S. Terbell, *N. Y. City.*
346. George W. Abbe, "
347. Sidney Mason, "
348. Charles Shields, "
349. George B. Dorr, "
350. Gardiner Pike, "
351. John C. Beatty, "
352. Lora B. Bacon, "
353. Charles H. Ludington, "
354. James Brown, "
355. Charles O'Conor, "
356. Charles B. Collins, "
357. John H. Wright, *Boston, Mass.*
358. Wm. S. Constant, *N. Y. City.*
359. Geo. W. Wales, *Boston, Mass.*
360. John L. Deen, *N. Y. City.*
361. T. Matlack Cheesman, "

SHARE

362. Maximilian Rader, *N. Y. City*
363. J. Hobart Herrick, "
364. Louis P. Griffith, "
365. Barrow Benrimo, "
366. Edward F. DeLancey, "
367. Samuel L. Breese, "
368. D. Henry Haight, "
369. John Adriance, "
370. Same, "
371. Joseph W. Alsop, "
372. Henry Chauncey, "
373. Frederick Chauncey, "
374. William Habirshaw, "
375. Henry A. Heiser, "
376. William H. Jackson, "
377. Elijah T. Brown, "
378. Henry K. Bogert, "
379. Addison Brown, "
380. Ernest Fiedler, "
381. J. Watts de Peyster, "
382. William Remsen, "
383. Walter M. Underhill, "
384. Samuel W. Francis, "
385. George Livermore, *Cambridge, Mass.*
386. Same, "
387. Same, "
388. Same, "
389. John F. Gray, *N. Y. City*
390. Henry G. Griffen, "
391. Thomas S. Berry, "
392. Calvin Durand, "
393. Robert B. Minturn, "
394. F. A. P. Barnard, "
395. William Bryce, "
396. James Bryce, "
397. Augustus Belknap, "
398. Andrew Wilson, "
399. William J. Van Duser, "
400. John C. Havemeyer, "
401. John T. Agnew, "
402. Same, "
403. Charles E. Beebe, "
404. Nathaniel W. Chater, "

SHARE

405. George C. Collins, *N. Y. City.*
406. William H. Goodwin, "
407. Charles G. Harmer, "
408. William Hegeman, "
409. Peter V. King, "
410. George W. Lane, "
411. Louis F. Therasson, "
412. Henry F. Sewall, "
413. Miss Elizabeth Clarkson Jay, *N. Y. City.*
414. William E. Dodge, "
415. William E. Dodge, Jr., "
416. George W. Robins, "
417. John D. Locke, "
418. John McKesson, "
419. Richard M. Hoe, "
420. Robert Hoe, "
421. Peter S. Hoe, "
422. Augustus W. Payne, "
423. William Oothout, "
424. Edward Oothout, "
425. Edward F. Hopkins, "
426. David E. Wheeler, "
427. John H. Sprague, "
428. Theodore Van Norden, "
429. George de Heart Gillespie, *N. Y. City.*
430. Benjamin G. Arnold, "
431. Coridon A. Alvord, "
432. Same, "
433. Same, "
434. Same, "
435. J. Otis Ward, "
436. James Lenox, "
437. Same, "
438. Jabez E. Munsell, "
439. Arnold C. Hawes, "
440. Jacob W. Feeter, "
441. Daniel Spring, "
442. John C. Green, "
443. David L. Holden, "
444. Joseph W. Patterson, "
445. Gordon W. Burnham, "
446. Samuel Wilde, Jr., "

SHARE

447. William B. Taylor, Jr., *N. Y. City.*
448. William V. Brady, "
449. Oliver Hoyt, "
450. Charles W. Lecour, "
451. John H. Swift, "
452. Hugh N. Camp, "
453. W. Woolsey Wright, "
454. Jed Frye, "
455. Henry Owen, "
456. William A. Young, *Albany,*
457. John Buckley, Jr., *N. Y. City*
458. D. Randolph Martin, "
459. Samuel L. M. Barlow, "
460. E. W. Ryerson, "
461. Samuel Shethar, "
462. Geo. Brinley, *Hartford, Conn.*
463. Augustus F. Smith, *N. Y. City.*
464. William H. Hurlbut, "
465. Henry A. Hurlbut, "
466. Mrs. Sophie H. Scott, "
467. The N. Y. Society Library, *New York City.*
468. Thomas K. Marcy, *N. Y. City.*
469. Jas. Y. Smith, *Providence, R. I.*
470. Wm. B. Bolles, *Astoria, N. Y.*
471. Gouv. Morris Wilkins, *New York City.*
472. James T. Fields, *Boston, Mass.*
473. Horace P. Biddle, *Logansport, Indiana.*
474. A. L. Roache, *Indianapolis, Indiana.*
475. Miss Eliza S. Quincy, *Quincy, Mass.*
476. Alfred Brookes, *N. Y. City.*
477. Henry Youngs, Jr., *Goshen.*
478. Jeremiah Loder, "
479. Thomas H. Armstrong, "
480. William C. Bryant, "
481. Matthew P. Read, "
482. Manning M. Knapp, *Hackensack, N. J.*
483. Lockwood L. Doty, *Albany.*

SHARE

484. Walter L. Newberry, *Chicago, Illinois.*
485. Hamilton Fish, *New York City.*
486. Wm. B. Towne, *Boston, Mass.*
487. Same, "
488. Same, "
489. Same, "
490. Sidney W. Dibble, *N. Y. City.*
491. Charles J. Seymour, *Binghamton, N. Y.*
492. D. A. McKnight, *Kansas City, Mo.*
493. Chas. H. Housman, *N. Y. City.*
494. James M. Chichester, "
495. William W. Greene, "
496. Francis F. Dorr, "
497. Charles W. Whitney, "
498. Robert D. Hart, "
499. George H. Mathews, "
500. Thomas Addis Emmet, "
501. Andrew J. Smith, "
502. William D. Maxwell, "
503. Charles A. Macy, Jr., "
504. Thomas W. Field, "
505. Charles Gorham Barney, *Richmond, Va.*
506. Benj. B. Atterbury, *N. Y. City.*
507. Richard W. Roche, "
508. Thomas H. Morrell, "
509. Smith Barker, "
510. Everardus B. Warner, "
511. Augustus T. Francis, "
512. Wm. A. Slingerland, "
513. Riley A. Brick, "
514. Same, "
515. Walter M. Smith, "
516. Henry Elsworth, "
517. John Hecker, "
518. Warren Ward, "
519. Charles G. Judson, "
520. J. Meredith Read, Jr., *Albany.*
521. John H. Van Antwerp, "
522. Wm. M. Van Wagenen, "
523. Wm. T. Ryerson, *N. Y. City.*

SHARE

524. Edwin Hoyt, *N. Y. City*
525. John Van Nest, "
526. Clinton Gilbert, "
527. J. Carson Brevoort, *Brooklyn.*
528. Same, "
529. Isaac D. Russell, *N. Y. City.*
530. Henry Oothout, "
531. Alexander P. Irvin, "
532. Beriah Palmer, "
533. Robert Schell, "
534. Alfred T. Ackert, *Rhinebeck.*
535. John H. Watson, *N. Y. City.*
536. Abraham Baldwin, "
537. Ezra A. Hayt, "
538. William L. Lambert, "
539. Charles S. Smith, "
540. Charles A. Macy, "
541. Samuel Raynor, "
542. Lucius Tuckerman, "
543. William Betts, "
544. William K. Strong, "
545. John D. Jones, "
546. Same, "
547. Thomas C. Doremus, "
548. Rudolph A. Witthaus, Jr., *N. Y. City.*
549. Fred'k W. Macy, *N. Y. City.*
550. Joseph N. Ireland, "
551. William Montross, "
552. Samuel R. Mabbatt, "
553. Jacob S. Wetmore, "
554. Marvelle W. Cooper, "
555. Abraham M. Cozzens, "
556. Jacob Van Wagenen, "
557. John H. Riker, "
558 Wm. Alexander Smith, "
559. George Dixon, Jr., "
560. Hamilton Odell, "
561. Charles B. Richardson, "
562. Horatio Nichols, "
563. George T. Hall, "
564. Henry A. Burr, "
565. Franklin H. Delano, "
566. James M. Deuel, "

SHARE
567. Richard Irvin, Jr., *N. Y. City.*
568. Dudley B. Fuller, "
569. Henry A. Smythe, "
570. Josiah S. Leverett, "
571. John S. Davenport, "
572. Bronson Peck, "
573. William A. Allen, "
574. William Dowd, "
575. David L. Baker, "
576. John G. Shea, "
577. Clarkson N. Potter. "
578. David D. Field, "
579. William H. Appleton, "
580. Samuel J. Tilden, "
581. James W. Gerard. "
582. Timothy G. Churchill, "
583. Parker Handy, "
584. Nathaniel Hayden, "
585. John G. Holbrooke, "
586. Robert H. McCurdy, "
587. Rush C. Hawkins, "
588. L. M. Ferris, Jr., "
589. Theo. Roosevelt, "
590. J. Butler Wright, "
591. George Palen, "
592. George Griswold, "
593. O. D. Munn, "
594. Frank Moore, "
595. William H. Lee, "
596. H. P. Crozier. "
597. Henry E. Clark, "
598. Jackson S. Schultz, "
599. John Carter Brown, *Providence, R. I.*
600. John Carter Brown, 2d, *Providence, R. I.*
601. Peleg Hall, *N. Y. City.*
602. Charles L. Anthony, "
603. George W. Hall, "
604. J. T. Leavitt, "
605. Joseph Howland, *Matteawan.*
606. John W. Munro, *N. Y. City.*
607. Parker Handy, "
608. Same, "

SHARE
609. Parker Handy, *N. Y. City*
610. George Griswold, "
611. Willard Parker, "
612. Alex'r W. Bradford, "
613. Benjamin L. Benson, "
614. Edward Schell, "
615. A. B. Kellogg, "
616. Joseph O. Brown, "
617. E. B. Oakley, "
618. Nathaniel Jarvis, Jr., "
619. David S. Duncomb, "
620. Augustus K. Gardner, "
621. L. Bayard Smith, "
622. Louis de V. Wilder, "
623. William E. Bird, "
624. Franklin B. Hough, *Lowville.*
625. Thomas P. Rowe, *N. Y. City.*
626. Samuel Osgood, "
627. Charles A. Meigs, "
628. Edward H. Purdy, "
629. Joseph F. Joy, "
630. Hezekiah King, "
631. Horace W. Fuller, "
632. William H. Post, "
633. Edward D. Butler, "
634. Henry B. Dawson, *Morrisania.*
635. Almon W. Griswold, *N. Y. City.*
636. S. Townsend Cannon, "
637. Theodore M. Barnes, "
638. Joel Munsell, *Albany.*
639. Same, "
640. Thomas A. Bishop, *N. Y. City.*
641. Same, "
642. Nicholas F. Palmer, "
643. J. L. Leonard, *Lowville.*
644. David C. Halstead, *N. Y. City.*
645. Thomas Morton, "
646. J. F. Sheafe, "
647. Henry A. Bostwick, "
648. Hiram D. Dater, "
649. George H. Williams, "
650. O. W. Reynolds, "
651. Silvanus J. Macy, "
652. Henry J. Scudder, "

SHARE
653. N. W. Stuyvesant Catlin, *N. Y. City.*
654. H. Tracy Arnold, *N. Y. City.*
655. Benjamin R. Winthrop, "
656. Same, "
657. Benj. R. Winthrop, Jr., "
658. Egerton L. Winthrop, *N. Y. City.*
659. Franklin Edson, *Albany.*
660. Robert C. Melvain, *N. Y. City.*
661. Archibald Russell, "
662. William I. Paulding, *Cold Spring.*
663. John Romeyn Brodhead, *N. Y. City.*
664. John L. Kennin, *N. Y. City.*
665. James Stokes, Jr., "
666. John A. Russell, "
667. E. M. Wright, "
668. Everardus Warner, "
669. Everardus B. Warner, "
670. John C. Hewitt, "
671. Peter Stryker, *Phila., Pa.*
672. Wilson M. Powell, *N. Y. City.*
673. Samuel H. Brown, "
674. Ellsworth Eliot. "
675. John T. Klots, "
676. Charles H. Dummer, "
677. Henry D. Bulkley, "
678. J. K. Hamilton Willcox, "
679. Appleton Sturgis, "
680. William T. Salter, "
681. William Rockwell, "
682. E. H. Janes, "
683. Thomas B. Newby, "
684. Louis de V. Wilder, "
685. Same, "
686. Samuel Coulter, "
687. Ralph Clark, "
688. Thomas F. De Voe, "
689. John Groshon, "
690. S. L. Boardman, *Augusta, Me.*
691. Charles J. Folsom, *N. Y. City.*
692. George Folsom, "

SHARE
693. Everardus Warner, *N. Y. City.*
694. George C. Eyland, "
695. C. F. Hardon, "
696. F. Wiley, "
697. Alexander Wiley, "
698. John W. Scott, *Astoria.*
699. Edward Anthony, *N. Y. City*
700. Chauncey P. Smith, *Wolcott.*
701. H'y Camerden, Jr., *N. Y. City.*
702. George Bancroft, "
703. Abraham R. Warner, "
704. James W. Purdy, *Suffern.*
705. Chas. Congdon, *B'klyn, N. Y.*
706. Long Island Historical Society, *Brooklyn, N. Y.*
707. Brooklyn Mercantile Library Association, *Brooklyn, N. Y.*
708. New Bedford Free Library, *New Bedford, Mass.*
709. John David Wolfe, *N. Y. City.*
710. Miss C. L. Wolfe, "
711. George W. Cook, "
712. James L. Woodward, "
713. William Frederick Poole, *Boston, Mass.*
714. Benjamin H. Field, *N. Y. City.*
715. Cortlandt De Peyster Field, *N. Y. City.*
716. John Fitch, *N. Y. City.*
717. Same, "
718. F. Augustus Wood, "
719. John H. Dillingham, *Haverford College, Pa.*
720. F. Augustus Wood, *N. Y. City.*
721. Charles A. Peabody, "
722. Edwin F. Corey, Jr., "
723. John G. Lamberson, "
724. Same, "
725. John E. Parsons, "
726. Gratz Nathan, "
727. B. F. De Costa, "
728. Henry C. Potter, "
729. Henry Nicoll, "
730. George E. Moore, "

SHARE
731. JOHN F. TROW, *N. Y. City.*
732. SAME, "
733. SAME, "
734. SAME, "
735. SAME, "
736. SAME, "
737. SAME, "
738. SAME, "
739. SAME, "
740. SAME, "
741. GEORGE H. MOORE, "
742. SAME, "

SHARE
743. GEORGE H. MOORE, *N. Y. City.*
744. SAME, "
745. SAME, "
746. SAME, "
747. SAME, "
748. SAME, "
749. SAME, "
750. SAME, "
751. WILLIAM J. HOPPIN, "
752. JAMES W. BEEKMAN, "
753. JOSEPH F. LOUBAT, "
754. CARLISLE NORWOOD, JR. "

SHAREHOLDERS BY TRANSFERS TO DECEMBER, 1872.

SHARE
41. JAMES A. ROOSEVELT, *N. Y. City.*
94. GEORGE H. MOORE, "
111. J. K. WIGGIN, *Boston, Mass.*
150. GEORGE H. PEEKE, *Jersey City, N. J.*
167. JOHN H. THOMPSON, *N. Y. City.*
174. LUCIE P. BENEDICT, "
187. J. K. WIGGIN, *Boston, Mass.*
284. SAMUEL C. BLACKWELL, *Somerville, N. J.*
321. SAMUEL Y. CLARK, *N. Y. City.*
358. ROBERT S. MILLER, "
426. EVERETT P. WHEELER, "
450. EUGENE H. LECOUR. "

SHARE
470. WILLIAM BOLLES HALSEY, *N. Y. City.*
508. JOSEPH SABIN, *N. Y. City.*
532. NATHAN B. WALKER, "
643. THE TRUSTEES OF THE LOWVILLE ACADEMY.
670. WM. P. PRENTICE, *N. Y. City.*
684. EDWARD C. WILDER, "
685. C. V. B. OSTRANDER, "
714. JOHN EVERITT, "
716. JAMES M. HUNT, "
719. HAVERFORD COLLEGE LIBRARY, *Haverford College, Pa.*
727. DAVID G. FRANCIS, *N. Y. City.*

FOR INDEX—SEE SUBSEQUENT VOLUME.

www.ingramcontent.com/pod-product-compliance
Lightning Source LLC
LaVergne TN
LVHW021321110826
845150LV00003B/642

* 9 7 8 1 4 2 5 5 5 6 6 6 2 *